HETERODOXY IN EARLY MODERN SCIENCE AND RELIGION

Heterodoxy in Early Modern Science and Religion

Edited by
JOHN BROOKE AND IAN MACLEAN

OXFORD
UNIVERSITY PRESS

OXFORD
UNIVERSITY PRESS

Great Clarendon Street, Oxford OX2 6DP

Oxford University Press is a department of the University of Oxford.
It furthers the University's objective of excellence in research, scholarship,
and education by publishing worldwide in

Oxford New York

Auckland Cape Town Dar es Salaam Hong Kong Karachi
Kuala Lumpur Madrid Melbourne Mexico City Nairobi
New Delhi Shanghai Taipei Toronto

With offices in

Argentina Austria Brazil Chile Czech Republic France Greece
Guatemala Hungary Italy Japan Poland Portugal Singapore
South Korea Switzerland Thailand Turkey Ukraine Vietnam

Oxford is a registered trade mark of Oxford University Press
in the UK and in certain other countries

Published in the United States
by Oxford University Press Inc., New York

British Library Cataloguing in Publication Data

Data available

Library of Congress Cataloging-in-Publication Data

Heterodoxy in early modern science and religion / edited by John Brooke and Ian Maclean
p. cm.
Includes index.
ISBN 0-19-926897-5 (alk. paper)
1. Religion and science 2. Heresy. 3. Science–Philosophy. 4. Philosophy.
5. Physics. I. Brooke, John Hedley. II. Maclean, Ian, 1945- III. Title.

BL240.3.H48 2005
201′.65′0903–dc22

2005019524

Typeset by SPI Publisher Services, Pondicherry, India
Printed in Great Britain
on acid-free paper by Biddles Ltd., King's Lynn

ISBN 0-19-926897-5   978-0-19-926897-9
3 5 7 9 10 8 6 4 2

Contents

Notes on the Contributors

John Brooke is Andreas Idreos Professor of Science & Religion and Director of the Ian Ramsey Centre at Oxford University, where he is also a Fellow of Harris Manchester College. His books include *Science and Religion: Some Historical Perspectives* (1991); *Thinking About Matter* (1995); (with Geoffrey Cantor), *Reconstructing Nature: The Engagement of Science and Religion* (1998 and 2000); and (co-edited with Margaret Osler and Jitse van der Meer), *Science in Theistic Contexts: Cognitive Dimensions* (2001).

William E. Carroll is Thomas Aquinas Fellow in Theology and Science at Blackfriars Hall and member of the Faculty of Theology of the University of Oxford. He is the author of *La Creación y las Ciencias Naturales: Actualidad de Santo Tomás de Aquino* (2002) and co-author of *Aquinas on Creation* (1997). He has also published several essays on Galileo and the Inquisition, including articles on Galileo and biblical exegesis.

Nicholas S. Davidson is University Lecturer in History and Tutorial Fellow of St Edmund Hall, Oxford. His main research interest is the religious, social, and intellectual history of early modern Italy. He is currently completing a study of the Inquisition in Venice, and writing a general history of Italy between 1500 and 1800.

David Boyd Haycock was a Junior Research Fellow at Wolfson College, Oxford (1998–2004), and is Wellcome Research Fellow in the Department of Economic History at the London School of Economics. He is the author of *William Stukeley: Science, Archaeology and Religion in Eighteenth-Century England* (2002) and co-editor with George S. Rousseau, Miranda Gill, and Malte Herwig of *Framing and Imagining Disease in Cultural History* (2003).

Cees Leijenhorst is a Lecturer in the history of modern philosophy at the Radboud University Nijmegen (The Netherlands). Among his publications are *The Mechanisation of Aristotelianism. The Late*

Aristotelian Setting of Thomas Hobbes's Natural Philosophy (2002), and, co-edited with Christoph Lüthy and J. M. M. H. Thijssen, *The Dynamics of Aristotelian Natural Philosophy from Antiquity to the Seventeenth Century* (2002). His research interests include Thomas Hobbes's natural and political philosophy, Renaissance natural philosophy, and Hermeticism.

Christoph Lüthy is a historian of science and philosophy working at the Radboud University Nijmegen (The Netherlands), and a Research Fellow of the Netherlands Royal Academy of Sciences. To date, most of his publications have dealt with the history of Renaissance and early modern natural philosophy and the emergence of experimental science. He is the co-editor, with John E. Murdoch and William R. Newman, of *Medieval and Early Modern Corpuscular Matter Theories* (2001), and with Cees Leijenhorst and J. M. M. H. Thijssen, of *The Dynamics of Aristotelian Natural Philosophy from Antiquity to the Seventeenth Century* (2002).

Ian Maclean is Professor of Renaissance Studies at the University of Oxford and a Senior Research Fellow of All Souls College. Among his publications are *The Renaissance Notion of Woman* (1980, frequently reprinted), *Meaning and Interpretation in the Renaissance: The Case of Law* (1992), *Montaigne philosophe* (1996), *Logic, Signs and Nature in the Renaissance: The Case of Learned Medicine* (2001), and an edition of Cardano's *De libris propriis* (2004).

Scott Mandelbrote is an Official Fellow and Director of Studies in History at Peterhouse, Cambridge, and Isaac Newton Trust Lecturer in the Faculty of History, Cambridge University. He is also a Fellow of All Souls College, Oxford. His publications include *Footprints of the Lion: Isaac Newton at Work* (2001) and he is an editorial director of the Newton Project.

Tabitta van Nouhuys read History and Law at Leiden University. In 1997 she completed her Ph.D. thesis, *The Age of Two-Faced Janus. The Comets of 1577 and 1618 and the Decline of the Aristotelian World View in the Netherlands* (published in 1998). In 1997 and 1998, she held postgraduate research fellowships at the Herzog August Bibliothek, Wolfenbüttel, and the Institut für europäische Geschichte in

Mainz. From 1998 to 2001, she was a Prize Fellow in History at Magdalen College, Oxford.

Margaret J. Osler is Professor of History and Adjunct Professor of Philosophy at the University of Calgary. Her major publications include: *Divine Will and the Mechanical Philosophy: Gassendi and Descartes on Contingency and Necessity in the Created World* (1994); 'How Mechanical Was the Mechanical Philosophy? Non-Epicurean Themes in Gassendi's Atomism', in *Late Medieval and Early Modern Corpuscular Matter Theories*, edited by Christoph Lüthy, John Murdoch, and William R. Newman (2001), 423–39; and numerous articles on the relationship between natural philosophy and theology in the seventeenth century.

Stephen D. Snobelen completed his Ph.D. in History and Philosophy of Science at the University of Cambridge and was a Junior Research Fellow at Clare College, Cambridge before taking up a position as Assistant Professor in the History of Science Programme at King's College, Halifax, Nova Scotia. He is also Adjunct Professor of History at Dalhousie University, a member of the Editorial Board of the Newton Project, and Director of the Newton Project Canada. Dr Snobelen has published several papers on Isaac Newton's theology and is the author of a forthcoming Icon Books biography of Newton.

David Wootton is Anniversary Professor of History at the University of York. He was educated at Cambridge and Oxford, and taught in Canada from 1980 to 1994, both in History and in Politics departments. He has published widely on the intellectual and cultural history of France, Italy, and the English-speaking countries from 1500 to 1800, particularly on the history of political philosophy. The present essay is related to his earlier work on The Family of Love, in Stuart Clark (ed.), *Languages of Witchcraft* (2001), and to work in progress, including an edition of Marlowe's *Faustus*.

Introduction

Ian Maclean

The papers united in this collection were originally given in a seminar series held in All Souls College, Oxford on thinkers in the early modern period (roughly 1500 to 1800) whose work touched on both science (understood in a broad sense[1]) and religion, and who in their time were associated with heterodox views in one, or the other, or both, spheres. Contributors to the series were asked to consider the following questions: how was heterodoxy determined in the case of each thinker? What was the effect (if any) of the thinker's heterodox scientific thinking on his religious views? What was the effect of his heterodox theological views (if any) on his science? Is there a homology between his heterodox views in both areas?

These questions presuppose that thinkers in the past were able to measure their deviation from agreed scientific and religious positions; clearly this is much easier at certain times and places, and in respect of certain issues, than others. Most early modern writers who venture into areas in which it is important to determine where they stand on contentious scientific and religious issues set down or imply their own relationship to the orthodoxies of their day; in each case it is important to recognize the particularities of the context in which such determinations are made. In the light of this caveat, contributors chose to discuss thinkers from all over Europe; the topics they discussed concern the soul and the nature of matter (Pomponazzi, Cardano, Lutheran philosophers on the physics of the eucharist, Vanini, Gassendi), cosmology, eschatology, and the question of human destiny (Donne, Galileo, van Lansbergen, Voetius, Fromondus, and Wendelin), and the confrontation of the new philosophies

---

[1] It is not the intention in this volume to engage in the debate about the use of the terms 'natural philosophy' and 'science'; see below, n. 3.

of the later seventeenth and eighteenth centuries with Christian beliefs and writings (Hobbes, Fatio de Duillier, Newton, Stukeley, Priestley). These issues are related to others which occur in many of the writings discussed, notably the nature of God and his ways of intervening in his creation, and the meaning to be attributed to statements found in Holy Writ about the universe ('mosaic' physics).[2] Not all the figures who are discussed in this volume are well known, but each was chosen to reveal in a symptomatic way issues intimately connected to heterodoxy.

The fact that theology and natural philosophy interacted throughout the early modern period in various institutions and contexts, and that their relative authority was a matter of contention, has of course never been in dispute. An early notorious expression of this contention is to be found in the condemnations at Paris of certain Aristotelian propositions about the world and human nature by Bishop Étienne Tempier in 1270 and 1277; these clearly set theology above natural philosophy, and refute the view that religion and philosophy are distinguished by different orders of truth. The Pomponazzi affair of the early sixteenth century revived this dispute, and is testament to its perennial nature (see below, 12–14). Throughout the period here under discussion, theology never relinquished its claim to determine the boundaries of human enquiry and the conclusions reached by philosophers about nature. By the nineteenth century, however, the struggle between theology and science came to be seen as one between prejudice and rationality; the erosion of the power of religion to constrain scientific enquiry was taken to be proof of the progressive liberation of the human spirit and the 'demagification' of the world. More recently still, this view has been challenged in turn; rather than see the projects of early modern natural philosophers as opposed in some way to theology, the importance of their religious motivation has been stressed, and the ways in which it informed their

---

[2] Lambert Daneau's *Physice Christiana* (Geneva, 1579), Franciscus Vallesius's *De iis quae scripta sunt physice in sacris literis* (Lyons, 1588), and Robert Fludd's *Philosophia moysaica* (Gouda, 1638) are three of many contemporary sources; see also Ann Blair, 'Mosaic Physics and the Search for a Pious Natural Philosophy in the Late Renaissance', *Isis*, 91 (2000), 32–58.

scientific projects investigated.[3] In an earlier study, John Brooke has analysed in some detail the strategies available to historians in the light of such interpenetration.[4] To offer new interpretations of the book of nature was not necessarily to abandon revealed truths in the form of Holy Writ and the traditions of the Church in favour of observation and experiment. A recurring goal was to adapt the insights of one sphere to the other. Galileo may have claimed that the book of nature was written in the language of mathematics; but in his view this did not entail that theology had suddenly relinquished its role as a privileged mediator of truth through the exegesis of Holy Writ and the determination of the correct interpretation of the traditions of the Church. In his *Letter to the Grand Duchess Christina*, circulated in 1615, Galileo argued that a sound knowledge of nature was one of the best aids to the understanding of Scripture (see below, 128–38).

Nevertheless, it was obvious to any contemporary by the time of the Galileo affair that there were competing orthodoxies in both religion and science, and that the issue of authority had become paramount in both spheres. Once Lutheranism had brought about schism in the Western Church, a series of attempts to define right doctrinal thinking occurred. These theological measures were not paralleled by formal statements of doctrinal differences in natural

---

[3] A pioneering study of this type is Walter Pagel's 'Religious Motives in the Medical Biology of the XVIIth Century', *Bulletin of the Institute of History of Medicine*, 3 (1935), 265–312; see also Amos Funkenstein, *Theology and the Scientific Imagination from the Middle Ages to the Seventeenth Century* (Princeton: Princeton University Press, 1986); David C. Lindberg and Ronald L. Numbers, *God and Nature: Historical Essays on the Encounter between Christianity and Science* (Berkeley: University of California Press, 1986); R. K. French and Andrew Cunningham, *Before Science: The Invention of the Friars' Natural Philosophy* (Aldershot: Scholar, 1996); David C. Lindberg and Ronald L. Numbers (eds.), *When Science and Christianity Meet* (Chicago: Chicago University Press, 2003). The battle lines of the strongly contested debate about the use of the terms 'natural philosophy' and 'science' in relation to this period, and the possibility of seeing medieval and early modern science as a purely secular undertaking, are clearly set out by Andrew Cunningham and Edward Grant in *Early Science and Medicine*, 5 (2000), 258–300. See also John Hedley Brooke, Margaret J. Osler, and Jitse M. van der Meer, *Science in Theistic Contexts: Cognitive Dimensions*, *Osiris*, 2.16 (Chicago: Chicago University Press, 2001).

[4] John Hedley Brooke, *Science and Religion: Some Historical Perspectives* (Cambridge: Cambridge University Press, 1991), 16–51.

philosophy, but as Charles Schmitt and others have shown, Aristotelianism also evolved into a multiplicity of doctrines in the course of the sixteenth century, and struggled to relate newly acquired empirical knowledge to the authoritative texts of the philosopher (as well as to serve confessional interests: see below, 89–109). In medicine too, relevant here because of the mind–body problem, there were a number of developments which threatened the unicity of the revived Galenism of the early years of the sixteenth century; these include both Paracelsianism and Hippocratism, as well as the new revisionist positions of figures such as Fracastoro, Fernel, and Argenterio. Orthodoxy expressed itself in different institutional ways: in theology, it was through councils and synods; in natural philosophy, right thinking was defined in this period by individual universities. Such 'right' thinking ranges from the doctrine, dangerously akin to the 'two truths' heresy, implied by the Albertine tenet 'de naturalibus naturaliter', to the theologically driven arts curriculum of Wittenberg designed by Melanchthon and the second scholastic developed by Iberian Catholics such as Suárez, Fonseca, and Toletus.[5]

The evolution of scientific enquiry was linked also to the way in which the relationship of the human mind to the world was viewed. Was there a homology between the mind and the (rational) order of nature which predisposed man to the understanding of his environment; an understanding that was in some sense his birthright? This was undoubtedly true for Galileo who saw human reason as a divine gift to be exercised, as for Kepler who saw in geometry a form of access to the divine mind.[6] Alternatively, was human (malign) curiosity more a symptom of the fall from grace?[7] Did the limitations of

[5] Sachiko Kusukawa, *The Transformation of Natural Philosophy: The Case of Philip Melanchthon* (Cambridge: Cambridge University Press, 1995); Eckhard Kessler, 'The Second Scholastic', in Charles B. Schmitt and Quentin Skinner (eds.), *The Cambridge History of Renaissance Philosophy* (Cambridge: Cambridge University Press, 1988), 507–18; Annabel S. Brett, *Liberty, Right and Nature: Individual Rights in Later Scholastic Thought* (Cambridge: Cambridge University Press, 1997).

[6] See below, 115–44, Rikva Feldhay, *Galileo and the Church: Political Inquisition or Critical Dialogue?* (Cambridge: Cambridge University Press, 1995), and Peter Barker and Bernard R. Goldstein, 'Theological Foundations of Kepler's Astronomy', *Osiris*, 16 (2001), 88–113.

[7] See Peter Harrison, 'Curiosity, Forbidden Knowledge, and the Reformation of Natural Philosophy in Early Modern England', *Isis*, 92 (2001), 265–90.

his senses and his reason set limits on his knowledge, such that his mind was the measure of all things, not the things themselves? Could that which was apprised through empirical investigations challenge the rational and metaphysical basis of religiously sanctioned scholastic physics? Could it further challenge the statements about the physical world found in Holy Writ (however these were to be interpreted)? Could there ever be a 'rational religion' (that is a religion wholly consistent with the processes of human enquiry and speculation about nature)? In the course of the seventeenth century, a shift in emphasis occurred from a concern with speculative and truth-centred knowledge informed by the questions set out above to an approach informed by quite different issues: how does nature work, and how can it be put to use? This is sometimes linked to millenarian aspirations to master nature, as in the case of the Hartlib circle. This shift, detectable in the increasing currency of mathematical and experimental approaches to knowledge, is marked also by the vernacularization and vulgarization of scientific enquiry, revealing the public as well as private dimensions of religion and science. The successive changes of religious practice in certain parts of Europe (from Roman Catholic, to Lutheran, to Calvinist) brought about by the change of ruler led eventually not only to the doctrine of 'cuius regio eius religio', but also such views as that of Hobbes, that religion was a form of public conduct regulated by the sovereign (see below, 195–7). In scientific terms, publicity (or privacy) also emerged as an issue, and is reflected both in the decision of audacious thinkers such as Giordano Bruno to expound doctrines previously thought too dangerous to communicate to untrained minds and (conversely) in the secrecy with which they shrouded some of their lines of speculation. Recent scholarship on Newton, for example, has stressed a parallel between the privacy of his conduct of natural philosophy (as he retreated from unpalatable controversy) and the necessary privacy of his heterodox religious life.[8]

It is pertinent here to say a preliminary word about the term 'heterodoxy' and its semantic field; this will not constitute a comprehensive survey of all languages and contexts, but rather an indicative

[8] See below, 223–62, and I. Bernard Cohen and George E. Smith (eds.), *The Cambridge Companion to Newton* (Cambridge: Cambridge University Press, 2002).

sample to highlight one or two features of the term having very strong resonances in the early modern period. The words 'heterodox' and 'heterodoxy' in Greek, Latin, and various vernaculars, have a long history, and long associations with deviancy, heresy, and error. They belong to a group of words, including 'paradoxa', 'amphidoxa', 'cacodoxa', and 'pseudodoxa', having the same Greek stem ('doxa'): this is usually translated into Latin as 'opinio', and often contrasted with the higher form of demonstrative knowledge known as 'scientia' ('epistēmē'). 'Opinio' was not viewed negatively by all disciplines in the early modern world: in law, the 'opinio communis doctorum' represents the authoritative understanding of the legal texts enshrined in the consensus of the greatest number of jurists or the best experts in a field as to their meaning.[9] 'Opinio' belongs to the order of the utilitarian; a given opinion needs only to satisfy the majority of the evidence in favour of a given proposition, whereas a 'scientific' proposition must be applicable universally.[10]

Of the group of terms under consideration here, 'paradox' was the first to be used in a significant cultural way in the post-medieval period. It was already well known to fifteenth-century humanists from the title of a Ciceronian text which expounds surprising moral propositions held to be true by the Stoics (*Paradoxa*); in the first part of the sixteenth century, it was given new life through its use by Martin Luther and other early religious reformers to describe their radical opposition to Roman Catholic doctrine and practice.[11] At the same time, it was employed in other fields to indicate opinions which

---

[9] Ian Maclean, *Interpretation and Meaning in the Renaissance: The Case of Law* (Cambridge: Cambridge University Press, 1992), 93–4.

[10] Ian Maclean, *Logic, Signs and Nature in the Renaissance: The Case of Learned Medicine* (Cambridge: Cambridge University Press, 2001), 114–47.

[11] Martin Luther, *Christianissimi Wittenbergensis Gymnasii, multarum Disputationum paradoxa et plane enigmata in Papistica illa mendaciis confusissima Ecclesia* (n.p., 1521); Martin Bucer (1491–1551), *Ein kurtzer warhafftiger bericht von Disputationem ... so zwischen Cunrat Treger Provincial der Augustiner, und den predigern des Evangelii zu Strassburg sich begeben hat ... Und hundert Paradoxa oder wunderreden vom gewalt der Schrifft, Kirchen und Concilien verteüscht* (Strasbourg, 1524); Sebastian Franck (*c.*1499–*c.*1542), *Paradoxa ducenta octoginta* (Ulm, 1534). I owe these references to Agnieszka Steczowicz, whose doctoral dissertation, shortly to appear, will be a major source for the history of Renaissance paradox in all disciplines. See also in general Rosalie Colie, *Paradoxia epidemica* (Princeton: Princeton University Press, 1966).

were either novel in respect of existing doctrine or in contradiction to it. The jurist Andrea Alciato (1492–1550) published a book of legal paradoxes in 1518, which used humanist philological scholarship to refute medieval interpretations of Roman law; following in the footsteps of the humanist doctor Niccolò Leoniceno (1428–1524), who published corrections to the *Natural History* of Pliny in the 1490s, the Tübingen professor Leonard Fuchs (1501–66) wrote a book in 1530 on errors in the writings of more recent physicians which he later termed medical paradoxes.[12]

From the orthodox point of view, Luther's 'paradoxical' views were attacked as heresy, especially after his conscientious stand at the Diet of Worms in 1521;[13] a little later, departure from the orthodoxy of established medical teaching began to be described analogously in the same terms (an understandable analogy for doctors to exploit, as the various ancient schools of medicine were already described as sects[14]). The radical physician and religious thinker Theophrastus Paracelsus (1493?–1541) gloomily records in the *Opus paragranum* (1529–30) that he was described as the Luther of medicine; soon after, Andreas Thurinus (1473–1543) in Florence, Jeremias Drivere (1504–54) in Louvain, Andrea Camuzio (1510?–78) in Pavia, and Gianfilippo Ingrassia (1510–80) in Naples use the epithets 'Lutheran' or 'heretic' to describe deviant thought in the sphere of medicine.[15] 'Paradox' is also used in the field of natural philosophy to denote departure from generally accepted doctrine; Copernicus's cosmology is described as paradoxical by Joachim Georg Rheticus and Bruno.[16] Through such usage, Galen and Aristotle are transformed into orthodoxies, even quasi-theological orthodoxies (Michel de Montaigne

---

[12] Alciato, *Paradoxorum ad Pratum libri sex* (Milan, 1518); Leonhart Fuchs, *Errata recentiorum medicorum* (Hagenau, 1530); *Paradoxorum medicinae libri iii* (Basle, 1535); Niccolò Leoniceno, *De Plinii et plurium aliorum in medicina erroribus liber* (Ferrara, 1492); Maclean, *Logic, Signs and Nature*, 20–2.

[13] See Diarmaid MacCulloch, *Reformation: Europe's House Divided, 1490–1700* (London: Allen Lane, 2003), 131 (on the dubious authenticity of 'hier steh ich: ich kann nicht anders, so hilf mir Gott').

[14] Maclean, *Logic, Signs and Nature*, 76–80.

[15] For these references, see below, 26 n.85

[16] Rheticus, *Narratio prima* (Basle, 1541), sig. a2r; Bruno, *La cena de le ceneri*, in *Œuvres complètes*, ed. Giovanni Aquilecchia, trans. Yves Hersant (Paris: Les Belles Lettres, 1994), ii. 37.

refers to Aristotle as the 'God of natural philosophy'[17]): this was the status they enjoyed in medieval universities, and retained as late as 1657, according to the chymist George Starkey (1627–66), who complains that 'whosoever should dare to swarve from [Galen and Aristotle] [is] looked upon as Heterodox'.[18]

'Paradox' did not only denote departure from established doctrine; it also referred to the new knowledge that was emerging in the course of the sixteenth century in the works of 'neoterici' who cited new data, or produced new theory, or did both. In the sphere of medicine, this included both previously unknown botanical and zoological specimens that were brought back by travellers to the New World and elsewhere, and previously unrecorded illnesses, of which the most famous is the Great Pox or French disease.[19] As the Paracelsian doctor Petrus Severinus (1542–1602) says in 1571, 'paradoxical (i.e. previously unrecorded) diseases called forth paradoxical physicians'.[20] In the sphere of natural philosophy, new knowledge could take various forms: it could be the recovery of ancient doctrines which had been lost, discarded, neglected, or forgotten (such as atomism); it could be the logical extension of the work of the ancients (most clearly seen in the field of mathematics and mechanics); it could be radical revision of Aristotelian physics and cosmology, as in the work of Nicholas Copernicus, Tycho Brahe, and Johannes Kepler.

In natural philosophy and medicine, 'heterodox' (and the more rarely used 'pseudodoxa' and 'cacodoxa') emerged in the following century as a variation on paradox. The Basle physician Felix Platter (1536–1614) seems to have used the two terms in an earlier version of the title of his posthumous book *Quaestiones paradoxae et endoxae* (1625), if we are to believe the title cited by his pupil Johann Heinrich

---

[17] *Essais*, ed. Pierre Villey (Paris: PUF, 1962), 539 (ii. 12).

[18] George Starkey, *Natures Explication and Helmont's Vindication* (London, 1657), 18. This reference, and those to the works of Browne, Biggs, and Hales below, are cited in the *Oxford English Dictionary*, s.v. heterodox, heterodoxical.

[19] Jon Arrizabalaga, John Henderson, and R. K. French, *The Great Pox: the French Disease in Renaissance Europe* (New Haven: Yale University Press, 1997).

[20] Petrus Severinus, *Idea medicinae philosophicae, fundamenta continens totius doctrinae Paracelsicae, Hippocraticae et Galenicae* (Basle, 1571), 3: 'paradoxi morbi paradoxos medicos peperere.' Cf. Jacopo Zabarella (1533–89), *Opera logica* (n.p. 1586–7), i sig. α3r, who defines 'paradoxa' as 'nova dogmata'.

Frölich in 1612 (*Sēmeiōtice phoibeia, paradoxis et heterodoxis D. Felicis Plateris adornata*); it seems here that 'heterodox' designates either an existing alternative version of a doctrine, or a deviant view which is different from, but not radically contrary to, an existing dogma, or an opinion expressed by someone else on a subject on which no doctrine of an authoritative kind is on record. 'Heterodoxy' thus appears as a sort of middle or neutral term, which can refer both to revisions of knowledge and to new knowledge; when Sir Thomas Browne refers in his *Pseudodoxia epidemica* of 1646 to a proposition as 'not only simply heterodoxicall, but a very hard Paradox, it will seeme, and of great absurdity, unto obstinate eares', and, a few years later, Noah Biggs talks in an equally polemical publication of a 'not simply heterodoxicall, but a very rough-hewed paradoxicall asseveration', they seem to be using 'heterodoxicall' in this sense.[21]

The domain of theology works in a somewhat different way. There, the more frequently encountered term is heresy (denoting the holding of heterodoxical opinions); it is used in the Acts of the Apostles (translated into Latin as 'secta') by Jews to describe early Christian communities, and on more than one occasion in the Pauline epistles to describe splinter groups which threaten Church unity; together with 'orthodoxy', it was given a clear institutional sense prior to the Reformation at the Council of Chalcedon in 451. Heresy is not merely the holding of opinions inconsistent with orthodoxy, but presupposes obdurate persistence in such error; it is thus a moral state as well as the holding of false (heterodox) beliefs. This obduracy can manifest itself not only by refusal to abandon false doctrine, but also by the extension and development of orthodox positions beyond the limits sanctioned by the Church.[22]

The Reformation brought with it a conscious rejection of Catholic orthodoxy, and a pressing need for the new Protestant groups to establish their own institutionally approved beliefs in contradistinction to each other and to the Church of Rome. At various councils

---

[21] Sir Thomas Browne, *Pseudodoxia epidemica* (London, 1646), ii. 3. 66; Noah Biggs, *Mataeotechnia medicinae praxeωs* (London, 1651), 214.

[22] Acts 24: 5, 28: 22; Gal. 5: 20; 1 Cor. 11: 19; Titus 3: 10. On heresy see the *New Catholic Encyclopaedia*, s.v; Bruno Neveu, *L'Erreur et son juge: remarques sur les censures doctrinales à l'époque moderne* (Naples: Bibliopolis, 1993). See also below, 87.

and meetings, Christian denominations produced their own versions of orthodoxy: the Roman Catholics at the Council of Trent, between 1545 and 1563; the Lutherans, first in Augsburg in 1530, then again in 1540 (the 'confessio variata', which set out to accommodate the views of other Protestant groups), and finally in 1577 (the Gnesio-lutheran 'Formula of Concord'); elsewhere in Europe, there were other agreed confessions (the Gallican in 1559, the Belgic in 1561, the Helvetic in 1561–2); the Synod of Dort (1618–19) represents in one sense a culmination of these declarations of doctrine which are for the most part of Calvinist inspiration. The Church of England meanwhile had enacted its thirty-nine articles by 1571.[23] These institutional acts by churches as self-conscious units establishing their own discipline, dogmas, structure, and catechisms occurred during the historical phase often referred to as 'confessionaliza-tion';[24] they were accompanied both by controversial theology, which proliferated from the second half of the sixteenth century onwards, and by the publication of guides to ancient and modern heresies issued by the various denominations.[25]

From the middle years of the sixteenth century, different groups of Protestants use 'orthodox' to denote consonance with their chosen confessions; the use of 'heterodox' comes later, and seems at first to refer to emerging or doubtful doctrine as well as error. In his Letter from Dort to Sir Dudley Charlton, Walter Balcanqual describes as 'heterodox' those articles of faith being drawn up by the Synod about which there was disagreement (or with which he himself

[23] MacCulloch, *Reformation*, 347–99.
[24] See Heinz Schilling, 'Die "Zweite Reformation" als Kategorie der Geschichts-wissenschaft', in Heinz Schilling (ed.), *Die reformierte Konfessionalisierung in Deutschland: das Problem der 'Zweiten Reformation'* (Gütersloh: Mohn, 1986), 387–437; Bodo Nischan, *Lutherans and Calvinists in the Age of Confessionalism* (Aldershot: Ashgate, 1999). I am grateful to Diarmaid MacCulloch for these references.
[25] An extensive bibliography of these works divided by denomination is given in Georgius Draudius, *Bibliotheca classica* (Frankfurt am Main, 1625), 296–301. See also, for a slightly earlier usage of a similar kind, *Tuba Iubilæi Lutherani. Hoc est, Explicatio dicti insignis Habacuc c. 2. 4. Iustus fide sua vivet: in qua nostra de iustificatione hominis coram Deo gratuita thesis orthodoxa confirmatur, antithesis Pontificiorum et heterodoxa in hoc articulo doctrina partim refutatur, partim indicatur, dictumque hoc a pravis Jesuitarum, Bellarmini, Costeri, Riberae expositionibus vindi-catur. Quam . . . in illustri Academia Rostochiensi 10. Decembris . . . Publice examinandam proponit Iohannes Tarnovius S.S. Theologiae Professor. Respondente Hermanno Lonero Strandens* (Rostock, 1617).

disagreed).[26] The same usage is found later in the title of Hamon l'Estrange's book of 1641, *God's Sabbath ... briefly vindicated from novell and heterodox assertions;* whereas that of the Dutch theologian Joannes Hoornbeeck (1617–66) in his *De paradoxis et heterodoxis Weigelianis* (1646) seems closer to medical usage in denoting by the term 'heterodox' the less reprehensible departures from orthodoxy in the beliefs of Valentin Weigel's followers. By the middle of the seventeenth century, 'heterodoxy' had strong institutional connotations in various disciplines; it was linked to new or recovered knowledge or doctrine as well as existing opinions, and could designate, as well as views which are less severe challenges to a given orthodoxy than its direct contradiction, a sort of penumbra of emerging opinion not yet fixed in its relation to established doctrine.

The interaction of theology and natural philosophy, of religious belief and theories about the physical world, is complex throughout this period. In any one institutional context, one might (in the most straightforward case) have 'orthodox' religious beliefs which coexist with 'orthodox' scientific ones; one might have 'orthodox' religious beliefs which are coupled with heterodox scientific ones; one might conversely begin from scientific beliefs which lead to religious orthodoxy or heterodoxy; one may also subscribe to a metaphysics or possess a mental predisposition which leads to heterodoxy in both spheres. One's agenda may be driven by religious preoccupations (as it is in the majority of cases), or by scientific ones. These questions can be posed in respect of an evolving range of issues in the early modern period which are discussed in the following chapters: the eternity of matter and the world, the distinction between superlunary and sublunary nature; the (im)materiality and (im)mortality of the soul; 'mosaic' physics; biblical hermeneutics; corpuscularianism and atomism; matter and spontaneous generation; the nature of God (including the 'necessary' limitations placed on his essence such as His incapacity to know singulars or to have complete foreknowledge); the doctrines of occasionalism and voluntarism, with the

---

[26] John Hales, *Golden Remains* (London, 1688), 524: 'upon Tuesday the canons of the first and second article were approved, except the last of the second article... and the second heterodox of the same Article. On Thursday morning it was reasoned whether the last heterodox should be retained.'

related issues of causality, occult properties, and gravity; the question of trinitarianism and unitarianism; *prisca theologia* and the history of religion. The chapters in this volume constitute a set of intriguing case studies which reveal a range of the ways in which these issues interact in the early modern period.

The editors would like to thank the Faculty of Theology, the Faculty of Modern History, and All Souls College, Oxford for their generous financial support of the seminar series on which this collection of papers is based; and Hilary O'Shea and Lucy Qureshi of the Oxford University Press for their unobtrusive efficiency in bringing the book into being.

1

Heterodoxy in Natural Philosophy and Medicine: Pietro Pomponazzi, Guglielmo Gratarolo, Girolamo Cardano

Ian Maclean

There were, of course, mute inglorious heterodox thinkers in the early modern period whose speculations were lost on the desert air: Carlo Ginzburg has given a fascinating account of one such village philosopher in *The Cheese and the Worms*.[1] But this study is about those who achieved notoriety or fame through the various means of disseminating knowledge available to early modern writers. The most celebrated of these means was the printing press: reformers such as Luther and Calvin and thinkers such as Girolamo Cardano showed themselves to be very conscious of the power of this medium.[2] Manuscript circulation of lectures and monographs, and the communication of ideas through epistolary exchanges and personal encounters were also effective, as the case of Pomponazzi will show; one of the reasons why early modern scholars and librarians expended so much effort in the pursuit of the unpublished *Nachlass* of innovative writers (such as Paracelsus, Cardano, Harriot, and

---

[1] Carlo Ginzburg, *The Cheese and the Worms: The Cosmos of a Sixteenth-Century Miller*, tr. John and Anne Tedeschi (Baltimore: Johns Hopkins University Press, 1992).
[2] Mark U. Edwards, *Printing Propaganda and Martin Luther* (Berkeley: University of California Press, 1994); Jean-François Gilmont, *Jean Calvin et le livre imprimé* (Geneva: Droz, 1997); Ian Maclean, 'Cardano and his Publishers, 1534–1663', in Eckhard Kessler (ed.), *Girolamo Cardano: Philosoph, Naturforscher, Arzt* (Wiesbaden: Harrassowitz, 1994), 305–33.

Descartes) was because it was suspected that it contained their most radical and explicit speculations. Thanks to these modes of transmission and the early pursuit of private papers, the roll-call of those who might be considered the most important heterodox thinkers of the sixteenth century has not altered very much since the beginning of the seventeenth century; the French scholar Gabriel Naudé's list of 'novateurs' is much the same as that found in the relevant chapter of the *Cambridge History of Renaissance Philosophy*, published in 1988.[3] These names all belong to the world of international (i.e. Latin) discourse; the vernacular, which has different implications for censorship, readership, and diffusion, is here not in question. Naudé lists those who were being falsely accused of magic and other religiously deviant thinking in the feverish Parisian atmosphere of the early 1620s; he omits to mention uncontroversial innovative figures such as the anatomist Andreas Vesalius, and a number of prominent anti-Aristotelians, such as Petrus Ramus, who did not stray into the disputed territory between natural philosophy and theology. Not all innovation attracts the obloquy of traditionalists.

To give an account of all of Naudé's 'novateurs' is beyond the scope of this chapter; I intend to concentrate on heterodox thinking in relation both to natural philosophy and to medicine in two of them (Pomponazzi and Cardano), with a brief look at a third figure (Gratarolo) who has links to both. There are two reasons for this choice, First, the same important issues arise in both disciplines: the nature of matter and of the soul; the unicity of the intellect; *spiritus*; and the astrological and magical relationship of the superlunary and sublunary realms, with its implications for occult causes, teleology, fate, chance, and determinism. Second, many innovative and deviant thinkers were trained as doctors: not only those named in the title of this chapter, but also Ficino, Agrippa, Paracelsus, Fracastoro, Fernel, Servetus, Simoni, to name but a few. This choice of focus has meant that I have set aside other issues over which Aristotelianism came into conflict with Christian thought (notably the eternity of the

---

[3] Gabriel Naudé, *Apologie pour tous les grands personnages qui ont esté faussement soupçonnez de magie* (Paris, 1625), 331; Alfonso Ingegno, 'The New Philosophy of Nature', in Charles B. Schmitt and Quentin Skinner (eds.), *The Cambridge History of Renaissance Philosophy* (Cambridge: Cambridge University Press, 1988), 236–63.

world and cosmology): these would have produced a different list of names, including Copernicus himself, Telesio, Bruno, and Campanella.

I

The three cases I have chosen to study were all three trained in Padua; and all three, it seems to me, evince the cast of mind of the North Italian learned physician. Their alma mater will no doubt call to mind the disputed thesis of J. H. Randall, according to which Paduan Aristotelianism marks a step forward on the path to the secular and naturalistic scientific outlook of the seventeenth century. As my own focus is more on the medical than the philosophical, I shall not engage with this debate.[4] The rational doctor, that is, the ideal product of the educational system of Renaissance medical faculties, was first taught the arts course, and was expected to be a competent logician, as well as knowing astrology, arithmetic, natural philosophy, pharmacopoeia, and ethics. He was trained then to deal with empirical data of various kinds, and to develop his powers of inference and prognosis.[5] He was, in Nancy Siraisi's words, 'a man of judgement who gained understanding from careful observation of patients which then led to a reasoned choice of remedies';[6] he combined rational analysis and empirical enquiry, 'ratio' and 'experientia', in a way strongly suggestive of the new science of the seventeenth century.[7]

[4] J. H. Randall, *The School of Padua and the Emergence of Modern Science* (Padua: Antenore, 1961); id., 'Paduan Aristotelianism Reconsidered', in E. P. Mahoney (ed.), *Philosophy and Humanism* (Leiden: Brill, 1976), 275–82; for a critique of Randall, see Charles B. Schmitt, 'Aristotelism in the Veneto and the Origins of Modern Science: Some Considerations of Continuity', in Luigi Olivieri (ed.), *Aristotelismo veneto e scienza moderna, Atti del 25o anno accademico del centro per la storia della tradizione aristotelica nel Veneto*, ii (Padua: Antenore, 1983), ii. 104–25.

[5] Ian Maclean, *Logic, Signs and Nature in the Renaissance: The Case of Learned Medicine* (Cambridge: Cambridge University Press, 2001), 68–100.

[6] Nancy G. Siraisi, 'Medicine, Physiology and Anatomy in Early Sixteenth-Century Critiques of the Arts and the Sciences', in John Henry and Sarah Hutton (eds.), *New Perspectives on Renaissance Thought: Essays in the History of Science, Education and Philosophy in Memory of Charles B. Schmitt* (London: Duckworth,1990), 214–29 (paraphrasing Mariano Santo).

[7] Maclean, *Logic, Signs and Nature*, 333–41.

Even if their relationship in institutional terms was not always harmonious, the faculties of philosophy and medicine had close links throughout the period.[8] Galen, medicine's principal authority in both the theoretical and practical aspects of the discipline, wrote a tract to establish that 'the best doctor is a philosopher'; another often-quoted tag stated that 'where the natural philosopher leaves off, the physician takes over', suggesting (on one reading at least) that medicine might in some sense be subordinated to natural philosophy.[9] It was often claimed that medicine took its dogmatic foundations (the elements, the humours, etc.) from natural philosophy, which enjoyed at the time the status of a science (in so far as it was based on the knowledge of causes).[10] This made natural philosophy's interest in things in themselves (its pursuit of 'veritas') superior to medicine's instrumental concerns (its pursuit of 'utilitas'). But it was also possible to argue that medicine was more advanced than natural philosophy in that its interest in the organs of the body and the rational calculus of diseases, causes, symptoms, cures, and prophylaxis is more evolved; even its empirical knowledge of particulars (as opposed to the more general concerns of philosophy) could be turned to its advantage. Most natural philosophers in the Italian schools are recognizably Aristotelian in their outlook, and impress their peripatetic outlook on the medical faculties of their universities.[11] Their version of Aristotelianism did not exclude the use of

---

[8]   On the remuneration attached to chairs of natural philosophy and medicine see David A. Lines, 'Natural Philosophy in Renaissance Italy: The University of Bologna and the Beginnings of Specialization', *Early Science and Medicine*, 6 (2001), 267–323; also Nicholas Jardine, (1997), 'Keeping Order in the School of Padua: Jacopo Zabarella and Francesco Piccolomini on the Offices of Philosophy', in Daniel A. Di Liscia, Eckhard Kessler, and Charlotte Methuen (eds.), *Method and Order in Renaissance Philosophy of Nature* (Aldershot: Ashgate, 1997), 183–210.

[9]   'Optimus medicus philosophus'; 'Ubi desinit philosophus, incipit medicus'. On these tags, see Charles B. Schmitt, 'Aristotle among the Physicians', in Andrew Wear, R. K. French, and Iain M. Lonie (eds.), *The Medical Renaissance of the Sixteenth Century* (Cambridge: Cambridge University Press, 1985), 1–15. See Maclean, *Logic, Signs and Nature*, 80–4, for the points made in this paragraph, with supporting references.

[10]   The Aristotelian locus is *De sensu et sensato*, 436^{a}17–436^{b}1.

[11]   Schmitt, 'Aristotle among the Physicians'; Nancy G. Siraisi, *Avicenna in Renaissance Italy: The Canon and the Medical Teaching in Italian Universities after 1500* (Princeton: Princeton University Press, 1987), 222–3 (mentioning Zimara, Achillini, Nifo, Pomponazzi, Zabarella, Cremonini, and Liceti).

empirical data where necessary, as Charles Schmitt has shown; professors of medicine probably owed some part of their naturalism and empiricism to their early training by their philosophical colleagues.[12]

The anatomical enterprise of Vesalius and others in the middle years of the century is the clearest manifestation of these features of their approach, and may be linked to a new spirit which set experience above reason, and both experience and reason above authority. The Spanish physician Gomez Pereira (1500–58?) expressed the first option clearly in his *Nova veraque medicina* of 1558: 'so enormous is the force of experience in discovering the truth that we must, when an apparent explanation is opposed to experience, place greater trust in the evidence of the senses than the explanation, and search for a better one'.[13] A half-century later, the Paduan professor Sanctorius Sanctorius (1561–1636) related an anecdote (which his friend Galileo repeated in the *Dialogue on the Two World Systems*) which aptly demonstrates the second option. At a dissection, a doctrinaire Aristotelian is made to witness that nerves originate in the brain and not in the heart (as Aristotle had claimed), whereupon he tells the anatomist demonstrator that he had been made to see the matter so palpably and plainly that if Aristotle's text were not contrary to what he had just seen with his own eyes, he would have been forced

---

[12] See e.g. Charles B. Schmitt, 'Experience and Experiment: A Comparison of Zabarella's View with Galileo's in *De motu*, *Studies in the Renaissance*, 16 (1969), 80–138, on the use of experiment by Zabarella, who was 'an empirical Aristotelian in the sense that experience is almost always utilized to corroborate and verify the philosophical and scientific problems of Aristotle'; also Schmitt, 'Girolamo Borro's *Multae sunt nostrarum ignorationum causae* (Ms Vat. Ross. 1009)', in E. P. Mahoney (ed.), *Philosophy and Humanism* (Leiden: Brill, 1976), 462–7 (on Girolamo Borro, and the Aristotelian loci supporting experiment in *De caelo*, iii, *Nicomachean Ethics*, vi. 8, and *De generatione et corruptione*, i); Jerome Bylebyl, 'The School of Padua: Humanistic Medicine in the Sixteenth Century', in Charles Webster (ed.), *Health, Medicine and Mortality in the Sixteenth Century* (Cambridge: Cambridge University Press, 1979), 335–70.

[13] Pereira cited by Iain M. Lonie, 'Fever Pathology in the Sixteenth Century: Tradition and Innovation', in W. F. Bynum and V. Nutton (eds.), *Theories of Fever from Antiquity to the Enlightenment* (London, *Medical History*, Suppl. no.1, 1981), 42: 'adeo ingentem vim ad dignotionem veritatis experimenta habere, ut teneamur cum ratio apparens experimento adversatur, plus fidere experimento, quam rationi: cogamurque potiorem rationem, quam fuerit prior inquirere'. This view can be traced progressively back through Galen, *De Morbis Vulgaribus*, iv. 2, Aristotle, *Physics*, viii. 3 to (ps.) Hippocrates, *Praecepta*, i.

to admit that what he had seen was true.[14] There are several things which might be said about this anecdote,[15] one of which concerns its implicit misrepresentation of authorities, who on closer inspection do not seem to require such blind loyalty from their disciples and even set out to 'disauthorize' themselves. Aristotle urges his readers to sacrifice their closest personal ties in defence of the truth; Galen's 'precept' is precisely to pay more attention to experience and theory than to books.[16] An emblematic expression of such independence is the oft-quoted saying 'Plato (or Socrates, or Aristotle, or Galen, or Paracelsus) is my friend, but truth is an even greater friend'.[17] Such a statement could not apply, however, to theology, where revealed truth and its source cannot be separated.

One of the features of the University of Padua at the end of the fifteenth century, as it had been of the University of Paris in the

---

[14] Sanctorius Sanctorius, *Methodi vitandorum errorum omnium, qui in arte medica contingunt libri quindecim* (Geneva, 1630), 315 (iii. 15); Galileo Galilei, *Dialogi sopra il due massimi sistemi del mondo tolomeico e coperniciano*, ed. Ottavio Besomi and Mario Helbing (Padua: Antenore, 1998), 116–17.

[15] Reasons were found by a number of early modern thinkers for such loyalty to orthodox thinking even in the face of empirical disconfirmation. The rhetoric of citing an authority in this way is a manner of declaring one's allegiance not only to that specific authoritative doctrine but also to the arguments and theories which underpin it. Cf. the ironical Ciceronian trope 'I prefer to err with a given authority (Plato, or Galen, or Aristotle, or Avicenna, or "neoterici", or the Council of Trent) than to be right with his (or its) detractors.' The locus classicus is in Cicero, *Disputationes Tusculanae*, i. 17. 77: 'errare mehercule malo cum Platone... quam cum istis vera sentire': Maclean, *Logic, Signs and Nature*, 192 n. cites a range of sixteenth-century adaptations.

[16] *Nicomachean Ethics*, i. 6, 1096^{a}16–17; Galen, *In Hippocratis de morbis vulgaribus*, vi. 2. quoted by Luis García Ballester, 'Medical Ethics in Transition in the Latin Medicine of the Thirteenth and Fourteenth Centuries: New Perspectives on the Physician–Patient Relationship and the Doctor's Fee', in Andrew Wear, Johanna Geyer-Kordesch, and R. K. French (eds.), *Doctors and Ethics: The Earlier Historical Setting of Professional Ethics* (Amsterdam: Rodopi, 1993), 40: 'illos qui magis credunt auctoribus quam experientiae et rationibus esse temerios'. To 'disauthorize' an authority is a verb attested in 1623: see M. Le Roux de Lincy (ed.), *Les Caquets de l'accouchée* (Paris: Vannet, 1855), 210.

[17] Henri de Guerlac, 'Amicus Plato and Other Friends', *Journal of the History of Ideas*, 39 (1978), 627–33; Leonardo Taran, 'Amicus Plato sed magis amica veritas: from Plato and Aristotle to Cervantes', *Antike und Abendland*, 30 (1984), 93–124. It is even used by Luther in his debate about free will with Erasmus: see ibid. 120. See also Peter Dear, '*Totius in verba*: Rhetoric and Authority in the Early Royal Society', *Isis*, 76 (1985), 145–61.

middle years of the thirteenth century, was the uneasy relationship between philosophy and theology over the very issue of truth.[18] This is often associated with the phrase 'de naturalibus naturaliter': the view here expressed is that it is possible to investigate nature in a way which does not come into conflict with the truth of religion. It is not quite the same as the claim that the truths of religion and philosophy are different truths (the heresy of 'duplex veritas'), which was explicitly refuted in Bishop Tempier's Parisian condemnations of the 1270s;[19] rather, it is linked to Albert the Great's more modest ambition to set aside the question of God's direct interventions in this world when investigating nature. For him, philosophical discussion can aspire only to the level of probability (in the scholastic understanding of that term[20]); as a result, there is no conflict with the revealed truth, which belongs to a higher order of discourse.[21] Where there is conflict between philosophy and theology, it must always be settled in the favour of the latter; but it is perfectly acceptable to treat the two domains as being entirely separate. This is not, however, how Pomponazzi was to portray the doctrine in the early years of the sixteenth century:

It is noteworthy that Albertus Magnus came to various conclusions which are against the faith; he avers however that he made such assertions because physics is not to be mixed with theology, and because theology understands things differently from philosophy. Therefore those little devils (*diabulini*) of

---

[18] C. H. Lohr, 'The Medieval Interpretation of Aristotle', in Norman Kretzmann, Anthony Kenny, and Jan Pinborg (eds.), *The Cambridge History of Later Medieval Philosophy* (Cambridge: Cambridge University Press, 1982), 88–92; J. M. M. H. Thijssen, *Censure and Heresy at the University of Paris, 1200–1400* (Philadelphia: University of Pennsylvania Press, 1998).

[19] J. F. Wippel, 'The Condemnations of 1270 and 1277 at Paris', *Journal of Medieval and Renaissance Studies*, 7 (1977), 169–201; Friedrich Niewöhner and Olaf Pluta, *Atheismus im Mittelalter und in der Renaissance* (Wiesbaden: Harrassowitz, 1999).

[20] Maclean, *Logic, Signs and Nature*, 181.

[21] Bruno Nardi, 'La dottrina d'Alberto Magno sull' Inchoatio formae', in *Studi di filosofia medievale* (Rome: Edizioni di Storia e Letteratura, 1960), 108–50; Albertus Magnus, *De generatione et corruptione*, 1. 1. 22 ad t. c. 14: 'dico quod nihil ad me de Dei miraculis cum ego de naturalibus disserram.' See also James A. Weisheipl (ed.), *Albertus Magnus and the Sciences: Commemorative Essays* (Toronto: Institute of Medieval Studies, 1980); on probability, see Maclean, *Logic, Signs and Nature*, 123–32, 181.

Dominican friars [i.e. inquisitors] should burn Albert; but instead they make him a saint.[22]

As well as Aristotle, Galen was treated as an authority whose writing needed to be reconciled with Christian doctrine.[23] Here the principal issues were the relationship of body to mind or soul (most explicitly discussed in the treatise *Quod animi mores*), the relationship between good regimen and divine precept on matters such as diet and sexuality, and astrological determinism.[24] Because the link between theology and medicine was less intimate than that between theology and philosophy, the conflict of views was less often debated, but physicians were aware of it. One of the clearest statements of the way it was usually resolved is found in the lectures of the Paduan professor Giambattista da Monte (1498–1552), who, in separating sharply theology from natural philosophy, repeats Pomponazzi's statement about Albert above, but seeks at one point not his authority but that of Duns Scotus;[25] and elsewhere, on the issue of the generation of mixed bodies, he interposes the following comment:

---

[22] 'Notandum quod Albertus Magnus determinavit plura contra fidem; tamen, inquit, dixi sic, quia phisica non sunt commiscenda cum theologia, quia theologia aliter sentit quam philosophia. Ideo fratres diabulini sancti dominici deberent comburere Albertum ... tamen faciunt Albertum sanctum': quoted by Bruno Nardi, *Studi su Pietro Pomponazzi* (Florence: Le Monnier, 1965), 27 n.

[23] He also had to be reconciled with Aristotle: the classic text on this, which was still being used as a textbook in the seventeenth century, is Pietro d'Abano's *Conciliator* of the early fourteenth century.

[24] See Ian Maclean, 'Naturalisme et croyance personnelle dans le discours médical à la fin de la Renaissance', *Journal of the Institute of Romance Studies*, 6 (1998), 177–92; id., *Logic, Signs and Nature*, 87–92.

[25] Giambattista da Monte, *In nonum librum Rhasis ad Mansorem Regem Arabum expositio* (Venice, 1554), 59–60: 'hic, si me rogeris, quid determinandum sit, possum dupliciter respondere secundum duplicem formam, quam possum induere. Si velim esse philosophus, et in principiis philosophiae consistere, non in fide nostra, non possum non Hippocrati et Galeno assentire. At si formam Theologicam volumus induere, quod certe debemus facere, dicendum est Arabum opinionem esse veram. Sed hoc, ut est re ipsa verum, ita sine demonstratione credi debet. nihil enim peius est, quam quaerere demonstrationes in iis, quae fide tendenda sunt. Quia agendae potius gratiae Deo, qui intellectum nostrum illuminavit, ut ea sciret, quae nullo medio naturali percipi possunt, et rogemus Dominum, ut augeat credulitatem in nobis. Et certe in hoc Scotus se optime gessit, qui cum tenuisset animam in via naturali et Peripatetica mortalem esse in 4 lib Sententiarum, quaestione 41 vel 43, postea conversus ad Dominum, egit illi gratias, quod id cognovisset, illuminatione divina esse verissimum, quod naturaliter falsum videbatur. Sed quia nunc in scholis

To this question theologians, philosophers and doctors will give different replies. I shall say something briefly on this issue, but what I shall say will be as an Aristotelian and a doctor. For if ever I wanted to talk about it in theological terms, it might well be that I would say exactly the opposite. I myself think that there is nothing worse in philosophy than to mix theology with it.[26]

Philosophers and doctors are here taken to be united (indeed, Paduan medical graduates were styled 'doctors of medicine and philosophy'); and both arrogate to themselves a robust independence from the claims of the Queen of Faculties.

The agreed relationship between Aristotle and Christianity (by which it was permitted philosophically to debate Aristotelian views which clashed with Catholic doctrine provided that the discussion was settled in favour of the Church) involved Aristotle's authoritative Arabic commentators, notably Averroes, whose name was also linked to heresies, most notably that which claimed that all mankind shares a single intellect. Averroism was seen by the Church in the later Middle Ages as a threat to Christianity's doctrine of individual responsibility and salvation; this threat was exacerbated by the development of Neoplatonist philosophy and the rediscovery, translation, and diffusion of ancient Greek commentators on Aristotle in the latter part of the fifteenth century. In 1489, pressure was put on the natural philosopher Nicoletto Vernia by Bishop Pietro Barozzi of Padua to publish a recantation of a treatise in which he had determined that on the matter of the soul, Averroes had correctly interpreted the text of Aristotle.[27] More than two decades later, the issue

profitemur nos esse philosophos et medicos, ex principiis philosophiae defendimus opinionem Galeni et Hippocratis, quia nihil deterius est arbitror, quam miscere philosophiam theologiae.' Cited by Siraisi, *Avicenna*, 291–2; see also Duns Scotus, *Quaestiones in quatuor libros Sententiarum*, xliii. 2.

[26] da Monte, *In nonum librum Rhasis expositio*, 31: 'In qua quidem generatione aliter respondent theologi, aliter philosophi, aliter medici. Ego brevissime de hac questione aliqua dicam, sed quaecunque dicam, dicam ut peripateticus, et ut medicus. Nam quando theologice de ea loqui voluero, totum forte oppositum dicam. Nihil autem existimo deterius in philosophia posse contingere quam cum ea theologiam commiscere'; cited (with other texts) by Siraisi, *Avicenna*, 248, and Maclean, 'Naturalisme et croyance personnelle', 185.

[27] Edward P. Mahoney, 'Nicoletto Vernia and Agostino Nifo on Alexander of Aphrodisias: An Unnoticed Dispute', *Rivista critica di storia della filosofia*, 23 (1968), 270–1; Eckhard Kessler, 'The Intellective Soul', in Schmitt and Skinner (eds.), *The Cambridge History of Renaissance Philosophy*, 492–3.

had not gone away; it gave rise to a discussion at the Fifth Lateran Council in Rome, which on 19 December 1513 condemned all who asserted that the intellectual soul in man is mortal, or that there is but one single intellective soul for the whole human race. It reiterated the doctrine affirmed two centuries before by Clement V at the General Council of Vienne that the intellectual soul is the form of the human body, that it is immortal, and that it is single for each individual human being; and it added that since one truth cannot contradict another truth, every assertion contrary to the truth of faith was defined as altogether false.[28]

II

Pietro Pomponazzi (1462–1525) would have been aware of Vernia's teaching and his problems; he began himself to teach natural philosophy in Padua in 1486, becoming a doctor of medicine in 1495, and continuing to teach with short breaks until 1509 (when the university closed because of war); he ended his career in Bologna (1511–25). He lectured and wrote on a wide range of issues arising from Aristotelian texts: some of his works were published in his lifetime, most notoriously his discussion of the immortality of the soul; others were circulated in manuscript, to be printed much later in the century. As he never mastered Greek, he was not able, as were some of his predecessors and contemporaries, to work from the Greek text of Aristotle; he relied on translations of the Stagirite's Greek commentators, and remained faithful to a scholastic mode of exposition of texts. His notoriety was not due to humanist learning, but more to his radical questioning of texts, his jaunty lecturing style, and his use of the commentaries on Aristotle by Averroes and Alexander of Aphrodisias.[29] Naudé's description of him as a 'pure peripatetic' is very appropriate; his life's work lay in investigating the

---

[28] Heinrich Denzinger, *Enchiridion symbolorum, definitionum et declarationum de rebus fidei et morum*, ed. Adolf Schönmetzer (Barcelona: Herder, 1976), 353–4 (no. 738); also ibid. 284 (no. 481).

[29] The best introduction to Pomponazzi is Martin L. Pine, *Pietro Pomponazzi, Radical Philosopher of the Renaissance* (Padua: Antenore, 1986).

peripatetic corpus, and in adjudicating between competing interpretations; his declared aim was to show the internal consistency of this corpus and to reveal the authentic views of Aristotle.[30] He states on more than one occasion that he is hostile to aspects of Averroes's interpretations; his approval of Alexander's reading of the *De anima* on the issue of the immortality and immateriality of the soul suggests that his was the preferred guide to Aristotle. But it would be wrong to underestimate Pomponazzi's independence of thought: in a way directly relevant to this discussion, he asserts that 'it is important for anyone in pursuit of the truth to be a heretic in philosophy'.[31]

His practice as a commentator is marked by his willingness to doubt both his own conclusions about the text and those of others, and to approach issues in an unconventional way by asking new 'quaestiones'. The manuscript of his commentary on Aristotle's *De partibus animalium*, delivered in 1522, gives an insight into his lively and irreverent approach to texts.[32] At one point, he admits, 'I have never understood this chapter, and don't at present. I doubt whether I'll ever understand it. But I'll read it to you to open the way'; elsewhere one finds comments such as 'I have only set out to have a conversation with you about this book, as if I were a fellow disciple'; 'I only want to teach you to doubt'; 'There are [not one, but] several plausible opinions about this material.'[33] This deliberate irreverence

---

[30] Henri Busson, 'Introduction', in Pietro Pomponazzi, *De naturalium effectuum admirandorum causis: Les causes des merveilles de la nature, ou les enchantements* (Paris: Rieder, 1930), 57 (citing Naudé); Pietro Pomponazzi, *Abhandlung über die Unsterblichkeit der Seele: lateinisch-deutsch*, tr. and introd. Burkhard Mojsisch (Hamburg: Meiner, 1990), 5: 'Aristotelis dictis consonare . . . sententiam Aristotelis revelare.'

[31] Pine, *Pomponazzi*, 18, citing Cesare Oliva, 'Note sull'insegnamento di Pietro Pomponazzi', *Girornale critico della filosofia italiana*, 7 (1926), 274, 'oportet enim in philosophia haereticum esse, qui veritatem invenire cupit.'

[32] Pomponazzi, *Expositio super libris De partibus animalium*, ed. Stefano Perfetti (Florence: Olschki, 2004).

[33] Cited by Stefano Perfetti, '*Docebo vos dubitare*. Il commento inedito di Pietro Pomponazzi al *De partibus animalium* (Bologna 1521–1524)', *Documenti e studi sulla tradizione filosofica medievale*, 10 (1999): 446, 460, 459: 'istud capitulum nunquam intellexi, nec intelligo. Nescio an in futurum intelligam. Sed ideo lego ut vobis viam aperiam'; 'tantum proposui habere sermonem vobiscum, ac si essem vester condiscipulus'; 'docebo tantum vos dubitare'; 'de ista materia . . . sunt enim plures opiniones': 'opiniones' here has the sense of 'endoxa' set out in Aristotle, *Topics*, i. 1, 100^b 18 ff.: 'those which commend themselves to all or to the majority or to the wise—that is to all of the wise or to the majority or to the most famous and distinguished of them.'

about his own and Aristotle's authority must have seemed very refreshing and very daring; but there are even more audacious passages about Christian witness. In referring to Aristotle's reliance on second-hand evidence, he says at one point:

You should know that Aristotle was not purveying true knowledge in this book, but hearsay, because he did not see all these things with his own eyes, and would not have been able to if he had lived a thousand years, but trusted those who saw them... he had the same knowledge of his subject matter as we Christians have of Christ: for we have not seen Christ, but believe that he existed from the writings of others.[34]

This is not quite heterodox, but it sets aside Christ's presence as experienced by the soul of the believer, and suggests a relativism which would most certainly have been seen as religiously offensive. His apparently undifferentiated use of both 'God' and 'gods' in some of his writings and his startling views about the astrologically occasioned rise and fall of religions are other symptoms of the same relativist outlook.[35]

Pomponazzi is best known for the affair caused by the publication of his monograph *De immortalitate animae* in 1516, although it would be misleading to suggest that the publication was alone responsible for the furore which followed; the contents of the book were known much earlier from lectures he had delivered at Padua, one of which directly addressed the question whether the rational soul is immaterial and immortal.[36] There has not been much dis-

---

[34] Cited by Perfetti, '*Docebo vos dubitare*', 458: 'debetis scire quod Aristoteles in hoc libro non habuit veram scientiam, sed credulitatem et fidem, quoniam Aristoteles non vidit ista omnia oculis suis, quoniam non vidisset si mille annis vixisset, sed fidem dedit illis qui viderunt haec... sic esse scripsit et libris mandavit. Et ipse Aristoteles de istis rebus habuit eandem scientiam quam nos christiani de Christo habemus: nos enim non vidimus Christum, sed credimus scribentibus eum fuisse.'

[35] Pietro Pomponazzi, *Opera: De naturalium effectuum admirandorum causis, seu, de incantationibus liber. Item de fato: libero arbitrio: praedestinatione: providentia Dei, libri V. in quibus difficillima capita et quaestiones theologicae et philosophicae ex sana orthodoxae fidei doctrina explicantur, et multis raris historiis passim illustrantur, per autorem, qui se in omnibus canonicae scripturae sanctorumque doctorum iudicio submittit*, ed. Guglielmo Gratarolo (Basle, 1567), 283 ff.; Lynn Thorndike, *A History of Magic and Experimental Science* (New York: Columbia University Press, 1941), v. 108; Pine, *Pomponazzi*, 235–75; Mojsisch in Pomponazzi, *Unsterblichkeit*, xi.

[36] Kessler, 'The Intellective Soul', 502 ('utrum anima rationalis sit immaterialis et immortalis'). See also Stefano Perfetti, '*An anima nostra sit mortalis. Una quaestio inedita discussa da Pietro Pomponazzi nel 1521*', *Rinascimento*, 8 (1998), 205–26.

agreement about what he meant, but a great deal about what he himself was personally committed to. In this treatise, as in other texts, he protests repeatedly that he was, like Albert, remaining within the bounds of philosophical discourse ('intra limites naturales'), thereby recognizing also the limitations of human knowledge;[37] elsewhere, he makes the explicit statement that the truths of philosophy are no more than 'probable', being both not fully scientific and incomplete; these statements prepare the reader for his formally recorded submission to the authority of the Catholic Church and its authoritative version of truth.[38]

His position is in a certain sense both anti-Platonist and anti-Averroist; he claims that Aristotle's doctrine of the soul determines that all intellectual activity is mediated through the senses, making the survival of the intellect without a body unprovable; that human consciousness requires both body and soul; and that the 'scala naturae' (the hierarchy of beasts, man, and divine intelligences) requires the human soul to be mortal, against Averroes's doctrine that the agent intellect in man is immaterial and shared by all men, and against the Neoplatonist tenet that the soul is separable from the body.[39] These conclusions are reached through a consideration of a logically distributed field of questions concerning mortality and immortality, and plural and single human natures. Although he, like Vernia, publicly abjured his position (or rather, had a text of recantation written by another scholar associated with his own), he continued to affirm Aristotle's authentic opinion to be that the soul was mortal.[40] He also lays stress on the political motivation for maintaining the immortality of the soul (that it keeps populations in the thrall of the powers that be, for fear that sins committed in this world will be punished in the next); this weakens the case in

---

[37] See above, n. 22.

[38] Pomponazzi, *Unsterblichkeit*, 236: 'haec itaque sunt, quae mihi in hac materia dicenda videntur, semper tamen me et in hoc et in aliis subiiciendo Dei Apostolicae'.

[39] Pine, *Pomponazzi*, 124 ff.

[40] Nardi, *Studi su Pomponazzi*, 252–3, quoting his commentary on *De generatione et corruptione*, ii, of 1522: 'vos scitis quod ego composui librum in quo teneo, secundum Aristotelem, animam esse mortalem, licet credam opinionem illam esse falsam, quoniam est contra fidem nostram.'

philosophical terms by making the thesis of immortality utilitarian rather than true per se.[41]

Between 1517 and 1519, attacks on his monograph came from various religious orders (especially the Dominicans, guardians of Thomist philosophy); the sale of the book was banned in Venice; a papal warning was issued in June 1518, requiring its author to bring it into consonance with the Lateran decree. The book was also referred to Pietro Bembo, then a cardinal in Rome, who gave it a clean bill of health; Pomponazzi defended himself with two tracts (one of which was initially refused a licence for publication in Bologna), against published critiques by his ex-pupil and churchman Gasparo Contarini, his philosophical rival Agostino Nifo, and the Dominicans Bartolomeo de Spina and Girolamo Fornario, *inter alios*.[42] In his two defences, he did not retreat from the argument *a decoro personae* (i.e. that he was setting out faithfully what the Aristotelian texts meant, in full knowledge that Aristotle was a pagan). It is worthy of note that at this stage, the debate was a wholly Italian affair; although his treatise came later to be discussed elsewhere in Europe, Pomponazzi was not an international figure in his lifetime.[43]

In 1520, he completed two monographs, the *De incantationibus* and the *De fato*. Both relate to the relationship of the superlunary and sublunary realms, and develop lines of argument that had been adumbrated in much earlier works; this shows Pomponazzi to be more of an accumulative thinker than one whose thought underwent development.[44] The former of these works (which found its way into the 1580 edition of the *Index librorum prohibitorum*[45]) touches on

---

[41] Pomponazzi, *Unsterblichkeit*, 197, 221–2.

[42] Pine, *Pomponazzi*, 124 ff.

[43] The last refutation of the *De immortalitate animae* was by the French Jesuit Antoine Sirmond, in 1635, in response to its reprinting at an undisclosed location (probably in Northern Europe) in 1634.

[44] See Busson, 'Introduction', 10 ff. (on *De actione reali* as a predecessor of the *De incantationibus*); Eckhard Kessler, 'Narturverständnisse im 15. und 16. Jahrhundert', in Lothar Schäfer und Elisabeth Ströker (eds.), *Naturauffassungen in Philosophie, Wissenschaft, Technik* (Munich: Karl Alber, 1994), 38–44 (on Pomponazzi's conception of nature).

[45] J. M. de Bujanda et al. (1994), *Index des livres interdits, ix: Index de Rome 1590, 1593, 1596. Avec étude des index de Parme 1580 et Munich 1582* (Quebec: Université de Sherbrooke/Droz, 1994), 163.

the difficult question of divine intelligences and demons, which had become fashionable through the work of Ficino. Pomponazzi here argues that the heavens regulate nature; such regulation may produce effects so infrequent as to cause them to appear miraculous, but they are not miracles.[46] He also denies that demons intervene directly in the sublunary world. In a characteristic gesture which both submits to theology and at the same time declares his independence from it, Pomponazzi begins his discussion with the statement that these latter are to be believed in as a religious truth, and yet are at the same time no more than explanatory devices allowing us to 'save the phenomena'; an argument which would be applied in due course to heliocentrism.[47] More daringly, he turns the discussion to miracles; with the same equivocality, he begins by saying that the raising of Lazarus is a miracle which only Christ could have accomplished, but then proceeds to claim that miracles can be explained by natural, if occult, causes (including the 'natural' cause of superlunary influence), and that the resurrection of the dead by natural means is indeed conceivable.[48] He even says (in a yet more audacious passage) that it is not impossible for a man born under (and determined to some degree by) a given constellation to be able to command the wind and waves (alluding to Luke 8: 25); the reader may be tempted to link this bold claim with that concerning the rise and fall of religions (including Christianity) under the influence of the stars.[49] The integrity of religious truth here comes under considerable pressure. The power of words over nature through incantation—a much-discussed medical topic—is also attributed to the action of the vital spirits of the body, as is the capacity of doctors to heal by harnessing the imagin-

[46] Pomponazzi, *Opera*, 294: 'non sunt autem miracula quia sint totaliter contra naturam et praeter ordinem corporum coelestium, sed pro tanto dicuntur miracula, quia insueta et rarissime facta et non secundum communem naturae cursum sed in longissimis periodis.'

[47] Ibid. 1567: 6: 'ut salvemus multa experimenta'; cf. Andreas Osiander's preface to Copernicus, most recently discussed by Anthony Corones, 'Copernicus, Printing and the Politics of Knowledge', in Guy Freeland and Anthony Corones (eds.), *1543 and All That: Image and Word, Change and Continuity in the Proto-scientific Revolution* (Dordrecht: Kluwer, 2000), 280–4.

[48] Pomponazzi, *Opera*, 81, 94.

[49] Ibid. 241: 'non est incredibile aliquem hominem sub tali constellatione natum ut imperat mari, ventibus et tempestatibus'; ibid. 283–4; Thorndike, *A History of Magic and Experimental Science*, v. 107.

ative powers of their patients.[50] It will, however, come as no surprise
that these daring asseverations are accompanied by a humble declaration of submission to the authority of the Church.[51]

The *De fato, libero arbitrio, praedestinatione, et providentia Dei*
looks at the vexed issues of determinism and free will. As Martin
Pine has shown, Pomponazzi evinces the same independence of
mind and the same willingness to ask new questions here as in his
other works; but his claim to investigate things wholly within the
realm of nature in so far as it is given to unaided reason to engage in
such investigation[52] is not so easily upheld, as he shows a very
sophisticated grasp of the discussions of theologians from Boethius
to Ockham who sought to reconcile the determinism implied in
God's foreknowledge with the need to assert future contingency,
without which there could be no space for freedom of the human
will. The term 'predestination' which appears in the title did not in
1520 have the contentious ring that it would have after the publication of Calvin's *Institutes* twenty years later; the Lateran Council of
1513 had not seen the necessity of regulating discussion on this issue,
as they had that of the immortality of the soul.

There seems to be a consistency in Pomponazzi's writing; in an
Albertine way, his protestations of submission to the Church can be
reconciled with his propensity to doubt, his programmatic survey of
Aristotle both from the point of view of correct interpretation and
from that of natural truth, and his conception of a cosmos in which
the superlunary realm influences hylomorphic human nature, the
immortality of whose intellect is undemonstrable. But how far he was
personally committed to this view remains unclear; and no further
light is shed upon it by the account of his deathbed conversation with
a pupil (written within two days of his death). Pomponazzi had
refused to take sustenance, and was heard to utter 'I am departing,
happily departing.' When asked where he was going, he replied,
'where all mortals go'. 'And where', enquired one of those present,

---

[50] Maclean, *Logic, Signs and Nature*, 112–13 n. (on incantation); Busson, 'Introduction', 33.

[51] Pomponazzi, *Opera*, 325: 'quantum autem religionem attinet, si quid in his
dictis nostris offendetur, quod sanctae Ecclesiae catholicae adversetur, vel ei minus
placeat, illud totum revoco, et humiliter eius correctioni me subiicio.'

[52] Ibid. 1010: 'stando in puris naturalibus et quantum dat ratio humana.'

'do all mortals go?' 'Where I am going', replied Pomponazzi, 'and others have gone.' Martin Pine suggests, I think rightly, that one cannot infer from this conversation that he intended to commit suicide by self-starvation; but it cannot be said that its evasiveness provides firm grounds for attributing to Pomponazzi a strong personal faith in salvation and human immortality.[53]

III

Pomponazzi's lectures were, like those of many sixteenth-century university figures, taken down by his pupils and circulated; so were his monographs.[54] Girolamo Cardano, who studied at Padua in 1524–5, had access to a manuscript of the *De fato*; both this work and the *De incantationibus* were procured in about 1536 by Guglielmo Gratarolo (1516–68), a student of medicine and member of a prominent Bergamese family, who would become responsible for their European diffusion in printed form. On completing his doctorate at Padua, Gratarolo returned to his native city to practise medicine, and underwent a conversion there to Protestantism in 1546; after suffering persecution by the local inquisition, he fled in 1549 to Basle, where he practised as a doctor and taught at the university.[55] He took the unusual step of issuing a broadsheet in 1552 in which he specified his own religious beliefs, and included a millenarian admonition to the faithful; he entered into contact with Calvin in Geneva, and reported to him on the reaction of his adopted city to the trial and execution of Michael Servetus; he associated with publishing circles, compiling an index to the Basle edition of Galen's works, and producing a number of short, cheaply made tracts on practical medical topics which he seems to have intended to const-

---

[53] Pine, *Pomponazzi*, 51–2, quoting a letter of Antonio Brocardo of 20 May 1525: 'abeo, loetus abeo'; 'quo ergo vultis abire domine?'; 'quo mortales omnes'; 'et quo erunt mortales?'; 'quo ego et alii'.

[54] Giancarlo Zanier, *Ricerche sulla diffusione e fortuna del "De incantationibus" di Pomponazzi* (Florence: La nuova Italia, 1975).

[55] He also taught for a short time at Marburg.

itute a sort of modest self-help encyclopaedia for educated laymen.[56] He also edited books for the humanist publisher, Heinrich Petri, who was famous for his production of medical and natural-philosophical works; among these were a group of alchemical treatises and the unpublished texts of Pomponazzi referred to above. The first Pomponazzi volume, containing only the *De incantationibus*, appeared in 1556, and was dedicated to the Lutheran bibliophile Count Palatinate Ottheinrich; the second was dedicated to his successor Frederick the Pious, who was more sympathetic to Philippism and Calvinism. The notoriety of Pomponazzi's book on the soul, with its Alexandrian reading of Aristotle, was noted by Gratarolo, who justified the publication of both the *De fato* and the *De incantationibus*, with its unorthodox account of miracles, by reference to Augustine's practice of setting down clear accounts of heresies before refuting them. Gratarolo's preface begins with a qualified approval of human intellectual curiosity, and a defence of the activities of publishers and others who are making interesting materials readily available to the Latinate public.[57]

Gratarolo does not believe all philosophers to be heretics, as he says some do; rather, he suggests that the best theologians were trained in philosophy. He also respects Pomponazzi for submitting himself to the authority of 'his' Catholic Church, and cites the contemporary historian Paolo Giovio as witness of Pomponazzi's piety. As the *De fato* is seen as a refutation of the views of Alexander of Aphrodisias, it counterbalances Pomponazzi's approval of this pagan commentator in the *De immortalitate animae*. Gratarolo's dedicatory letter ends with an exhortation to the irenic Frederick to uphold the 'holy and orthodox church' (not presumably, the Cath-

---

[56] Guglielmo Gratarolo, *Opuscula de memoria reparanda, augenda, conservanda; de praedictione morum naturamque hominum; de mutatione temporum, eiusque signis perpetuis*, in Joannes ab Indagine, *Introductiones apotelematicae elegantes in hysiologiam, astrologiam naturalem, complexiones hominum, naturas plantarum, cum periaxiomatibus de faciebus signorum et canonibus de aegritudinibus hominum* ... (Oberursel,1603); Nancy G. Siraisi, 'Medicine and the Renaissance World of Learning', *Bulletin of the History of Medicine*, 78 (2004), 1–36.

[57] The dedicatory letter in Pomponazzi, *Opera*, sig. a4v refers to Petri as 'magnificus et doctus typographus', and implies that he, together with Frederick the Pious, subsidized its publication. On curiosity, see Lorraine Daston, 'Curiosity in Early Modern Science', *Word and Image*, 11: 4 (1995), 391–404.

olic Church of Pomponazzi); it recalls to the reader the titlepage with its reference to yet another concept of orthodoxy (more Gratarolo's than Pomponazzi's, although attributed to the latter): 'difficult topics and theological and philosophical questions are explained through the sound doctrine of orthodox faith ... by the author, who submits himself in all things to the judgment of Canonical Scripture, the saints and the doctors [of the Church]'.[58] This constellation of orthodoxies—Roman Catholic, Philippist, and Calvinist—may seem surprising: it could only have come from the pen of someone like Gratarolo, whose faith is defined minimally (in the broadsheet he distributed) by the Apostle's, Athanasian, and Nicene creeds, together with the text of Holy Writ.[59] In the text itself, Gratarolo shows less tolerance, and allows himself to remove or attenuate Pomponazzi's references to the Roman Church;[60] but there is no commentary on the divergence of views over predestination between Calvin and Pomponazzi. Gratarolo himself seems to have taken a moderate position on this issue; his account of physiognomy in his booklet on the subject asserts that all animals are determined absolutely as to character by their physical being, whereas man is only predisposed to certain virtues or vices as a result of his facial and bodily characteristics; he has free will precisely to combat the evil tendencies of his psychophysical nature.[61]

IV

Gratarolo did not achieve the fame of either Pomponazzi or Cardano, but he is of note here as the maker of Pomponazzi's

---

[58] 'In quibus difficillima capita et quaestiones Theologicae et Philosophicae ex sana orthodoxae fidei doctrina explicantur, et multis raris historiis passim illustrantur, per autorem, qui se in omnibus Canonicae scripturae sanctorumque doctorum iudicio submittit.'

[59] *Confessione di fede, con una certissima et importantissima ammonitione a tutti gli huomini che credono l'eterna vita* (Basle, 1552).

[60] Manuela Doni, 'Il "de Incantationibus" di Pietro Pomponazzi e l'edizione di Guglielmo Gratarolo', *Rinascimento*, 15 (1995), 183–230.

[61] His stance is similar to that of the Philippist philosopher and doctor Nicolaus Taurellus, on whom see Maclean, *Logic, Signs and Nature*, 89–90.

international reputation, and in himself affords an interesting example of the philosophical and medical sensitivity to theological issues in the middle years of the century. Moreover, he provides a bridge between the other two figures of this chapter: when Girolamo Cardano passed through Basle in 1553 on his way back to Milan from Scotland, he was a guest of Gratarolo, and through him obtained an introduction to the world of publishing in the city. Cardano (1501–76) was by then an acknowledged polymath and established medical professor (at Pavia). His education (as an illegitimate child) had been unconventional; his father taught him mathematics, but not Latin, and he did not acquire Greek until his fortieth year. But he did attend the universities of Pavia and Padua, and obtained a doctorate in medicine. His intellectual interests encompassed mathematics, logic, practical medicine, astrology, moralistic writing, history, fictional writing, natural philosophy, and medicine. Unlike many of his contemporaries, he was aware that publication was a road to fame, and he was fortunate that a list of his unpublished works, which he caused to be printed at the end of a treatise on arithmetic, published in his native Milan in 1539, was noticed by the agent of a prominent German publisher, Joannes Petreius of Nuremberg; from there, he found his way into print in France and, with Gratarolo's help, in Switzerland, where Heinrich Petri published for him until his death.[62]

Like Pomponazzi, he suffered the attentions of the Inquisition in Bologna late in his life, and underwent a short spell of imprisonment there in 1570. Also like Pomponazzi, he protested his orthodoxy, and submitted to censure, writing a tract of corrections to his works; he also wrote to the Congregation of the Index of Prohibited books, offering to compose a set of retractions of his errors, but stressing that they were no more than errors; neither he nor anyone in his household, he averred, had been associated in any way with heresy.[63] Furthermore, Cardano proudly advertised his authorship of a number of unpublished devotional works, including the lives of Saint Martin and the Virgin, and a hymn to God.[64] He records that he

---

[62] Maclean, 'Cardano and his Publishers'.

[63] Nancy G. Siraisi, *The Clock and the Mirror: Girolamo Cardano and Renaissance Medicine* (Princeton: Princeton University Press, 1997), 225–6.

[64] Girolamo Cardano, *Opera omnia*, ed. Charles Spon (Lyons, 1663), i. 41.

destroyed a large body of manuscripts after his release from custody. It is not possible to be certain which these were, but they almost certainly included all or part of three early works (his life of Christ, the *De fato*, and most of the *De arcanis aeternitatis*, which were looked on with suspicion as early as 1538), as well as the *De rebus supernaturalibus* and those sections of the *Problemata* which dealt with theologically sensitive issues.[65] Rather than being deliberately bold, Cardano seems to have been naive about his writing and his contacts: he was open about his correspondence with prominent Italian protestant exiles, and this, together with his publication by Northern publishers such as Sebastian Gryphius and Heinrich Petri and his respectful geniture of Martin Luther, would have attracted the suspicions of the Bologna Inquisition, which was noted for its rigour and its strong loyalty to Rome. In 1580, all his works except those dealing with medicine found their way *nisi corrigantur* into the Index of forbidden books.[66]

In 1562, Cardano produced a map of the whole of human knowledge, in which he detailed his own contributions to many of its domains.[67] Not all of these contributions were heterodox, either in religious or scientific terms; but few were respectful of established astrological, medical, and philosophical authority. Cardano's spur to write was in many cases a reaction to an existing writer or doctrine. He began collecting his disputatious *Contradicentia medica* very early in his career; later, he systematically opposed Luca Gaurico's astrology, as Anthony Grafton has shown; his mathematics involved him in bitter personal disputes.[68] I shall set aside his mathematics and astrology here for reasons of space, and survey his refutations of Pomponazzi, his *De subtilitate*, and his medical works.

---

[65] Ian Maclean, 'Introduction', in *Girolamo Cardano: de libris propriis* (Milan: FrancoAngeli, 2004), 45.

[66] Maclean, 'Cardano and his Publishers'.

[67] de Bujanda, *Index des livres interdits*, ix. 108; Guido dall'Olio, *Eretici e inquisitori nella Bologna del Cinquecento* (Bologna: Istituto per la Storia di Bologna, 1999).

[68] Anthony Grafton, *Cardano's Cosmos: The Worlds and Works of a Renaissance Astrologer* (Cambridge, Mass.: Harvard University Press, 1999), 97–103; António Cândido Simões Capelo, 'Gerolamo Cardano, il matematico', in Emilio Gabba and Riccardo Galetto (eds.), *Gerolamo Cardano nel quinto centenario della nascita* (Pavia: Edizioni Cardano, 2001), 22–8.

Pomponazzi's work, which was well known to him, provoked him to surpass or refute it. In 1533 he wrote a *De fato* in supersession of Pomponazzi's (which he describes variously as thin and incomplete); in the same work he also dismisses the treatises on the same subject by Cicero and Alexander of Aphrodisias. He records the chapter titles of his *De fato* in the *De libris propriis* of 1557; from this we can learn something of their contents. There is discussion of the proofs for the existence of fate (including empirical proofs), of the relationship between fate, free will, and chance, fate and God, fate and religion, fate and prophecy, and fate's role in the history of the world. Like Pomponazzi, Cardano is aware of the difficulty which arises if it is asserted both that future contingency is possible, and that there is a finite number of causes which produce future events, entailing a form of determinism; but where Pomponazzi chooses to examine the answers given by medieval theologians, Cardano claims to write only as a philosopher, and devises his own eccentric solution to the problem.[69]

The same claim is made in his *De animorum immortalitate*, which he wrote some eleven years after the *De fato* to refute Pomponazzi's work. This is a somewhat rambling discussion of the subject, in contrast to Pomponazzi's tightly structured argument; it is both exegetical and analytic, where Pomponazzi had confined himself to the task of interpreting Aristotle correctly. Unlike his predecessor, Cardano offers his own account of the rational soul: the human intellect is not a substance, but a power ('virtus'); it is a sort of eternal and impassive light, flowing from one source, distributed among the bodies of individual men; it is a complex of the agent intellect (which contains the 'total substance': i.e. the combination of the light and the 'simulachra'), the material intellect (the light itself), and the passive intellect (which receives the 'simulachra rerum'). The reason why the intellect is not always active, and why it is diverse in its power in different men, and absent from beasts altogether, is the interference of matter (which is compared to clouds which obscure the sun).[70]

This eclectic account—part Neoplatonist, part Aristotelian—is not however the sole focus of the text, which also discusses many

---

[69] Cardano, *Opera*, i. 62–3, 98–100.   [70] Ibid. ii. 529–30.

of the themes which emerge elsewhere in Cardano's writings, including demonology, miracles, and the principles of good exegesis.[71] His belief in the existence of demons (expressed also in other of his writings) distinguishes his work from that of Pomponazzi,[72] as does the steadfast claim that the rational soul is immaterial. It is therefore somewhat ironic that he should come to be classed by posterity as a materialist through his association with those figures such as Vanini who cite his work with approval.[73] Unusually for a graduate of Padua, Cardano chooses to obey the injunction of the Lateran Council, and sets out to prove the immortality of the soul from natural reasoning alone; he is explicit in this work as elsewhere about his religious orthodoxy.[74] In direct contradiction of Pomponazzi, he writes that there is only a minimal difference between the view of the soul held by theologians and that held by philosophers, the latter being less fully worked out than the former; that the end of man is seen to be the same in both disciplines; and that it is not for philosophers to speak of God and miracles (an injunction he himself fails to obey; like Pomponazzi, he allows himself to say at one point that what has in the past been taken for a miracle may in fact have a natural cause).[75]

---

[71] According to ibid. ii. 492, one of the major causes of error among recent thinkers lies in the confusion of hermeneutics with true philosophy; his contemporaries are accused of not distinguishing the following two questions: what did the philosopher mean by his words? And is it true in the light of reason?: 'causa tanti erroris fuit, quod [Philosophi] haec duo quaesita, confuderunt, quid senserit Philosophus? Quid ex ratione naturali est manifestum?' On Cardano's hermeneutics, see Maclean, *Logic, Signs and Nature*, 206–33.

[72] Gabriel, 'Vita Cardani, ac de eodem Iudicium', in Cardano, *Opera*, i sig. i1–o2 comments unfavourably on this.

[73] The anti-libertine writings of Garasse and others of the 1620s strongly suggest that Cardano believed the soul to be material; a view repeated in 1737 by Boyer: see Naudé, *Apologie*; Jean-Baptiste de Boyer, marquis d'Argens, *La Philosophie du bon sens* (1737), ed. Guillaume Pigeaud de Gurbert (Paris: Champion, 2002), 303–4, 331–2. I am grateful to Richard Scholar for this reference.

[74] The brief remarks which follow are to be seen in the context of the studies of Eugenio Di Rienzo, 'La religione di Cardano. Libertinismo e eresia nell'Italia dello Controriforma', in Eckhard Kessler (ed.), *Girolamo Cardano, Philosoph, Naturforscher, Arzt*, 49–76, and Marco Bracali, 'Filosofia italiana e Riforma. Appunti su Cardano', in Marialuisa Baldi and Guido Canziani (eds.), *Cardano, le opere, le fonti, la vita* (Milan: FrancoAngeli), 81–104.

[75] Cardano, *Opera*, ii. 529: 'una igitur Philosophorum, at religionis naturae de anima ferme sententia est, differens solum velut imperfectum a perfecto: velut puer a viro; sic delineatio a pictura'; Cardano, *De immortalitate animorum* (Lyons, 1545),

There are also discreet references to contemporary religious strife in the work, which suggest a less ideologically committed stance. The schism with Germany, and the proliferation of councils which it has produced, are the results of a 'tiny error', which Cardano seems to regard as forgiveable. Even more strikingly, he uses sectarian disagreement to show the dangers of dialectical judgements which 'by being so finely poised can incline to one or the other view'.[76] This passage is strangely reminiscent of the passage in the 1550 text of the *De subtilitate*, in which he shows an apparent indifference as to which of the four competing religions (those of Christians, Jews, Muslims, and pagans) wins the day: a passage which he saw fit to amend in later editions.[77] Elsewhere in the text, Cardano seems to be led to a comparative and implicitly relativist approach to religious truth (about the notion of paradise, for example) in so far as he sets out to show how arguments from natural reason can produce the same metaphysical result in all religions.[78] What is more, the political justification for the doctrine of the immortality of souls, found also

316: 'finis hominis secundum Theologos et Philosophos unus, et qualis sit'; Cardano, *Opera*, ii. 486: 'Ego sane cum multa difficilia fere in omnibus disciplinis invenerim, nec quicquam frustra quaesierim quantumvis arduum, atque aditum, de Deo tamen me tantum scire fateor, quantum ex fide, atque religione accepi, praeter quam quod sit'; ibid. ii. 487: 'miracula ad Deum pertinere, sed non esse Philosophi, qui secundum naturam loquitur, ea admittere'; ibid. iv. 471, cited by Alfonso Ingegno, *Saggio sulla filosofia di Cardano* (Florence: La nuova Italia, 1980), 59 n.: 'ut olim miracula sic nunc multarum rerum scientia innotuit...': also n. 45 above.

[76] Cardano, *Opera*, ii. 492: 'Haec enim quanquam (ut Philosophus recte dicebat) parva in principio sint, maxima tamen evadunt in fine: sic minimo errore legati tota Germania a religione abalienata est: sic supra Synodos Synodus, et super Consilia Consilia, quare ne illud etiam nobis periculum adiicitur ut pro fidei articulo credendum constanter sit, Aristotelem voluisse animum humanum, vel unum in omnibus tantum esse, vel esse mortalem'; ibid. ii. 469 (on a variety of opinions about the immortality of soul sometimes causing more harm than good): 'ut cum nostris temporibus totus mundus religionis contentione pessundatur: Lutherani Catholicos oppugnant, cum Christum utrique tamen colant: et Persae cum Turcis ob id gravissima bella gessere, cum utraque gens Mahumethem adoret... igitur bonum hoc per se, si bonum est veritati insistere... non igitur haec probant, quae in utramque partem quasi ex aequilibrio possunt inclinare.'

[77] In the early editions of *De subtilitate*, xi, there is the phrase 'his arbitrio victoriae relictis', which was amended in 1560 to 'sed haec parum Philosophi attinent, pro quibus institutus est sermo' (see Cardano, *Opera*, iii. 552).

[78] Ibid. ii. 530 (on the various versions of paradise in different religions). But cf. *De sapientia*, iii, ibid. i. 534, where Cardano attacks Erasmus for writing ambiguously to please both Catholics and Protestants.

in Pomponazzi, is sometimes given precedence in the *De immortali-tate animorum* over the religious one.[79] It would seem from this that Cardano had a certain leaning towards religious relativism, but I do not myself believe that he ever allowed this to inflect his own personal belief or his institutional commitment to the Roman Catholic Church.

His most successful work, the *De subtilitate* (1550, revised in 1554), contains a radical modification of Aristotelian physics; according to Cardano, there are five principles (matter, form, spirit, place, and movement: but not privation or time), three (not four) elements (earth, water, and air), and two (not four) qualities (hot and moist).[80] This, together with many other unconventional opinions, so outraged his contemporary Julius Caesar Scaliger that he was moved to write his exhaustive *Exotericae exercitationes* to refute the numerous errors of the text in the name of orthodox peripatetic thinking: this appeared in 1557. Scaliger's frequently republished work became (in Germany at least) a handbook of Aristotelian orthodoxy, and ensured that Cardano's *De subtilitate* was seen as the very opposite.[81] But Cardano's text deals with more than just Aristotelian physics: much of it is about the world of everyday experience and man's interaction with it. Here, as elsewhere in his writing, he evinces a strong pride in his practical achievements and discoveries (which, in the form of the universal joint, are with us still today). In the *De subtilitate*, Cardano sets out to speak as a philosopher, not a theologian; but he strays too far from his brief when making the incautious aside about world religions recorded above. He, like Pomponazzi, also speculates about the history of religions and their astrologically inspired rise and decline; his ill-judged geniture of Christ, which was withdrawn from his published collection of horoscopes after 1571, is of course consonant with this discussion.[82]

[79] Ibid. ii. 460, 471, 477, 488, 518.

[80] Ibid. iii. 357–411. On the impossibilia of Aristotelian physics (vacuum, infinity in act, and coexistence in the same place at the same time) and on the Aristotelian doctrine of the eternity of the world he expresses complex positions: see ibid. iii. 360; ii. 713–19; i. 143.

[81] Ian Maclean, 'The Interpretation of Natural Signs: Cardano's *De Subtilitate* versus Scaliger's *Exercitationes*', in Brian Vickers (ed.), *Occult and Scientific Mentalities in the Renaissance* (Cambridge: Cambridge University Press, 1984), 231–52.

[82] Cardano, *Opera*, v. 221–2.

I turn finally to his medical works.[83] His earliest medical publications, the *De malo recentiorum medicorum medendi usu* and the *De simplicium medicinarum noxa* (1536) attacked the medical orthodoxy of his day. They were the product of his seven years of experience as a town physician in Sacco. When he was eventually elected (in 1544) to a chair of medicine in Pavia, he developed a strong critique of Galen and enthusiastically expounded the works of Hippocrates, on whose whole œuvre he planned to write a commentary,[84] to supplant those of Galen which were authoritative at the time.[84] As a result of this he was accused by a colleague of medical heresy. Opposition to established medical teaching had begun to be described in terms of heresy in the 1530s (an understandable analogy for doctors to exploit, not only because of the rise of Lutheranism, but also because the various ancient schools of medicine were themselves described as sects[85]). Andrea Camuzio's *Disputationes* of 1563 attack Cardano by name for his criticism of Galen and ill-judged promotion of Hippocrates.[86]

---

[83] The best account of these is that of Siraisi, *The Clock and the Mirror*.

[84] Cardano was not alone in the middle years of the century in looking on Hippocrates as the better ancient authority: see Iain M. Lonie, 'The "Paris Hippocratics": Teaching and Research in Paris in the Second Half of the Sixteenth Century', in Andrew Wear, R. K. French, and Iain M. Lonie (eds.), *The Medical Renaissance of the Sixteenth Century* (Cambridge: Cambridge University Press, 1985), 155–72, and Vivian Nutton, 'Hippocrates in the Renaissance', *Sudhoffs Archiv*, suppl. 27 (1989), 420–39.

[85] Maclean, *Logic, Signs and Nature*, 76–80. The radical physician and religious thinker Paracelsus (1493?–1541) gloomily records in the *Opus paragranum* (1529–30) that he was described as the Luther of medicine; soon after, Andreas Thurinus (1473–1543) in Florence, Jeremias Thriverus (1504–54) in Louvain, Andrea Camuzio (1510?–78) in Pavia, and Gianfilippo Ingrassia (1510–80) use the epithets 'Lutheran' or 'heretic' to describe deviant thought in the sphere of medicine. See Paracelsus, *Sämtliche Werke von Theophrast von Hohenheim genannt Paracelsus: 1. Abteilung, Medizinische naturwissenschaftliche und philosophische Schriften*, ed. Karl Sudhoff (Munich: Oldenbourg, 1922–33), viii. 62–5; Andreas Thurinus, *Ad Matthaeum Curtium de vena in curatione pleuritidos incidenda* (Bologna, 1533), 24r; Jeremias Thriverus, *Paradoxa de vento, aere, aqua et igni* (Antwerp, 1542), sig. A6; Andrea Camuzio, *Disputationes, quibus Hieronymi Cardani magni nominis viri conclusiones infirmantur, Galenus ab eiusdem iniura vindicatur, Hippocratis praeterea aliquot loca diligentius multo, quam unquam alias, explicantur* (Pavia, 1563), cited by Siraisi, *The Clock and the Mirror*, 68, 145; Giovanni Filippo Ingrassia, *Galeni ars medica* (Venice, 1574), sig. *5r. See also Charles Webster, 'Conrad Gessner and the Infidelity of Paracelsus', in John Henry and Sarah Hutton (eds.), *New Perspectives on Renaissance Thought: Essays in the History of Science, Education and Philosophy in Memory of Charles B. Schmitt* (London: Duckworth, 1990), 13–23.

[86] Camuzio, *Disputationes*, cited by Siraisi, *The Clock and the Mirror*, 68, 145.

Cardano replied to these disputations in the preface to his *Ars curandi parva*, a manual of therapy and surgical procedures intended for the layman, which appeared in 1566, by which time he had lost his professorship at Pavia, perhaps as a result of Camuzio's attack. He shows how stung he was by the accusation of being a heresiarch, and, in rejecting it, recalls his orthodox defence of the immortality of the soul, claiming that he would no more call into question either this or 'the most constant authority of our religion' than he would doubt that an egg is an egg.[87]

V

This chapter has reviewed the works and attitude to orthodoxy of three medically trained writers, with respect to issues about soul, matter, and astral determinism. Not all three of them have recourse to the empirical validation of theory which is characteristic of anatomical enquiry at this time; but they all share an anti-authoritarian attitude, expressed in the philosophically 'heretical' exegesis of Pomponazzi, Cardano's polemical works, and even, to some degree, in the self-help manuals of Gratarolo. This independence of mind does not, however, extend to theology; it seems that both Pomponazzi and Cardano were always willing, while asserting the independent nature of philosophical enquiry, to proclaim their submission to Roman orthodoxy (albeit in a way which would not have been found adequate by the Roman Church); it is more easy to credit Cardano with sincerity in this than Pomponazzi. Gratarolo, with a different orthodoxy in mind, respected the same limitations, even approving of Pomponazzi's pious submission to a Church whose authority he, Gratarolo, did not recognize. It is thus possible to say that Pomponazzi and Cardano treated their beliefs in theology and in natural philosophy as belonging to different disciplinary domains (although Cardano allowed that there was some convergence); Gratarolo seems

---

[87] Cardano, *Opera*, vii. 143: 'cum non plus ego dubitarem de animorum immortalitate etiam citra religionis nostrae constantissimam auctoritatem, quam quod ovum ovum esset.'

to have allowed a bridge to exist between them, at least in so far as personal piety was a prerequisite for the right sort of natural curiosity.

The medical predisposition to challenge authority and confront theory with empirical data, seen most clearly in the sixteenth century in the work of anatomists, is more fully worked out in Cardano, who practised as a doctor, than in Pomponazzi, who did not, although it should be pointed out that the older scholar refers to the dangers of hearsay and the need for eye witnessing in the lectures on zoology which he delivered late in his career.[88] As a self-proclaimed philosophical heretic, he also would have had no difficulty in laughing at the anatomical anecdote recorded above about the origin of nerves. Indeed, Pomponazzi makes a protestation in a spirit wholly opposed to that of Sanctorius's Aristotelian:

> You are saying straightaway to yourselves that it's very presumptuous of me to give an exposition of this book [Aristotle's *De partibus animalium*], which no-one else has expounded. I reply that I'm not doing this out of presumption, I don't presume to expound, and don't want to teach you in this, but rather be your companion. I have only come to this book because I'm older than you, not because I'm more learned. It's intellectual curiosity which has made me do this, and so I want here to submit myself to your judgement, and be taught by you.[89]

We have already met this modesty of approach and this proclamation of the provisional nature of philosophical doctrine in other quotations from Pomponazzi's lectures: it comes as more of a surprise to find it in the more vainglorious Cardano, whose words can act as a coda to this chapter, and as an attestation of independence in the face of authority characteristic of the Padua-trained philosopher and doctor:

> I love and honour Galen ... and although I disagree with him on this matter [the nature of the soul] in the name of truth—a dearer friend to me

---

[88] Perfetti, 'Docebo vos dubitare', 457–9.

[89] Ibid. 446: 'sed vos statim dicetis me valde temerarium esse presumere exponere hunc librum, cum nullus exposuerit. Et ego respondeo quod non temeritate facio hoc, nec presumo me exponere et in hoc nolo vos docere, sed volo esse comes vester. Et non ut doctior huc accessi, sed quia senior. Et amor scientiae me compulit ad hoc et ideo volo me subiicere ferule, et volo a vobis doceri.'

than even he—no-one has exalted him with a more ardent will than I, insofar as it was in my power. But when I saw that in his haste, impelled by such desire for glory and such vain ambition for popular favour, he wrote things full of error that can be of harm to many because of his authority, I considered it necessary to counsel everyone that they should believe only as much as reason itself dictates, and that it is not sufficient to have said to themselves, 'Aristotle states' or 'Plato', or 'Archimedes', or 'Ptolemy', or 'Galen'; but that they should weigh the force of the argument; and in respect of my own pronouncements, if ever they should come to have any authority, I not only freely permit this, but require it to be done.[90]

---

[90] Cardano, *Opera*, ii. 475: 'Galenus amamus, colimus, . . . et quamvis hac in parte ob veritatem, quae nobis magis etiam quam ille amica est, ab eo dissentiamus, nullus tamen ardentiore voluntate illum, quantum per vires licuit, extulit. Sed cum adeo cupidum illum gloriae, ambitionis inanisque aurae properantem aliqua perperam scribere videmus quae multis ob authoritatem iacturae esse possunt, necessarium duximus, omnes admonendos ut tantum cuique credant, quantum ratio ipsa coegerit, nec sufficiat illis dixisse, Aristoteles dixit, vel Plato, aut Archimedes, vel Ptolomaeus, aut Galenus: sed vires argumentorum pensitent: quod et in nostris placitis, si aliqua unquam futura est nobis autoritas, non solum libenter permittimus, sed requirimus.' Cf. n. 17 above.

2

John Donne's Religion of Love

David Wootton

John Donne was in love with love. He was, of course, a love poet, and
in the love poems he presents himself as one of 'Love's divines, (since
all Divinity | Is love or wonder', and as 'love's martyr'.[1] He hoped his
God would 'ravish' him ('Batter my heart, three person'd God').[2] He
believed 'there is a religion in friendship'; his friends often heard him
say 'I love you'; and when he signs his letters he is sometimes 'your
very affectionate friend and servant and lover'.[3] He described himself
as a member of the 'sect' of 'the philosophy of love'.[4] My suggestion is
that Donne's preoccupation with love and the religion of love ('Thy

Earlier versions of this paper were given to The Society Belief and Culture Seminar at
the Institute of Historical Research in London (as a memorial to Alan Bray); to the
Heterodoxy seminar in Oxford; and to David Norbrook's seminar in Oxford. I am
grateful to David Colclough for reading a late draft; an invaluable introduction to the
vast literature on Donne is provided by David Colclough (ed.), *John Donne's Professional Lives* (Woodbridge: D. S. Brewer, 2003).

[1] John Donne, *'The Elegies' and 'The Songs and Sonnets'*, ed. Helen Gardner
(Oxford: Oxford University Press, 1965), 68 ('A valediction: Of the book'), 91 ('The
funeral').

[2] John Donne, *The Divine Poems*, ed. Helen Gardner (Oxford: Oxford University
Press, 1952), 11.

[3] Edmund Gosse, *The Life and Letters of John Donne* (2 vols.; New York: Dodd,
Mead, 1899), i. 290, 218, 177. In the absence of a modern scholarly edition, I quote
Donne's letters from Gosse. Recent scholarship has sought to correct the addressees
given in the *Letters* of 1651 and to establish a chronology for them (see M. Thomas
Hester's facsimile edition: Delmar, NY: Scholars' Facsimiles and Reprints, 1977), but
the argument presented here would, if accepted, require that these questions be
revisited.

[4] Gosse, *Life and Letters*, i. 291.

law's abridgement, and thy last command | Is all but love': 'Father, part of his double interest') carried him so far that he become a member of the Family of Love, a religious sect which had numerous adherents in late sixteenth- and early seventeenth-century England.[5] Donne was born a Catholic; the Church into which he was ordained was dominated by Calvinism; the Church in which he died was controlled by Laud; and Donne's religious writings are traditionally read in this triple context of Catholicism, Puritanism, and Anglicanism. In 1581, however, the Jesuit Robert Parsons wrote that there were four, not three, religions in England. They were Catholicism, Protestantism, Puritanism, and the Household of Love.[6] It is in the context of this fourth religion, sometimes called Familism or the Family of Love, that I propose to read Donne.

In reading Donne in this way I have a distinguished precursor, William Empson. From 1935, when he published *Some Versions of Pastoral*, until his death in 1984, Empson sought to defend a coherent account of the core preoccupations underlying Donne's love poetry, but his efforts met with little success. 'Why will nobody believe a word I have to say about Donne?' he asked in 1973.[7] Two themes struck Empson in Donne's love poetry, and he believed these two themes were braided together. The first theme is the discovery of new worlds, not only new continents but new planets and new stars. Each lover's tear becomes a world, each dewdrop becomes a star, as if the

---

[5] Donne, *Divine Poems*, 12. On the Family of Love in England see Christopher Marsh, *The Family of Love in English Society, 1550–1630* (Cambridge: Cambridge University Press, 1994), Peter Lake, *The Boxmaker's Revenge* (Manchester: Manchester University Press, 2000), and David Wootton, 'Reginald Scot / Abraham Fleming / The Family of Love', in Stuart Clark (ed.), *Languages of Witchcraft* (London: MacMillan, 2000), 119–39. A central puzzle raised by Marsh's book (119–22) is that of Elizabeth I's attitude to the Family of Love: I intend to present elsewhere evidence that she was indeed 'receptive' to Familist doctrines.

[6] Robert Parsons, *A Brief Discours contayning certayne reasons why Catholiques refuse to goe to Church*, 'Douai' [East Ham], 1580, sig. ‡3r (I owe this reference to Johann Sommerville). So too *Leicester's Commonwealth* (1584) takes the three major religious groupings in England to be 'Papists, Puritans, Familians': *Leicester's Commonwealth*, ed. D. C. Peck (Athens, Ohio: Ohio University Press, 1985), 185.

[7] Quoted in John Haffenden's introduction to William Empson, *Essays on Renaissance Literature*, i. *Donne and the New Philosophy* (Cambridge: Cambridge University Press, 1993), 1–61, at 58. The present chapter would not exist had Alison Mark not urged me to read Empson's 'Donne the Space Man' (1957), now in *Donne and the New Philosophy*, 78–128.

telescope and the microscope had hopelessly relativized our sense of scale. The second theme is the religion of love, in which the lovers worship each other, and become divine. Donne thinks there is 'some Deity in love' (indeed he writes a poem called 'Love's deity'), and some deity in lovers too.[8] Empson believed these themes reinforced each other. In a Copernican universe in which there may be many inhabited planets, particular historical events on earth, such as the Incarnation and Crucifixion, lose their universal significance: Copernicus thus undermines orthodox Christianity. On the other hand if love is the true deity, God is incarnated whenever love takes on flesh. Empson consequently attributed to Donne a view of the divine which made God local and human; such a view, Empson maintained, was held by an obscure, contemporary sect called the Family of Love and Donne, had he been consistent with his own principles, would have become a Familist.

We might add to these a third preparation for Familism which Empson did not stress: the discovery of yet another new world, that of the inner life. At the heart of the Familist undertaking lay an exploration of the hidden depths of the soul, the inner recesses of the self. As the founder of Familism, Hendrick Niclaes, expressed it: 'The whole outward world, is very great and unmeasurable: and how great and unmeasurable soever the same is, yet is notwithstanding the inward world without comparison much greater, inwardly in us.'[9] Donne too employs what Anne Ferry has called an 'inward language'.[10] He was 'content to look inward upon myself'.[11] His advice was 'Seek we then ourselves in ourselves.'[12] Donne's sermons are above all an exploration of this inner world.

Is your soul less than your body because it is in it? How easily lies a letter in a box which if it were unfolded would cover that box? Unfold your soul and you shall see that it reaches to heaven; from thence it came and thither it should pretend, whereas the body is but from that earth, and for that earth

---

[8] Donne, *Elegies*, 82 ('Farewell to Love'); 47–8 ('Love's Deity').

[9] Quoted from *Dicta HN* in Marsh, *Family of Love*, 20.

[10] Anne Ferry, *The 'Inward' Language: Sonnets of Wyatt, Sidney, Shakespeare, Donne* (Chicago: University of Chicago Press, 1983).

[11] Gosse, *Life and Letters*, ii. 16.

[12] John Donne, *The Satires, Epigrams, and Verse Letters*, ed. W. Milgate (Oxford: Oxford University Press, 1967, 70 ('To Mr Rowland Woodward').

upon which it is now, which is but a short and inglorious progress ... the soul is larger than the body, and the joys of heaven larger than the honours and the pleasures of this world.[13]

It is precisely because Donne's sermons look inward that they are so different in character from those of Lancelot Andrewes. Andrewes's Christianity is a historical faith; Donne's is a spiritual faith.

As far as I can tell, Empson never read any of Donne's sermons: whenever he quotes them he turns out to be quoting other people quoting them. This was not laziness, but a deep-seated aversion to Christianity. In this chapter I want to argue that the Donne we find in the sermons is surprisingly close to the Donne that Empson had found in the love poetry, and that the religion of this Donne, the dean of St Paul's, is derived from that of the Family of Love. The same religion, I would add, is to be found in the Divine Poems. In presenting this account of Donne as influenced by Familism I have an additional advantage over Empson, beyond my willingness to read the sermons, for two recent studies have transformed our knowledge of English Familism: Christopher Marsh's *The Family of Love in English Society, 1550 to 1630* (1994) established that there were numerous Familists at the court of Elizabeth in the 1580s; most immediately relevant is Peter Lake's *The Boxmaker's Revenge* (2000) which takes the story of English Familism through into the Jacobean period. As a result of Marsh's and Lake's pioneering studies we now know a great deal more about Familism than Empson ever could.

Familism was founded in the Low Countries in the 1540s. It was disseminated in England by Hendrick Niclaes's disciple, Christopher Vittels, in the 1570s. Familists believed that Christ is reborn in each believer, who becomes, in Niclaes's best-known phrase 'Godded with God'. (As Etherington described it, they held 'every one of his [Niclaes's] family of love to be Christ, yea and God, and himself God and Christ in a more excellent manner, saying that he is Godded with God and codeified with him and that God is hominified with him.')[14] We know that in the early seventeenth century there were a

---

[13] *The Sermons of John Donne*, ed. George R. Potter and Evelyn M. Simpson (10 vols.; Berkeley: University of California Press, 1953–62), ii. 338.

[14] Etherington, *Discovery of the Errors of the English Anabaptists* (1623), quoted in Lake, *Boxmaker's Revenge*, 150; Etherington was paraphrasing Niclaes's *First Exhortation*: cf. Alastair Hamilton, *The Family of Love* (Cambridge: James Clarke, 1981), 35.

number of Familist groupings in London. We are told there were Castalian Familists, Gringletonian Familists, Familists of the mountain, Familists of the valley, Familists of the cap, Familists of the scattered flock.[15] John Etherington, who in 1610 may well have been a Familist of the scattered flock, was by 1623 an ex-Familist prepared to assert that there were Familists who were clergymen in the Church of England, that some were even to be found in the king's chapel (where Donne, of course, preached every year).[16] Looking back in 1645 he repeated and extended this claim: 'There have been and are great doctors of divinity, so called [Donne received a doctorate of divinity in 1615], yea and some great peers and persons of quality and estate in this land ... that have taught and entertained the same [Familism] with great affection and high applause.' He himself had spoken to such people 'forty years ago and sundry times since'.[17]

John Donne was born in 1572 into a devout Catholic family. Two of his uncles were Jesuits, and his brother died in Newgate prison, held for sheltering a priest, in 1593.[18] Donne was clearly passing as an Anglican by 1597, when he began a career in government service which was wrecked by his secret marriage to Anne More in 1601. Donne's career never recovered from this blow, or not at least until he agreed to be ordained in 1615, which led to his becoming dean of St Paul's in 1621. In 1625 he preached the first sermon to the new king, Charles I. He died in 1631. The bulk of the evidence I will be considering derives from the sermons, and so from the period 1615–31. Some of Donne's religious poems clearly postdate his ordination, but others (we are about to look at one which must predate 1608) belong to the period between his marriage in 1601 and his ordination in 1615. The two letters that particularly interest me are undated; they survive only in the edition of 1651. In that edition modern scholars believe the names of addressees were arbitrarily altered, so we not only do not know when but we do not even know to whom they were written; but they too surely date to the period between marriage and ordination. I should stress that the whole of this

[15] Nigel Smith, *Perfection Proclaimed* (Oxford: Clarendon, 1989), 148; Lake, *Boxmaker's Revenge*, 180.

[16] Lake, *Boxmaker's Revenge*, 151, 182.   [17] Ibid. 155.

[18] John Carey, *John Donne: Life, Mind and Art* (London: Faber & Faber, 1981), reads Donne's biography in the context of his Catholic upbringing.

chapter is about married Donne, seventeenth-century Donne; it is an exploration of where Donne's quest for the deity in love, which in his youth had taken him from mistress to mistress, but which after his marriage turned into a quest for God, eventually led him.

Let us begin with two poems. The first contains a well-known textual crux:

'The Relic'

When my grave is broke up again
Some second guest to entertain,
(For graves have learned that woman-head
To be to more than one a bed)
    And he that digs it, spies
A bracelet of bright hair about the bone
    Will he not let us alone,
And think that there a loving couple lies,
Who thought that this device might be some way
To make their souls, at the last busy day,
Meet at this grave, and make a little stay?

If this fall in time, or land,
Where mis-devotion doth command,
Then, he that digs us up, will bring
Us, to the Bishop, and the King,
    To make us relics; then
Thou shalt be a Mary Magdalen, and I
    A something else thereby;
All women shall adore us, and some men;
And since at such time, miracles are sought,
I would have that age by this paper taught
What miracles we harmless lovers wrought.

First, we loved well and faithfully,
Yet knew not what we loved, nor why,
Difference of sex no more we knew,
Than our guardian angels do;
    Coming and going, we
Perchance might kiss, but not between those meals;
    Our hands ne'er touched the seals,
Which nature, injured by late law, sets free:
These miracles we did; but now alas,

> All measure, and all language, I should pass,
> Should I tell what a miracle she was.

The problem here is what is meant by 'Thou shalt be a Mary Magdalen and I a something else thereby.' Redpath, Empson, and Ricks have all pointed out that we seem to be invited to make a substitution for 'a something else', and the only substitution which scans is 'a Jesus Christ'. Empson says: 'Donne in the love poems often presents himself as a Christ of True Love, founding a colony or teaching a school to promulgate his new doctrine; when you realize this you are no longer tempted to deny the obvious meaning of the lines in 'The Relic': Thou shalt be a Magdalen, and I | A something else thereby,' the obvious meaning being that Donne would be taken to be Jesus Christ.[19] At this point other commentators have come to a sharp stop, for how can one be *a* Jesus Christ; and how could Christ, who ascended into heaven, leave a relic behind him? When he first insisted on this idea, in 1957, Empson seems not to have known that the Family of Love believed that every Christian was a Mary Magdalen, a sinner rescued from sin; and that every Christian was reborn through faith as a Jesus Christ. Every Familist was a Jesus Christ, but (and here is the resolution of the paradox that seems at first insoluble) everyone of them is capable of leaving a relic at his death. This poem only makes sense if it is read in the context of Familism, a context in which Empson placed it in 'Rescuing Donne' (1972).

The Relic is generally thought to have been addressed to Magdalen Herbert; the next poem, which must predate her marriage to Lord Danvers in 1608, is explicitly addressed:

> To Mrs Magdalen Herbert: Of St Mary Magdalen
>
> Her of your name, whose fair inheritance
>   Bethina was, and jointure Magdalo:
> An active faith so highly did advance,
>   That she once knew, more than the Church did know,
> The Resurrection; so much good there is
>   Delivered of her, that some Fathers be
> Loth to believe one woman could do this;

---

[19] Empson, *Donne and the New Philosophy*, 191–2; see also 13, 16, 87; for Ricks, see John Donne, *The Complete English Poems*, ed. A. J. Smith (Harmondsworth: Penguin, 1971), 398.

> But, think these Magdalens were two or three.
> Increase their number, Lady, and their fame:
>   To their devotion, add your innocence;
> Take so much of th'example, as of the name;
>   The latter half; and in some recompense
> That they did harbour Christ himself, a guest,
>   Harbour these hymns, to his dear name addressed.

Mary Magdalen was the first to meet the risen Christ, the first to know of the Resurrection. There was a moment then when she knew more than the apostles; but the true Church, the bride of Christ, is incapable of error, and no one can know more than that Church, which is informed by the Holy Spirit. Moreover the Church came into existence, not with the Resurrection, but at Pentecost. To say that Mary Magdalen once knew more about the Resurrection than the Church did is to problematize the ideas both of the Church and of the Resurrection. One needs here to know that the Family of Love believed that membership of a church was not what counted. The Family of Love was neither a church (in the normal sense) nor a sect. Familists believed (as Donne repeatedly said he did) that salvation could be found within all the Christian churches; they also believed in a true, spiritual, or invisible Church—a Church not on seven hills, like that of Rome, or on one hill, like that of Geneva, but on no hill.[20] They were consequently willing to adopt any official creed alongside their private devotions. Central to those devotions was the conviction that the resurrection which matters is the resurrection that takes place within each believer when his sinful self dies and he is reborn as Christ. Mary Magdalen may thus be said to have experienced the resurrection as soon as she was cured of sin (the miracle of which Donne speaks in 'The Relic'), before even her brother Lazarus was raised from the dead, and long before she met Christ risen from the dead.

I have suggested the poem quietly problematizes the ideas of the Church and the Resurrection. Directly, it problematizes the identity of Mary Magdalen herself. To suggest that there were several Magdalens, that these Magdalens (the sinner, the sister of Lazarus, the

---

[20] Donne, *Divine Poems*, 15: 'Show me dear Christ', l. 8. For Geneva's hill, see L. Erne, 'Donne and Christ's Spouse', *Essays in Criticism*, 51 (2001), 208–29.

witness to the Resurrection) were two or three was not a problem for Donne, for each could be substituted for the others: it was three times, not once or even twice, that Magdalen had had a special knowledge of the resurrection. For Familists, a true understanding of the first of these resurrections, the resurrection from sin ('this is that holiness and newness of life which the scripture so commendeth unto us, by the names of vivification, renovation spiritual and the first resurrection', said the Familist T.L.; 'we were elemented and compacted of nothing but sin, till we come to this resurrection, this mortification, which is indeed our vivification', says Donne), which is indeed a harbouring of Christ, had been lost by the Church, until it was rediscovered by Hendrick Niclaes.[21] Thus all three Magdalens stand for the same knowledge, and to make of Magdalen Herbert a fourth Magdalen was to make of her too a privileged witness to the Resurrection: in this case, presumably Donne's own resurrection from sin, his becoming a Christ. If the other Magdalens harboured Christ, this Magdalen has harboured Donne, which is why he is repaying her with poetry. It might be thought that if Donne, in this poem as in 'The Relic', is thinking of himself as a Christ, then he might as well address his religious poetry to himself, but this would be to apply the wrong sort of logic to Donne's religion, which is all about God speaking to God: 'Hear us, O hear us Lord ... Hear thyself now, for thou in us dost pray' (A Litany, xxiii); 'the Spirit of God, that dictates them [sermons, but it could equally be religious poems] in the speaker or writer and is present in his tongue or hand meets himself again (as we meet ourselves in a glass) in the eyes and hearts of the hearers and readers'.[22] God, we might say, is always reflected in man ('I was your prophet in your younger days, | And now your chaplain, God in you to praise': To the Countess of Huntingdon).[23]

Donne's letters and poems to Magdalen Herbert were perhaps his first experiments with the language of extravagant compliment which, in its highest development in *The Anniversaries*, seemed to Jonson positively blasphemous, appropriate only if addressed to the

---

[21] T.L., 'An advertisement to Queen Elizabeth' (1589), quoted in Lake, *Boxmaker's Revenge*, 132—this is the second usage of 'vivification' recorded in *OED*—and Donne, *Sermons*, iv. 58.

[22] Donne, *Divine Poems*, 24; Gosse, *Life and Letters*, ii. 123.

[23] Donne, *Satires*, 88.

Virgin Mary. Indeed Donne's language of compliment often seems so excessive as to require some sort of additional explanation, beyond the conventions of the day, such as would be provided by the belief that one can find God in (wo)man:

> Madam,
> Reason is our soul's left hand, Faith her right,
> By these we reach divinity, that's you ...[24]

Everything he writes in this vein is intended to be explicable as mere 'thoughts of women's worthiness'; but at times the explanation seems forced.[25] Through much of his work Donne seems to have cultivated a careful doubleness: what he has to say makes some sense if read in the context of orthodox Christianity, but problems and doubts remain (in the case of 'To Mrs Magdalen Herbert' the reader must puzzle over whether there is some sense in which Magdalen Herbert knows more than the Church about the Resurrection); it makes much better sense when read in the context of Familism, a reading which consistently eliminates the problems that leap from Donne's page.

Let me take a last example from the poems. There are numerous commentaries on the Holy Sonnet 'Show me dear Christ, thy spouse, so bright and clear.'[26] All assume that Donne's problem is to choose among the various existing Churches. None considers the possibility that God may not have revealed his spouse to our sight. Anthony Randall, however, a Devon vicar deprived of his living on suspicion of Familism in 1581, insisted that he was a member neither of the Church of England, nor of the Roman Catholic Church, 'but hoped yet there was a third Church, which should stand where both these shall fall'. There were others who believed 'There is no church, nor visible Christian in the world as yet.'[27] They too were waiting for Christ to show them his spouse. It is only because Donne is writing about a Church so spiritual that it is yet to appear on earth that he can risk, can bear the extraordinary paradox of comparing it to a prostitute, 'open to most men'—it is the actually existing Church

---

[24] Ibid. 90 ('To the Countess of Bedford').

[25] Gosse, *Life and Letters*, ii. 179.   [26] Donne, *Divine Poems*, 15.

[27] Marsh, *Family of Love*, 37; and see Henoch Clapham's *Error on the Right Hand* (1608), quoted in Lake, *Boxmaker's Revenge*, 173.

which prostitutes itself, taking in all and sundry, while the spiritual Church is accessible only to 'adventuring knights', to those who have an 'amorous soul', but even they must not make the mistake of thinking it can be found in some existing institution. For the Familists the Church, at least for the moment, consisted only of 'living stones', of true believers, and was consequently invisible, at least to the uninformed observer.[28]

Only once in the letters does Donne write, as he does in 'The Relic', in a fashion that seems straightforwardly incompatible with any orthodox religion. The letter in question is undated, and (according to the *Letters* of 1651) was written to 'Sir H. R. '. Donne and his addressee share in common the fact that they have 'friends, who are of other impressions than you or I in some great circumstances of religion'.

You know I never fettered nor imprisoned the word Religion, not straightening it friarly, *ad Religiones factitias* (as the Romans call well their orders of Religion), nor immuring it in a Rome, or a Wittemberg, or a Geneva; they are all virtual [i.e. operative] beams of one Sun, and wheresoever they find clay hearts, they harden them and moulder them into dust; and they entender and mollify waxen. They are not so contrary as the North and South Poles, and that they are co-natural pieces of one circle. Religion is Christianity, which being too spiritual to be seen by us, doth therefore take an apparent body of good life and works, so salvation requires an honest Christian.

These are the two elements ... the body of Religion, which is moral honesty and sociable faithfulness ... the soul, Christianity.[29]

We learn from this letter that Donne's religion is not conventional, that it is distinct from the religions of Rome, Wittemberg, and Geneva. He makes no mention of the sacraments, but implicitly rejects the Catholic doctrine that Christ takes on an 'apparent body' in the Mass. At the same time, though, he rejects the Protestant doctrine of salvation by faith alone—salvation requires 'good life and works'. What is this spiritual religion, shared by Donne and his correspondent, which differs 'in some great circumstances' from those men have made for themselves (*religiones factitias*)? Donne is not simply an irenicist, keen to stress those beliefs that all Christians

---

[28] Lake, *Boxmaker's Revenge*, 100–6.   [29] Gosse, *Life and Letters*, i. 226–7.

have in common, for he believes the true faith has been 'fettered' and 'immured'. The true faith is to be sought outside the constraints of any Church. Only Familists believed this.

Before we turn to the sermons, which provide the most extensive evidence in support of my interpretation, we need to pause to consider *Biathanatos*, apparently written in 1608. Unpublishable until the Civil War, *Biathanatos: A Declaration of that Paradoxe or Thesis, That Self-Homicide Is Not So Naturally Sin That It May Never Be Otherwise* was so important to Donne that he took careful measures to ensure it would not be destroyed on his death (including giving a copy to Lord Herbert of Cherbury, Magdalen Herbert's son, for preservation in his library, where it would find itself in the company of other unorthodox works).[30] The 'paradox' (in the sense of an argument contrary to received opinion) or thesis of *Biathanatos* is that suicide is not always a mortal sin; but the key move in the argument is the treatment of martyrdom as a form of self-killing. Even Christ's death on the cross involved a voluntary compliance on his part, and was thus a form of self-homicide. Donne argues that, inspired by Christ's example, the desire for martyrdom became a 'disease' of the early Church, that the early Church was 'enamored of death' and that far from being an overcoming of a natural fear of death, the desire for martyrdom is 'too obedient to nature', for in all societies people have been prone to kill themselves.[31] The logic of Donne's argument here is clear: one should be intensely suspicious of the motives of those who embrace martyrdom. His argument seems designed to encourage the reader to sympathize with the view propounded by Helchesar (even though he was condemned as a heretic) who taught 'that in time of persecution, so we kept our heart at anchor safe, we were not bound to testify our religion by any outward act, much less by dying'.[32]

Thus Donne's real subject is a paradox in the sense of a statement which is internally contradictory: suicide is a sin, but martyrdom is admirable. Donne claims that the arguments of his opponents 'fight with themselves and suffer a civil war of contradiction', for they both

---

[30] Gosse, *Life and Letters*, ii. 125.

[31] John Donne, *Biathanatos*, facsimile of 1st edn., ed. J. William Hebel (New York: Facsimile Text Society, 1930), 63, 66, 64.

[32] Ibid. 68.

say we ought to have a horror of death, and that we ought to die willingly rather than betray our faith.[33] He offers, by contrast, an entirely unparadoxical statement of his own intention, which is 'to encourage men to a just contempt of this life, and to restore them to their nature, which is a desire of supreme happiness in the next life by the loss of this'; yet his arguments too are at war with each other, for this statement of his position fails to acknowledge his earlier attack on martyrdom.[34] How is one to resolve this civil war of contradiction? By recognizing that there is 'nothing so evil, that is never good', so that, like the telling of a lie, suicide can be 'wholesome in desperate diseases, but otherwise poison'.[35] Donne's argument, in asking us to reassess suicide, requires us also to reassess martyrdom. In doing so, in showing us the merit of Helchesar's position, Donne is (I would suggest deliberately) inviting us to sympathize with one of the central claims of the Familists: that we are under no obligation to bring persecution upon ourselves by declaring our faith to the authorities, but are instead entitled to claim to believe whatever the authorities require of us. As Niclaes said, 'Wherever ye come or dwell, there submit you obediently under the rulers and magistrates of the same land: and show all reverence unto them.'[36] According to Etherington, the Familists 'outwardly submit to any kind of religion and to any idolatrous service whatsoever, pretending it is not the body that can sin, but the soul'.[37] *Biathanatos* is a defence, not only of suicide, but also of Nicodemism, and as such it fits neatly into the larger pattern I am exploring here.

A fundamental part of Familist doctrine was that, just as believers experience the Resurrection in themselves, so too for believers the Last Judgement is past, and heaven is here and now. As Niclaes expressed it: 'the coming of the kingdom of God cometh not to pass with outward appearance, as that men may say: Lo, here or there it is. For behold: The kingdom of God, and the life of the heavenly being, is inwardly, within us.'[38] Again and again Donne tells

[33] Ibid. 214.
[34] Ibid. 216.
[35] Ibid. 36, 217.
[36] Quoted from *Exhortatio I* in Marsh, *Family of Love*, 25.
[37] Etherington, *A Discovery of the Errors of the English Anabaptists* (1623), quoted in Lake, *Boxmaker's Revenge*, 151.
[38] Quoted from *Comoedia* in Marsh, *Family of Love*, 24.

us in the sermons, as the Familists did, that we can have heaven upon earth: 'even here I have Goshen in my Egypt, incorruption in the midst of my dunghill, spirit in the midst of my flesh, heaven upon earth'.[39] Christ told the thief on the cross, who was about to die, that this day he would be with him in heaven; but Donne believes the same promise is made to those who are not about to die: 'If you will hear his voice this day, *hodie eritis*, this day you shall be with him in paradise, and dwell in it all the year, and all the years of an everlasting life'.[40] 'My soul is united to my Saviour, now in my life, as in death, and I am already made "one spirit with him": and whatsoever death can do, this kiss, this union can do, that is give me a present, an immediate possession of the kingdom of heaven'.[41] 'The joy of heaven, God opens to our discovery, and delivers for our habitation even whilst we dwell in this world'.[42] 'By our conversation in heaven here (that is, a watchfulness that we fall not into sin) we have *lucem essentiae*, possession and fruition of heaven'.[43] 'You shall have a Resurrection and an Ascension, an inchoation and an unremovable possession of heaven itself in this world'.[44] 'Into another world no man is gone, for that heaven which God created and this world is all one world'.[45] 'Heaven, to men disposed, is everywhere.' ('Epithalamion at the marriage of the Earl of Somerset'.)[46]

Donne quotes Chrysostom to prove Paul, as a result of his conversion on the road to Damascus, was in heaven on earth:

It is but a little way that St. Chrysostom goes, when he speaks of an inferior transubstantiation, of a change of affections, and says that here is another manner of lycanthropy than when a man is made a wolf; for here a wolf is made a lamb, says that father. A bramble is made a vine, cockle and tares become wheat, a pirate becomes a safe pilot, the lees are come to swim on the top, and the last is grown first, and he that was born out of time has not only the perfection but the excellency of all his lineaments. St. Chrysostom goes farther than this; he that was the mouth of blasphemy is become the mouth of Christ; he that was the instrument of Satan is now the organ of the

---

[39] Donne, *Sermons*, v. 249.   [40] Ibid. vi. 9.   [41] Ibid. iii. 15.
[42] Ibid. vii. 1.   [43] Ibid. iii. 17.   [44] Ibid. vii. 280.
[45] Ibid. vii. 383.
[46] John Donne, *The Epithalamions, Anniversaries, and Epicedes*, ed. W. Milgate (Oxford: Oxford University Press, 1978), 12.

Holy Ghost. He goes very far when he says, being yet upon earth he is an angel, and being yet but a man, he is already in Heaven.[47]

Donne not only maintains, with Chrysostom, that the true Christian believer is already in heaven, but insists that he is transformed into Christ himself. To make this claim he has to go even beyond Chrysostom who had described Paul as an angel on earth: 'He goes very far when he says, being yet upon earth he is an angel, and being yet but a man, he is already in Heaven. Yet St. Paul was another manner of sacrament, and had another manner of transubstantiation than in all this; as he was made the same spirit with the Lord, so in his very body he had Stigmata, the very marks of the Lord Jesus.' The normal view, of course, was that St Francis was the first to bear the stigmata, though Donne is following the Vulgate text, which attributes to Paul the *stigmata Christi*. 'Here was a true transubstantiation [i.e. Paul's conversion], and a new Sacrament. These few words, "Saul, Saul, why persecutest thou me," are words of consecration. After these words, Saul was no longer Saul, but he was Christ: "It is not I that live," not I that do anything, "but Christ in me." ' Donne has gone beyond Chrysostom here to preach a new doctrine.

Paul's Christness—I hesitate to say Christlikeness, for this would be a symbolic not real presence of Christ in Paul, not a true transubstantiation at all—is evident in the fact that he dies daily (we must 'die even so daily with Christ', said the Familist author of *An Apology*),[48] that he constantly relives Christ's passion. Like Christ, we too are crucified:

so when my crosses have carried me up to my Savior's cross, I put my hands into his hands, and hang upon his nails, I put mine eyes upon his, and wash off all my former unchaste looks, and receive a sovereign tincture, and a lively verdure, and a new life into my dead tears, from his tears. I put my mouth upon his mouth, and it is I that say, 'My God My God, why hast thou forsaken me?' and it is I that recover again, and say, 'Into thy hands O Lord I commend my spirit.' Thus my afflictions are truly a cross, when those afflictions do truly crucify me, and supple me, and mellow me, and knead me, and roll me out, to a conformity with Christ.[49]

---

[47] Donne, *Sermons*, vi. 169. [48] Quoted in Marsh, *Family of Love*, 42.
[49] Donne, *Sermons*, ii. 14.

Such an emphasis on the need to identify completely with Christ's life, passion, and death is characteristic of Niclaes's writing.

Over and over again Donne insists that we, like Paul, are as good as, or indistinguishable from, or identical to Christ. Thus 'every Christian truly reconciled to God is a beam and an abridgement of Christ himself.'[50] We experience 'a transfusion, a transplantation, a transmigration, a transmutation into him', so that we 'grow strong enough' by Christ's blood 'to meet David's question, *quis homo?* "What man?" with Christ's answer, *ego homo*, "I am the man in whom whosoever abideth shall not see death." '[51] We experience 'a metamorphosis, a transformation, a new creation in Jesus Christ, and thereby ... become *semen dei*, the seed of god, and *filium dei*, the child of god, and *participem divinae naturae*, partaker of the divine nature itself'.[52]

Donne is aware that there are various ways in which I might be said to be divine (this is in part the subject of his poem on Mr Tilman's ordination).[53] God, when he looks at my sins, may see instead Christ's innocence: this is Luther's notion of justification. In such circumstances there is nothing godlike about me, though God chooses to see me as Christlike. But Donne insists that we are not only capable of putting on Christ's outward uniform, not only capable of going further than this and conforming ourselves inwardly to Christ; we are capable of becoming that which Christ is. We are to put on Christ, he says,

so as the son puts on his father, that we may be of the same nature and substance as he, and that God may be in us, *non tanquam in denario*, not as the king is in a piece of coin or a medal, but *tanquam in filio*, as he is in his son, in whom the same nature, both human and royal, doth reside. There is then a double *induere*, a twofold clothing, we may *induere* 1. *vestem*, put on a garment, 2. *personam* put on a person; we may put on Christ so we shall be his [wear his livery, or be stamped with his image like a coin] and we may put him on so as we shall be *He*.[54]

Donne's sermons usually follow the Bible text very closely: *semen dei*, *filium dei*, *participem divinae naturae* are all perfectly accurate quotations from the Vulgate. He was not alone in turning to the

---

[50] Donne, *Sermons*, vi. 14.   [51] Ibid. ii. 9.   [52] Ibid. vii. 135.
[53] Donne, *Divine Poems*, 32–3.   [54] Donne, *Sermons*, v. 7.

Greek fathers and finding in them an account, based on such texts, of the believer's first resurrection, and his deification. But Familists did not hold that we are reborn in Christ; strictly speaking, they did not even hold that we become Christ; but rather that the old Adam dies in us and a new self, a new Christ is born in us. Donne too argues, not that we are reborn in Christ, but that Christ is born in us, and in doing so he finds himself on territory where there are no supporting biblical quotations, and where there is no theological tradition to which he can appeal. Yet we find him preaching this characteristically Familist doctrine on a Christmas day in St Paul's:

Christ Jesus who came only for the relief of sinners, is content to be known to have come, not only of poor parents but of a sinful race, and though he exempted his blessed mother, more than any, from sin, yet he is now content to be born again of sinful mothers. In that soul that accuses itself most of sin, in that soul that calls now to mind (with remorse and not with delight) the several times and places and ways wherein she hath offended God, in that soul that acknowledgeth itself to have been a sink of uncleanness, a tabernacle, a synagogue of Satan, in that soul that hath been as it were possessed with Mary Magdalen's seven devils, yea with him whose name was Legion, with all devils, in that sinful soul would Christ Jesus fain be born this day, and make that soul his mother, that he might be a regeneration to that soul.[55]

If Christ is to be born in us, then each of us must be the Virgin Mary. The Familists held that 'Christ is come forth in their flesh, even as he came forth of the Virgin Mary'.[56] Donne does not baulk at this comparison: 'Be thou a Mother where the Holy Ghost would be a Father; conceive by him ...'[57] 'Let us present our own will as a mother to the father of light, and the father of life, and the father of love, that we may be willing to conceive by the overshadowing of the Holy Ghost and not resist his working upon our souls, but with the obedience of the Blessed Virgin may say, "Behold the servant of the Lord, be it done unto me according to thy Word." '[58]

Thus each one of us relives the incarnation, the crucifixion ('Every man ... must be crucified upon the cross', said the Familist Leonard

---

[55] Ibid. vi. 17.   [56] Hamilton, *Family of Love*, 118.
[57] Donne, *Sermons*, vii. 1.   [58] Ibid. i. 8.

Romsey[59]), and the resurrection. This suggests that the Bible is to be read metaphorically not literally. According to Etherington, the Familists turn 'the holy writings and sayings of Moses and the prophets, of Christ and the apostles, and the proper names, persons, and things mentioned and contained therein into allegories'.[60] Miracles such as the virgin birth cease to be important as actual events; what is important is the spiritual truth they symbolize, and that spiritual truth is our delivery from sin. 'It is a less miracle to raise a man from a sick bed than to hold a man from a wanton bed, a licentious bed; less to overcome and quench his fever than to quench his lust. Joseph that refused his mistress was a greater miracle than Lazarus raised from the dead.'[61] 'And truly, in our spiritual raising of the dead, to raise a sinner putrefied in his own earth, resolved in his own dung … To raise a man resolved into diverse substances, scattered into diverse forms of several sins, is the greatest work.'[62]

Such a metaphorical reading of the Bible means that the Bible need no longer be read chronologically: Familists held that 'when Adam sinned, then Christ was killed'.[63] Donne never says this, but he does say that where Adam sinned, there Christ was killed ('Hymn to God my God, in my sickness'), that Christ was crucified from the moment that a second Adam was promised to the first, in Paradise, and that Christ's mystic body was crucified in Abel (A Litany, X).[64] Such a reading means that Satan himself becomes simply a symbol for sin. Familists believed that the devil only exists inside the soul of man; it follows that he first came into existence at the Fall. Donne, too, believes that God created men first, and then hell. It is striking that Donne quotes Chrysostom's view that we have each 'a bosom devil, and could tempt ourselves, though there had been no other tempter in this world', that we have *spontanaeus daemon*, in no less than seven

---

[59] Jean Dietz Moss, *'Godded with God': Hendrick Niclaes and the Family of Love* (*Transactions of the American Philosophical Society*, 71/8) (Philadelphia: American Philosophical Society, 1981), 191.

[60] Etherington, *A Brief Discovery* (1645), quoted in Lake, *Boxmaker's Revenge*, 367.

[61] Donne, *Sermons*, iv. 5.   [62] Ibid. iv. 13.

[63] Etherington, *A Discovery of the Errors of the English Anabaptists* (1623), quoted in Lake, *Boxmaker's Revenge*, 150.

[64] Donne, *Divine Poems*, 19–20, 50; Donne, *Sermons*, viii. 208.

sermons.[65] His view is that 'man not only is the herd of swine, | But he's those devils too, which did incline | Them to a headlong rage ...'[66]

To be Christ is to be incapable of sin. Familists held that those who were reborn in Christ were incapable of sin, or, if they sinned, this sin did not mean that they were by nature fallen. So too Donne insisted (although cautiously) that

There's the fullness of power: in Christ I can do all things—I can want or I can abound, I can live or I can die. And yet there is an extension of power beyond all this, in this, being born of God in Christ, I cannot sin. This that seems to have a name of impotence, I cannot, is the fullest omnipotence of all, I cannot sin; not sin to death; not sin with a desire to sin; not sin with a delight in sin; but that temptation which overthrows another, I can resist, or that sin which being done casts another into desperation, I can repent.[67]

And to be Christ is to be one substance with God himself. Again, Donne follows one of the Greek fathers, this time in his exposition of the Eucharist:

What the bread and wine is, or what becomes of it, Damascene thinks impertinent to be inquired. He thinks he hath said enough (and so may we do) *Migrat in substantiam animae*; There is the true transubstantiation, that when I have received it worthily, it becomes my very soul; that is, my soul grows up into a better state, and habitude by it, and I have the more soul for it, the more sanctified, the more deified soul by that sacrament.[68]

But this does not only happen through the sacraments: 'we are translated even into the nature of God. By his precious promises we are made partakers of the Divine nature.'[69] 'God's eye not only turns us to himself, but finally turns us into himself, so that we are not only his but He.'[70]

'We shall be like the angels,' says Christ; in that wherein we can be like them, we shall be like them, in the exalting and refining of the faculties of our souls, but they shall never attain to be like us in our glorified bodies. Neither had God only reserved this treasure and dignity of man to the next world, but

---

[65] Donne, *Sermons*, i. 179, 226; iii. 121; vi. 150, 187; vii. 217, 446.
[66] Donne, *Satires*, 80 ('To Sir Edward Herbert, at Juliers').
[67] Donne, *Sermons*, ix. 2.   [68] Ibid. vii. 12.
[69] Ibid. v. 7.   [70] Ibid. ix. 367.

even here he hath made him *filium Dei*, the Son of God, and *semen Dei*, the seed of God, and *consortem divinae naturae*, partaker of the divine nature, and *deos ipsos*, Gods themselves, for *ille dixit Dii estis*, he hath said we are Gods. So that, as though the glory of heaven were too much for God alone, God hath called up man thither, in the ascension of his Son, to partake thereof; and as though one God were not enough for the administration of this world, God hath multiplied gods here upon earth, and imparted, communicated, not only his power to every magistrate, but the divine nature to every sanctified man. David asks that question with a holy wonder, *Quid est homo?* 'What is man that God is so mindful of him?' But I may have his leave, and the holy Ghost's, to say, since God is so mindful of him, since God hath set his mind upon him, What is not man? Man is all.[71]

This again is the teaching of the Familists, that we can be, as they put it, Godded with God.

Where in traditional Christianity, Incarnation, Crucifixion, Resurrection represent a temporal sequence, for the Familists they were constantly repeated in each believer. The same is true for Donne: 'This day [Easter day] we celebrate his [Christ's] resurrection; this day let us celebrate our own. Our own, not our one resurrection, for we need many. Upon those words of our saviour to Nicodemus, *oportet denuo nasci*, speaking of the necessity of baptism, *non solum denuo, sed tertio nasci oportet*, says St. Bernard, he must be born again and again ...'[72] Repeated too was Christ's baptism. Believers may be baptized, but they are rebaptized each time they repent. The water of baptism represents tears of repentance; Etherington writes of 'the baptism of a thousand tears' and Donne too writes of the baptism of tears.[73] (The anonymous author of *A Discovery of the Abominable Delusions of ... The Family of Love* [1622] thought the phrase 'tears is the water of baptism' to be indicative of Familism.)[74] In his sermons, for example, on Christ weeping and in his religious poetry it is through tears that Donne seeks his salvation:

> You which beyond that heaven which was most high
> Have found new spheres, and of new lands can write,
> Pour new seas in my eyes that so I might

[71] Ibid. vi. 15.   [72] Ibid. iv. 359.
[73] Lake, *Boxmaker's Revenge*, 92, 160, 368; Donne, *Sermons*, vii. 7.
[74] Lake, *Boxmaker's Revenge*, 156.

> Drown my world with my weeping earnestly.[75]
> ('I am a little world made cunningly')[76]

I have drawn out a series of correspondences between Donne's Christianity and the beliefs of the Family of Love. I would like now to draw attention to a peculiar argument to which Donne recurs, and which may be a consequence of seeking to bring the original Familist teaching, that heaven is only in this life, which implies a denial of the immortality of the soul, into a more orthodox framework. In a letter, perhaps to Sir Thomas Lucy, an associate of the Herberts, Donne argues with care that there is no good evidence that *every* person has an immortal soul.[77] In the sermons he seems repeatedly to tell us we acquire a spirit or soul through salvation: our immortal soul is in fact the birth of Christ in us. Thus, interpreting St Paul, 'I pray God your spirit, and soul, and body may be preserved blameless,' he insists 'it is not so absurdly said (though a very great man [Calvin] call it an absurd exposition) that the soul, *anima*, is *qua animales homines* (as the apostle calls them), that by which men are men, natural men, carnal men, and the spirit is the spirit of regeneration, by which man is a new creature, a spiritual man'.[78] Here the soul appears to be mortal, something which men have in common, as he argues in the letter, with horses and elephants; the spirit, by contrast, is immortal. Of St Paul he says that God chose 'to reinanimate him with his spirit, or rather to preinanimate him; for, indeed, no man has a soul till he has grace'.[79] The same thought is expressed catachrestically: 'though the soul be *forma hominis*, it is but *materia dei*; the soul may be the form of man, for without that man is but a carcass; but the soul is but the matter upon which God works; for except our soul receive another soul, and be inanimated with grace, even the soul itself is but a carcass.'[80] Here the Familist doctrine, that something new is born in us at the moment of our salvation, that it is when we are 'implanted into Christ' that we are 'made alive', seems to have been reinterpreted and rethought in order to address the question of immortality.[81] For although Donne sometimes writes about the

---

[75] Donne, *Sermons*, iv. 324–44.   [76] Donne, *Divine Poems*, 13.
[77] Gosse, *Life and Letters*, i. 173–7.   [78] Donne, *Sermons*, v. 65.
[79] Ibid. vi. 172.   [80] Ibid. vii. 108–9.
[81] Quoted from *Evangelium Regni* in Marsh, *Family of Love*, 22.

soul as if its immortality was indisputable, at other times he maintains that it is immortal by preservation, not by nature, and suggests
that the belief that the soul is naturally immortal was unknown to the
early Church.[82] Donne, I would suggest, unlike the Familists, believes
in the immortality of the regenerate spirit; but, like the Familists, he
does not believe in the immortality of the soul.

Of course you may suspect that the similarities I have identified are
accidental. Perhaps his views were entirely conventional for a Jacobean cleric. Or, if not, perhaps there was a recognized tradition of
theology on which he could draw.

There is an instructive comparison to be drawn with Lancelot
Andrewes, who, like Donne, was much influenced by the Greek
fathers. For Andrewes it was primarily through the sacraments that
we become partakers of the divine nature. For Andrewes true happiness is to be found only in the next world—our rebirth in this
world is only to the hope of a better life; we must wait for our
inheritance. He recognizes that there is a first resurrection in this
life, but he limits, rather than develops its significance. Thus preaching at Easter he says 'You thought you should have come to Christ's
resurrection today, and so you do. But not to his alone, but even to
Mary Magdalen's resurrection too. For in very deed a kind of resurrection it was, was wrought in her, revived as it were and raised from
a dead and drowsing to a lively and cheerful estate.'[83] This falls short
of Donne's notion of deification, and there is nothing in Andrewes to
suggest that Christ is born in us.[84]

Of course Donne did have sources to draw on. He quotes Augustine, for example, on the spiritual resurrection which believers experience in this life, and whenever possible he calls on Calvin's
authority.[85] More importantly, as we have seen, Damascene and
Chrysostom provide him with a crucial legitimacy, even though he

---

[82] Donne, *Sermons*, viii. 97; ii. 201; v. 385.
[83] Easter 1620, in Lancelot Andrewes, *Sermons*, ed. G. M. Story (Oxford: Clarendon 1967), 215.
[84] This is not to say that Andrewes does not have a concept of deification, but it is
not nearly as radical as Donne's concept: see Nicolas Lossky, *Lancelot Andrewes* (Paris:
Éditions du Cerf, 1986), 188–95, 212, 247–70.
[85] For Augustine, Donne, *Sermons*, iv, 359.

acknowledges going beyond Chrysostom.[86] There may have been other, more recent, sources for Donne to draw on. Castellio had translated the *Theologia Germanica*, which itself had been a source for Niclaes: hence, it has been suggested, the existence of 'Castalian' Familists.[87] In the mid-sixteenth century Andreas Osiander, an unorthodox Lutheran, had argued that 'Justification itself consists not in a mere juridical pardon, but in the indwelling of the divine nature of the Logos, Jesus Christ. Christ in the Christian justifies ... and then becomes the basis of the Christian's renewal in the image of God.'[88] Donne refers to Osiander in passing, and would certainly have known of him from Calvin's attacks upon him; but by the early seventeenth century Osiander's works on grace must have been hard to obtain, and I think it unlikely, though not impossible, that Osiander was a major influence. Even if he was, this would take Donne well outside the boundaries of orthodox Protestantism.

The work of Marsh and Lake has shown that Familism was widespread in Donne's England, and it is to Familism, and not just to Chrysostom, that we should first look for an understanding of Donne's theology, for any educated Familist trying to preach within the formal limits of orthodoxy would certainly have developed themes such as those we find in Donne's sermons. The similarities I have drawn out between Donne and the Familists do not mean, of course, that Donne when he was a clergyman in the Church of England was a member of the Family of Love: Peter Lake has shown how ex-Familists might continue to use much of the language of Familism, and echo Familist doctrines. But it is worth remembering that we know of several clergymen who were Familists, and that Familism itself insisted on the need for outward conformity to the established Church.

I do not think that the question of whether Donne was or was not a Familist after 1615 is a particularly profitable one because we do

---

[86] Donne's reliance on the Greek fathers needs to be placed in the context of H. R. Trevor-Roper, 'The Church of England and the Greek Church in the Time of Charles I', in his *From Counter-Reformation to Glorious Revolution* (London: Secker & Warburg, 1992), 83–111.

[87] Smith, *Perfection Proclaimed*, 148.

[88] Mickey Mattox, 'Andreas Osiander', in Trevor A. Hart (ed.), *Dictionary of Historical Theology* (Carlisle: Paternoster, 2000). I am grateful to A. Gregg Roeber for bringing Osiander to my attention.

not know enough about the views of the various sub-groups which existed within Familism by the early seventeenth century: Donne's peculiar views may have been those of a Familist sub-group, or his own personal synthesis between Familism and orthodoxy. Certainly Donne was much more orthodox than many Familists. Familists in the 1570s are supposed to have denied the Trinity and the Resurrection of the Body; Donne, while insisting on the difficulties both beliefs present (one of his central themes is the near-impossibility but yet necessity of belief in the Resurrection of the Body) emphasizes his belief in both over and over again. But, for all his relative orthodoxy, Donne stood outside the boundaries of conventional Anglicanism, Calvinism, and indeed Catholicism—so far outside that not even Greek Orthodoxy, only Familism can explain his peculiar beliefs.

My claim is that the sermons Donne preached in St Paul's, at Whitehall, and in the presence of the King were tinged with Familist thinking, but were acceptable because they remained close to the text of the Bible and were unquestionably orthodox on key questions such as the Resurrection of the Body and the Trinity. Like most other Familists, Donne was successful in living out his religious life while outwardly conforming to the established Church. But I want to end by drawing attention to a number of sermons that Donne preached to audiences that were more nearly private than public. We have already seen a striking example in Donne's rejection of the Lutheran and Calvinist doctrine of forensic justification. It is perhaps no coincidence that this plain speaking occurred at a christening (whose christening, unfortunately, we do not know), an almost private gathering. But what was going on, we might wonder, when Donne preached at the marriage of Sir Francis Nethersole (secretary to Donne's patron, Viscount Doncaster) to Lucy Goodyer, the daughter of Donne's closest friend, Henry Goodyer, and the servant and godchild of Donne's patron, the Countess of Bedford? If ever there was a marriage within Donne's inner circle, this was it, and the Countess so strongly approved of the match that she was reported to have given the couple over a thousand pounds.[89] Yet having preached what Evelyn Simpson thinks is a deeply unsatisfactory sermon,

---

[89] R. C. Bald, *John Donne: A Life* (New York: Oxford University Press, 1970), 367.

Donne ends lamely by saying that those who marry should be suited to each other:

there is a moral fitness … and there is a civil fitness … and there is a spiritual fitness, in the unanimity of religion, that they be not of repugnant professions that way. Of which, since we are well assured in both these, who are to be joined now, I am not sorry if either the hour, or the present occasion, call me from speaking anything at all, because it is a subject too mis-interpretable and unseasonable to admit an enlarging in at this time.[90]

What was so misinterpretable and unseasonable about the religion of Nethersole and his bride?[91]

Equally striking is another sermon delivered at a christening in which he directly attacks the orthodox Protestant idea that perfection can only be attained in the next life:

some … see no way of admitting these perfections in this life. But St. Paul saw a way, when he said of the elect, even in this life, 'God which is rich in mercy *convivificavit, conresuscitavit, considere fecit*, he hath quickened us, he hath raised us, he hath made us sit together in the heavenly places in Christ Jesus.' That is, as he is our head, and is there himself, and we with Christ Jesus as we are his members, we are with him there too.[92]

But the most striking of all these sermons is the one he delivered on 1 July 1627 at the memorial service for Magdalen Herbert, by then Lady Danvers.[93] Indeed this is a most exceptional sermon, for it is the only sermon by Donne printed in his lifetime not to have been included in the three volumes of collected sermons which appeared in the seventeenth century. (The mystery only deepens if one thinks it was intended to be included. The twenty-six sermons of 1660 are missing a sermon numbered 9, which occupied sheet R4, and which

---

[90] Donne, *Sermons*, ii. 17.
[91] Another unseasonable marriage was that between Magdalen Herbert and Sir John Danvers in 1609. 'Young Danvers is likewise wedded to the widow Herbert (mother to Sir Edward) of more than twice his age,' wrote John Chamberlain (Bald, *John Donne*, 183). Contemporaries doubted whether marriages to women past childbearing age were properly legitimate (Laura Gowing, *Common Bodies* (New Haven: Yale University Press, 2003), 77–8). Unseasonable marriages were, however, common in the Family of Love, where pressure to marry within the religious community was high, and the supply of potential partners was restricted: Marsh, *Family of Love*, 147–8.
[92] Donne, *Sermons*, v. 4.   [93] Ibid. viii. 61–93.

must have been pulled from the volume while it was in the press). It survives in a tiny duodecimo volume, where it is accompanied by George Herbert's poems in Latin and Greek in memory of his mother, and was not reprinted until 1839.[94]

This sermon contains one of Donne's most remarkable passages on the Christian's transformation into Christ, one in which, charactistically, he cites Chrysostom only to go beyond him:

He is not only my rule and my example, but my surety and my promise, that where he is I shall be also; not only, where he is in Glory now, but in every step that he made in this world; if I be with him in his afflictions, I shall be with him in his eluctation, in his victory, in his triumph. St. Chrysostom, falling upon such a meditation as this, is loath to depart from it. He insists upon it thus: *Illine qui a dextris Dei sedet, conforme fiet hoc corpus?* Will God make this body of man like that that now sits at his right hand? Yes, he will. *Illi, quem adorant Angeli?* Like him, whom all the angels worship? Yes, like him. *Illi, cui adstant incorporales virtutes?* Like him to whom the Thrones and Powers and Dominations and Cherubins and Seraphins minister? Yes, he will do all that says that Father. But allow me the boldness to add thus much: *Cum illo,* I shall be with him before, with him wheresoever he was in this world. I shall be with him in his agonies and sadness of soul, but in those agonies and sadness, I shall be with him still in his *Veruntamen,* in his surrender of himself: Not my will but thine O Father be done. I shall be with him upon his cross, but in all my crosses and in all my jealousies and suspicions of that *Dereliquisti,* that God my God hath forsaken me; I shall be with him still in his *In Manus,* in a confidence and assurance that I may commit my spirit into his hands. For all this I do according to his promise that where he is I shall be also.[95]

Let me end with a lengthy quotation, in which Donne speaks on behalf of the true believers in his audience:

we, for all his [the devil's] scorns, for all these terrors, shall have an answer to his *Quis vos?* and be able to tell him that we are that *gens sancta* and that *regale sacerdotium* that this apostle speaks of; that holy people, made holy by

[94] For Herbert's poems, *Memoriae Matris Sacrum,* see *The Latin Poetry of George Herbert: A Bilingual Edition,* trans. Mark McCloskey and Paul R. Murphy (Athens, Ohio: Ohio University Press, 1965). If the argument presented here is accepted, it has considerable implications for our understanding of the upbringing of both George Herbert and Herbert of Cherbury.

[95] Donne, *Sermons,* viii. 74.

his covenant and ordinances, and that royal priesthood which, as priests, have an interest in his sacrifice, his son; and as kings have an interest in that crown which, for his son's sake, he hath ordained for us. We are they who have seen the marks of his election in their first edition, in the scriptures, and seen them again in their second edition, as they are imprinted in our consciences, in our faith, and in our manners, and so we cannot mistake, nor be deceived in them. We are that *semen dei* that Malachai speaks of, the seed of God which he hath sowed in his Church; and by that extraction we are *consortes divinae naturae*, partakers of the divine nature itself; and so grow to be *filii dei*, the sons of God; and by that title *cohaeredes Christi*, joint-heirs with Christ; and to be *Christi ipsi*, Christs ourselves, as God calls all his faithful, his anointed, his Christs; and from thence we grow to that height to be of the quorum, in that commission, *dii estis*, I have said you are Gods, and not only Gods by representation, but *idem spiritus cum Domino*, so become the same spirit with the Lord that as a spirit cannot be divided in itself, so we are persuaded that neither death nor life, nor any creature, shall be able to separate us from God. ... So then you see what fellowship of the faithful, what household of the righteous, what communion of saints it is that falls under this denomination, We—we that have laid our foundations in faith, and made our superedifications in sanctimony and holiness of life, we that have learnt, and learnt by the right rule, the rule of Christianity, how to put a right value upon this world ... if we can say of the fires of tribulation as Origen says ... that all our fiery tribulations fall under the nature and definition of sacraments, that they are so many visible signs of invisible grace, that every correction from God's hand is a rebaptization to me, and that I can see that I should not have been so sure of salvation without this sacrament, without this baptism, without this fire of tribulation ... if I can bring these fires to this compass and to this temper, I shall find that as the ark was in the midst of the waters, and yet safe from the fire, so, though St. Jerome say (and upon good grounds) *grandis audaciae est, puraeque conscientiae*, it is an act of greater boldness than any man, as man, can avow, and a testimony of a clearer conscience than any man, as man, can pretend to have *regnum dei postulare, et iudicium non timere*, to press God for the day of judgement and not to fear that day (for upon all men, considered but as men, falls that severe expostulation of the prophet Amos, 'Wo unto you that desire the day of the Lord; to what end is it for you? The day of the Lord is darkness and not light'), yet I shall find that such a family, such a society, such a communion there is, and that I am of that quorum that can say, 'Come what scorns can come, come what terrors can come, *in Christo omnia possumus*, though we can do nothing of ourselves, yet as we are in Christ, we can do all things, because we are fixed in him, *secundum promissa* ... God shall impart to us all a mysterious gavelkind, a mysterious equality of fullness of glory, to us all ... And God shall say to us all *sedete a dextris*, sit ye all on my right hand, for from the left hand there is no prospect to the face of God; and to us all *hodie genui vos*, this day I have begotten you all; begotten you in the confirmation of my first baptism, in the ratification of my first election; and to us all *ponam inimicos vestros*, I will make all your enemies your footstool, for God shall establish us there *ubi non intrat inimicus, nec amicus exit*, where no man shall come in that troubles the company, nor any, whom any of the company loves go out, but we shall all, not only have but be a part of the righteousness that dwells in these new heavens and new earth, which we, according to his promise, look for.[96]

I began by suggesting that Donne's two poems inspired by Magdalen Herbert invite us to question the nature of the Resurrection and the Church, and in so doing insinuate Familist beliefs; let me end by suggesting that as Donne preached at her memorial service there were present in the congregation a significant number of Familists, and that it was to them that these words were particularly addressed. For who but the Familists would have been prepared to envisage themselves as the fellowship of the faithful, the household of the righteous, a holy people, a royal priesthood, not the Church but the seed of God sown in the Church, already safely embarked in the ark of salvation, already partaking in the same spirit as God himself, already Christs, already Gods? Who but the Familists would have felt entitled to ignore the prophet Amos and St Jerome, and declare they had no fear of the day of judgement? It is in this sermon, I would suggest, that we hear most clearly the language that Donne would have liked always to employ when he spoke about his God, for as Donne preached this sermon he was speaking to as well as of Magdalen Herbert, who had known more than the Churches about the Resurrection.

[96] Donne, *Sermons*, viii. 70.

3

'Le plus beau et le plus meschant esprit que ie aye cogneu': Science and Religion in the Writings of Giulio Cesare Vanini, 1585–1619

Nicholas S. Davidson

Vanini's heterodoxy was recognized in his own lifetime. Ascanio Spinola, for example, the minister of the London Italian Church, who met him in 1612, believed him 'to bee of no religion, but a profane person, a filthy speaker and a grosse fornicatour', and he prohibited Vanini from preaching in his Church.[1] His books were swiftly condemned too: the Sorbonne repudiated his *De admirandis* on 1 October 1616, just a month after its publication.[2] His execution as an atheist and blasphemer on the orders of the Parlement of Toulouse at the tender age of 34 confirmed this reputation. The earliest surviving report of his death described his beliefs as diabolical and scandalous, and the vicar-general of the archbishop of Toulouse issued a condemnation of his two published books in the summer of 1620. The *De admirandis* was added to the Catholic Church's official Index of Prohibited Books in 1623.[3]

---

[1] Émile Namer, *Documents sur la vie de Jules-César Vanini de Taurisano* (Bari: Adriatica editrice, 1965), 75.

[2] Ibid. 89–90.

[3] Didier Foucault, 'Documents toulousains sur le supplice de Vanini', *La Lettre clandestine*, 5 (1996), 29; Namer, *Documents*, 134–5; *Index Librorum prohibitorum Alexandri VII* (Rome: Ex typographia Reurendae Camerae Apostolicae, 1664), 93, 323.

More amplified legends about Vanini began to develop very soon after his death. The first accounts of his execution, written and published in 1619, describe his courage as he approached his death, publicly affirming his beliefs and expressing a determination to die as he had lived:

he died with as much steadfastness, patience and will as any man that one had ever seen. He came out from the Conciergerie [where he had been held in prison] joyous and lively, and pronounced these words in Italian: 'come along, let's die cheerfully as a philosopher'. And as if to demonstrate even more strongly his constancy in the face of death and the lack of expectation in his soul, when he was asked if he would beg God for mercy, he said these words in the presence of a thousand people: 'there is neither God nor devil. For if there were a God, I would pray him to launch a thunderbolt on the wholly unjust and iniquitous Parlement here; and if there were a devil, I would pray him to swallow it up in the realm below. But because neither one nor the other exists, I will do nothing.'[4]

Pierre Bayle was later to use Vanini's conduct during his trial and execution as evidence that atheism could produce its own martyrs.[5] But within just a few years of Vanini's death, a different story was already being told. The Jesuit François Garasse in 1623 had him dying not with calm courage but 'enragé', and twenty years later, Gabriel de Gramond described how he had hypocritically received the sacraments in prison before his execution, and then displayed fear at the end, howling horribly like a slaughtered animal.[6] What we see in the emergence of this later version, of course, is the conventional picture of the heretic or unbeliever: an uncontrolled, dishonest, and cowardly individual who has no faith in the false beliefs he had formerly tried to persuade others to adopt. And throughout the seventeenth and eighteenth centuries, Vanini's name appeared prom-

---

[4] Foucault, 'Documents toulousains', 30. Cf. ibid. 18–20, 25–6; *Mercure françois*, v (Paris: Richer, 1619), 64–5; Didier Foucault, 'Giulio Cesare Vanini, un libertin martyr à l'âge baroque: Mise au point bio-bibliographique', *Le Bulletin de la Société d'Histoire Moderne et Contemporaine* (1996), 90.

[5] Pierre Bayle, *Pensées diverses, écrites à un docteur de Sorbonne, à l'occasion de la Cométe qui parut au mois de Decembre 1680* (Rotterdam: Reinier Leers, 1683), 567–71.

[6] François Garasse, *La Doctrine curieuse des beaux esprits de ce temps ou pretendus tells* (Paris: Sébastien Chappelet, 1623), 146–7; Gabriel de Gramond, *Historiarum Galliae ab excessu Henrici IV* (Toulouse: Arnald. Colomerium, 1643), 210.

inently in the published lists of men deemed responsible for spreading atheism. The French Minim Marin Mersenne included him, along with Machiavelli, Cardano, and others, among the atheists whose arguments he repudiated in his *Quaestiones celeberrimae in Genesim* in 1623. Robert Burton named him in the third edition of *The Anatomy of Melancholy*, published in 1628, along with Machiavelli and Aretino; and Jean de Silhon associated Pomponazzi, Cardano, and Vanini in his *De l'immortalité de l'âme*, published in 1634.[7] Henry More, the Cambridge Platonist, linked Vanini with Pomponazzi in his *Immortality of the Soul* published in 1658; Jenkin Philipps included Pomponazzi, Cardano, Aretino, and Vanini in his *Historia atheismi*, perhaps the first systematic history of atheism, published in 1709.[8] Passages from Vanini's writings were incorporated in the notorious *Traité des trois imposteurs*, printed at the end of the seventeenth century, and in the early eighteenth century, his name appeared on the title page of the published text of the *Theophrastus redivivus*.[9]

By then, however, Vanini had become more of an icon than an object of serious study, and it is clear that those authors who criticized him most fiercely in the seventeenth and eighteenth centuries had often not actually read his books very closely. In 1623, Garasse called him the patriarch of atheists, and summarized his *De admirandis* as an 'Introduction à la vie indevote'; in the 1640s, Gijsbert

---

[7] Marin Mersenne, *Quaestiones celeberrimae in Genesim* (Paris: Sumptibus Sebastiani Cramoisy, 1623), cols. 286–8, 393–5; Robert Burton, *The Anatomy of Melancholy*, ed. Thomas C. Faulkner, Nicolas K. Kiessling, and Rhonda L. Blair (Oxford: Clarendon, 1989–2000), iii. 405 and vi. 430; Jean de Silhon, *De l'immortalité de l'âme* (Paris: Pierre Billaine, 1634), 47–8. Cf. also Garasse, *La Doctrine curieuse*, 1013–14.

[8] Henry More, *The immortality of the soul, so farre forth as it is demonstrable from the knowledge of nature and the light of reason* (London: J. Flesher, 1659), unpaginated preface, cap. 6; Jenkin Philipps, *Historia atheismi breviter delineata* (Basle, 1709), 66–75. Cf. also Jenkin Philipps, *Dissertatio historico-philosophica de atheismo* (London, 1716), 97–114.

[9] *Trattato dei tre impostori: La vita e lo spirito del Signor Benedetto de Spinoza*, ed. Silvia Berti (Turin: Einaudi, 1994), 96–8, 110–14, 124–8, 150–2, 272–4, 278–9, 282–3, 290; Francesco Paolo Raimondi, 'Vanini e il *De tribus impostoribus*' in *Ethos e cultura: Studi in onore de Ezio Riondati*, i (Padua, Antenore, 1991), 268, 284–5; Tullio Gregory, ' "Libertinisme érudit" in Seventeenth-Century France and Italy: The Critique of Ethics and Religion', *British Journal for the History of Philosophy*, 6 (1998), 324, 328–9; Antonio Perrino, 'Giulio Cesare Vanini nel *Theophrastus redivivus*', *Bollettino di storia della filosofia dell'Università degli Studi di Lecce*, 10 (1990–2), 201.

Voet referred to him as the apostle of atheism.[10] Later in the century,
the English satirist John Oldham went so far as to call him its 'Bless'd
Saint', and an anonymous German pamphlet of 1686 even named
him as 'the vicar of Lucifer'.[11] In the eighteenth century, there were
some attempts to examine his life and writings more carefully.
Johannes Schramm published the first biography in 1709, while
Peter Arpe's 1712 *Apologia pro Julio Cesare Vanino* suggested that
Vanini was innocent of the charges laid against him.[12] And Vanini's
two books continued to be quite widely available: Andrzej Nowicki
has traced at least 119 surviving first editions of his *Amphitheatrum*,
and 87 of the *De admirandis*.[13]

But it has to be admitted that these texts are still not easy to
interpret. They do not actively assert any heterodox ideas—on the
contrary, in fact, for Vanini claimed that he wrote them to refute
error. In addition, much of their content is copied verbatim from
other sources: what we have is a major exercise in plagiarism, one
that serves to disguise Vanini's own views. And many areas of his life
remain undocumented, too. No letters or other personal documents
seem to have survived, for example, and the records of his trial in
Toulouse have still not been found. How then can we get behind the
myths and the literary theft to the beliefs of the man himself?

We can begin with some biographical information.[14] Giulio Cesare
Vanini was born at Taurisano, in the heel of Italy, in 1584 or 1585. His
mother was Spanish, and his father, who came from Liguria, managed the local estates of the duke of Taurisano, the Spanish nobleman
Francisco de Castro, who was appointed viceroy of Naples in 1600

[10] Garasse, *La Doctrine curieuse*, 641; Gijsbert Voet, *Selectarum disputationum theologicarum. Pars prima* (Utrecht: Apud Joannem à Waesberge, 1648), 136.

[11] John Oldham, *The Poems of John Oldham*, ed. Harold F. Brooks (Oxford: Clarendon, 1987), 179; Andrzej Nowicki, 'Vanini et la philosophie de la culture', *Tijdschrift voor de Studie van de Verlichting*, 2 (1974), 168.

[12] Johannes Schramm, *De vita et scriptis famosi athei Julii Caesaris Vanini* (Cus-trini: Typis & sumptibus Godofredi Heinichii, 1709); Peter Arpe, *Apologia pro Julio Cesare Vanino* ('Cosmopoli' [i.e. Rotterdam]: Typis Philaletheis, 1712).

[13] Andrzej Nowicki, 'Gli incontri tra Vanini e Campanella', in *Tommaso Campa-nella (1568–1639): Miscellanea di studi nel 4 centenario della sua nascita* (Naples: F. Fiorentino, 1969), 483.

[14] The best introductions to Vanini's life are now Didier Foucault's two articles, 'Giulio Cesare Vanini, un libertin martyr', 81–90, and 'Chronologie sommaire de la vie de Vanini', *Kairos*, 12 (1998), 329–30.

and was later to serve as Spanish Ambassador to the Holy See. Vanini may have been educated as a boy by the Jesuits, and by the early years of the seventeenth century, he had moved to the University of Naples, where he completed his Arts degree and some medical studies before taking his doctorate in both laws in June 1606.[15] Three years earlier, he had entered the Carmelites, receiving the name Gabriele in religion, and subsequently been ordained priest. Later, probably in 1608, he moved to Padua, where he apparently studied theology and got to know a fellow-Carmelite from Genoa named Giovanni Maria Ginocchi. In 1611, he served as a Lent preacher at St Mark's in Venice. His career seemed to be flourishing, and he was later to acquire a reputation as a talented preacher.[16] But in January of the following year, he and Ginocchi were ordered by the general of their order, Enrico Silvio, to leave Padua. Ginocchi was to go to Pisa, and Vanini to the Terra di Lavoro, near Capua.[17] We do not know the reason for this decision, though it is possible that the ecclesiastical authorities were concerned that Vanini and Ginocchi were mixing in the wrong intellectual and political circles in Venice.[18] Certainly, the two men had already made some contact with the English community in the city, for instead of observing the general's order, they persuaded the English Ambassador to the Republic, Dudley Carlton, to send them to London, where they arrived in June. In the following month, Vanini renounced his Catholic faith and was received into the exiled Italian church in London. For the next two years, he lived as a guest of the archbishop of Canterbury, George Abbot, first at Lambeth Palace and later in Croydon.[19]

During his stay in England, he made formal visits to both Cambridge and Oxford, where he was apparently hospitably treated; but he reportedly told friends in Oxford that he had tired of

---

[15] Papuli, Giovanni, 'Per una revisione della biografia di Giulio Cesare Vanini', in Michele Paone (ed.), *Studi di storia pugliese in onore di Giuseppe Chiarelli*, iii (Galatina: M. Congedo, 1974), 118–20; Francesco De Paola, 'Nuovi documenti per una rilettura di Giulio Cesare Vanini', *Bruniana e campanelliana*, 5 (1999), 190–9.

[16] Francesco Paolo Raimondi, 'Documenti vaniniani nel'Archivio Segreto Vaticano', *Bollettino di storia della filosofia dell'Università degli Studi di Lecce*, 8 (1980–5), 189, 197.

[17] Antonio Corsano, 'Postille Vaniniane', in Paone, *Studi di storia pugliese*, iii. 34.

[18] De Paola, 'Nuovi documenti', 192.

[19] Namer, *Documents*, 38, 72–8.

Protestantism and wished to return to the Continent. By means of the Spanish ambassador in London, Vanini and Ginocchi in 1613 made contact with Guido Bentivoglio, the papal nunzio in Flanders, asking for a formal pardon for their apostasy; but the following year, before they could leave England, Abbot had them both arrested. Under questioning, according to the archbishop's own account, Vanini revealed his continued commitment to Catholicism. Shocked by this discovery—'never did I finde in all my life more impudent and unworthy varletts', he wrote—Abbot excommunicated Vanini, and planned to exile him to Bermuda, 'there to digge for his living'; but Vanini made his escape in the spring of 1614, again possibly with the assistance of the Spanish Ambassador, and travelled to Brussels, where he was received back into the Roman Church and granted a dispensation from his Carmelite vows.[20]

By the end of July 1614, Vanini had moved to Paris, from where the papal nunzio Roberto Ubaldini authorized his transfer to Rome so that he could present to the Congregation of the Holy Office a book he claimed to have written on the Council of Trent. He seems to have left Paris around the end of August 1614; but on the way south, he stopped off in Genoa, where he joined the household of Scipione Doria as tutor to his sons.[21] Here he met up again with Ginocchi, who had also fled from London. However, when Ginocchi was arrested by the local Inquisition in January 1615, Vanini decided to head back to France for his own safety.[22] He went first to Lyons, where several other members of the Vanini family had been resident for some years.[23] There, in June 1615, and possibly with the assistance of these relatives, he published his _Amphitheatrum aeternae prouidentiae diuino-magicum_[24] as a contribution to the debate about atheism in France that followed the death in Paris of Catherine

---

[20] Ibid. 74, 76, 77, 88–9; Raimondi, 'Documenti vaniniani', 189–90, 196–7.

[21] Raimondi, 'Documenti vaniniani', 190, 197.

[22] Ibid. 190–1, 198.

[23] Didier Foucault, 'Gli ambienti lionesi che accolsero il Vanini al momento della pubblicazione dell'_Amphitheatrum_ (1615)' in Francesco Paolo Raimondi (ed.), _Giulio Cesare Vanini e il libertinismo_ (Galatina: Congedo, 2000), 153–65.

[24] Giulio Cesare Vanini, _Amphitheatrum aeternae prouidentiae diuino-magicum, Christiano-physicum, nec non astrologo-catholicum, Aduersus veteres_ [sic] _philosophos, atheos, Epicureos, peripateticos, et Stoicos_ (Lyons: Apud viduam Antonii de Harsy, 1615).

de' Medici's Italian astrologer, Cosme Ruggieri, who had reportedly died rejecting belief in God.[25] The book was published by the widow of the Protestant Antoine de Harsy, but it received its *imprimatur* from Jean-Claude de Ville, the local Catholic archbishop's official censor of books, and from François du Soleil, the archbishop's vicar-general, as well as from the requisite government officials.[26] Two months later, he was back in Paris.[27] Here he entered the household of François, baron de Bassompierre, later marshal of France, and in September 1616, his more radical *De admirandis naturae reginae deaeque mortalium arcanis* was published by the Protestant Adrien Perier.[28] Both his published books were printed with the formal approval of both the ecclesiastical and the secular authorities of the day, but the Sorbonne subjected the *De admirandis*, as we have seen, to a further investigation as soon as it appeared. The two ecclesiastical censors who had registered their consent for publication in the previous May, the Franciscans Edmond Corradin and Claude Le Petit, claimed that Vanini had published a different text from the manuscript they had approved. The Sorbonne's subsequent condemnation of the *De admirandis*, dated 16 October 1616, was couched in very general terms, but Vanini nonetheless fled from Paris after the decision. He moved first to Guyenne and by 1617 had arrived in Toulouse, where he adopted the name Pompée Usciglio and joined the household of Adrien de Monluc, Count of Cramail and Governor of the Comté of Foix, as a tutor.[29] Monluc was known to Bassompierre (like him, he was later imprisoned by Richelieu), and it is possible that Vanini went to Toulouse precisely because of this connection.

Vanini now became a member of the circle of mostly young intellectuals that gathered around Monluc, and for a year or so, his false name seems to have protected him. In 1618, however, rumours

[25] Garasse, *La Doctrine curieuse*, 154–7; Nicholas Davidson, 'Unbelief and Atheism in Italy, 1500–1700', in Michael Hunter and David Wootton (eds.), *Atheism from the Reformation to the Enlightenment* (Oxford: Clarendon, 1992), 74.

[26] Foucault, 'Gli ambienti lionesi', 165–7.

[27] Raimondi, 'Documenti vaniniani', 191.

[28] Giulio Cesare Vanini, *De admirandis naturae reginae deaeque mortalium arcanis* (Paris: Apud Adrianum Perier, 1616).

[29] De Paola, 'Nuovi documenti', 199–201; Namer, *Documents*, 89–90, 113; Raimondi, 'Vanini e il *De tribus impostoribus*', 268–71.

of his teaching reached Father Cotton, the Lent preacher at St Sernin, who visited Vanini and 'came away from their conversation more astonished than instructed'. On 2 August 1618, Vanini was arrested on the orders of the Capitouls, the city government. After a lengthy investigation lasting six months, in which Father Cotton's evidence was apparently corroborated by that of a nobleman called Tersac Monbérant, Sieur de Francon, the Parlement of Toulouse found Vanini guilty of atheism, blasphemy, impieties, and other unspecified crimes, and condemned him to death. On 9 February 1619, a placard recording his crime, 'Atéiste et blasphémateur du nom de Dieu', was hung from his neck, and he was taken first to the cathedral of Saint-Étienne, and then to the Place du Salin, where his tongue was cut out before he was strangled. After death, his body was burned and his ashes scattered to the wind.[30] Guillaume de Catel, whose report to the court was in part responsible for Vanini's conviction, included a brief mention of his death in a letter he sent to Pierre Fabri de Peiresc a few days later: 'he died an atheist, persisting to the end. *Le plus beau et le plus meschant esprit que ie aye cogneu*.'[31]

Since the trial records have not been recovered, we cannot tell precisely why the Parlement decided on such a harsh sentence. The decision to hand down an exemplary punishment may have been related to recent changes on the Toulouse Capitoulat, allied with a desire to tighten discipline among the local clergy.[32] Nobody, it seems, made the connection between Pompée Usciglio and the author of the *Amphitheatrum* and the *De admirandis* until after his death. Those two books remain, however, our only major source for his beliefs. None of the other books he claimed to have written—several mentioned in the *Amphitheatrum* and the *De admirandis*, plus the apology for the Council of Trent mentioned by nunzio Ubaldini—appear to have been published. Garasse claimed to have

---

[30] Foucault, 'Documents toulousains', 29–30; Garasse, *La Doctrine curieuse*, 145–6; Andrzej Nowicki, *Giulio Cesare Vanini (1585–1619): La sua filosofia dell'uomo e delle opere umane* (Wroclaw: Zakllad Narowowy im. Ossolinskich, 1968), 5; Cesare Vasoli, 'Vanini e il suo processo per ateismo', in Friedrich Niewöhner and Olaf Pluta (eds.), *Atheismus im Mittelalter und in der Renaissance* (Wiesbaden: Harrassowitz, 1999), 139; Namer, *Documents*, 113–14.

[31] Foucault, 'Documents toulousains', 25.

[32] Ibid. 26; De Paola, 'Nuovi documenti', 201–2.

read his book on wisdom, perhaps in manuscript, but we may doubt whether Vanini did actually write them all, as we shall see.[33]

The *Amphitheatrum* is dedicated to his father's employer, Francisco de Castro, a devout Catholic, and the *De admirandis* to Vanini's patron in Paris, François de Bassompierre, a man whose orthodoxy was later doubted by Mersenne.[34] The *Amphitheatrum* opens with a complaint: that atheism is increasing, in both Catholic and non-Catholic territories. The key atheistic belief, Vanini claims, is a rejection of divine providence, a denial that he links with a rejection also of miracles, immortality, and the authority of Scripture. It is clear, he continues, that the reason for the growth of atheism is the intellectual inadequacy of the traditional arguments presented in support of the doctrine of divine providence. The purpose of his book, therefore, is to demonstrate the truth of that doctrine anew.[35] The text of the book is constructed as a series of 'exercises', each one dealing with a particular doctrinal question: exercise II, for example, is headed 'Deus quod sit'.[36] This was a recognized academic format at the time, though Vanini's text is perhaps arranged more coherently than most examples of the genre.[37] On the surface, therefore, the *Amphitheatrum* appears to be a fairly conventional sort of book. As we shall see, however, it is in reality a good deal more subversive than it might at first appear. Vanini's second published volume, the *De admirandis*, is constructed in an equally familiar literary genre. The text here is set out in four books, each subdivided into a series of dialogues, sixty in all, between Alexander and Julius Caesar; they are

[33] Garasse, *La Doctrine curieuse*, 1015; Arpe, *Apologia*, 5–7; Giulio Cesare Vanini, *Le opere di Giulio Cesare Vanini e le loro fonti*, ed. Luigi Corvaglia, ii (Galatina: Congedo, 1990–1991), 277–9; Pierre Boiteau, 'Au temps de l'Inquisition: J.-C. Vanini et la notion d'évolution au début du XVIIe siècle', *La Pensée*, 127 (1966), 102; Ivan Jadin, 'Pomponace mythique: La sincérité religieuse de Pietro Pomponazzi dans le miroir de sa réputation française', *Tijdschrift voor de Studie van de Verlichting en van het vrije Denken*, 14–15 (1986–7), 33; Adele Spedicati, 'Indice del *De admirandis* di G.C. Vanini', *Bollettino di storia della filosofia dell'Università degli Studi di Lecce*, 9 (1986–9), 309–10.

[34] Don Cameron Allen, *Doubt's Boundless Sea: Skepticism and Faith in the Renaissance* (Baltimore: Johns Hopkins University Press, 1964), 66.

[35] Vanini, *Le opere*, i. xviii–xx. I have used this modern edition of Vanini's works, with its invaluable citations from his plagiarized sources, in the notes below.

[36] Ibid. 5–7.

[37] Jean-Robert Armogathe, 'Jules-César Vanini: Une rhétorique de la subversion', *Kairos*, 12 (1998), 148–9.

joined in the fourth book by a further character, an atheist from
Amsterdam. Although it is clear that the dialogues are the author's
invention, the figure of Julius Caesar is clearly meant to stand for
Vanini himself. On one page, indeed, Julius Caesar admits that he no
longer holds to all the teaching he had presented in his *Amphitheatrum*. In line with this hint, the *De admirandis* is in fact more openly
unorthodox than his earlier book, something we might easily guess
from its title alone, which refers to nature as 'the queen and goddess
of mortals'.[38]

　　Both these books are at times very funny, and also very clever. But
it is not at all easy to draw from them a coherent doctrinal position.
The fragmented structure of exercises and dialogues prevents (probably deliberately) the presentation of any systematic analysis. In
addition, both books are constructed from a mass of quotations
lifted from earlier authors. Often, therefore, when we think we are
hearing Vanini's own voice, we discover he has borrowed the words
of other people. But the selection of these quotations, and the
methods adopted to reconstruct them into two new books, are
conscious, skilful, and careful. And his use of his plagiarized texts is
anything but uncritical. Both the *Amphitheatrum* and the *De admirandis* borrow massively from Giulio Cesare Scaligero's *Exotericarum
exercitationum ... de subtilitate*, first published in 1557, a response
to Girolamo Cardano's critique of Aristotelianism, *De subtilitate*, of
1550.[39] Vanini's views on some subjects—including his views on
Cardano—often simply repeat those already advanced by Scaligero.[40]
On other occasions, however, he prefers to echo the views of Cardano, and at one point he refers to Cardano as 'a man who can never
be praised enough'.[41] His use of Pomponazzi is equally inconsistent.[42]

　　What we have then is a more creative use of plagiarism than we
might at first suppose. And a close reading of the two books reveals a

---

[38] Vanini, *Le opere*, ii. 318–19; cf. 287, 289, 304.
[39] Girolamo Cardano, *De subtilitate libri XXI* (Nuremberg: Apud Ioh. Petreium,
1550); Giulio Cesare Scaligero, *Exotericarum exercitationum liber quintus decimus, de
subtilitate, ad Hieronymum Cardanum* (Paris: Ex officina typographica Michaelis
Vascosani, 1557).
[40] Vanini, *Le opere*, iii/1. 137–8.　　　[41] Ibid. i. 261.
[42] Ibid. ii. 281; iii/1. 84.

number of different ways in which Vanini puts his sources to use. The most straightforward among these is when he borrows a passage directly from another author to state an argument for him, whether he agrees with it himself or not. The *De admirandis* in particular, which as we have seen is constructed in dialogue form, often simply presents one set of quotations against another to advance the debate. Sometimes, though, Vanini clearly and deliberately abuses his sources. Many passages are incorporated in such a way that, torn from their original context, they seem to lead to the opposite conclusion to the one their authors had intended. In exercise xxvii of the *Amphitheatrum*, for example, he takes as his starting-point a passage from Scaligero's *Exotericarum*, arguing that the immortality of the soul can be proved from physical principles; but Vanini builds his text up from there so that it reaches the conclusion that immortality cannot be proved.[43] Sometimes, he shifts the implication of a passage by providing a different answer to a rhetorical question than that expected in the original. And on other occasions, he deliberately alters the phrasing of his borrowed texts, perhaps only by a single word, or adds something of his own to them, thus radically changing their meaning. In dialogue li of the *De admirandis*, for instance, he compiles a long list of examples of fraudulent religious beliefs and practices in the ancient world, drawn from Pomponazzi's *De incantationibus*, first published in 1556, and from Cardano's *De rerum varietate* of 1557 as well as his *De subtilitate*.[44] Here he appears to be echoing the familiar Christian idea that pagan religions were invented by rulers and priests to secure their own power and authority. He inserts into the discussion, however, some additional examples drawn from the Middle Ages, and at one point he slips subtly into the present tense, thus leaving open the possibility that the beliefs and practices of the contemporary Christian Church might also be considered fraudulent.[45]

[43] Ibid. i. 97–8; cf. Giulio Cesare Vanini, *Anfiteatro dell'eterna providenza*, tr. Francesco Paolo Raimondi and Luigi Crudo (Galatina: Congedo, 1981), 179.

[44] Pietro Pomponazzi, *De naturalium effectuum causis, siue de Incantationibus* (Basle: Per Henrichum Petri, 1556); Girolamo Cardano, *De rerum varietate libri XVII* (Basle: Per Henrichum Petri, 1557).

[45] Vanini, *Le opere*, i. 17; ii. 276–84; cf. ii. 271, 289–93; Vanini, *Anfiteatro*, 63–4; Didier Foucault, 'Fondaments d'une ontologie matérialiste dans l'*Amphitheatrum* et le *De admirandis* de Vanini', *Kairos*, 12 (1998), 45, 49–50; Armogathe, 'Jules-César Vanini', 154.

A further tactic is to pile up quotations from his orthodox sources in such a way that their argument begins to look ridiculous. A good example appears early in the *Amphitheatrum*, where Vanini constructs a long set of quotations from three different chapters of Scaligero's *Exotericarum*, all designed to describe the attributes of God:

He is not being, but essence; he is not good, but goodness; he is not wise, but wisdom; he is not omnipotent, but omnipotence. ... He has always existed, but is outside time. ... He reigns everywhere, but is located nowhere; he is unmoving, but without rest, indefatigable, but never moves. He is entirely outside of everything, in all things, but not contained by anything, outside of everything, but not excluded from anything. ... He is totality without parts, unchanging, but producing change in other things. ... He is everything, over everything, outside everything, in everything, beyond everything, before everything and after everything.[46]

All the words in this passage appear in Scaligero's book, where they are used to demonstrate the mystery of God. Thrown together by Vanini, they appear instead to make the concept of God sound irrational, incoherent, and meaningless. By thus exposing the inconsistencies and inadequacies of established beliefs—and of their expression by the authors he plunders so mercilessly—he produces a subversion of the Christian system from within.

Vanini therefore uses his sources to undermine orthodoxy. But this is not the only way he works against the Church's doctrine. Another method is to make a powerful presentation of an explicitly heterodox argument, following it with nothing more than a token restatement of the Catholic counter-argument that fails to meet it adequately. One example can be found in exercise ix of the *Amphitheatrum*, in which a major argument against the working of divine providence is presented in a discussion of the views attributed to the ancient Greek philosopher Diagoras of Melos. In a providential universe, it is suggested, good would be rewarded and evil punished. Since this is manifestly not the case, the world cannot be subject to the working of divine providence. Vanini's version of the Christian response that follows this argument is wholly unconvincing, leaving the reader

---

[46] Vanini, *Le opere*, i. 6–7; cf. Vanini, *Anfiteatro*, 44–5.

with no defence against the doubts raised by his own text.[47] Time and again, in fact, he draws the reader's attention to the weakness of the traditional Christian case. In the *Amphitheatrum,* for instance, he directly criticizes the writings of theologians who defend the immortality of the soul as writing 'in such a silly and foolish way' that they serve only to strain belief in the truth of their teaching. 'Even I', he adds, 'Christian and Catholic, could scarcely bring myself to believe in the immortality of the soul had I not been led to it by the Church.'[48]

Elsewhere, he arranges his arguments so that unorthodox assertions remain unchallenged. In the fourth book of the *De admirandis,* for instance, a number of objections to Christianity are argued at length by the 'unhappy atheist' of Amsterdam without any serious response from either of the other two speakers in the dialogue, Alexander and Julius Caesar.[49] Sometimes, he manages to avoid commenting directly on such beliefs by referring to other books he claims to have written, so that he does not need to discuss them further in this one. Since however, these books were never published, and were probably never written, the purpose of his tactic seems fairly clear.[50] On occasion, Alexander and Julius Caesar even offer words of praise in response to arguments that undercut Christian teaching, or ask awkward questions that are never answered.[51] And in a particularly cheeky section, Julius Caesar refuses to explain anything about his views on the immortality of the soul on the ground that 'I swore an oath to my God that I would not occupy myself with this question until I was old, rich and German.'[52]

By piecing together an understanding of his rhetorical methods, it becomes possible to identify more securely the theological arguments Vanini is trying to convey. And his texts become especially revealing when we strip out the quotations from the other authors and expose Vanini's own interpolations. In summary, what he argues in these two books is that there is no spiritual world separate from the material world we see around us every day. The Christian notion of a spiritual God is therefore untenable, as is belief in any other

---

[47] Vanini, *Le opere,* i. 45–52.   [48] Ibid. i. 97–8; cf. i. 171–2.
[49] Ibid. ii. 267–72.   [50] Ibid. ii. 271–2.
[51] Ibid. ii. 288, 362; cf. Armogathe, 'Jules-César Vanini', 155.
[52] Vanini, *Le opere,* ii. 365; cf. Armogathe, 'Jules-César Vanini', 152–3.

spiritual beings: 'No reason can persuade me', he writes, using his own words, 'that demons exist. They are fabrications of the human intellect.'[53] Religions, miracles, scriptures, prayers, and immortality are therefore all fraudulent, invented by rulers or priests to maintain their own power. And in the middle of a passage in dialogue L of the *De admirandis*, which reworks an argument from Pomponazzi's *De incantationibus*, we find another crucial interpolation by Vanini which is not drawn from any of his sources: 'There is only one law of Nature, for Nature is God.'[54]

This notion brings us to another fascinating aspect of Vanini's work, the use he made of information drawn from his understanding of the natural world. The idea that 'Nature is God' appears also in exercise XLII of the *Amphitheatrum*, where it is inserted by Vanini into a passage from Scaligero's *Exotericarum*. The effect is to transform the meaning of Scaligero's words entirely and to make nature not (as Scaligero had intended) ultimately subordinate to God, but eternally independent of him.[55] This 'de-spiritualizing' of the world is accompanied by a statement about the nature of the universe, in which—in contrast to Aristotelian thinking—Vanini insists that the sublunary and celestial spheres are made of the same matter: 'I deny that celestial matter (*coeli materia*) is any more noble than that here below (*nostri ... materia*), for as I have argued in more detail in my *Philosophical commentaries*, celestial matter is no different from that of men or beetles.' And this conviction in turn is associated with another idea drawn from natural philosophy, the eternity of matter. In a passage in the *Amphitheatrum* constructed from words by Scaligero, in which the meaning of the original is changed to refute Scaligero's view, he says 'in reality, matter does not change its being.... For if the celestial matter is unchangeable, so too must be matter here on earth; its essence is eternal and unchanging. In fact, it is never corrupted, though the things made of it may corrupt. I therefore believe that we must reject the theory according to which matter tends to corruption.'[56]

---

[53] Vanini, *Le opere*, ii. 318; cf. ii. 260.   [54] Ibid. ii. 276.
[55] Ibid. i. 279.
[56] Ibid. i. 17; cf. i. 99; ii. 260, 275, 286, 288; Vanini, *Anfiteatro*, 63–4.

Vanini also argues that the senses are our only reliable source of information, for human beings are part of the natural world, and not superior to any part of it. 'What in humans is called "reason" is called "instinct" in animals', he asserts, here using his own words.[57] Human behaviour is conditioned entirely by the physical and social environment in which humans find themselves—by the balance of humours in their bodies, by the impact on them of the air they breathe and the food they eat, by their education and their inheritance. But it is not just their physical appearance that is determined by the parental seed from which they develop, but also their personality traits. In a marvellous passage, he explains how the behaviour patterns of a host of '*vilissimi homines*, such as sailors, drivers, porters, carriers, etc., whenever they are ... aggressive or inhospitable, showing neither fear nor reverence', are entirely a consequence of the dreadful food they have to eat. And adding an observation from his own experience about the British to an assertion about the Tartars taken from Cardano, he concludes: 'The Tartars are cruel, because they drink the blood of horses; the British are gentle, because they drink cold beer.'[58]

In fact, Vanini suggests that everything that exists or happens in the world has a purely natural explanation, and that only the uneducated can think otherwise. In dialogue li of the *De admirandis*, for example, he discusses a number of apparitions, each one of which is presented as the product of natural causes. Quoting directly from Cardano's *De rerum varietate* of 1557, he points to the frequency with which people mistake what they think they see. In support of this contention, he takes an observation from Agrippa's *De occulta philosophia*, first published in 1531, to suggest that visions of celestial armies fighting great battles in the sky are merely the reflection there, during certain atmospheric conditions, of human battles taking place far away. And he similarly borrows from Cardano's *De subtilitate* to explain that the ghosts that people think they have seen in cemeteries are just the vapours that rise naturally from graves that have been recently dug or occupied.[59] In later dialogues, he deals with a series of

[57] Ibid. i. 261; ii. 258.   [58] Ibid. ii. 255–7, 261–2.
[59] Ibid. ii. 276–80, 307–8; cf. ii. 283–4; Giovanni Papuli, 'Il Vanini e i miracoli: le "Gregoriane apparizioni" ', *Bollettino di storia della filosofia dell'Università degli Studi di Lecce*, 9 (1986–9), 100–2, 106–9.

spiritual conditions. Here he uses material drawn variously, not only from Pomponazzi and Agrippa, but also from Girolamo Fracastoro's *De sympathia et antipathia rerum* and his *De contagione et contagiosis morbis et curatione* of 1546, from the Flemish physician Levinus Lemnius's *Occulta naturae miracula,* first published in its final form in 1567, and from parts of Jean Fernel's *Medicina,* first published as a collection (after the author's death) in 1567.[60] Vanini insists that people who believe themselves to be possessed by demons are really suffering from poor health. The best way to treat their complaints, he says, is to give them the appropriate medicines. Those who suffer from the torments of demons in their sleep, however, are afflicted with indigestion, nothing more. Turning them over in bed will do more good than invoking the name of Jesus, while those who enter an ecstatic state and speak in tongues are suffering from an excess of humours, a condition that revives their forgotten knowledge of foreign languages. They are easily cured by a bucket of cold water. (And it does not need to be holy water, he adds, helpfully.) Miracle cures are also dismissed. At a famous shrine in his home region of Apulia, he reports, the sick are cured not because of any spiritual powers inhering in the place, but because they are obliged to drink the local sea water, which washes the poison of the disease out of their systems.[61]

But if matter is eternal, how can we explain the origins of life, and more especially the existence of the first human beings? In dialogue XXIX of the *De admirandis,* Vanini appropriates the ancient idea of abiogenesis, according to which living animals can be generated spontaneously in and from non-living matter. This theory had

---

[60] Girolamo Fracastoro, *De sympathia et antipathia rerum liber unus: de contagione et contagiosis morbis et curatione libri III* (Venice: Apud heredes Lucaeantonii Juntae Florentini, 1546); Levinus Lemnius, *Occulta naturae miracula, ac varia rerum documenta, probabili ratione atque artifici coniectura explicata* (Antwerp: Apud Guilielmum Simonem, 1567); Jean Fernel, *Universa medicina, tribus et viginti libris absoluta* (Paris: Apud A. Wechelum, 1567).

[61] Vanini, *Le opere,* ii. 302–4, 322, 333, 335, 361–2; cf. Andrzej Nowicki, 'Il Vanini e le *voces peregrinae*', *Bollettino di storia della filosofia dell'Università degli Studi di Lecce,* 9 (1986–9), 82–3; Papuli, 'Il Vanini e i miracoli', 86–94; Jean-Pierre Cavaillé, 'Vanini e gli equivoci', in Raimondi (ed.), *Giulio Cesare Vanini e il libertinismo,* 70–2.

been discussed at length in Aristotle's *History of Animals*, and was adopted by a number of sixteenth- and seventeenth-century scientific writers in Italy.[62] Vanini could thus repeat Aristotle's assertion that a number of lower animals, including some fish, eels, worms, and mice, develop as a result of the action of the heat of the sun on rotting flesh or vegetation, or on mud. As evidence, he pointed to the spontaneous appearance of frogs in the summer when new rain falls in dry ditches. He claimed that he owed this observation to his old friend Giovanni Maria Ginocchi, who, he says, had noticed the phenomenon while the two men were living in Padua. In fact, however, Ginocchi's alleged observation simply echoes a passage in Scaligero's *Exotericarum*, and the rest of the dialogue draws equally generously on material found in Cardano and Agrippa.[63] But Vanini extends this idea about the spontaneous generation of lower animals and applies it to greater animals as well. In dialogue xxvii, he suggests that humans, too, can be generated in a similar way. Here he takes his wording directly from Scaligero, though he changes its intention, and misattributes the view he presents to Cardano. In his own words, he then goes on to suggest that the ancestors of all humans might have been spontaneously generated from the decaying carcasses of monkeys, pigs, or frogs.[64]

But lurking in these discussions about spontaneous generation is another idea entirely. In dialogue xxx, again taking his lead from passages in Scaligero and Pomponazzi, he points out that the seed of an ass in a horse's womb becomes a mule, and caterpillars naturally turn into butterflies. More mischievously, he adds that the staffs of Pharaoh's magicians recorded in the Book of Exodus were transformed into serpents. So why should not living animals of one kind be transformed into another, by equally natural processes? Why indeed should not fish or animals turn into human beings?[65] The idea that one sort of creature or substance might be transformed into another was not entirely new at the time. An even more

---

[62] Aristotle, *The Complete Works of Aristotle*, ed. Jonathan Barnes, i (Princeton: Princeton University Press, 1984), 852, 856, 858, 863–5, 869–71, 877–8, 894–6; Davidson, 'Unbelief and Atheism', 62–3; Henry Harris, *Things Come to Life: Spontaneous Generation Revisited* (Oxford: Oxford University Press, 2002), 1–8.

[63] Vanini, *Le opere*, ii. 152–4; cf. ii. 143–4.   [64] Ibid. ii. 178–9.

[65] Ibid. ii. 156–7.

thoroughgoing notion of transformation had apparently been considered a few years earlier by Federico Cesi, one of the founding members of the Accademia dei Lincei, to explain the existence of the fossil woods found in the area around his home town of Acquasparta in Umbria. According to Francesco Stelluti, a fellow-Linceian, who wrote a brief report on Cesi's findings after his friend's death, these objects were generated not from plants 'but only from a type of earth, containing much clay, which is slowly transformed into wood ... with the assistance of the heat of subterranean fires. ... The earth itself is the seed and mother of this wood.' And some pieces of the wood were subsequently petrified, so that they bear the 'semblance of wood, but the substance (is) entirely of stone'. The earth thus becomes living wood, and the wood stone.[66] Cesi had begun his work on the local fossils by 1611. There is no reason to suppose that Vanini was aware of it; but the idea he expressed in the *De admirandis* develops a similar theme. In the text of dialogue XXXVII, he makes Julius Caesar use the words of Scaligero to refer to the belief that certain kinds of humans—cannibals, pygmies, Ethiopians—might even be descended directly from monkeys. If that were the case, interrupts Alexander, would they not still want to walk on all fours? Indeed, replies Julius Caesar, human beings did once walk on all fours; and human babies still do, says Alexander. But over time, Julius Caesar concludes, now using Vanini's own words, human beings learned to walk upright.[67] Vanini is here presenting, in an abbreviated form, a theory of evolution.

In Vanini's two books, then, we can see a clear correspondence between his ideas about religion and his ideas about the natural world, and he drew at length on what we might now consider scientific writings to reinforce his religious and philosophical heterodoxy. Here again, though, his plagiarism was selective and creative. In his discussions of the world around him, he continued to lift some

---

[66] Francesco Stelluti, *Trattato del legno fossile minerale* (first published 1637) in Andrew C. Scott and David Freedberg, *The Paper Museum of Cassiano dal Pozzo. Series B, Natural History; Part 3, Fossil Woods and Other Geological Specimens* (Turnhout: Harvey Miller, 2000), 384–6; cf. Andrew C. Scott, 'Federico Cesi and his Field Studies on the Origin of Fossils between 1610 and 1630', *Endeavour*, 25/3 (2001), 93–103.

[67] Vanini, *Le opere*, ii. 178–9.

sections of text from the publications of Scaligero, Pomponazzi, and Cardano (not always honestly, as we have seen). There is no evidence that he was familiar with Cardano's medical works, however, and in the *De admirandis*, his most common sources for scientific matters are Lemnius and Fernel. His discussion in dialogue XLIX about the environmental determinants of human behaviour, for example, reworks some lengthy passages from Lemnius's *Occulta naturae miracula*, and Fernel was the source for his insistence on the importance of the food we eat. The same dialogue contains a very detailed description of the human respiratory system that is borrowed verbatim from Fernel. Elsewhere in the book, Vanini used the same sources when discussing bad dreams and human reproduction.[68] He may have been led to Fernel's works by references in Scaligero, but it is clear from his use of them that he had direct access to Fernel's own texts while he was writing the *De admirandis*, as he often conflates passages or alters them to serve his own purpose.[69] Some other scientific names appear too: Fracastoro, as we have seen; Galen and Hippocrates; even Kepler's response of 1610 to Galileo's *Sidereus nuncius* is mentioned once, in dialogue IX of the *De admirandis*, almost in passing.[70] But it is equally interesting to note the names of scientific writers he does not use. Neither Copernicus nor Paracelsus appears among his sources. Galileo and Fabrizi do not appear either, even though both were teaching at the University of Padua while Vanini was resident there. He makes no reference either to the work of Cesare Cremonini, professor of philosophy at Padua at that time, or of Paolo Sarpi, whom he almost certainly knew in Venice. Other celebrated contemporaries or near-contemporaries, such as Bernardino Telesio, Giordano Bruno, and Tommaso Campanella, are also absent.

The fact that he does not use the work of these writers does not, of course, prove that he was unfamiliar with their work. A number of contemporaries describe him as very learned, and ideas from other

[68] Ibid. ii. 256–7, 261–2, 302, 322, 361–2.

[69] Cf. ibid. iii/3. 507, 533–6, 544–63, and Marilena De Pietro, 'Vanini e Fernel: Antropologia e medicina', *Bollettino di storia della filosofia dell'Università degli Studi di Lecce*, 11 (1993–5), 334–7.

[70] Vanini, *Le opere*, ii. 36, 361.

authors reappear in his own writings quite frequently. It is therefore possible that he deliberately chose not to make use of everything he had read.[71] But it is also worth remembering that he spent much of his life as a vagrant, and that he cannot have carried a large library around with him as he travelled. Back in 1614, George Abbot had reported that Vanini's favourite reading while he was in London were the Italian works of Aretino and Machiavelli, books that were presumably available to him there.[72] Copies of Machiavelli's *Il Principe*, *Historie fiorentine*, and other works survive even now with Archbishop Abbot's gold-tooled arms on the binding in Lambeth Palace Library. Vanini was therefore unusually dependent on the books he could find locally as he wrote, and this alone might be enough to explain the rather eccentric collection of authors he plagiarized so cleverly for his own books. His extensive use of Scaligero's *Exotericarum* could be explained by the fact that the widow of Antoine de Harsy, who published the *Amphitheatrum* in Lyons, had previously produced a new edition of Scaligero's book as well, and a copy of it may therefore have been conveniently available to him as he put his own text together.[73] One of Fernel's medical works had similarly been printed in sixteenth-century Paris by a member of the Perier publishing family, who also published Vanini's *De admirandis* in 1616.[74] In any case, Vanini never felt constrained by his sources, and he treated his scientific authors with the same cavalier disregard as he did his theologians. His discussion of human creation from the decaying corpses of lower animals in dialogue XXXVII of the *De admirandis*, for example, takes its lead from references in Scaligero and Pomponazzi; but he uses his own words to apply the idea to all human beings.[75] This willingness to take a hint from one author and then to expand or vary its application is characteristic of Vanini's

---

[71] Foucault, 'Documents toulousains', 25, 29; Andrzej Nowicki, 'Vanini e il concetto di recreazione', in Raimondi, *Giulio Cesare Vanini e il libertinismo*, 34.

[72] Namer, *Documents*, 76.

[73] Giulio Cesare Scaligero, *Exotericarum exercitationum liber XV: De subtilitate ad Hieronymum Cardanum* (Lyons: Sumptibus viduae Antonii de Harsy, 1615); cf. Foucault, 'Fondaments d'une ontologie matérialiste', 41–2; Foucault, 'Gli ambienti lionesi', 164–5.

[74] Jean Fernel, *De abditis rerum causis libri duo* (Paris: Apud Christianu[m] Wechelum ... apud Carolum Perier, 1540).

[75] Vanini, *Le opere*, ii. 156–7, 177–9.

technique, and he used it frequently. In dialogue XLIX, for instance, he expanded a suggestion found in the Jesuit Alessandro degli Angeli's *In astrologos coniectores* (published in Lyons in the same year as the *Amphitheatrum*) and develops from it a very different theory that derives human sin from poor health.[76] In dialogue LX, he cites Hippocrates as his authority for the idea that bad dreams are caused by indigestion; but his use of that idea to explain away the nocturnal torments of demons is entirely his own.[77] Here again, we find that his creative exploitation of his plagiarized sources can help us to identify his own views: that reason is nothing more than instinct, that human behaviour is environmentally determined, and that humans first emerged from decaying matter or evolved from other animals.

Vanini therefore drew his material from both theology and science, and the assessment of the contemporary ecclesiastical and secular authorities in Italy, England, and France, who saw him as a serious threat to orthodox religion, was therefore surely accurate. But he was a good deal more than simply a plagiarist. He was a skilful writer, whose methods of conveying his own arguments were both original and amusing. He was also clearly very personable, a man who won the trust of many of the leading clerics and nobles who met him, and an effective speaker and teacher. Nicolas de Saint-Pierre, who may have been involved professionally in Vanini's trial as an advocate, and who penned one of the early accounts of his trial and execution, provides us with an indication of his impact on those who met him:

although his words seemed designed to disguise his intentions, it was as if, despite himself, that little artery that leads from the heart to the tongue conveyed his most secret thoughts, carrying them from his heart to his mouth, so that they evaporated from his mouth to distil in the ears of his listeners, thoughts full of blasphemy against God.[78]

---

[76] Alessandro degli Angeli, *In astrologos coniectores libri quinque* (Lyons: Sumptibus Horatij Cardon, 1615); Vanini, *Le opere*, ii. 260.

[77] Ibid. ii. 361–2.

[78] Foucault, 'Documents toulousains', 18.

4

The Confessionalization of Physics: Heresies, Facts and the Travails of the Republic of Letters

Christoph Lüthy

THE LEGEND OF THE IRENIC RÉPUBLIQUE DES LETTRES

According to a time-honoured view, there existed in an early modern Europe lacerated by confessional wars, ravished by famines, and decimated by the black plague, an élite of intellectuals who tenaciously functioned according to the rules of later centuries; who were the true precursors of the Enlightenment; and who engaged in measured scholarly discourse across confessional divides. These were the self-appointed members of the République des Lettres, an international alliance of reasonable people who followed higher rules of conduct than those prescribed by the warlords, preachers, and pamphleteers of their times. This Republic, 'at a time of almost

Research for this article was made possible by a fellowship from the Royal Netherlands Academy of Arts and Sciences. I wish to thank Ian Maclean, Carla Rita Palmerino and Cees Leijenhorst for their insightful criticism of earlier versions of my argument.

continuous war..., was essentially peaceful'.[1] Erasmian by inspiration, its 'concern for "bonae litterae" united its far flung members in a fellowship which transcended barriers of nation and even of religion and which was characterized by the display of mutual 'humanitas' and 'benevolentia" '.[2]

When one looks more closely at the intellectual relations among early modern thinkers, this idyllic image loses, however, much of its credibility. The presumed avant-garde of that "period of transition", which allegedly led the way from the religious revivals of the Renaissance to the secularizing trends of the Enlightenment, looks decidedly less pacific once the epistolary record is scrutinized: what one finds is, above all, 'dissonances and rivalries', in the words of a recent survey of seventeenth-century philosophy.[3]

The correspondence of Marin Mersenne, the famous early champion of international and inter-confessional scientific dialogue, shows just how high the barriers were that had to be taken down before any reasonable communication between early modern intellectuals was at all possible. This man, who in the course of his life came to be called Secrétaire de la République des Lettres, is usually portrayed as an irenic monk who in the cell of his Parisian convent (for Mersenne was a member of the vegetarian order of the Minims) would receive the great minds of his time—Pierre Gassendi, René Descartes, Thomas Hobbes, Blaise Pascal, Nicholas Fabri de Peiresc, Christiaan Huygens—to discuss philosophical, physical, and math-

---

[1] Adrian Johns, 'The Ideal of Scientific Collaboration: The "Man of Science" and the Diffusion of Knowledge', in Hans Bots and Françoise Waquet (eds.), *Commercium Litterarium. La communication dans la République des Lettres 1600–1750* (Amsterdam: APA-Holland University Press, 1994), 3–222, at 13.

[2] J. E. Platt, 'Sixtinus Amama (1593–1629): Franeker Professor and Citizen of the Republic of Letters', in G. Th. Jensma, F. R. H. Smit, and F. Westra (eds.), *Universiteit te Franeker 1585–1811. Bijdragen tot de geschiedenis van de Friese hogeschool* (Leeuwarden: Fryske Akademy, 1985), 236–48, at 239.

[3] The changing view of the Republic of Letters can be traced in the various editions of the *Überweg Grundriss der Philosophie*. In earlier editions, the seventeenth century was defined as 'The Period of Transition', with the emphasis put on the role of the avant-garde republicans of letters. In the general editor's preface to the new and completely revised edition, the intellectual climate of the seventeenth century is described negatively ('dissonances and rivalries'). See Jean-Pierre Schobinger (gen. ed.), *Grundriss der Geschichte der Philosophie, begründet von Friedrich Überweg. Die Philosophie des 17. Jahrhunderts*, i.i. *Allgemeine Themen, Iberische Halbinsel, Italien* (Basle: Schwabe, 1998), p. xlvi.

ematical problems, and who paid no attention to the confessional adherence of these interlocutors. True, towards the end of his life, Mersenne did begin to resemble this image: Protestants called him 'the Huguenot monk' for his tolerance, and the editors of his corres- pondence write that 'it is true to say that he had no enemies'.[4] But the ecumenical stance of his mature years was very much the result of the unprofitableness of his earlier behaviour. For when we read Mer- senne's publications of the early 1620s and the first two volumes of his published correspondence, we encounter quite a different man, namely a counter-reformational soldier of the *ecclesia militans*, for whom science represented, alongside faith and the evidence of Scrip- ture, a divine weapon in the battle against heretics.[5] In his early writings, Mersenne is a mud-slinging polemicist who mingles argu- ment with invective. In his *Quaestiones celeberrimae in Genesim* of 1623, insults such as *cacomagus* or *haereticomagus* alternate with *Satanas, atheorum princeps*, or such benevolent expressions as *brevi- bus submergendus fluctibus aeternis*.[6] A century later, Anton Maria Salvini would say of the Republic of Letters that it reigned 'wherever one finds kindness, politeness and civil behaviour'.[7] If this was the standard, the Republic's secretary, in his younger years, clearly fell short of it.

[4] Paul Tannery, Cornelis de Waard, and René Pintard (eds.), *Correspondance du P. Marin Mersenne religieux minime*, i. *1617–1627* (Paris: Beauchesne, 1932), p. li.

[5] In the early 1620s, Mersenne defined his interest in the natural sciences very much in terms of his membership in the *ecclesia militans* and of his duty to combat heretics, as the opening lines of the Preface to his *L'Impiété des déistes, athées et libertins de ce temps* (Paris: Pierre Bilaine, 1624; repr. Stuttgart-Bad Cannstatt: Frommann, 1975) demonstrate: 'L'eglise militante ressemble à l'air qui n'est jamais sans nuages, exhalations, vapeurs, ou tonnerres, car elle est toujours combattue de quelques heresies, et erreurs, mais elle est jamais abbattuë, parce qu'elle est assistée de toute puissance de Dieu, qui l'esclere par les raisons de la foy, et par la communica- tion qu'il luy faict du verbe Eternel, et de la science.'

[6] Marin Mersenne, *Quaestiones celeberrimae in Genesim, cum accurata textus explicatione* (Paris: Sébastien Cramoisy, 1623), *passim*.

[7] Salvini's definition of the Republic of Letters as being 'partout où l'on trouve de la gentillesse, de la politesse et de la civilité' is quoted in Nicolò Tommaseo and Bernardo Bellini (eds.), *Dizionario della lingua italiana* (Turin: L'Unione, 1865–79), s.v. 'Repubblica'.

MERSENNE V. AMAMA

The charge of heterodoxy was always close at hand in the early seventeenth century. In Mersenne's early writings, any view that was formulated by a member of a religious confession other than Roman Catholic was taken to be suspicious on a priori grounds. It is obvious that such an attitude is diametrically opposed to the presumed ecumenical spirit of the République des Lettres. One of the reasons behind Mersenne's subsequent conversion to a combination of erudite scepticism and confessional tolerance was that the charge of heterodoxy he levelled against interlocutors was utterly ineffective. Take the example of his early literary exchange with the Calvinist Sixtinus Amama, professor of Hebrew at the University of Franeker in the Dutch province of Frisia. In his *Quaestiones celeberrimae in Genesim*, Mersenne had attacked Amama for his attempt, in the *Censura Vulgatae* of 1620, to demonstrate that the Vulgate was not a divinely inspired work, but contained errors of translation. Mersenne, though his knowledge of Hebrew was inferior to Amama's, vehemently defended the authority of the Vulgate and the correctness of its translation, and he did so in a language that belied his preferred self-description as *Minimorum minimus*. Besides calling Amama a 'worm' and a 'nocturnal mushroom too shortlived to see the light of the day', Mersenne poured his standard list of insults at the Calvinist, who was, of course, 'impious', a 'heretic' and 'blasphemer', and one whose arguments concerning Hebrew grammar had, a fortiori, to be a 'lie'.[8] Four years later, in 1627, Amama responded to these attacks in a letter to Mersenne. He had just finished a treatise entitled *Anti-Barbarus Biblicus* and wished to alert Mersenne to the fact that this book also contained a refutation of the philological contestations of the *Quaestiones celeberrimae*. Amama's letter to Mersenne is quite remarkable, not least because it makes some strong claims concerning the irrelevance of confessional standpoints for the domain of facts. At a certain moment,

---

[8] Mersenne, *Quaestiones in Genesim*, col. 1027 ff: 'Aman alius', 'Amama haereticus', 'impia haereticorum progenies', 'Amamae impudentia', 'mendacium Amamae', 'unius noctis fungum', 'blasphemus', 'impius', etc.

Amama interrupts the flow of his words and writes these terse sentences:

> Stop insulting and speak to the point. You continuously call me a heretic, and all your arguments are studded with this type of rhetorical decoration. But to what end, Mersenne? We stopped long ago being sensitive to that obloquy; sensible people laugh at it. Under the tyrants, the crime of *lèse-majesté* was the only one that could be committed by anyone. That place has by now been taken up by the crime of heresy. I could retaliate, but what end will there be to it? *Ego tibi haereticus? Tu mihi*—Am I a heretic for you? You are one for me. But what is the use of see-sawing in this fashion? What is the use of burning this stigma into each other's skin? If in order to be a heretic, one needs to be stubborn (*pertinax*), then I confidently deny being heretical. Try to convince me with the authority, not of the Roman Church, but of the Holy Scripture, and I will give you my hand.[9]

This remarkable rebuke contains three elements, which not only shed light on Mersenne's subsequent softening *vis-à-vis* his non-Catholic correspondents, but which are more generally symptomatic of the difficulties of inter-confessional dialogue in the early modern period.

Let us first take a closer look at the phrase 'stop insulting and speak to the point' (*rem ipsam dic*). Amama implies that there is a way of talking about matters of fact without involving points of faith and that by limiting their discourse to such matters, members of different confessional groups can converse not only politely with one another, but also in a mutually beneficial way. However, these are by no means obvious assumptions, and Mersenne, for one, had implicitly denied them in his early writings. One of the reasons why he had mingled refutations with insults in an apparently indiscriminate fashion was his assumption that allegedly factual statements often served a grim religious agenda. If Amama was a Calvinist, and hence

---

[9] 'Mitte male loqui et rem ipsam dic. Haereticum me perpetuo vocas atque id genus flosculis universa tua vernat oratio. Cui bono, mi Mersenne? Jampridem occalluimus ad hoc convitium et rident cordiatores. Crimen laesae majestatis sub tyrannis unicum eorum erat, qui omni vacabant. In illius locum successit hodie crimen haereseos. Retaliare possem ego, sed quis finis? Ego tibi haereticus? Tu mihi. Quid reciprocamus hanc serram? Quid hoc stigma nobis inurimus invicem? Si nullus haereticus nisi qui pertinax, ego me haereticum esse confidenter nego. Convince me non Ecclesiae Romanae, sed S. Scripturae authoritate et dabo manus'. Sixtinus Amama, letter to Marin Mersenne of 20 February/2 March 1627 (quoted from Tannery, de Waard, and Pintard (eds.), *Correspondance*, i. 532–3).

a heretic, his Hebrew scholarship had to be fundamentally flawed. In such an embattled field as biblical exegesis, Mersenne's suspicion is understandable, all the more because in his *Censura Vulgatae*, Amama had accused the Catholic Church of having neglected the study of the holy languages for many centuries and of having thereby allowed the true biblical message to become distorted. The correctness, or incorrectness, of the Vulgate translation and the reliability of the then available Hebrew versions of the Old Testament were thus clearly an issue of confessional strife, and it was not evident whether one could talk about it as a *res ipsa*, in objective and factual terms.[10]

Indeed, not just scriptural interpretation, that weary mother of modern hermeneutics, but almost any other domain of knowledge constituted a confessional battleground, with such possible exceptions as numismatics or Roman poetry. We shall see later how even such a seemingly neutral discipline as physics had become so strongly confessionalized in the sixteenth century that it was unclear how members of different religious groups could reach a consensus in that field. A general aura of suspicion had thus come to surround all knowledge claims. In this situation, Mersenne had the legitimate choice between dismissing Amama's call to 'speak to the point' as begging the question and to continue treating his correspondent as the heretic that, from the Catholic standpoint, he clearly was, or else accepting the uncertain notion that there existed a domain of *res ipsae* that was protected from confessional infestation by a kind of doctrinal *cordon sanitaire*. Sixtinus Amama implied that philology constituted just such a domain, in which there existed objective standards—despite the fact that these standards allowed for certain anti-Catholic conclusions, such as the fallacy of the Vulgate translation. Amama's invitation to Mersenne to accept Hebrew philology as a neutral ground could thus have been interpreted as a trap, and it speaks in Mersenne's favour that he subsequently jumped over his

---

[10] See on this above all J. C. H. Lebram, 'Ein Streit um die Hebräische Bibel und die Septuaginta', in Th. H. Lunsingh Scheurleer and G. H. M. Posthumus Meyjes (eds.), *Leiden University in the Seventeenth Century. An Exchange of Learning* (Leiden: E. J. Brill, 1975), 21–64.

own shadow and acknowledged Amama's superior skills in the field of Hebrew philology.[11]

The second point to be mentioned about Amama's admonition concerns the phrase, *Ego tibi haereticus? Tu mihi.* At a first glance, Amama says, of course, something very obvious: There exists a perfect symmetry between two members of rivalling churches accusing each other of heterodoxy, who are thus caught up in an argumentative stalemate. Nevertheless, Mersenne would have been obliged to reject this argument from symmetry. In the long history of Christianity, it was typically the break-away group that insisted on the symmetry of dissent. From the second century onwards, when Christianity's battle against heterodox movements began, the orthodoxy of the true Church was always defined in terms of its direct apostolic succession and hence by the revealed antiquity of its doctrines. In contradistinction to other theologically erroneous statements such as *propositiones theologice erroneae, sententiae haeresi proximae,* or *sententia haeresin sapiens,* only those views were considered properly heretical that unambiguously contradicted a clearly defined doctrinal position ('dogma') of the Church. Seen from this angle, all Protestant sects were non-apostolic and doctrinally devious recent upstarts, and hence clearly heretical. Amama's talk of a symmetry between mutually exclusive doctrinal interpretations—*Ego haereticus tibi? Tu mihi*—should thus in the eyes of most Catholic theologians have constituted in itself a clear sign of his heresy.[12]

And yet, however much Amama's *Ego tibi, tu mihi* must have been theologically unacceptable in Mersenne's eyes, it reflected the political reality of a schismatized Europe. As in the case of the *rem ipsam dic,* Mersenne faced once more the choice between two options. Just as he could have denied the existence of matters of fact, he could have insisted on Amama's heterodoxy. There are lots of counter-reformational figures who would have found this the only possible response.

---

[11] See Mersenne's interest in obtaining Amama's grammatical texts and his invitation to the Frisian scholar to advise him on a point of translation, in Tannery, de Waard, and Pintard (eds.), *Correspondance,* ii. letters 121 and 126.

[12] This still constitutes the Vatican perspective, as we may see from the document *Dominus Jesus,* issued in 2000 by the papal Curia, which reaffirms, in s. 17, the traditional position that 'ecclesiastical communities that have not preserved the valid Episcopate and the genuine and integral substance of the Eucharistic mystery are not Churches in the proper sense', but apostatic sects.

However, Mersenne would not have become the Secrétaire de la République des Lettres had he done likewise. Although it is true that in his first epistolary reply, he did invite Amama to return to the true and Catholic faith (with Amama subsequently reciprocating the invitation with predictable symmetry), Mersenne quickly realized that insisting on his interlocutor's heretical standing was no winning strategy and subsequently ignored the issue.[13]

The third point that needs to be made with regard to Amama's outburst concerns the word *pertinax*—'stubborn'—and the way Amama perverts its meaning. In his letter, Amama says that the heretic is by definition 'stubborn', but that he himself lacks that quality. Since Saint Augustine, *pertinacia* had indeed been seen as the main characteristic of the heretic, because whereas all Christians are fallible and may therefore be mistaken in their beliefs, only the heretic perseveres in his error. Indeed, an erroneous belief becomes a formal heresy only when a dogma is being denied consciously and stubbornly; that is, if the heretic is unwilling to recant. To cite an example with which both Mersenne and Amama would have been acquainted: in 1600, the Great Inquisitors handed Giordano Bruno over to the secular courts to be burnt at the stake because of his *pertinacia*, as he had been unwilling to recant, though repeatedly invited to do so. From the days of Emperor Constantine and in Northern Europe up to the Treaty of Westphalia in 1648, the state was involved in the persecution of heretics, treating the latter's supposed lack of respect for the deity analogously with the crime of *lèse-majesté*—an analogy that explains Amama's remark regarding the ubiquitous application of these two crimes.

But when Amama says of himself that he is not stubborn, he certainly does not imply that he is willing to recant and thus take the step back from heterodoxy to orthodoxy. He means something

---

[13] Mersenne's first letter to Amama is lost, but we can reconstruct some of its contents on the basis of Amama's reply of 13/23 February 1628 (Tannery, de Waard, and Pintard (eds.), *Correspondance*, ii. 21), which opens with the following sign of reconciliation: 'Dolorem istum quem ex tuarum invectarum lectione conceperam, edulcavit, fateor, tuae epistolae humanitas'. Amama's explanation for why he does not feel that he needs to become a Catholic and his call upon Mersenne to convert to Calvinism are found ibid. 23. In a subsequent letter to André Rivet, a Calvinist theologian at the University of Leiden, Mersenne even explains how he will go about quenching the flames of his public polemic with Amama (ibid. letter 121).

quite different, namely that he is willing to *ignore* the fact that his correspondent belongs to the opposite confessional camp. Considering that this letter was written during the Thirty Years' War, this reinterpretation of 'stubbornness' is significant, for it allows us to see one of the roots of what would later be called the spirit of Dutch tolerance, and which had nothing to do with accepting divergent views, let alone cherishing multiculturalism, but consisted simply in turning a blind eye on one's neighbour's particular heterodoxy. And once again, it is unlikely that Mersenne accepted Amama's redefinition of *pertinacia*, as his initial attempt to persuade Amama to return to the Catholic faith indicates. But what is relevant for our story is that in his subsequent letters, he behaved as if he had accepted it, by ignoring what in truth continued being, legally speaking, heretical stubbornness. The oxymoronic epithet of 'Huguenot monk', bestowed on Mersenne some years later, is clearly the result of this decision to insist no longer.

THE CONFESSIONALIZATION OF NATURAL PHILOSOPHY

Mersenne and Amama's little exchange succinctly reflects the intellectual drama described so well in Richard Popkin's *History of Scepticism*. Popkin there links the emergence of scepticism, including the type of constructive or mitigated scepticism he associates with the later Mersenne, to what he calls the 'intellectual crisis of the Reformation' and the concomitant breakdown of all accepted criteria of truth.[14] The first Reformers had desired to replace ecclesiastical authority by direct scriptural evidence to establish the truth of genuinely Christian belief and behaviour. But since the Bible did not always speak unambiguously nor seemed to say the same thing to every interpreter, they quickly faced the problem of who should, and who should not, be given the theological authority to decide on the true meaning of Scripture. Was truth revealed to the faithful, or

[14] Richard H. Popkin, *The History of Scepticism from Erasmus to Spinoza* (Berkeley: University of California Press, 1979), title of ch. 1.

to the divinely inspired, or to the theologically instructed? This question became all the more pressing as the Protestant camp soon after the Lutheran revolt fragmented into various sects, which in turn accused each other of heterodoxy—Zwinglians, Calvinists, Anabaptists, Socinians, and innumerable other groups.[15] The consequence was that when Protestant preachers told their flock about the contradictory decisions taken throughout history by councils and popes, Catholic theologians answered by pointing to the inability of Protestant theologians to establish scriptural truth with any greater coherence. Describing this situation, Popkin poignantly speaks of 'each side trying to sap the foundations of the other'.[16] The consequence of this reciprocal sapping was a growing sense of epistemological scepticism among those who possessed the level of education to understand the weight of the respective argumentative strategies.

Let us now turn to the effects that this condition provoked in the field of natural philosophy. The situation just sketched, in which all traditional criteria for the settling of theological controversy were undermined, at first saved Aristotelian philosophy. Luther, Zwingli, and Calvin alike had intitially expressed their scorn for Aristotle's pagan philosophy and the corruptions it had brought about in the minds of medieval theologians. But prominent Protestant academic foundations such as Wittenberg, Geneva, Herborn, or Marburg soon discovered that they had no other philosophy with which to equip their theologians for their battle against enthusiasts and rival churches. What did the first Lutheran community at Wittenberg do when Anabaptists showed up in town rousing the rabble with religious visions and calls for renewed baptism? It sent out Melanchthon, who braved the enthusiasts with his Latin terminology, demanded that they define their terms and tenets, dichotomized their answers, and proved before the astonished populace that they

---

[15] Cf. Paul Hazard, *La Crise de la conscience européenne 1680–1715* (Paris: Gallimard, 1961), 85: 'Si le Protestantisme, en effet, parmi ses manifestations diverses comporte une révolte de la conscience individuelle contre l'ingérence de l'autorité dans les matières de la foi, de quel droit une autorité s'imposera-t-elle aux consciences? Qui fixera le point où cesse l'orthodoxie, et où l'hétérodoxie commence?'

[16] Popkin, *History of Scepticism*, 14.

could not make their case coherently.[17] But while a bunch of peasant enthusiasts might have been relatively easy to handle, what could a Reformer do when an equally trained rival attempted to demonstrate, on the basis of definitions of divine ubiquity or substantial transformation, that his own particular doctrine of the sacraments was correct and that of his opponent heterodox? As a reaction, the Reformer would typically decide to overhaul his local university's curriculum by adjusting Aristotelian metaphysics and natural philosophy in such a way that its graduates would be able to derive suitable conclusions from it and rebut those of rival theologians. The result of this strategy, which is observable at all early modern universities, was the emergence of an Aristotelian natural philosophy or physics that was distinctly Lutheran, Calvinist, Arminian, or indeed Catholic.

The emergence of denominationally specific Aristotelianisms in response to apologetic needs is a particularly interesting aspect of the sixteenth- and seventeenth-century fragmentation of the philosophical culture that we have already mentioned. It must be obvious that the resolve to maintain Aristotle's authority intact as the common terminological basis of theological debate was undermined by these adjustments of philosophy to confessional needs. If the idea had been to decide between rival interpretations of Scripture on the basis of a shared metaphysics, physics, and logic, the fact that these three philosophical disciplines were being redefined according to theological demands produced a vicious circle.[18]

THE CASE OF THE EUCHARIST

There is no better example to illustrate the confessional fragmentation of natural philosophy than the adjustment of such key concepts

[17] Sachiko Kusukawa, The Transformation of Natural Philosophy: The Case of Philip Melanchthon (Cambridge: Cambridge University Press, 1995), convincingly argues that this key event led Philip Melanchthon to reform the Lutheran University of Wittenberg on the basis of a modified form of Aristotelianism.

[18] See Cees Leijenhorst and Christoph Lüthy, 'The Erosion of Aristotelianism. Confessional Physics in Early Modern Germany and the Dutch Republic', in C. H. Leijenhorst, C. H. Lüthy, and J. M. M. H. Thijssen (eds.), The Dynamics of Aristotelian Natural Philosophy from Antiquity to the Seventeenth Century (Leiden: Brill, 2002), 375–412.

as space, place, or causality in support of mutually incompatible explanations of the Eucharist. True, the interpretation of the Eucharist was an old problem, but with the Reformation, dormant disputes flared up anew and new ones were kindled.

Recall that the gospels of the three Synoptic evangelists each contain a report of the Last Supper (or Lord's Supper).[19] In the Latin of the Vulgate, the phrase Jesus uses to speak of the relation of the bread he breaks to his body is: 'Hoc est corpus meum' ('this is my body'). To the standard account of Jesus breaking the bread and offering it and the chalice to his disciples during the paschal dinner only Luke adds that Christ called upon his disciples to repeat this ceremony in his memory. From the Apostle Paul's First Letter to the Corinthians, it emerges that the first Christian communities followed Luke and that they regarded the ceremony as a sacramental act, as the celebration of eucharistic communion.[20]

Early on, however, disputes erupted over the exact nature of this sacrament. Had Jesus used the phrase 'This is my body' in the same metaphorical way in which he had said, for example, 'I am the door' or 'I am the vineyard'? Or was one to suppose that something physical, though preternatural and thus miraculous, had happened during the Lord's Supper, which repeated itself on every occasion that the ceremony was carried out? The two main sources to bring this unresolved issue to the attention of the Latin Middle Ages were the Church fathers Ambrose and Augustine. Ambrose's interpretation was that the sacramental bread and wine physically and actually changed into the body and blood of Christ, whereas Augustine insisted on the non-identity of the bread and wine with the body and blood of Christ and claimed that Christ was present in the Eucharist only in spirit and in power. During the ninth, tenth, and eleventh centuries, the Augustinian and Ambrosian interpretations both had their following. The open-endedness of this discussion came to a close when in 1059, Berengar of Tours was required, by the Synod of Rome, to make the following public declaration:

In my heart and in word I profess that I have the same belief concerning the sacrament of the Lord's table as my lord the venerable Pope Nicholas and this holy synod by evangelical and apostolic authority have given and

---

[19] Matt. 26: 26–8; Mark 14: 22; Luke 22: 19.   [20] 1 Cor. 11: 23.

commanded me to hold. That is, that the bread and wine placed on the altar are, after the consecration, not merely the sacrament of, but also the true body and blood of our Lord Jesus Christ: that these are not only sacramentally but truly handled and broken by the hands of the priests and ground by the teeth of the faithful.[21]

It was with Berengar's enforced declaration that this physical, indeed carnal, interpretation of the Eucharist, which has been called 'eucharistic realism', started to be seen as the orthodox position, and its denial as heterodox. But whereas the Synod of Rome clearly insisted on the doctrine of the real presence by saying that the faithful consume the very body of Christ, it did not attempt to explain how this miracle happened. But in 1079, when Berengar was once more asked to make a public declaration of faith, we find, for the first time, the expression *substantialiter converti*—'to be substantially transformed'.[22] But in order for this expression to turn into the doctrine of transubstantiation, additional developments had to take place. For a certain period, three interpretations of the meaning of 'converti' coexisted. Peter of Capua distinguished, around 1201/2, the following positions: 'Some say that there is not any mutation here; rather, while the substance of bread and the substance of wine remain, when the words of consecration are spoken, the flesh and blood of Christ begin to be present beneath the same appearances, though at first

---

[21] 'ore et corde profiteor de sacramento dominicae mensae eam fidem me tenere, quam dominus et venerabilis papa Nicolaus et haec sancta Synodus auctoritate evangelica et apostolica tenendam tradit mihique firmavit: *scilicet panem et vinum, quae in altari ponuntur, post consecrationem non solum sacramentum, sed etiam verum corpus et sanguinem Domini nostri Iesu Christi esse, et sensualiter, non solum sacramento, sed in veritate, manibus sacerdotum tractari et frangi et fidelium dentibus atteri* …' Latin text and English translation taken from James F. McCue, 'The Doctrine of Transubstantiation from Berengar through Trent: The Point at Issue', *Harvard Theological Review*, 61 (1968), 385–430, at 387.

[22] 'Ego Berengarius corde credo et ore confiteor, panem et vinum, quae ponuntur in altari, per mysterium sacrae orationis et verba nostri Redemptoris substantialiter converti in veram et propriam ac vivificatricem carnem et sanguinem Iesu Christi Domini nostri'. 'I, Berengar, believe in my heart and confess aloud that the bread and wine which are placed on the altar are substantially changed, through the mystery of the sacred prayer and the words of our Redeemer, into the true, the living, the very own flesh and blood of our Lord Jesus Christ'. Latin Text and translation taken from McCue, 'Doctrine', 387.

only the substance of bread and wine were present.'[23] This view was later to be called 'consubstantiation'. It implied that the bread and wine remained substantially intact, but were joined by the substances of Christ's body and blood. This was to be Martin Luther's position. Here are the other two positions mentioned by Peter of Capua: 'Others say that the substance of bread and wine are totally annihilated and, while the appearances remain the same, there begins to be present only the flesh and blood of Christ.... We say (and this is what the commentators assert) that the very substance of the bread is changed into the true flesh of Christ....'[24] But while Peter of Capua did not think it was necessary for theologians to choose between these three physical explanations, the position to which he himself happened to adhere would soon become the one, only, and orthodox explanation. The Fourth Lateran Council of 1215 stated, in a declaration of faith *contra Albigenses et Catharos*, that '[Christ's] body and blood are truly contained in the sacrament of the altar under the appearances of bread and wine—the bread being transubstantiated into his body and the wine into his blood by the divine power.'[25]

Transubstantiation had thus become the favoured interpretation. In their respective *Sentence Commentaries*, Albert the Great and his disciple Thomas Aquinas argued linguistically, saying that if the bread had remained intact after the blessing, Christ would not have said, *Hoc est corpus meum*, but *Hic est corpus meum* ('here is my body') or *Hic panis est corpus meum* ('this bread is my body'). This

---

[23] 'De conversione triplex est opinio. Quidam dicunt quod non est ibi aliqua mutatio, sed remanente substantia panis et substantia vini ad prolationem illorum verborum incipit sub eisdem speciebus esse caro et sanguis Christi, cum prius non esset ibi nisi substantia panis et vini...' The Latin is quoted from Hans Jorissen, *Die Entfaltung der Transsubstantiationslehre bis zum Beginn der Hochscholastik* (Münster: Aschendorff, 1965), 24, and the English translation from McCue, 'Doctrine', 390.

[24] 'Alii dicunt quod substantia panis et vini penitus adnihilatur et manentibus speciebus eisdem incipit ibi esse sola caro et sanguis Christi...Nos dicimus et expositores hoc asserunt, quod ipsa substantia panis convertitur in carnem Christi veram quam traxit de Virgine...' Latin text from Jorissen, *Die Entfaltung*, 24; English translation from McCue, 'Doctrine', 390.

[25] 'Iesus Christus, cuius corpus et sanguis in sacramento altaris sub speciebus panis et vini veraciter continentur, transsubstantiatis pane in corpus, et vino in sanguinem potestate divina'. Latin and English translation quoted from McCue, 'Doctrine', 393.

grammatical analysis of the meaning of the Eucharist was intended to undermine the possibility of consubstantiation (that is, the view that bread and wine remained substantially intact even after receiving the additional substances of Christ's body and blood). But Aquinas now added, in contrast to previous authors, that all explanations apart from transubstantiation were heterodox. Duns Scotus, who agreed, furthermore introduced the false notion that it had been the Fourth Lateran Council that elevated transubstantiation to the status of a dogma.[26]

However, the elimination of rival explanations was not just due to an aberrant historiography and a determinate semantic analysis, but had to do with the introduction of Aristotelian philosophy, in whose terminology the orthodox view was now regularly expounded. Duns Scotus, for example, argued *ex Aristotele* that it was impossible for two substances to be in one place—an argument that did away with consubstantiation. And he wrongly assumed that the theory of annihilation implied that the substantial forms were first converted into prime matter before turning into the substance of Christ's body and blood, a possibility he happily rejected by arguing, again *ex Aristotele*, that prime matter can never exist *in actu*. Historians have always been bewildered by this successful introduction of Aristotelian hylemorphism as the main pillar of the theory of transubstantiation, not only because there is probably no other ancient philosopher whose philosophy could be more remote from sacramental theology, but also, because the dogma that the accidents of bread and wine remain intact while the substance changes from wine and bread into Christ's body and blood blatantly contradicts the premises of Aristotelian physics.

In fact, as Paul Bakker's *La Raison et le miracle* documents, a number of scholastics were fully aware of the fact that transubstantiation was not the most plausible theory.[27] There were many problematic issues that provided greater difficulties for the transubstantiationalist than for the consubstantiationalist, for example the famous question of why the consecrated host, if left uneaten, behaves like any old piece of

[26] Ibid. 300–403.
[27] Paul Bakker, 'La Raison et le miracle: les doctrines eucharistiques (c.1250–c.1400): Contribution à l'étude des rapports entre philosophie et théologie' (Ph.D. Thesis, Nijmegen, 1999).

bread by getting dry or mouldy. But the general assumption was that transubstantiation was an article of faith. As Durand of Saint-Pourçain argued in the early fourteenth century:

If [consubstantiation] were in fact true, many of the problems which arise concerning this sacrament when one supposes that the substance of bread does not remain would be solved. ... But because this explanation must in fact not be held—for the Church, which in such matters is not presumed to err, has decided the opposite—I therefore in fact hold the other position.[28]

In the name of this dogma, John Wyclif was condemned by the Council of Constance in 1415 for the view that 'the substance of the material bread and, in a similar way, the substance of the material wine, remain in the sacrament of the altar'.[29] When we turn from unsuccessful Reformers to successful ones, we find that both Luther and Zwingli, who were thoroughly acquainted with the history of the eucharistic controversies, tried to undo what, according to them, had gone wrong in the thirteenth and fourteenth centuries. Luther wrote, in his *Babylonian Captivity of the Church*: 'The church kept the true faith for more than twelve hundred years, during which time the holy fathers never and nowhere mentioned this transubstantiation (a monstrous word and a figment), until Aristotle's fake philosophy began to proliferate within the church in these last three hundred years.'[30] But unfor-

---

[28] Durand of Saint-Pourçain, *In IV libros Sententiarum*, lib. IV, dist. xi, quaest. 1, no. 15 (in the 1571 Venice edition, this is vol. II, fo. 318^{v}b): 'Si autem iste modus [sc. consubstantiatio] esset verus de facto, multae dubitationes quae occurrunt circa hoc sacramentum (tenendo quod substantia panis non remaneat) essent solutae. ... Sed quia hic modus non debet teneri de facto, cum ecclesia determinaverit oppositum quae non praesumitur errare in talibus, ideo teneo de facto aliam partem.' Translation from McCue, 'Doctrine', 411 n. 44. The three versions of Durand's doctrine of the Eucharist and the polemical reactions to it are discussed in Bakker, *La Raison et le miracle*, i. 94–119.

[29] One of the 'errores' of Wyclif was 'Substantia panis materialis et similiter substantia vini materialis remanent in sacramento altaris.' Quoted from McCue, 'Doctrine', 412. See Paul de Vooght, *Hussiana* (Leuven: Publications Universitaire de Louvain, 1960), 292–99 ('La présence réelle dans la doctrine eucharistique de Wiclif').

[30] Martin Luther, 'De captivitate Babylonica ecclesiae praeludium. 1520', in *D. Martin Luthers Werke. Kritische Gesamtausgabe* (Weimar: Böhlau, 1883–), vi (1935), 484–573, at 509: 'Sed et Ecclesia ultra mille ducentos annos recte credidit nec usquam nec unquam de ista transsubstantiatione (portentoso scilicet vocabulo et somnio) meminerunt sancti patres, donec cepit Aristotelis simulata philosophia in Ecclesia grassari in istis trecentis novissimis annis ...'

tunately, Zwingli wished to undo many more medieval decisions than did Luther. While Luther derided the pseudo-Aristotelian doctrine of transubstantiation as a typical sign of scholastic perversion, he continued to adhere to the doctrine of the real presence of Christ in the host. For Zwingli, by contrast, the Lord's Supper was not a physical, but a merely spiritual matter. What Christ had given to his disciples had been a spiritual gift, namely the gift of redemption; no physical presence was required by the faithful to receive that same gift, but only faith on the part of the participant in the sacramental act. Zwingli's Augustinian views forced Luther to defend the Catholic Church's decisions to enforce the Ambrosian view on Berengar of Tours: 'Therefore, the enthusiasts are wrong... if they chastize Pope Nicholas for having forced Berengar to the following confession: that he crushes and grinds with his teeth the true body of Christ. Would to God that all the popes had acted in so Christian a manner in all matters as this pope did with Berengar with respect to this confession.'[31]

The Marburg Colloquy of 1529, arranged by the Landgrave Philip of Hesse, did not bring about any agreement on that question between Luther and Zwingli. According to contemporary reports, Luther began the discussion by writing on the table the words 'This is my Body' and announced that he 'was not going to argue whether *is* can mean *is a sign of*. Zwingli, by contrast, could not reconcile himself to the cannibalist view that the faithful ate their Lord as they worshipped Him. And so, twelve years after its beginning, the Reformation had produced its first doctrinal schism.

When the Catholic Church somewhat belatedly gathered at the Council of Trent to deliberate on the frightening developments within Christianity, they showed no willingness to review the historical evidence against transubstantation as a church dogma. The records of their deliberations state that 'By the consecration of the bread and wine, a change takes place in which the whole substance of

---

[31] Martin Luther, *Vom Abendmahl Christi, Bekenntnis*. In *D. Martin Luthers Werke. Kritische Gesamtausgabe*, xxvi (1909), 241–509, at 442: 'Darumb thun die Schwermer unrecht, so wol als die glosa im geistlichen recht, da sie den Papst Nicolaus straffen, das er den Berenger hat gedrungen zu solcher bekendnis, das er spricht: Er zu drücke und zureibe mit seinen zenen den wahrhaftigen leib Christi. Wolt Gott, alle Pepste hetten so Christlich in allen stuecken gehandelt, als dieser Papst mit dem Berenger inn solcher bekendnis gehandlet hat...'

bread is changed into the substance of the body of Christ our Lord'— a position, they added, which the 'Holy Catholic Church fittingly and properly names transubstantiation'. At the same time, the Council of Trent condemned both the Zwinglian and the Lutheran position. The assembled cardinals and theologians declared as anathema both the Zwinglian view that 'Christ is present in the Sacrament only as a sign or a figure, or by his power', and the less radical, Lutheran view that 'the substance of the bread and wine remains in the holy sacrament of the Eucharist together with the body and blood of Christ our Lord'.[32]

We mentioned earlier the problem confronting Reformers in situations such as this one, where each found his respective sacramental theology under a double siege by both Catholic theologians and Protestant rivals. It is blatantly obvious why, willy nilly, these circumstances forced them to return to that Aristotelian vocabulary they so much despised for its pagan connotations. One of the key moments of this return to the scholastic terminology occurred already during the Marburg Colloquy. So as to explain Christ's real presence without needing transubstantiation, Luther had recourse to the doctrine of ubiquity, which stated that after he had risen, Christ, the man, had physically joined God, the Father, and had come to share in all the latter's attributes and hence also in ubiquity. This explained how it was possible that Christ, though sitting at the right hand of God, could physically be present at a great number of altars simultaneously. Zwingli responded that

[32] Council of Trent, session XIII, *Decretum de SS. Eucharistia*, ch. 4: 'per consecrationem panis et vini conversionem fieri totius substantiae panis in substantiam corporis Christi Domini nostri, et totius substantiae vini in substantiam sanguinis eius. Quae conversio convenienter et proprie a sancta catholica Ecclesia transsubstantiatio est appellata.' Ibid., *Canones de SS. Eucharistia*: 'Can. 1. Si quis negaverit, in sanctissimae Eucharistiae sacramento contineri vere, realiter, et substantialiter, Corpus et Sanguinem una cum anima et divinitate Domini nostri Iesu Christi, ac proinde totum Christum; sed dixerit, tantummodo esse in eo ut in signo vel figura, aut virtute: anathema sit. Can. 2. Si quis dixerit, in sacrosancto Eucharistiae sacramento remanere substantiam panis et vini una cum Corpore et Sanguine Domini nostri Iesu Christi, negaveritque mirabilem illam et singularem conversionem totius substantiae panis in Corpus et totius substantiae vini in Sanguinem, manentibus dumtaxat speciebus panis et vini, quam quidem conversionem catholica Ecclesia aptissime transsubstantationem appellat: A.[nathema] S.[it]'. Quoted from Heinrich Denzinger, *Enchiridion symbolorum, definitionum et declarationum de rebus fidei et morum*, 12th edn. (Freiburg im Breisgau: Herder, 1913), 287 and 290.

localitas, being in a place, was an essential property of any body whatsoever; consequently, the attribution of ubiquity to Christ's body implied that it possessed some non-corporeal properties, which was not only absurd, but could not explain the phrase 'This is my body'. In his rebuttal, Luther accepted Zwingli's scholastic premise that God could not do what involved a contradiction, but he insisted that no contradiction was involved here: 'As a general rule, it is well thus that bodies are contained in places, but God can easily conserve bodies outside of any place whatsoever'.[33] Luther explained this possibility by having recourse to the scholastic distinction of being in a place either *circumscriptive*, that is, in the normal way in which bodies are limited by a place on account of their finite dimensions, or *definitive*, that is, as the soul is in the body, or angels are in the world, without their spatial limits being defined. He added that Christ's body was also present *repletive*, that is, in God's omnipresent way of being.[34]

Calvin, finally, was content with neither explanation. Like Luther, he favoured Christ's real presence, but unlike Luther, he did not think ubiquity was the right lever for the proof, but looked instead for help to the pneumatological tradition. He argued that during the Lord's Supper, Christ remained physically limited to a clearly defined *localitas* next to God. It is not He, but the faithful, who accomplish the spatial displacement, for upon partaking in the Holy Communion, they are lifted up to Heaven in an act of faith and through the working of the Holy Spirit. Calvin did not intend to describe a mentally uplifting experience, but was convinced that the faithful take part in an actual spiritual communion with Christ's real presence.[35]

No wonder, then, that sixteenth- and seventeenth-century theologians and philosophers ended up talking and writing so much about *substantia, accidentia, localitas,* or *ubiquitas*. Given that aspiring

---

[33] 'Respondit Lutherus: Ordinatione generali ita quidem esse, ut corpora locis contineantur, sed deum conservare extra locum omnem corpora facile posse.' *Das Marburger Gespräch und die Magdeburger Artikel von 1529*, in *D. Martin Luthers Werke. Kritische Gesamtausgabe*, xxx/iii (1910), 92–171, at 139.

[34] See Luther, *Vom Abendmahl Christi*, 225 ff. For a discussion of Luther's arguments, see Hartmuth Hilgenfeld, *Mittelalterlich-traditionelle Elemente in Luthers Abendmahlsschriften* (Zurich: Theologischer Verlag, 1971), 183 ff.

[35] See Kilian McDonnell, *John Calvin, the Church, and the Eucharist* (Princeton: Princeton University Press, 1967), 239 ff.

theologians everywhere first had to study philosophy, and thus also Aristotelian physics or natural philosophy, it was obvious why professors frequently made them debate *theses de loco* in the prescribed disputational practices. At Protestant universities of all denominations, the theses to be refuted, from the 1590s onwards, were usually taken out of Cardinal Robert Bellarmine's *Disputations*. Protestant students were routinely required, first, to refute Bellarmine's physical arguments in favour of transubstantiation, and second, the arguments in favour of rival Protestant sects. This explains why the most important German philosophers of the period between 1550 and 1650, including such men as Jakob Schegk, Bartholomaeus Keckermann, Johann Heinrich Alsted, or Balthasar Meisner, developed Aristotelian philosophy in a direction that would prove the physical doctrines of the confessional group to which they adhered, with the consequence that they adjusted the use of their Aristotelian terminology according to necessity.[36]

For certain Protestants such as Sixtinus Amama, the Franeker professor of Hebrew we encountered earlier, this renewed scholastic bickering over the correct definition of scholastic terms constituted a proof that something about the Reformation had gone awry: After a short-lived Erasmian emergence from linguistic ignorance, the 'barbary' of Thomistic scholasticism had obviously regained the upper hand.[37] But as mentioned, though Europe's religious division granted the scholastic vocabulary a second life, the fragmentation of Aristotelian natural philosophy into confessionally specific schools could not but undermine the very purpose of its prolonged existence. Interconfessional disputes could not be settled if the terms were given divergent definitions.

After its Christianization in the twelfth and thirteenth centuries, then, Aristotelian natural philosophy underwent a process of confessionalization in the sixteenth and seventeenth. But although this development destroyed the usefulness of Aristotelianism as a common platform, attempts to replace it by a new philosophy were frowned upon everywhere and oftentimes censored and condemned.

---

[36] See Cees Leijenhorst, 'Place, Space and Matter in Calvinist Physics', *The Monist*, 84 (2001), 520–41; and Leijenhorst and Lüthy, 'The Erosion of Aristotelianism', 384–95.

[37] Amama, *De barbarie oratio*, preface to the *Anti-Barbarus Biblicus*.

Too much was at stake, politically and confessionally. Descartes, *novateur par excellence*, was placed on the index of forbidden books because of the incompatibility of his natural philosophy with the dogma of transubstantiation: the Eucharist turned out, to use Stephen Menn's phrase, to be his "greatest stumbling block".[38]

THE ARMINIAN ISSUE, TIME, AND MATTER THEORY

That there was no end to the confessionalization of natural philosophy is well demonstrated by the Arminian controversy, which did not only rage between one university and another, but within the very same universities, and which split Dutch Calvinism into two camps—with mutual accusations of heterodoxy. The initial conflict between Jacob Arminius, professor of theology at Leiden, and his colleague, Franciscus Gomarus, was originally about the niceties of the doctrine of predestination. But the question of whether God had predestined everything *ab initio* and *ab aeternitate*, just like the question regarding Christ's presence in the Eucharist, was ultimately about the way in which the divinity physically interacts with His created world. At the most general level, the Arminian controversy resembled many others in that it was about the way in which the omnipotent, omniscient, and omnipresent Creator could be kept at an appropriate distance from his creation, in such a way that he was, on the one hand, its unrivalled lord while, on the other hand, not being responsible for everything evil that happened in it. While the battles over the Eucharist were about the degree of spatial separation between Christ and the host, the battles over predestination were about the degree of temporal separation between God's intentions and the historical events in the world. Arminius combated the predominant Calvinist

[38] Stephen Menn, 'The Greatest Stumbling Block: Descartes' Denial of Real Qualities', in Roger Ariew and Marjorie Green (eds.), *Descartes and His Contemporaries. Meditations, Objections, and Replies* (Chicago: University of Chicago Press, 1995), 182–207. Pietro Redondi, *Galileo Heretic* (Princeton: Princeton University Press, 1987), has claimed, though somewhat implausibly, that Galileo's condemnation of 1633 was also due to the incompatibility of his matter theory with the Eucharist.

theory of predestination, which assumed that God's eternity implied that everything that happened on earth had been foreseen and willed by him *ab aeterno*, including the damnation of the sinners and the election of the saints.

When Arminius died in 1609, the Arminian faction chose a highly competent German theologian by the name of Conrad Vorstius as his successor. Vorstius had for years been teaching at the Gymnasium Illustre of Steinfurt, not far from the eastern Dutch border. His mastery of metaphysics and his logical approach to theology had terrorized the Jesuits at nearby Münster in Westphalia, who had routinely rejected the invitation to debate publicly with him. Vorstius had composed a detailed refutation of Bellarmine's sacramental theology, which had become something of a bestseller among Calvinists. But precisely what made him so successful in the battle against the Jesuit theologians made him look, in the end, quite dangerous to the Dutch anti-Arminians. For Vorstius had felt that the best way of settling theological questions was by establishing an ontological definition of God from which everything of doctrinal relevance would result by deduction, including the true way of conceiving of the Eucharist and of predestination. The premise of Vorstius's ontology was that there existed 'first and most general principles of sound philosophy, which hold no less true of God than they do indubitably hold true for all other entities in general, or substances, or spirits, as far as they are based on unchanging foundations'.[39]

In other words, this ontology subjected everything from God down to the elements to the same criteria of being. Everything that existed was said by Vorstius to be numerically one and fully in existence. And being one, it was confined in space and had to act in time. This was true even for God, whose omnipresence therefore implied that he could extend himself through space and make his power felt everywhere—this was a point scored against the Catholics and Lutherans—and whose eternity meant that he was everlasting

---

[39] Conrad Vorstius, *Tractatus theologicus de Deo sive De natura et attributis Dei* (Steinfurt: Theophil Caesar, 1610), 'Ad lectorem', fo. 1ᵛ: 'vel denique primis ac communissimis illis sanae philosophiae principiis, quae de Deo non minus, quam de aliis in genere vere entibus, aut substantiis, aut spiritibus, indubitato vera sunt, tanquam immotis fundamentis nituntur'.

within, not without, the category of time and therefore was not forced to abide by his own eternal decrees—and this was a point scored on behalf of the Arminians.

Though predominantly couched in a scholastic vocabulary, Vorstius's ontology represents a veritable departure from Aristotelian philosophy, and a departure, we may add, that was more successful than that of the first Refomers. His first philosophy dispenses with Peripatetic potentialities and entelechies and contains only actually existing, numerically indivisible, entities. In his attack on the doctrine of transubstantiation, Vorstius rejects, together with their specific use of *localitas, multilocalitas, illocalitas*, and *ubiquitas*, the Aristotelian definition of *locus*, 'place', as the innermost surface of the medium surrounding a body, replacing it with a concept of general space (*spatium*) he had patched together from Plato, Peter Ramus, Nicolaus Taurellus, and Julius Caesar Scaliger, and which was to become universally accepted a hundred years later as a consequence of Newtonianism. According to Vorstius's ontology, then, bodies are not in specific *loci*, but in a general *spatium*, which is the receptacle of all things.

According to this view, we affirm to be true that not only the ultimate celestial sphere, but also every single creature, whether corporeal or spiritual, nay, even God (when understood correctly) and whatever really and substantially exists, is in some place, that is, in a space that is by itself incorporeal and always adequate to what is placed in it.[40]

According to this ontology, God behaves like all substantial beings in that His own being is defined in space and time. When the theologians of the anti-Arminian faction read about these views, they found not only conclusions that disturbed them profoundly, but they

---

[40] Conrad Vorstius, *Tessaradecas anti-Pistoriana, hoc est, Responsio ad librum D. Johannis Pistorii Nidani*, 2 vols. (Hanau: Wilhelm Anton, 1607), i. 244: 'Causa etiam erroris adversariorum de corporis utopia, et speciatim de supremo caelo, tanquam nullo loco existente, est falsa loci definitio ab Aristotele in 4. Physicorum tradita, quod Locus sit superficies corporis continentis, etc. Cui non solum Platonis definitionem, quam etiam Ramus, Taurellus, Scaliger, et alii praestantissimi viri, approbant, merito praeferimus: iuxta quam non modo caelum supremum, sed etiam omnem omnino creaturam, sive corpoream, sive spiritualem, imo etiam (si recte intelligatur) ipsum Deum, et quidquid uspiam vere et substantialiter existit, in loco aliquo, hoc est, spatio per se prorsus incorporeo, et rei locatae semper adaequato, etc. vere esse affirmamus.'

discovered heresies galore. This is not the place to retell the harrowing story of what happened to the ill-fated Vorstius after he had made the fatal error of accepting the Leiden chair. Suffice it to say that once King James I had decided to refute Vorstius's main theological work, the *Tractatus theologicus de Deo, sive De natura et attributis Dei*, the Leiden appointment turned into an international political scandal, which incidentally also brought out the worst in some of the foremost members of the Republic of Letters, as can be seen from the published record.[41] When it eventually transpired that Vorstius had direct contacts with the much dreaded Polish Socinians, the newly appointed professor was sent away from Leiden even before he had delivered his first lecture, to spend the rest of his life defending himself against charges of subscribing to the most horrendous heresies, one of them being materialism. In fact, both the members of Heidelberg's theological faculty and King James accused Vorstius of having physicalized God in his ontology. The very first Vorstian thesis condemned by the English King was: 'God is not essentially immense, nor simply infinite; but he is a quantity, finite, in a place, in some way bodily, composed as it were of matter and form.'[42] In his defence, Vorstius argued that he had not intended to perpetrate any heresy, but to the contrary, that he had tried to provide an unassailable metaphysical basis from which true theological conclusions could be derived. But of course, since his conclusions did not please, his general premises were not accepted either. Here, then, we encounter confessionalized metaphysics and natural philosophy at their most dramatic.

While Vorstius is forgotten by today's historians of philosophy and of science, his disciple, David van Goorle, known to the world as

---

[41] For King James's reasons for meddling with the Vorstius appointment, see Frederick Shriver, 'Orthodoxy and Diplomacy. James I and the Vorstius Affair', *The English Historical Review*, 85 (1970), 449–74. For the published literary exchanges accompanying this affair, see Philip van Limborch (ed.), *Praestantium ac eruditorum virorum epistolae ecclesiasticae et theologicae ...* 3rd augmented edn. (Amsterdam: François Halma, 1704).

[42] '1. Deus non est essentialiter immensus, nec simpliciter infinitus: sed est quantum, finitum, in loco, quodammodo corporeum, constans quasi ex materia et forma.' Quoted from Vorstius's *Christiana et modesta responsio, ad articulos quosdam, nuper ex Anglia transmissos, et typis hic descriptos, passimque in vulgus late dispersos* (Leiden: Thomas Basson, 1611), 1.

David Gorlaeus, is not. Gorlaeus has a reputation as one of the seventeenth century's first outspoken atomists and as the father of certain positions defended several decades later by Dutch Cartesians such as Henricus Regius.[43] But it has been overlooked that Gorlaeus was by no means a physicist and that his main objective was not at all to reform physics in the modern sense of the word. In 1611, when he wrote his main work, the *Exercitationes philosophicae*, Gorlaeus was a 20-year-old theology student at Leiden, and the controversy surrounding Vorstius had reached its peak. Gorlaeus in fact radicalized the ontology he found in the Arminian professor's writings. We have already mentioned that according to Vorstius's *prima philosophia*, all entities, from God down to the simplest substances, are all actually existing and numerically indivisible entities placed in a potentially empty framework of space and time. What Gorlaeus did was to spell out that while the largest entity was God, the smallest was the atom— a move he accomplished on the basis of ideas he had gathered from the works of Nicholas Cusanus, Julius Caesar Scaliger, and Nicholas Taurellus. Gorlaeus's long *Exercitationes* begin with the question 'What is philosophy?', and his answer is that it is 'the naked knowledge of entities' which he calls *entia per se*.[44] With these self-subsisting, indestructible entities, he meant everything from the infinitely large deity to the finitely small atom. Gorlaeus's ontological *prima philosophia* was presented as the master discipline that defined God's nature and everything else; theology was relegated to the task of helping us obtain paradise and avoid hell. Whereas Vorstius's theology had still tried to maintain an Aristotelian vocabulary (though it subverted the significance of much of its terminology),

[43] On Gorlaeus, see Kurd Lasswitz, *Geschichte der Atomistik vom Mittelalter bis Newton* (Hamburg and Leipzig: Leopold Voss, 1890; repr. Hildesheim: Georg Olms, 1964), i. 332–5 and 455–63; Christoph Lüthy, 'David Gorlaeus' Atomism, or: The Marriage of Protestant Metaphysics with Italian Natural Philosophy', in C. H. Lüthy, J. E. Murdoch, and W. R. Newman (eds.), *Late Medieval and Early Modern Corpuscular Matter Theories* (Leiden: Brill, 2001), 245–90. On the role of Gorlaeus's philosophy in the Cartesian *Querelle d'Utrecht*, see Theo Verbeek, ' "Ens per accidens". Le origini della *Querelle* di Utrecht', *Giornale critico della filosofia italiana*, 6th ser., 71 (1992), 276–88.

[44] David Gorlaeus, *Exercitationes philosophicae post mortem auctoris editae, quibus universa fere discutitur philosophia theorica, et plurima ac praecipua Peripateticorum dogmata evertuntur* (Leiden: Widow of Johannes Commelius, 1620), 1: 'Quid sit philosophia': '... nuda entium cognitio'.

Goriaeus self-confidently rejected Aristotelianism. Forms and poten
cies are now officially rejected and atomism made to triumph over
hylemorphism.

In a certain way, Gorlaeus's dismissal of scholastic natural philosophy may be seen as a repetition of the anti-Aristotelianism of the
Reformers, a century earlier. One might even argue that he only
pulled away a fig leaf that had barely managed to hide a fake
terminological consensus. However, the main difference between
Gorlaeus and the Reformers lies, of course, in the young Dutchman's
faith in the powers of a reformed philosophy and his subjugation of
theology under a newly developed ontological, first philosophy.

This belief in the supremacy of rational deductions, together with
the Arminian thrust of the arguments employed, explains why decades after Gorlaeus's premature death in 1612, Gijsbert Voetius, that
stalwart of orthodox Calvinism, would still be attacking his atomist
ontology. Voetius called Gorlaeus an 'atheist', an 'Averroist', and a
'heretic', and insulted all those from whom Gorlaeus had drawn
inspiration.[45] His onslaughts are quite in keeping with Voetius's
usual linguistic habits, which display, especially in his disputations,
a mixture of menace and argument, insult and proof. One is
reminded of the tone of Mersenne's early works, until one discovers,
to one's bafflement, that Voetius in fact often and very much approvingly cites the fierce Minim, just as he applauds the sternest of
Spanish Jesuits. He cites them not, of course, because of their doctrinal views, which to him are naturally 'heretical', but because they,
too, insist on the superiority of theology over philosophy and de-
mand that rational argument bow to the diktat of theologically
interpreted revelation.[46]

---

[45] G. Rodis-Lewis: 'Problèmes discutés entre Descartes et Regius: L'âme et le
corps', in Theo Verbeek (ed.), *Descartes et Regius. Autour de l'explication de l'esprit
humain* (Amsterdam: Rodopi, 1993), 35–46, esp. 41 and 44; Theo Verbeek, *René
Descartes et Martin Schoock: La Querelle d'Utrecht* (Paris: Les Impressions Nouvelles,
1988), esp. 143; Lüthy, 'Gorlaeus' Atomism', 271.

[46] Gijsbert Voetius's manners, breach of etiquette, and applause for Mersenne and
the Spanish Jesuits can best be seen in action in his *Selectarum disputationum
theologicarum pars I* (Utrecht: Johannes a Waesberge, 1648). On Voetius's reasons
for disliking the new philosophical systems, see the excellent study by J. A. van Ruler,
The Crisis of Causality. Voetius and Descartes on God, Nature, and Change (Leiden: E. J.
Brill, 1995).

With this strange alliance between the Calvinist theologian and the Parisian Minim, we have almost come full circle—but not quite. Because the Mersenne invoked by the ageing Calvinist in the 1640s was the young ecclesiastical militiaman of the early 1620s, not his true contemporary, the meek, mitigated, scientific sceptic. It is true, as we have already seen, that when Mersenne wrote his first books, he felt that he had to defend Aristotelian natural philosophy against heterodox views. It was as clear to him as, I hope, it will be to the reader of this article after all that has been said, that natural philosophy was by no means a value-neutral field, but that it was heavily dependent on metaphysics, and metaphysics on religious doctrines. This explains why the young Mersenne did not only attack Protestant philologists like Sixtinus Amama, but also authors of works on natural philosophy. We may thus not be surprised if in Mersenne's *Quaestiones celeberrimae in Genesim*, we find Gorlaeus, together with Francis Bacon, Robert Fludd, Sébastien Basson, and Nicholas Hill, listed as 'recent members of the Calvinist, Lutheran, or other heretical sects' that had to be refuted.[47] In his *L'Impiété des Déistes, Athées, et Libertins de ce temps*, Mersenne even announced the publication of 'an Encyclopedia which I am preparing in support of all the truths against all kinds of lies, and in which I shall examine more diligently what has been put forward by Gorlaeus, Charpentier, Basson, Hill, Campanella, Bruno, Vanini, and some others'.[48] This noteworthy list is made up of Protestants and of Catholics condemned or executed for heresy. For the young Mersenne, there was really no difference between one category and the other. All these men had, in one way or another, demonstrated their apostasy from the truth of the Catholic Church and the right kind of physics that supported its dogmas. However, by the time he was being quoted by Voetius, Mersenne had undergone a profound change in words and behaviour. Not only had he come to behave as an irenic 'Huguenot monk', but he had

---

[47] Mersenne, *Quaestiones celeberrimae*, col. 1838: 'recentiores Calvinistae, Lutheranae, vel alterae hereticae sectae addicti'.
[48] Mersenne, *L'Impiété des déistes*, i. 237–8: 'en l'Encyclopedie, laquelle je prepare en faveur de toutes le véritez contre toutes sortes de mensonges, dedans laquelle j'examineray plus diligemment ce qu'on avancé Gorlée, Charpentier, Basso, Hill, Campanelle, Brun, Vanin et quelques autres'.

discovered the natural sciences as a supra-confessional, and in this sense ecumenical, field of activity.

ASEPTIC SCIENCE AND THE CULTURE OF OBSERVATIONAL AND EXPERIMENTAL FACTS

This chapter has focused on the obstacles that stood in the way of interconfessional dialogue. It has emphasized the ubiquitous distrust that reigned in the intellectual commerce of the seventeenth century and the difficulties involved in overcoming it.[49] But a few words should also be said about one of the most important ways in which these barriers were lowered. After all, the seventeenth century was characterized not only by the ongoing counter-reformation, the terror of the Thirty Years War, indexed books, and inquisitorial activities, but also by rather successful attempts to develop the natural sciences in a direction that was acceptable across most (though by no means all) confessional divides. The key lay in the development of a hypothetical, experimental, and thus predomin-antly fact-finding physics.

When writing about the so-called 'Scientific Revolution', historians are inclined to describe the detachment of the observational fact from the old philosophico-theological edifice of natural philosophy as a victory of science, and notably of a mathematical and empirical mentality, over metaphysics and as a sign of practical progress in quantification, instrumentation, observation, and experimentation. But it could also be argued, on a more sombre note, that the new emphasis on facticity is just as much an act of scientific liberation as it is the effect of censorship from without and within, in the sense that it constituted the only safe way of speaking about the created world without hurting religious feelings and triggering unpleasant private or public reactions. This negative element is clearly evident in the

---

[49] On this theme, cf. J. Bouwsma's appropriately titled essay, 'Anxiety and the Formation of Early Modern Culture', in Barbara C. Malament (ed.), *After the Reformation: Essays in Honour of Jack H. Hexter* (Philadelphia: University of Penn-sylvania Press, 1980), 215–46.

case of Mersenne himself. His so-called 'mitigated scepticism' was presented as the solution to the problems sketched before, and it entailed a disavowal of knowledge of the essences of things and causal knowledge—a type of knowledge only God possessed—and an insistence on the 'ignorance of true causes', and devices to protect religious dogma by insisting on the mere probability of all human knowledge.[50] As Alistair Crombie has poignantly described, Mersenne's emphasis on mathematical precision came at the expense of causal explanations: a mathematical formula could be said to describe only the phenomenal world, not the transcendental world of causal agencies. Significantly, Mersenne's potentially dangerous interest in Copernican and Keplerian cosmology was accompanied by an intense hatred of those, like Giordano Bruno, who attempted to erect an independent, un-Christian philosophy on that very cosmology.[51]

Mersenne's development is characteristic of a larger seventeenth-century development. For the case of Italy, Leonardo Olschki has claimed that after the condemnation of Galileo, philosophy and literature were suppressed to such a degree that only 'fact-finding scholarship' was possible, and that the speculative Italian temperament was forced to keep itself busy with the production of scientific facts, until revolutionary French troops at the end of the eighteenth century released its speculative genius once more from the dungeon.[52] Despite its desire to pass itself off as the heir to Galileo's scientific legacy, the Tuscan Grand Duke's Accademia del Cimento had, for example, to limit itself to uninterpreted experimental

---

[50] On Mersenne's 'mitigated scepticism', see Popkin, *History of Scepticism*; on the theme of the 'ignorance of true causes', see Mersenne, *Les Questions théologiques, physiques, morales, et mathematiques: où chacun trouvera de contentement, ou de l'exercise* (Paris: Henri Guenon, 1634), 18–19; on the nature of his science and philosophy of science, see Robert Lenoble, *Mersenne ou la naissance du mécanisme* (Paris: Vrin, 1943) and Peter Dear, *Mersenne and the Learning of the Schools* (Ithaca: Cornell University Press, 1988).

[51] See Alistair C. Crombie, 'Marin Mersenne', in Charles C. Gillispie (ed.), *Dictionary of Scientific Biography* (New York: Scribner, 1970–90), ix. 316–22. On the theme of mathematical precision and its relation to causal accounts, see also Peter Dear, *Discipline and Experience. The Mathematical Way in the Scientific Revolution* (Chicago: University of Chicago Press, 1995), esp. ch. 1.

[52] Leonardo Olschki, *The Genius of Italy* (Ithaca: Cornell University Press, 1954), 380–1.

reports. As the Proemium of their famous *Saggi* of 1667 emphasizes, the Tuscan academicians had absolutely no intention of getting involved in any doctrinal disputes and stray remarks were put down as mere lapses: 'if sometimes in passing from one experiment to another, or for any other reason whatever, some slight hint of speculation is given, this is always to be taken as the opinion or private sentiment of the academicians, never that of the Academy, whose only task is to make experiments and to tell about them'.[53] But precisely what to most academicians involved appeared to constitute an act of intellectual castration and retrospectively to Olschki a sign of the suppression of Italy's genius is nowadays celebrated as 'the beginning of modern physics': that moment where investigation of facts separates itself from the heavy shadows of old philosophical and theological constraints.[54]

Given the differences between Tuscany labouring under the inquisition and Restoration London, it may at first sight seem strange to hear how the Fellows of the recently established Royal Society received the *Saggi* with honest enthusiasm and celebrated it as a confirmation of their own way of doing science. However, as a result of two influences of a somewhat different order, the Royal Society had effectively arrived at a comparable manner of conducting science. There was, on the one hand, the legal, Baconian rhetoric of 'establishing matters of fact' 'by trial', which culimated in the claim, found in Thomas Sprat's *History of the Royal Society* of 1667, that the members of the Royal Society 'only deal in matters of Fact'.[55] There was, on the other hand, a sceptical strand of thought, born out of religious disputes and very much influenced by Mersenne's arguments. The mutual sapping of the bases of the rivalling confessions,

---

[53] Lorenzo Magalotti (ed.), *Saggi di naturali esperienze fatte nell'Accademia del Cimento sotto la protezione del Serenissimo Principe Leopoldo di Toscana e descritte dal Segretario di essa Accademia* (Florence: Giuseppe Cocchini, 1667), 'Proemio'. Translation from W. E. Knowles Middelton, *The Experimenters. A Study of the Accademia del Cimento* (Baltimore: Johns Hopkins University Press, 1971), 89–92.

[54] Martha Ornstein [Bronfbrenner], *The Role of Scientific Societies in the Seventeenth Century* [1913] (New York: Arno, 1975), 89.

[55] See the notable study of this tradition by Barbara J. Shapiro, *A Culture of Fact. England, 1550–1720* (Ithaca: Cornell University Press, 2000). The quote (given on p. 112 of Shapiro's book) is from Thomas Sprat, *The History of the Royal Society*, ed. Jackson Cope and H. W. Jones (St Louis: Washington University Studies, 1959), 70.

with which this article began, led in England first to an attitude of constructive scepticism in the field of theology, notably in the works of William Chillingworth. From there, it entered the field of natural philosophy thanks to scientifically active theologians such as John Wilkins and Joseph Glanvill, both of which were instrumental in shaping the experimental philosophy of the Royal Society and its probabilistic view of explanations.[56] However different, then, the respective cultural reasons behind the reluctance of Italians and Englishmen to engage in causal speculations, of which Newton's *hypotheses non fingo* is the most programmatic expression, they resulted in a shared culture that allowed gentlemen of different creeds to talk freely and fearlessly about the phenomenal world uncovered by such recent 'philosophical instruments' as telescopes, microscopes, and vacuum-pumps. In a climate that frequently associated philosophical discussions 'in the way of Speculative *Reasoning*, and upon the Principles of Philosophy' with 'atheism' (in Samuel Clarke's words), it was prudent, and indeed advisable, to depict scientific activity as a probing investigation into the stunning phenomena of God's majestically subtle but ultimately incomprehensible creation.[57] This approach allowed for an ecumenical joining of voices to a pious tune that was free of metaphysical and religious dissonances.

Admittedly, the Royal Society's neutralizing, fact-finding mentality was frequently ridiculed as vacuous and occasionally chastised as spurious, most famously by Thomas Hobbes. According to a credible interpretation, what angered Hobbes was 'Boyle's segregation of facts from the physical causes that might account for them'—a segregation that was very much in keeping with the overall claim of the experimental philosophers that they had found 'a new and exclusive way of behaving', by which they 'could now resolve contentions safely', that is to say, without giving political and religious

---

[56] This has been studied in detail by Henry G. van Leeuwen, *The Problem of Certainty in English Thought, 1630–1690* (The Hague: Martin Nijhoff, 1963).

[57] Samuel Clarke, *A Discourse Concerning the Being and Attributes of God*, 9th edn. (London: W. Botham, for J. Knapton, 1738), 167, quoted by Michael Hunter, 'Science and Heterodoxy: An Early Modern Problem Reconsidered', in David C. Lindberg and Robert S. Westman (eds.), *Reappraisals of the Scientific Revolution* (Cambridge: Cambridge University Press, 1990), 437–60, at 450.

offence.[58] The pan-European success of the Royal Society in the 1660s and 1670s, to which Hobbes's own notoriety as an atheist was of course no obstacle, testifies to the credibility of that claim.

Marin Mersenne, the Accademia del Cimento, and the Royal Society may have had different reasons for limiting their activities to the establishment of facts and for their reluctance to insert them into causal theories and natural philosophical edifices; they may also have used different rhetorical strategies to justify their methodology and the results of their labours. During his triumphant visit to the Royal Society, the Cimento's secretary, Count Magalotti, must surely have been aware of the cultural abyss that separated London and Florence. But the crucial point is that this abyss could easily be bridged by the Count and the English gentlemen as they talked about experimentally induced phenomena, ways of replicating or improving them, and better and more accurate instruments to be devised.

In the French Académie des Sciences, a similar view had taken root. As their *secrétaire perpetuelle*, Bernard Le Bovier de Fontenelle, was to point out:

Particularly when one writes about facts that have some link with religion, it is quite difficult, depending on the party to which one adheres, not to attribute to a false faith advantages that it does not deserve; or to attribute to a true faith false advantages that it does not need. However, one ought to persuade oneself that one can never add truth to the religion that is true, nor give truth to those that are false.[59]

If one follows this logic, it is precisely because the truth of the right faith and the falseness of any other are in no need of factual proof that one should stop using facts in support of religious views and keep them value-neutral.

---

[58] Steven Shapin and Simon Schaffer, *Leviathan and the Air-Pump: Hobbes, Boyle, and the Experimental Life* (Princeton: Princeton University Press, 1985), 19–20, 306.

[59] 'Surtout quand on écrit des faits qui ont liaison avec la religion, il est assez difficile que, solon le parti dont on est, on ne donne à une fausse religion des avantages qui ne lui sont point dus, ou qu'on ne donne à la vraie de faux avantages dont elle n'a pas besoin. Cependant on devrait être persuadé qu'on ne peut jamais ajouter de la vérité à celle qui est vraie, ni en donner à celles qui sont fausses...' Bernard le Bouvier de Fontenelle, *Histoire des oracles* (Paris: G. de Luyne, 1687), dissertation 1, ch. 4.

All of this goes to show how the new stress on empirical facticity introduced a new common denominator and helped the ideal of the Republic of Letters to become a genuine reality. Just as in the political realm, religious tolerance was the solution to the problem of the survival of republics in the face of religious pluralism, so experimental science became, for the Republic of Letters, the solution to the fragmentation of philosophical world-views. The parallels between societies and the nascent community of scientists go even further: in real republics as much as in the virtual Republic of Letters, a distinction was now being drawn between the public behaviour of the individual citizen and his private conscience.[60] In the political field, the *libertas conscientiae*, guaranteed by the Peace of Westphalia of 1648, created the possibility that citizens in a state could function collectively despite their religious differences. Within the Republic of Letters, it allowed for the type of scientific commerce of which Mersenne had been one of the early champions. It was sufficient to distinguish between the facts and calculations reported by an interlocutor and the hidden depths of his metaphysical convictions. It was sufficient, in other words, to accept Amama's heterodox notion of stubbornness—and to stop being stubborn by ignoring the possible heterodoxies buried in the bosom of one's interlocutor.

To be sure, there were lots of individuals, religious groups, and even entire geographical areas that did not take that step and consequently did not participate in the commerce of the nascent Scientific Republic.[61] The Iberian peninsula, for example, did so quite collectively, and elsewhere certain religious groups behaved in the same way. Their refusal was often motivated in a traditional manner by reference to the heterodoxy of the interlocutors. However, within the confessional melting pot of northern Europe, such notions of orthodoxy had become so thoroughly undermined that it was possible for the Pietist Gottfried Arnold, in his *Impartial History of the*

[60] On the topic of the survival of republics in the face of confessional and ideological pluralism, see Reinhart Koselleck, *Kritik und Krise. Eine Studie zur Pathogenese der bürgerlichen Welt* (Frankfurt: Suhrkamp, 1973); and Winfried Schulze, 'Pluralisierung als Bedrohung: Toleranz als Lösung', in Heinz Durchardt (ed.), *Der Westfälische Friede. Diplomatie—politische Zensur—kulturelles Umfeld—Rezeptionsgeschichte* (*Historische Zeitschrift*, NS 26; Munich: R. Oldenbourg, 1998), 115–40.

[61] See Peter van Rooden, 'Sects, Heterodoxies, and the Diffusion of Knowledge in the Republic of Letters', in Bots and Waquet, *Commercium Litterarium*, 51–64.

Churches and Heresies of 1699, to celebrate heresy as a sign of a divine vocation and to condemn orthodoxy as the pretentiousness of the egotists, the intolerant—and, indeed, of the stubborn.[62] And it is no coincidence that it is in those countries and in those social circles where unstubborn tolerance had gained the upper hand that modern science emerged.

[62] Gottfried Arnold, *Unparteyische Kirchen- und Ketzer-Historie von Anfang des Neuen Testamtents bisz auff das Jahr Christi 1688* (Frankfurt: Thomas Fritsch, 1699–1700).

5

Galileo Galilei and the Myth of Heterodoxy

William E. Carroll

On the occasion of the publication in March 1987 of the Catholic Church's condemnation of *in vitro* fertilization, surrogate motherhood, and fetal experimentation, there appeared a cartoon in the Roman newspaper, *La Repubblica*, in which two bishops are standing next to a telescope. In the distant night sky, in addition to Saturn and the Moon, there are dozens of test-tubes. One bishop turns to the other, who is in front of the telescope, and asks: '*This* time what should we do? Should we look or not?' The historical reference to Galileo was clear. In fact, at a press conference at the Vatican, Cardinal Ratzinger was asked whether he thought the Church's response to the new biology would not result in another 'Galileo affair'. The Cardinal smiled, perhaps realizing the persistent power, at least in the popular imagination, of the story of Galileo's encounter with the Inquisition more than three hundred and fifty years before. The Vatican office which Cardinal Ratzinger headed, the Congregation for the Doctrine of the Faith, is the direct successor to the Holy Roman and Universal Inquisition. Or consider the recent remarks of the American philosopher Paul Kurtz who, in referring to 'the intrusion of religion into science with a ban on cloning', derided attempts to 'censor scientific research in the name of religious morality', by exclaiming: 'Hark, hark back to the days of Galileo'.[1]

---

[1] *The New York Times*, 24 August 2002.

The legend of Galileo's encounter with the Inquisition is a powerful and persistent feature of the modern world's understanding of what it means to be modern. Galileo has come to represent modern science fighting to free itself from the clutches of blind faith, biblical literalism, and superstition. The legend of Galileo the scientist sees him as breaking with the scientific views of Aristotle and thereby helping to lay the foundations of modern science. Both features of the generally accepted story of Galileo, that is, Galileo the challenger of Aristotelian orthodoxy in science, and Galileo the rejecter of Counter-Reformation Catholic biblical exegesis, are essential parts of what I would call the myth of Galileo's heterodoxy. I think that, in fact, Galileo's science represents far less of a break with the traditions of Aristotelian science than is generally accepted and that, when it comes to the relationship between the Bible and the natural sciences, Galileo agreed more than he disagreed with his theological opponents in the Inquisition.

GALILEO AND ARISTOTELIAN SCIENCE

In the front of his own copy of the *Dialogue Concerning the Two Chief World Systems*, Galileo wrote:

Take care, theologians, that in wishing to make matters of faith of the propositions attendant on the motion and stillness of the Sun and the Earth, in time you probably risk the danger of condemning for heresy those who assert the Earth stands firm and the Sun moves; in time, I say, when sensately or necessarily it will be demonstrated [*quando sensatamente o necessariamente si fusse dimostrato*] that the Earth moves and the Sun stands still.[2]

Here we find both Galileo's commitment to demonstrations in science, a commitment which he shares with Aristotle, and his admis-

---

[2] 'Avvertite, teologi, che, volendo fare materia di fede le proposizioni attenenti al moto ed alla quiete del sole e della Terra, vi esponete a pericolo di dover forse col tempo condennar d'eresia quella che asserissero, la Terra star ferma muoversi di luogo il sole: col tempo, dico, quando sensatamente o necessariamente si fusse dimostrato, la Terra muoversi e 'l sole star fisso.' Galileo, *Dialogo sopra due massimi sistemi del mondo* (Turin: Einaudi, 1970), 55.

sion that there is not yet such a demonstration for the motion of the earth. The passage also reaffirms a key principle Galileo set forth in his 'Letter to the Grand Duchess Christina': that when investigating physical questions one should not begin with biblical texts. Galileo warns the theologians to avoid acting imprudently, lest they be faced with the unpleasant task of condemning as heretical those propositions which they now declare to be orthodox.

Interpretations of Galileo's science have run the gamut from emphases on the role of experimental procedures to versions of mathematical Platonism to principles of Archimedes to some kind of 'a combination between experiment and mathematical deductivism'.[3] We can see an example of this debate in the recent work of Ron Naylor, who concludes that Galileo's claims, in 1602, that 'there was one simple law governing all cases of natural linear motion, and a directly related simple law governing all possible cases of the motion of a circular quadrant' were the result of mathematical and not experimental reasoning. Galileo's commitment to Copernican cosmology, according to Naylor, led Galileo to the idea that 'the same principles of circular motion might ultimately apply to terrestrial motion as well'.[4] I want to leave aside the intricacies of specific conclusions in Galileo's sciences of motion, many of which are at variance with specific conclusions in Aristotelian physics. In the analysis that follows, I have accepted an understanding of Galileo as a participant in a broad Aristotelian project, at least with respect to his commitment to the importance of the ideal of scientific demonstration. As will be apparent, I have found the interpretation of scholars such as William Wallace especially persuasive.

Galileo the scientist shares with Aristotle and Aquinas, and with major figures of the Inquisition such as Cardinal Roberto Bellarmino, the view that science deals with the truth of things. Scientific knowledge for Aristotle is knowledge of what is necessarily so, that is, cannot be otherwise, because it is based on the discovery of the causes that make things be what they are. Such sure, certain knowledge is

---

[3] R. Feldhay, 'The Use and Abuse of Mathematical Entities: Galileo and the Jesuits Revisited', in P. Machamer (ed.), *The Cambridge Companion to Galileo* (Cambridge: Cambridge University Press, 1998), 101.

[4] R. Naylor, 'Galileo, Copernicanism and the Origin of the New Science of Motion', *British Journal for the History of Science*, 36/2 (June 2003), 180–1.

quite different from the product of probable or conjectural reasoning: reasoning which lacks certitude because it falls short of identifying true and proper causes. Galileo, despite his disagreements with many seventeenth-century Aristotelians, never departed from Aristotle's ideal of science as sure, certain knowledge. Whether Galileo was arguing about the movement of the earth or about laws that govern the motion of falling bodies, his goal was to achieve true, scientific demonstrations. When Galileo writes his *Two New Sciences*, near the end of his life, he argues that he deserves credit for establishing *new* sciences because his arguments employ 'necessary demonstrations' which proceed from 'unquestionable foundations' (*primarii e indubitati fondamenti con necessarie dimostrazioni provate*).[5]

Although we must distinguish among different senses of demonstration in this context, in its most general sense, a sense shared by Galileo and Bellarmino, for example, a demonstration is a syllogistic argument which results in sure and certain knowledge in terms of causes. We know how Galileo used the lecture notes of Jesuit natural philosophers at the Collegio Romano in his early professional years at the University of Pisa. These Jesuits, who traced their intellectual heritage either to Coimbra or Salamanca, participated in what some scholars have come to call a 'progressive Aristotelianism' which has its sources in the work of scholars in the thirteenth and fourteenth centuries at the University of Paris. In these notes we find the beginning of Galileo's notion of demonstration in mathematical physics: through the making of appropriate *suppositiones* and then reasoning *ex suppositione* to seek demonstrative knowledge.[6]

---

[5] W. A. Wallace, *Galileo and His Sources* (Princeton: Princeton University Press, 1984), 99.

[6] 'With regard to these "suppositions," however, both Galileo and the Jesuits [in Rome] recognized that ... some are capable of verification, either by induction from sense experience or by measurement to within a specified degree of accuracy. In all of Galileo's serious scientific writings up to, but not including, the *Dialogo*, he is at pains to identify and verify the suppositions on which his reasoning is based, so as to justify his claims for strict proof, and he continues the same procedure in the *Due nuove scienze* and its supporting documents.' W. A. Wallace, 'Galileo and Aristotle in the *Dialogo*', *Angelicum*, 60/3 (1983), 326. For recent analyses of the contributions of the Jesuits to science in the seventeenth century, see M. Feingold (ed.), *Jesuit Science and the Republic of Letters* (Cambridge, Mass.: MIT, 2003).

These lecture notes [*reportationes*] of Jesuits such as Antonius Menu, Paulus Valla, Mutius Vitelleschi, and others contain commentaries on Aristotle's *Posterior Analytics* and, in particular, on how causes are used to secure scientific proof. Whether or not, or to what extent, mathematical *suppositiones* are appropriate categories for reaching true conclusions about nature divided thinkers in the broad Aristotelian tradition of the late sixteenth and seventeenth centuries. By the late 1580s mathematical astronomy was being taught at the Collegio Romano, concurrently with Aristotle's *De caelo*, and 'calculatory' arguments were being discussed in tracts on the continuum. Christopher Clavius, the great Jesuit mathematician, whom Galileo met on his first visit to Rome in 1587, was especially influential in making sure that young Jesuits were trained in pure and applied mathematics. The Aristotelianism at the Collegio Romano, in its openness to the role of mathematics in the study of nature, stands in marked contrast to the more Averroistic type of Aristotelianism embraced in other Italian universities. The importance of this 'progressive Aristotelianism' at the Collegio Romano for Galileo's own development has been examined extensively by the late Alistair Crombie of Oxford and by William Wallace in the United States. In particular, Wallace has shown how discussions of the connection between the method of scientific argument set forth in the *Posterior Analytics* and the use of that method in Aristotle's works in natural philosophy are characteristic of Renaissance Aristotelianism, and that they were an important resource for Galileo.[7] Jacopo Zabarella's commentary on the *Posterior Analytics*, a key text for the Renaissance Aristotelian exposition of the 'demonstrative *regressus*', is especially important for understanding the background to Galileo's methodology.[8] In the late sixteenth century at Padua, Zabarella gave the classic formulation of *regressus* theory: 'a kind of reciprocal demonstration in which, after we have demonstrated an unknown

---

[7] W. A. Wallace, *Galileo's Logic of Discovery* (Dordrecht: Boston Studies in the Philosophy of Science, 1992), and id., 'Galileo's Regressive Methodology, Its Prelude and Its Sequel', in D. A. DiLiscia, E. Kessler, and C. Methuen (eds.), *Method and Order in Renaissance Philosophy of Nature: The Aristotelian Commentary Tradition* (Aldershot: Ashgate, 1997), 229–52.

[8] W. A. Wallace, *The Modeling of Nature: Philosophy of Science and Philosophy of Nature in Synthesis* (Washington, DC: Catholic University of America Press, 1996), 300–8; id., 'Galileo's Regressive Methodology', 230–1.

cause through the known effect, we convert the major proposition and demonstrate the same effect through the same cause'.[9] The natural sciences must use a method of discovery, which includes an inductive process, as a first step in disclosing the truths of nature. It is, of course, the second half of the procedure, the demonstration from cause to effect, which yields true scientific knowledge in the Aristotelian sense. Wallace argues that Galileo frequently employed the 'paradigm of the demonstrative *regressus* to make the claims he did for the "new sciences" he was so intent on discovering'.[10] Galileo, for example, in a treatise on the sphere (1602), first argues that the various aspects and phases of the moon are probably caused by its spherical shape, illuminated by the sun. In order to arrive at a scientific demonstration, Galileo 'employs principles of projective geometry [to show] that *only* external illumination falling on a shape that is approximately spherical will cause the moon to exhibit the phases it does at precise positions and times observable from the earth'.[11] There is an elaborate intermediate stage of reasoning between the initial stage of discovery and the final stage of scientific demonstration.

At the beginning of the regress, knowledge of the moon's aspects and phases is in some sense conjectural—a partial and obscure grasping of the truth about them, what Zabarella would call 'confused' knowledge of their cause, and Galileo [would call] grasping that cause 'materially.' By the time the regress is completed the obscurity is gone, the confused has become the distinct, and the cause is grasped 'formally,' precisely as it is the cause and thus able to provide the basis for scientific knowledge.[12]

Recently, scholars at the Max Planck Institute for the History of Science in Berlin have reinforced these claims, pointing out that Galileo shared with his contemporaries an adherence to the fundamental principles of Aristotelian physics.

When historians of science discuss the general state of ideas in the seventeenth century, they tend to portray medieval Aristotelian scholasticism

---

[9] Wallace, *The Modeling of Nature*, 301; H. C. Kuhn, 'Non-regressive Methods and the Emergence of Modern Science', in DiLiscia, Kessler, and Methuen (eds.), *Method and Order in Renaissance Philosophy of Nature*, 321.
[10] Wallace, 'Galileo's Regressive Methodology', 250.
[11] Wallace, *The Modeling of Nature*, 306.   [12] Ibid. 308.

merely as the counter position against which Galileo's theory of motion gained its profile as a new science, neglecting the potential of Aristotelianism as a generic knowledge resource available to Galileo and his contemporaries. Galileo's unpublished commentaries on Aristotelian physics ... make it not only amply clear that he had thoroughly appropriated the immense knowledge accumulated in the scholastic tradition of elaborating and commenting [on] Aristotle, but also that he had thus acquired a resource of knowledge that provided essential assets of the new science of motion, assets such as the conceptualisation of acceleration in terms of the changing degrees of a quality. This conceptualisation was in fact part of the doctrine of intension and remission [of forms] transmitted by the lively scholastic tradition of the time, a tradition from which contemporary intellectuals could hardly escape, whether they encountered it in the college of La Flèche, as was the case for Descartes, or in the lecture notes of Jesuit professors of the Collegio Romano, as was the case for Galileo.[13]

All these scholars have built on the famous essay by John Hermann Randall, 'The Development of Scientific Method in the School of Padua', in which he argued that it was an Aristotelian method which was the method of modern science and that 'the father of modern science in fact turns out to be none other than the Master of those who know'.[14]

It is true that Galileo rejects several conclusions which Aristotle and his followers had accepted as true, especially cosmological claims about the incorruptibility of the heavens,[15] geocentricity, the immobility of the earth, and the like. But neither geostatic nor geocentric cosmology, for example, is an essential feature of Aristotelian natural philosophy; that is, their rejection does not necessarily entail a rejection of the fundamental principles of Aristotelian physics. It is fair to say that the emergence of modern science occurred both 'against [a certain] Aristotelian context and within [a certain]

---

[13] J. Büttner, P. Damerow, and J. Renn, 'Traces of an Invisible Giant: Shared Knowledge in Galileo's Unpublished Treatises', in J. Montesinos and C. Solís (eds.), *Largo Campo di Filosofare: Eurosymposium Galileo 2001* (The Canaries: Fundación Canaria Orotava de Historia de la Ciencia, 2001), 190–1.

[14] J. H. Randall, 'The Development of Scientific Method in the School of Padua', *Journal of the History of Ideas*, 1 (1940), 177–206.

[15] For a good discussion concerning debates about the fluidity of the heavens, see M. Bucciantini, 'Teologia e Nuova Filosofia: Galileo, Federico Cesi, Giovambattista Agucchi e la discussione sulla fluidità e corruttibilità del cielo', in *Sciences et Religions de Copernic à Galilée (1540–1610)* (Rome: École française de Rome, 1999), 411–42.

Aristotelian context'.[16] Galileo was quick to point out that were Aristotle to have the evidence of the new telescopic discoveries he would have accepted the conclusions Galileo drew from them. Galileo, however, never thought that his telescopic observations alone provided sufficient evidence to prove that the earth moved; they served as strong encouragement for him to seek such a demonstration, a demonstration in which he hoped to show that the only cause for the ocean tides was the double motion of the earth.

Galileo's commitment to the importance of mathematics in studying nature does represent an *emphasis* not found in the Aristotelian traditions; nevertheless, it is, I think, consistent with the Aristotelian notion of an intermediate science—intermediate, that is, between physics and mathematics—in which the principles of mathematics are applied to the study of natural phenomena. Aristotle, in the second book of his *Physics*, considers such intermediate sciences to be in some sense branches of mathematics which come nearest to the study of nature: optics, harmonics, and astronomy. Referring to such a mixed science, Thomas Aquinas writes: 'it does not belong to the mathematician to treat of motion, although mathematical principles can be applied to motion.... The measurements of motions are studies in the intermediate sciences between mathematics and natural science.'[17] In this view, the work of Galileo, and later Newton, can be seen to represent not so much a rejection of Aristotle but a great advance in the intermediate science of mathematical physics.[18] As Rivka Feldhay has pointed out, it is important to examine Galileo's 'mathematical strategies' against the background of the debate on the certitude of mathematics, the nature of mathematical entities, and the relationship among mathematics, natural philosophy, and metaphysics which was especially lively in the late sixteenth and early seventeenth centuries—and especially among Jesuit scholars.[19]

---

[16] Kuhn, 'Non-regressive Methods', 320.

[17] Thomas Aquinas, *The Division and Methods of the Sciences* [*In Boethium De trinitate*, qq. 5–6], tr. A. Maurer (Toronto: Pontifical Institute of Mediaeval Studies, 1963), 36.

[18] W. E. Carroll, 'The Scientific Revolution and Contemporary Discourse on Faith and Reason', in T. Smith (ed.), *Faith and Reason* (South Bend, Ind.: St Augustine's Press, 2001).

[19] Feldhay, 'The Use and Abuse of Mathematical Entities', 200.

Although Christopher Clavius argued for the importance of the study of mathematics, his views concerning this topic did not go unchallenged in the Collegio Romano.[20] A traditional counter-argument advanced was that the intermediate sciences, being types of applied mathematics,

imported improper principles into the science of nature when they used mathematics to solve physical problems. ... Still faithful to the ideals of the *Posterior Analytics*, [these other Jesuits] would claim that true demonstrations could be found in Aristotle's writings on philosophy and in scholastic treatises on theology, but that they could rarely if ever be attained in the newer type of physics that made extensive use of mathematics.[21]

Thus we see an important source of the scepticism which greeted claims that mathematical astronomers could do anything more than 'save the appearances'—a scepticism which informed the views of theologians of the Inquisition in their condemnation of Copernican astronomy.

GALILEO AS THEOLOGIAN

Galileo's theological acumen, especially concerning the relationship between the Bible and science, has been celebrated by diverse commentators,[22] and it plays a central role in claims about his

---

[20] J. Lattis, *Between Copernicus and Galileo: Christopher Clavius and the Collapse of Ptolemaic Cosmology* (Chicago: University of Chicago Press 1994).

[21] W. A. Wallace, 'The Problem of Apodictic Proof in Early Seventeenth-Century Mechanics', *Science in Context*, 3/1 (1989), 80.

[22] On several occasions, Pope John Paul II has praised the astuteness of Galileo's theological observations on the relationship between science and Scripture. In ceremonies commemorating the 100th anniversary of the birth of Einstein (1979), the Pope, referring to the fundamental compatibility between science and the Bible, quoted approvingly from Galileo's 'Letter to the Grand Duchess Christina', in which Galileo observed that God is author of all truth, both the truth of nature and the truth of Scripture. In 1992, as part of an official ceremony in which he accepted the findings of a commission of historical and theological enquiry into the Galileo affair, the Pope noted that the theologians of the Inquisition failed to re-examine their criteria of scriptural interpretation in the context of 'the new science'. Galileo, 'a sincere believer', paradoxically 'showed himself to be more perceptive' in his biblical hermeneutics 'than the theologians who opposed him'. John Paul II, 'Address to the Pontifical Academy of Sciences, 31 October 1992', *Origins*, 22/1 (1992), 372.

heterodoxy, at least in the context of the early seventeenth century. Discussions of Galileo the theologian necessarily involve analyses of his understanding of the nature of science and, in particular, his commitment to the ideal of demonstrations in the natural sciences. As I have already suggested, claims about Galileo's revolutionary role in the history of science are often tied closely to claims about his understanding of the relationship between science and Scripture. There is an obvious reciprocity in such claims about Galileo's innovations in the realms of both science and theology.

Giorgio di Santillana, in his influential book *The Crime of Galileo*, offers effusive praise for Galileo the theologian:

In his concern with enduring things, in his confessional simplicity, Galileo spans the centuries. … The elaborate baroque formulas of submissiveness do not prevent the reader from feeling that here is someone like Ambrose, Augustine, or Bonaventure, reprehending sleepy shepherds and degenerate epigones. He speaks in the name of the community of the faithful which joins the ancient dead to the yet unborn. … [H]e deserves heeding no less than Aquinas himself.

He was not wrong either, as a matter of record. The content of his spurned and incriminated theological letters has become official Church doctrine since 1893. Had there been in Rome, at the time of the first crisis of 1616, a youthful Aquinas to take up his lead, instead of an aged Bellarmine—but there was no Aquinas, and there was no time.[23]

Occasionally, Galileo's exegetical sophistication *vis-à-vis* his theological opponents is compared to their sophistication in matters scientific. Walter Brandmüller remarks that, paradoxically, whereas the Inquisition erred in matters of biblical interpretation, Galileo was wrong in his claims for the truth of the new astronomy.[24] Paul Feyerabend praises the Inquisition for its caution and sees its position as an anticipation of contemporary attempts 'to temper the

---

[23] G. di Santillana, *The Crime of Galileo* (Chicago: University of Chicago Press, 1955), pp. x–xi.

[24] 'Ci troviamo così di fronte al paradosa di un Galilei che sbaglia nel campo delle scienze e di una Curia che sbaglia nel campo della teologia. Viceversa, la Curia ha ragione nel campo scientifico e Galilei nella interpretazione della Bibbia.' W. Brandmüller, *Galileo e la Chiesa ossia il diritto ad errare* (Vatican City: Libreria Editrice Vaticana, 1992), 196.

totalitarian and dehumanising tendencies of modern scientific objectivism'.[25]

Among recent studies of Galileo's understanding of the relationship between the Bible and science, the most detailed analysis of Galileo's principles of biblical exegesis can be found in the work of Mauro Pesce of the University of Bologna. For Pesce, Galileo represents a missed opportunity for the Catholic Church in the seventeenth century to discover a *modus vivendi* between modernity and religion [*una convivenza tra modernità e religione*]. According to Pesce, it was not until Pope Leo XIII's encyclical, *Providentissimus Deus* (1893), that the Church would accept, even in an attenuated form, the principles enunciated by Galileo. For Pesce, the fundamental issue from 1616 to 1893 was not really the acceptance of Copernican astronomy, but rather the unwillingness of the Church to accept Galileo's hermeneutical principle that the truth of Scripture is religious and not scientific.[26] Pesce claims that it was this distinction between science and religion which constituted the core of Galileo's understanding of the Bible, and, furthermore, that it was the rejection of this distinction which lies behind the condemnation of heliocentric astronomy.[27]

Galileo's theological arguments concerning the relationship between science and Scripture are found principally in a series of letters and notes he writes from 1613 to 1615.[28] In them, Galileo sets forth

[25] P. Feyerabend, *Farewell to Reason* (London: Verso, 1987), 259.

[26] 'tra il febbraio 1616 … e il 1893, esiste una continuità di rifiuto ufficiale della proposta galileiana di accordo tra religione e scienza'. M. Pesce, 'Momenti della ricezione dell'ermeneutica biblica galileiana e della *Lettera a Cristina* nel XVII secolo', *Annali di storia dell'esegesi*, 8/1 (1991), 56.

[27] 'il punto fondamentale della questione non riguarda l'accettazione o meno del copernicanesimo da parte dell'autorità ecclesiastica, ma l'accettazione o meno della tesi ermeneutica per la quale la verità della Scrittura non è scientifica bensì soltanto religioso. Questa era la tesi che Galileo difese nella *Lettera al Castelli* e perfezionò nella *Lettera a Cristina*. Ed è il rifiuto di questa ermeneutica che portò alla censura delle due proposizione copernicane nel 1616.' Ibid. See also G. Stabile, 'Linguaggio della natura e linguaggio della scrittura in Galilei dalla *Istoria* sulle macchie solari alle lettere copernicane', *Nuncius*, 9/1 (1994), 37–64, for the same claim.

[28] In the letters to Benedetto Castelli, Piero Dini, and the Grand Duchess Christina, Galileo offers a systematic response to objections from academic and theological opponents: priests and professors who were convinced that Copernican astronomy and its apparent implications for Aristotelian physics, cosmology, and metaphysics presented a serious threat to the traditional interpretation of the Bible as well as to the

two general principles. First, there can be no contradiction between the truths of science and the truths of faith. God is the author of all truth: both the truth known through revelation and the truth known through reason alone.

The views that truth does not contradict truth and that rational enquiry has a competence of its own are hardly alien to Catholic culture. Augustine and Aquinas admit as much, as did Cardinal Bellarmino. In a 1615 letter to the Carmelite priest, Paolo Foscarini, the Cardinal observed that were there to be a demonstration that the earth moved, then the Church could not maintain that the Bible revealed the opposite.[29] Indeed, as I have said, Cardinal Bellarmino and Galileo shared the same broad Aristotelian understanding of what a demonstration in science is. Science for them was necessary knowledge in terms of causes. Galileo, in sketching his response to Bellarmino's letter to Foscarini, writes:

The motion of the earth and the stability of the sun could never be against Faith or Holy Scripture, if this proposition were correctly proved to be physically true by philosophers, astronomers, and mathematicians, with the help of sense experience, accurate observations, and necessary demon-

whole edifice of Catholic theology. See E. McMullin, 'Galileo on Science and Scripture', in P. Machamer (ed.), *The Cambridge Companion to Galileo* (Cambridge: Cambridge University Press, 1998), 271–347.

[29] 'Third. I say that if there were a true demonstration [*ci fusse vera dimostrazione*] that the sun is in the center of the universe [*nel centro del mondo*] and the earth in the third sphere, and that the sun does not circle the earth but the earth circles the sun, then one would have to proceed with great care in explaining the Scriptures that appear contrary [*che paiono contrarie*], and say rather that we do not understand them than what is demonstrated is false. But I will not believe that there is such a demonstration until it is shown to me [*Ma non crederó che ci sia tal dimostrazione, fin che non mi sia mostrata*]. Nor is it the same to demonstrate that by supposing the sun to be at the center and the earth in the heaven one can save the appearances, and to demonstrate that in truth [*che in verità*] the sun is at the center and the earth in heaven; for I believe the first demonstration may be available, but I have very grave doubts [*grandissimo dubbio*] about the second, and in the case of doubt one must not abandon [*non si de[v]e lasciare*] the Holy Scripture as interpreted by the Holy Fathers.' Bellarmino to Foscarini, April 1615. M. Finocchiaro (ed.), *The Galileo Affair: A Documentary History* (Berkeley: University of California Press, 1987), 68. There has been considerable debate on how to understand Bellarmino's first sentence. Rivka Feldhay defends a straightforward reading of Bellarmino's claim and surveys other interpretations, 'Recent Narratives on Galileo and the Church or the Three Dogmas of the Counter-Reformation', in J. Renn (ed.), *Galileo in Context* (Cambridge: Cambridge University Press, 2001), 219–37.

strations. However, in this case, if some passages of Scripture were to sound contrary, we would have to say that this is due to the weakness of our mind, which is unable to grasp the true meaning of Scripture in this particular case. This is the common doctrine, and it is entirely right, since one truth cannot contradict another truth. On the other hand, whoever wants to condemn it judicially must first demonstrate it to be physically false by collecting the reasons against it. ... If the earth *de facto* moves, we cannot change nature and arrange for it not to move. But we can rather easily remove the opposition [*la repugnanza*] of Scripture with the mere admission that we do not grasp its true meaning [*il suo vero senso*]. Therefore the way to be sure not to err is to begin with astronomical and physical investigations, and not with scriptural ones.[30]

The second general observation by Galileo concerning the relationship between the Bible and science is that the main purpose of God's revelation in Scripture is not to teach natural philosophy but to lead all to salvation. What so many see as particularly modern in Galileo's understanding of the relationship between the Bible and science is but the reaffirmation of traditional Catholic thinking. Despite Galileo's explicit claim that he is only reaffirming 'the common doctrine', Pesce, Giorgio Stabile, Paolo Lombardi, and others think that Galileo's hermeneutical principles were as unacceptable to the Church 'as they were new'. In particular, they claim that Galileo denies to the Bible any authority in determining truths of nature and that this denial is a radical departure from traditional Catholic thinking.[31]

---

[30] *Considerazioni circa l'opinione copernicana*, in Galileo Galilei, *Le opere di Galileo Galileo*, ed. A. Favaro *et al.* (Florence: Barbèra, 1968), v. 364–5; Finocchiaro, *The Galileo Affair*, 80–2.

[31] 'La proposta esegetica di Galileo è *tanto ineccepibile quanto nuova* [my emphasis], ed è esattamente quella già implicitamente presupposta (si nota il concetto di *repugnanza*) dai brani delle *Lettere sulle macchie solari*. ... Galilei rovesciava sui teologi l'onere della prova, e nelle divergenze tra dettato scritturale e natura, attribuiva a quest'ultima il ruolo di autorità dirimente: non è la *fictio* verbale che può falsificare la realtà dell'effeto, ma esattamente il contrario. L'*interpretatio scripturae*, che lavora sui significati del linguagio biblico, dev'essere assoggettata all'*interpretatio naturae*, che indaga direttamente sui significati naturali, tutte le volte che i due ordini interferiscono. ... [The contradiction is only apparent] tra contento incontrovertibilmente fattuale del Verbo reificato ed erronea interpretazione del Verbo proferrito [a distinction Stabile had already made].' Stabile, 'Linguaggio della natura', 62–3. Mauro Pesce claims that Galileo goes even further than either Augustine or Aquinas

Although Galileo does emphasize more than do his contemporaries the distinction between an essentially religious purpose of the Bible and other truths which it may contain, he does not really anticipate a radical separation between religious truths and other truths in the Bible.

Galileo's excursion into biblical exegesis had a practical end. In the 'Letter to the Grand Duchess Christina', he sought to persuade the Church not to condemn Copernican astronomy, especially since he was convinced that he was on the verge of proving that the earth moves. In the attempt to protect the new astronomy from the charge of heresy, Galileo appealed to theological principles which were shared by the theologians of the Inquisition. In fact, Galileo uses arguments found in Melchior Cano (1509–60) and Benedictus Pererius (1535–1610), whose works were fundamental for Counter-Reformation Catholicism.[32] Galileo quotes verbatim this observation by Pererius: 'in dealing with the teachings of Moses, do not think or say anything affirmatively ... which is contrary to the manifest evidence and arguments of philosophy or the other disciplines. For since every truth agrees with every other truth, the truth of Sacred Scripture cannot be contrary to the true arguments and evidence of the human sciences.'

When Pererius comments on the passage from Genesis [1: 6–8] concerning God's placing the firmament in the midst of the waters, with waters above and below, he concludes that the passage must be taken either metaphorically or as describing a miracle, since it must be not read as contrary to Aristotle's doctrine of the natural place of water.

---

in that he makes an epistemological claim in distinguishing science from religion when he observes that the Book of Nature is read quite differently from the Book of Scripture. Thus Galileo, at least implictly, lays the groundwork for a modern conception of religion. 'Ho allora [in his 1987 article] sostenuto che Galileo distingue la natura dalla Scrittura da un punto di vista epistemologico e perviene così non solo a distinguere scienza da religione, ma ad individuare, seppure implicitamente, la natura propria di ciò che è religione.' Pesce, 'Momenti della ricezione', 57.

[32] In the letter to the Grand Duchess, Galileo makes explicit reference to Pererius, Paolo di Burgos (1353–1435), Alfonso Tostado, bishop of Avila (1400–55), and Diego de Zuñiga (1536–84), in addition, of course, to Augustine, Jerome, Aquinas, and Pseudo-Dionysius.

Galileo does not claim that the Bible is silent about the world of nature. He observes that when we seek to examine what the Bible says about the physical world we must remember that, although the Bible cannot err, this inerrrancy concerns the Bible's true meaning [*il suo vero sentimento*] and not what 'its bare words' may signify [*che suona il puro significato delle parole*]. A slavish adherence to the 'unadorned grammatical meaning' [*nel nudo suono literale*] of any particular passage may lead to follies, error, and heresy. One may come to think, for example, that God has hands, feet, eyes, that He gets angry and is subject to other emotions. The Bible often contains passages written in a mode 'to accommodate' these passages to 'the capacities of the common people, who are rude and unlearned' [*per accomodarsi all capacità del vulgo assai rozo e indisciplinato*].[33]

Too many translators of (as well as commentators on) these texts miss an important distinction. When Galileo refers to 'il nudo' or 'il puro', 'significato delle parole', 'il nudo suono literale', or similar phrases, he does not mean the literal sense of Scripture. As Aquinas and others had observed, the literal sense of the Bible, which is always true, is 'what the author intended, but the author of Sacred Scripture is God'.[34] Galileo, observing this same distinction between what we might call a literalistic and a literal reading of the Bible, distinguishes between a naive literalism and 'il vero sentimento' of the text. The literal sense is not always the same as what the bare words signify. Galileo, thus, is embracing, not challenging, a traditional Catholic principle of biblical exegesis. It is a principle affirmed not only by Augustine and Aquinas, but by all sixteenth- and seventeenth-century Catholic theologians.

Cardinal Bellarmino was well aware of the difficulties in discovering the truths in Scripture. Every sentence in the Bible has a literal or historical meaning, i.e. 'the meaning which the words immediately present'. The literal meaning is either *simple*, 'which consists of the proper meaning of the words', or *figurative*, 'in which words are transferred from their natural signification to another'. When the Bible refers to 'the right hand of God', the simple literal sense would

---

[33] Finocchiaro, *The Galileo Affair*, 92; Galileo Galilei, *Lettere*, ed. F. Flora (Turin: Einaudi, 1978), 130.

[34] Thomas Aquinas, *Summa theologiae* I q. 1 a. 10; see also I q. 68, aa. 2–3; q. 69 a. 2 ad 3; q. 70 a. 1 ad 5; q. 74 a. 2 ad 2, a. 3 ad 3.

mean a part of God's body; whereas the figurative literal sense means God's power. As Richard Blackwell notes, Bellarmino distinguishes the literal sense (with all its senses) from the 'spiritual' or 'mystical' senses, which involve references to something else other than which the words immediately signify. The spiritual senses are in addition to the literal sense, not a substitute for it. Bellarmino distinguishes three distinct spiritual senses: (1) the allegorical (signifies something pertaining to Christ or the Church); (2) the tropological (signifies something which pertains to morality); and (3) the anagogical (signifies something which pertains to eternal life).[35]

Bellarmino had argued that serious exegetical errors can arise 'either by reading figuratively what should be taken as simply literal or by reading as simply literal what should be taken as figurative'. The Cardinal, in distinguishing between the simple literal sense and the figurative literal sense, often writes that one must distinguish between *res quae dicuntur* (what is said) and *modus quo dicuntur* (the way it is said).[36] There are as many different types of figurative meanings as there are types of literary figures, but all these figurative meanings are part of the literal sense of Scripture.[37]

On the basis of distinctions between what the bare words signify and the true sense of the Bible (and the examples Galileo uses concern passages in the Bible which ascribe certain human attributes to God, and with which obviously Bellarmino would agree), Galileo with rhetorical deftness advances a *wider* argument:

---

[35] R. Blackwell, *Galileo, Bellarmine, and the Bible* (Notre Dame, Ind.: University of Notre Dame Press, 1991), 33–4. See also R. Fabris, *Galileo Galilei e gli orientamenti esegetici del suo tempo,* Scripta varia, 62 (Vatican City: Pontifical Academy of Sciences, 1986), 34–6.

[36] In this respect he was following a tradition which can be seen from Augustine on. In a dispute concerning divine inspiration, with a professor (Estius) at Douai, Bellarmino rejects the view that there is a single literal/historical sense. In defending his view of the plurality of literal senses, Bellarmino liked to quote Augustine's observation about his [Augustine's] own reading of Scripture: *in ipsis sanctis Scripturis multo nescio plura quam scio.* 'Bellarmin, dans la tradition augustinienne, précise bien qu'elles [les deux Testaments] sont susceptibles de *plusieurs* sens littéraux (figurés).' J.-R. Armogathe, 'La Vérité des Écritures et la nouvelle physique', in id. (ed.), *Le Grand Siècle et la Bible* (Paris: Beauchesne, 1989), 50.

[37] When Paolo Lombardi examines Galileo's claims concerning the way to read biblical passages concerning physical matters, he concludes that the Church was not able to accept Galileo's arguments to interpret allegorically (*allegoricamente*) those passages of the Bible which appeared to contradict the hypotheses of Copernicus,

whenever the Bible has occasion to speak of any physical conclusion [*alcune conclusione naturale*] (especially those which are very abstruse and hard to understand), the rule has been observed of avoiding confusion in the minds of the common people which would render them contumacious toward the higher mysteries. ... Who, then, would positively declare that this principle [of accommodation] has been set aside, and the Bible has confined itself rigorously to the bare and restricted sense of its words [*i puri ristretti significati delle parole*], when speaking but casually of the earth, of water, of the sun, or of any other created thing? ...

[Therefore] ... in discussions of physical problems [*problemi naturali*] we ought to begin not from the authority of scriptural passages [*non si dovrebbe cominciare dalle autorità di luoghi scritture*], but from sense experience and necessary demonstrations [*ma alle sensato esperienze e dalle dimostrate necessarie*] ... It is necessary for the Bible, in order to be accommodated to the understanding of every man [*per accomodarsi all'intendimento dell'universale*], to speak many things which appear to differ from the absolute truth [*dal vero assoluto*] so far as the bare meaning of the words [*al nudo significato delle parole*] is concerned.[38]

Ugo Baldini thinks that Galileo's wider application of the principle of accommodation was unacceptable to Bellarmino because the cardinal embraced a 'Mosaic physics' instead of an Aristotelian cosmology.[39] Baldini also thinks that in Galileo's extension of the principle of accommodation to biblical discussions of physical

since the Church reserved such allegorical interpretations to the heavens, whereas biblical references to terrestrial realities were taken only in the literal sense. According to Lombardi, for the Church to concede to Galileo's hermeneutical principles would involve, so leaders of the Inquisition feared, a return to the heresies of Origen. But the 'allegorical sense' to which Lombardi refers, when he invokes Galileo's arguments, is equivalent to what Bellarmino calls the figurative sense of the literal. P. Lombardi, *La Bibbia contesa: Tra umanesimo e razionalismo* (Florence: La Nuova Italia, 1992), 217.

[38] Galileo, *Lettere*, 130. See also S. Drake (ed.), *Discoveries and Opinions of Galileo* (Garden City, NY: Doubleday, 1957), 182, and Finocchiaro, *The Galileo Affair*, 92–3.

[39] 'La lettura fondamentalistica del *Genesi* e di altri testi biblici che autorizzava la scissione tra "fisici mosaica" e cosmologia aristotelica imponeva dunque al cardinale il rifiuto della più radicale tra le innovazioni astronomiche, il principio eliocentrico. ... [C]ome per Galileo, anche per il cardinale la concordanza tra Scrittura e natura era un assioma, ma l'indagine umana sulla seconda (fallibile, come mostrava il collasso del cosmo aristotelico) trovava un fondamento di verità in espressioni non equivoche della prima. ... Le proposte galileiane non potevano non entrare in rotta collisione con la visione bellarminiana del nesso Scrittura-scienza: per Galileo i passi biblici di contenuto astronomico andavano interpretati in modo da risultare congruenti con risultati ottenuti per via scientifica, che così costituivano un *prius* logico;

phenomena there is a clear break with the hermeneutical principles of Cardinal Bellarmino. According to Baldini, Bellarmino places physical phenomena in the same category as historical events and, thus, will not grant the possibility of their being interpreted in a figurative sense.[40] Baldini does admit, ultimately, that Bellarmino and Galileo do share common ground in their exegetical stances, but Bellarmino, concerned with defending the authority of the Church (and the traditional interpretation of Scripture), was not well disposed to entertain sympathetically Galileo's arguments.[41]

Although many passages from an earlier 1613 letter to Benedetto Castelli appear verbatim in the 1615 letter to the Grand Duchess, several changes indicate Galileo's awareness of subtle theological distinctions. With respect to the opening of the second passage just quoted: in 1613, Galileo writes to Castelli using almost the same words he will employ in 1615, save for the observation that: 'in physical disputes [*disputi naturali*] it [the Bible] should be reserved to the last place [*ella doverebbe esser riserbata nell'ultimo luogho*]'. In 1615, in the passage quoted above, Galileo argues that 'we ought not to begin from the authority of scriptural passages'. This change, from reserving the Bible to last place in discussing scientific questions to the admonition not to begin from the authority of Scripture, is indicative of the rhetorical thrust of the letter to the Grand

se non consentivano simile interpretazione quei passi erano da considerare metafore, o casi di adeguamento ad espressioni consuete.' U. Baldini, 'L'astronomia del cardinale Bellarmino', in Paolo Galluzzi (ed.), *Novità celesti e crisi del sapere* (Florence: Barbèra, 1984), 303.

[40] '[E]ssa porta a ritenere che, se una frase enuncia un evento nel suo puro senso fisico, e non in uno metaforico o simbolico, non è lecito attriburle un significato diverso da quello che risulta possibili, infatti, si doverebbe ammettere che Dio non ha curato che la rivelazione fosse interpretabile univocamente, o perfino che essa include affermazioni non vere, cosa che le *Controversiae* [II, cap. xii] escludono espressamente.' U. Baldini, 'Bellarmino tra vecchia e nuova scienza: epistemologia, cosmologia, fisica', in G. Galeota (ed.), *Roberto Bellarmino: Arcivescovo di Capua, Teologo e Pastore della Riforma Cattolica, Atti del Congresso Internazionali di Studi*, ii (Capua: Istituto Superiore de Scienze Religiose, 1990), 660–1.

[41] The principles of biblical exegesis affirmed by Galileo 'entro in una stessa gamma i atteggiamenti [with those of Bellarmino], dei quali il suo fissa l'estremo di massima elasticità, mentre l'altro di massima rigidità. Tale gamma, nel suo insieme, individua un atteggiamento che per brevità si può dire concordista.' Ibid. 670.

Duchess.[42] For the real audience Galileo addresses is not the Grand Duchess, but theologians and Church officials in Rome.

In explaining that the purpose of the Bible is to lead men to salvation and not to disclose information extraneous to that purpose, Galileo writes the following to Castelli in 1613:

> I should believe [*Io crederei*] that the authority of Holy Writ had *only* the aim of persuading [*l'autorità delle Sacre Lettere avesse avuto solamente la mira a persuadere*] men of those articles and propositions which, being necessary for salvation [*sendo necessarie per la salute loro*] and overriding all human reason [*superando ogni umano discorso*], could not be made credible by another science, or by other means than the mouth of the Holy Ghost itself.[43]

In the letter of 1615, Galileo alters this passage; he writes:

> I should judge that the authority of the Bible had the aim *principally* of persuading [*l'autorità delle Sacre Lettere avesse avuto la mira a persuadere principalmente*] men of those articles and propositions which, surpassing all human reasoning, could not be made credible by another science, or by any other means than through the mouth of the Holy Ghost.[44]

In 1613, Galileo wrote that the purpose of the Bible was *only* [*solamente*] to persuade men of those truths which surpassed human

---

[42] There is another difference: in the letter to Castelli, Galileo writes that in Scripture there are 'proposizioni le quali quanto al nudo significato della parole, hanno aspetto diverso dal vero', but in the letter to the Grand Duchess, he writes: 'molte cose diverse, in aspetto e quanto al nudo significato delle parole, dal vero assoluto'. This was one of the sentences in the letter to Castelli which was rendered differently in the text which the Inquisition had (and which was pointed to as troublesome by the consultors in Rome): 'Che nella Santa Scrittura si trovano molte proposizioni false quanto al nudo senso delle parole.' For an illuminating discussion of these differences see Finocchiaro, *The Galileo Affair*, 331 n. 6; M. Pesce, 'Una nuova versione della lettera di G. Galilei a Benedetto Castelli', *Nouvelles de la Republique des Lettres* (1991), 89–122; and id., 'La versioni originali della lettera "copernicana" a B. Castelli', *Filologia e Critica*, 2 (1992), 35–56. Even those scholars who discuss Galileo's principles of biblical exegesis in considerable detail (e.g. Blackwell, Pesce, Fabris, Stabile) do not distinguish between Galileo's arguments in the letter to Castelli and his arguments in the letter to the Grand Duchess.

[43] Galileo, *Lettere*, 106.

[44] 'Stimerei per questo che l'autorità delle Sacre Lettre avesse avuto la mira a persuadere principalmente a gli uomini quegli articoli e proposizioni, che, superando ogni umano discorso, non potevano per altra scienza ne per altro mezzo farcisi credibili, che per la bocca dell'istesso Santo Spirito.' Ibid. 131. Drake's translation of the 1615 text (*Discoveries and Opinions of Galileo*, 183): 'I should judge that the

reason. In 1615, he changes the adverb to 'principally' [*principalmente*]; thereby, he does not exclude from the purpose of the Bible the revelation of truths which are within the realm of human reason. Notice also, that the 1615 text omits the phrase 'being necessary for salvation'; in these changes Galileo eliminates a restriction concerning the subject of the articles and propositions which come under the 'authority of the Bible'. Thus, Galileo admits that there may be truths in the Bible which are not directly connected to the Bible's purpose of leading human beings to salvation. Mauro Pesce refers to this passage from the letter to the Grand Duchess as an example of Galileo's radical break with traditional Catholic biblical exegesis. According to Pesce, Galileo rejects granting any authority to the Bible in matters scientific. Pesce seems to understand *principalmente* as *solamente*, but, as we have seen, Galileo himself changed *solamente* to *principalmente*.[45]

authority of the Bible was designed to persuade men of those articles and propositions which, surpassing all human reasoning, could not be made credible by science, or by any other means than through the very mouth of the Holy Spirit.' He misses completely the thrust of 'principalmente', and he also omits the 'altra' in 'altra scienza', whereas he does not omit the 'altra' in his translation of the 1613 letter. To use the adjective 'altra' indicates that the Bible/sacra scrittura is a science/knowledge. In his translation of the letter to Castelli (1613) Drake does include 'only' and the phrase 'being necessary for our salvation'. (*Galileo at Work* (Chicago: University of Chicago Press, 1978), 226.) Finocchiaro, in his translations of these passages, uses 'merely' for 'solamente' (1613 letter) and 'chiefly' for 'principalmente' (1615 letter). (*The Galileo Affair*, 51 and 93.) R. Fabris quotes a major part of the above passage from the letter to Castelli with the following introduction: 'l'intenzione *primaria* [my emphasis] della Scrittura è quella di enunciare "gli articoli concernenti alla salute e allo stabilimento della fede;" articoli o proposizioni "che sendo necessarie per la salute degli uomini e superando ogni umano discorso non potevano per altra scienza né per altro mezzo farsi credibili, che per la bocca dell'istesso Spirito santo." ' (*Galileo Galilei e gli orientamenti esegetici del suo tempo*, 16.) Fabris conflates the two distinct passages from the letters to Castelli and the Grand Duchess and, accordingly, misses the very important change in the text.

[45] 'L'affermazione è radicale: l'autorità della Scrittura riguarda "articoli e proposizioni" che *superano ogni umano discorso*, cioè: l'autorità della Scrittura riguarda *solo* [my emphasis] le verità *irraggiungibili* con la scienza umana. Tutto ciò che può essere dimostrato razionalmente viene sottratto all'autorità della Bibbia.' Thus, for Pesce, Galileo affirms a 'disomogeneità epistemologica tra Scrittura e natura che non si può usare la Scrittura nelle "disputi di problemi naturali" ... In sostanza, la Scrittura è limitata in due modi convergenti: negli argomenti, e cioè fede costumi salvezza, e per il modo di conoscenza, perchè non rientra sotto la sua autorità tutto ciò che può essere dimostrato scientificamente.' 'L'interpretazione della Bibbia nella lettera di

It is important to recognize the Catholic tradition in which Galileo participates. The 'Letter to the Grand Duchess' is richly laced with quotations from the Church fathers, principally Augustine, all left in Latin: passages which lend authority to his arguments.[46] The passages quoted reinforce the general principles of the complementarity of science and Scripture, and the need to avoid naive, literalistic interpretations of the sacred text.[47]

In the absence of a scientific demonstration for the motion of the earth, Cardinal Bellarmino in 1615 had urged prudence: do not challenge the traditional readings of those biblical passages which have been interpreted as affirming the mobility of the sun and the immobility of the earth. The Cardinal was acutely aware of Protestant challenges to the Catholic Church's claim to be the sole, legitimate interpreter of God's word. It seems that Bellarmino was more concerned with maintaining the authority of the Church to be the authentic interpreter of Scripture than he was in refining principles of biblical exegesis.[48] Nevertheless, on the level of fundamental principles concerning the relationship between science and Scripture, Cardinal Bellarmino and Galileo were in agreement, just as they were in agreement concerning the Aristotelian requirements for scientific knowledge.

Galileo a Cristina di Lorena e la sua ricezione. Storia di una diffocltà nel distinguere ciò che è religioso da ciò che non lo è ', *Annali di storia dell'esegesi*, 4 (1987), 250–1. Pesce has recently responded to my criticisms: id. 'Gli ingegni senza limiti e il pericolo per la fede', in J. Montesinos and C. Solís (eds.), *Largo Campo di Filosofare: Eurosymposium Galileo 2001* (The Canaries: Fundación Canaria Orotava de Historia de la Ciencia, 2001), 637–59.

[46] There are twenty-seven citations of authors; fifteen from Augustine (all from *De Genesi ad litteram*); see Pesce, 'L'interpretazione della Bibbia', for some analysis of these citations.

[47] Galileo quotes Augustine's advice that one should be prudent in interpreting those passages of Scripture which deal with 'matters that are obscure and far beyond our vision since different interpretations are sometimes possible without prejudice to the faith we have received. In such a case, we should not rush in headlong and so firmly take our stand on one side that, if further progress in the search for truth justly undermines this position, we too fall with it. That would be to battle not for the teaching of Holy Scripture but for our own, wishing its teaching to conform to ours, whereas we ought to wish ours to conform to that of Sacred Scripture.' *De Genesi ad litteram*, I. 36.

[48] See Blackwell, *Galileo, Bellarmine, and the Bible*, 24, and Fabris, *Galileo Galilei e gli orientamenti esegetici del suo tempo*, 43–4.

There is something more in Galileo's arguments, more than the traditional affirmation that God is the author of the book of nature and the book of Scripture and that the truths of nature and the truths of Scripture cannot really be in conflict. In the letter to the Grand Duchess there is an additional argument, not well developed in his earlier letters on the subject: an argument which concerns the role of science in discovering the true senses of those scriptural texts which address scientific questions.

When one is in possession of knowledge about questions of nature which are not matters of faith, based on indubitable demonstrations or sensory experience, since such knowledge is also a gift from God, one must apply it to the investigation of the true meanings [*veri sensi*] of Scripture in those places which apparently seem to read differently. These senses would unquestionably be discovered by wise theologians [*indubitatamente saranno penetrati da' sapienti teologi*], together with the reasons for which the Holy Ghost sometimes wished to veil itself under words with a different meaning [*velare sotto parole di significato diverso*].[49]

Galileo argues that there is not simply a complementarity between the Bible and science, in that the truth of one cannot contradict the truth of the other, but that there also must be a concordance between science and those passages in the Bible which appear to make claims about the physical nature of the universe.

In a March 1615 letter to Piero Dini, a friend in Rome, who had advised Galileo about objections to Copernican astronomy from Cardinal Bellarmino, based on verses from Psalm 19 in which the

---

[49] In two other passages Galileo makes the same point:
'[H]aving become certain of any physical conclusions [*venuti in certezza di alcune conclusioni naturali*], we ought to utilize these as the most appropriate aids in the true exposition [*alla vera esposizione*] of the Bible and in the investigation of those meanings which are necessarily contained therein [*quei sensi che in loro necessariamente si contengono*], for these [meanings] must be concordant [*concordi*] with demonstrated truths [*le verità dimostrate*].'
'[Since] two truths cannot contradict one another [*due verità non possono contrariarsi*] ... it is the function of wise expositors [of Scripture] to seek out the true senses [*i veri sensi*] of scriptural texts. These will unquestionably accord [*indubitabilmente saranno concordanti*] with the physical conclusions [*conclusioni naturali*] of which we are already certain and sure [*certi e sicuri*] through manifest sense or necessary demonstrations [*senso manifesto o le dimostrazioni necessarie*].' Galileo, *Lettere*, 131, 134, and 145; Drake, *Discoveries and Opinions of Galileo*, 183, 186, and 199; and Finocchiaro, *The Galileo Affair*, 93, 96, and 105.

Sun 'comes out' of the tent pitched for it by God and runs its course through the heavens, Galileo offers an elaborate exegesis of these verses, showing how the new astronomy allows one to read the biblical text with greater insight. Galileo observes: 'when sacred texts have to be reconciled with new and uncommon physical doctrines, it is necessary to be completely informed about such doctrines, for one cannot tune two strings by listening to just one'.[50] Here again we see Galileo's commitment to a concordance between the Bible and science.

In the 1613 letter to Castelli and then, more amply, in the 1615 letter to the Grand Duchess, Galileo examines the passage from the Book of Joshua in which the sun stands still: a passage frequently referred to as being inconsistent with the new astronomy. Galileo notes that if one were to take Joshua's words according to their surface meaning 'this passage shows clearly the falsity and impossibility of the Aristotelian and Ptolemaic world system, and on the other hand agrees very well with the Copernican one. ... It is absolutely impossible to stop the sun and lengthen the day in the system of Ptolemy and Aristotle, and therefore either the motions must not be arranged as Ptolemy says or we must modify the meaning of the words [*alterar il senso delle parole*] of Scripture.'[51]

In the letter to the Grand Duchess, Galileo concludes his exegesis of the story of Joshua's commanding the sun to stand still by pointing out that theologians who now find biblical statements contrary to Copernican astronomy do so only because they consider the new astronomy to be false. But these same theologians who consider such passages incapable of being interpreted consistently with the new astronomy, 'as long as they regard it to be false [*mentre la reputan falsa*], would find highly congenial interpretations for these passages [*ne troverebbono interpretazioni molto ben congruenti*], if the new astronomy were known to be true and demonstrated [*quando ella fusse conosciuta per vera e dimostrata*]'. Such congenial or concordant interpretations would surely follow if these theologians 'were to add

[50] '[Q]uando si abbino a concordar luoghi sacri con dottrine naturali nuovi e non communi, è necessario aver intera notizia di tali dottrine, non si potendo accordar due corde insieme col sentirne una sola.' Galileo, *Lettere*, 119; Finocchiaro, *The Galileo Affair*, 62–3.

[51] Finocchiaro, ibid. 53.

some knowledge of the astronomical sciences to their expertise about Holy Writ. ... Just as now, when they consider it [Copernican astronomy] false, they think that whenever they read Scripture they only find statements repugnant to it, so if they thought otherwise they would perchance find an equal number of passages agreeing with it [*altrettanti di concordi*].'[52]

R. Hooykaas is correct when he observes: 'In Galileo's view ... Scripture, which at first sight was accommodating itself to the vulgar opinion on the world system, was using this opinion as a veil through which the learned could perceive scientific truth. The supposed conformity of the two Books, Scripture and Nature, which led literalists to the condemnation of the Copernican system, served Galileo for its verification, and in this respect he used the same method as his opponents.'[53]

The key for theologians in Rome, as well as for astronomers and philosophers, is Galileo's conditional statement: 'quando ella fusse conosciuta per vera e dimostrato'. In the absence of such a demonstration, how ought the theologians to proceed? Despite all the rhetoric of necessary demonstrations throughout the letter to the Grand Duchess,[54] Galileo never offers a demonstration for the motion of the earth and the stability of the sun.[55]

Frequently scholars have been troubled by what they consider to be an inconsistency between Galileo's claim that the Bible is not relevant to the natural sciences and Galileo's use of passages from the Book of Joshua to support Copernican astronomy.[56] But as we have seen,

[52] Ibid. 115.

[53] R. Hooykaas, *Religion and the Rise of Modern Science* (Edinburgh: Scottish Academic Press, 1972), 126.

[54] For an analysis of Galileo's rhetoric, see J. D. Moss, *Novelties in the Heavens: Rhetoric and Science in the Copernican Controversy* (Chicago: University of Chicago Press, 1993).

[55] There is considerable disagreement concerning Galileo's ultimate judgement concerning his proposed demonstration for the motion of the earth based on the phenomena of the tides. In 1615 and 1616 he was convinced that such a demonstration would work, although he had yet to perfect it. William Wallace argues that by the time Galileo writes the *Dialogo* he has come to recognize the inadequacy of the argument. ('Galileo and Aristotle in the *Dialogo*', 311–32.)

[56] E. McMullin, 'Introduction', in *Galileo, Man of Science*, ed. E. McMullin (New York: Basic Books, 1967), 32–5; and id. 'From Augustine to Galileo', *The Modern Schoolman*, 76 (January/March 1999), 183–94.

Galileo does not deny all authority to the Bible in discovering the truths of nature.[57] Furthermore, we must remember the rhetorical or strategic unity in the letter. Galileo was employing every argument at his disposal to persuade the Inquisition not to condemn the new astronomy.[58] Similarly, when Galileo, in other passages, notes that unproved physical propositions which contradict biblical passages ought to be rejected (on the grounds that truth cannot contradict truth), he is convinced that he is on the verge of demonstrating the truth of Copernican astronomy.

Galileo's confidence in discovering the true senses of biblical passages concerning natural phenomena sets Galileo apart from the more circumspect positions of Augustine and Aquinas. It is a confidence shared by Galileo's opponents in the Inquisition, although they reached a different conclusion when they examined the particular case of Copernican astronomy.[59] The theologians of the Inquisition concluded [in 1616] that the claim that the sun was immobile and at

[57] The passage quoted by McMullin to support his claim that Galileo does affirm that it is not the purpose of the Bible to provide scientific truths is the translation by Drake which omits the adverb 'principalmente' and thus reads: 'the authority of the Bible was designed to persuade men of those articles and propositions which, surpassing all human reason ...'

[58] Mauro Pesce observes that the inconsistencies, or alleged inconsistencies, in the letter to Christina need to be seen as part of a 'funzione tattica'. Pesce thinks that the principal problem is the concordist position at the very end of the letter when Galileo uses the story of Joshua to support Copernican astronomy. Pesce does not see the concordist principles that Galileo has already enunciated. But Pesce is correct, I think, to recognize that 'Al criterio della coerenza interna va sostituito quello della coerenza strategica, senza però rinunciare affatto a individuare un nucleo più autenticamente galileiano nel pensiero ermeneutico delle lettere.' 'Una nuova versione della lettera di G. Galilei a Benedetto Castelli', 105.

[59] That the theologians of the Inquisition came to a conclusion different from the one reached by Galileo concerning a reading of the Bible in the light of Copernican astronomy does not mean that they did not share fundamentally the same principles of biblical interpretation, especially the principle of accommodation. In addition to the general analysis of R. Hooykaas and the extensive discussion by R. Blackwell, see I. A. Kelter, 'The Refusal to Accommodate: Jesuit Exegetes and the Copernican System', *Sixteenth Century Journal*, 262 (1995), 273–83; F. Laplanche, 'Herméneutique biblique et cosmologie mosaique', in *Les églises face aux sciences du Moyen Age au XXe siècle* (Geneva: Librairie Droz, 1991), 29–51; G. Leonardi, 'Verità e libertà di ricerca nell'ermeneutica biblica cattolica dell'epoca galileiana e attuale', in *Galileo Galilei e Padova: Libertà di Indagine e Principio di Autrorità—Atti del Convegno e del Simposio Novembre 1982–Gennaio 1983*, Rivista di Scienze Religiose (Padua: Studia Patavina, 1983), 109–47; A. Fantoli, *Galileo: Per il Copernicanesimo e per la Chiesa* (Vatican City: Specola Vaticana, 1993); and McMullin, 'Galileo on Science and Scripture'.

the centre of the universe was 'foolish and absurd in philosophy, and formally heretical since it explicitly contradicts in many places the sense of Holy Scripture, according to the proper sense of the words and according to the common interpretation and understanding of the Holy Fathers and the doctors of theology'.[60] The theologians also concluded that the claim that the earth moves was foolish and absurd in philosophy and, 'in regard to theological truth it is at least erroneous in faith'.[61]

The first part of each of the two conclusions reached by the theologians of the Inquisition is that Copernican astronomy 'is false and absurd' [*stultam et absurdam*] philosophically. Why should the theological experts of the Inquisition care whether Copernican astronomy is false scientifically? First of all, there is the ancient Catholic commitment to the safeguarding of reason since, as Aquinas would say, reason is a way to God. Aquinas, himself, will refer to those propositions about God, such as that he exists, which serve as preambles to faith. More importantly for our purposes, I think, is that these theologians were committed to the complementarity

[60] 'Omnes dixerunt dictam propositionem esse stultam et absurdam in philosophia, et formaliter haereticam, quatenus contradicit expresse sententiis sacrae Scripturae in multis locis secundum proprietatem verborum et secundum communem expositionem et sensum Sanctorum Patrum et theologorum doctorum.' S. M. Pagano, and A. G. Luciani (eds.), *I documenti del processo Galilei* (Vatican City: Libreria Editrice Vaticana, 1984), 99 [punctuation added]. Finocchiaro (*The Galileo Affair*, 344 n. 35) observes that the original Vatican MS (fo. 42r) has a semicolon after 'philosophia' and Favaro's *Le opere* of Galileo (xix: 321) has a comma. Finocchiaro notes that Pagano's transcription 'conveys the impression that biblical contradiction is being given as a reason for ascribing both philosophical-scientific and theological heresy'. When Pesce ('L'interpretazion della Bibbia nella letter di Galileo a Cristina di Lorena e la sua ricezione ...', 264) quotes this text he omits any punctuation.

[61] 'Omnes dixerunt, hanc propositionem [the second] recipere eandem censuram in philosophia; et spectando veritatem theologicam, ad minus esse in fide erronea.' The expression 'in fide erronea' distinguishes the second condemnation from the first. The scriptural affirmations concerning the stability of the earth permit a broader interpretation than do those concerning the motion of the sun. This same distinction can be found in a 1613 letter to Galileo from Cardinal Conti concerning the relationship between Scripture and Copernican astronomy: 'e questa pare meno conforme alla Scriptura: perchè, se bene quei luoghi dove si dice la terra sii stabile et ferma, si possono intendere della perpetuità della terra, nondimeno dove si dice che il sole giri e i cieli si muovono, non puole havere altra interpretazione, se non che parli conforme al commun modo del volgo; il quale modo di interpretare *senza gran necessità non si deve ammettere*.' (Galileo, *Le opere*, xi. 354–5; my italics.) Note how similar this is to Bellarmino's observation that 'if there were a demonstration ...'

between science and Scripture. In reaching the conclusion that Copernican astronomy *contradicts* the Bible, the theologians accepted as incontrovertibly true a particular geocentric cosmology, and on the basis of such an acceptance, they insisted that the Bible be read in a certain way. Thus, in part, they subordinated scriptural interpretation to a physical theory. They proceeded in this manner because, like Galileo, they were convinced that the Bible contained scientific truths and that, on the basis of what is known to be true in the natural sciences, one could discover the same truth in related biblical passages.[62] Rinaldo Fabris observes that the 'orientamento concordista nell'interpretare i testi biblici' was characteristic of theologians contemporary with Galileo. He notes that Nicolò Serario (1555–1609), Giovanni De Pineda (1558–1637), and others when they discussed briefly Copernican astronomy declared that this 'opinion' was at variance with both philosophy and sacred Scripture.[63]

Galileo's theological claims are part of the traditional heritage of Catholicism, and further, they are a part of the theological

---

[62] Walter Brandmüller points out that Galileo's theological opponents failed to interpret the literal sense of Scripture in an adequate way, even though they had at their disposal both a tradition (from Augustine and Aquinas) and the views of contemporary exegetes which would have been sufficient for the task. 'L'errore dell'Inquisizione fu proprio questo. Prigoniera dell'assolutizzazzione della lettera biblica, la maggior parte degli esegeti di quel tempo non fu in grado di fare propria, per esempio, la posizione già presa dal cardinale Tommaso De Vio, detto il Gaetano, oppure di presagire i risultati dell'ermeneutica biblica del secolo XX. Non si faceva ancora parola dei diversi modi di esprimersi della Bibbia: i cosidetti *generi letterari.*' Recognizing that Galileo invokes principles of biblical interpretation that have their origin in Augustine, Brandmüller unfortunately (so it seems to me) continues: 'Galileo aveva proposto un metodo di interpetazione che oggi qualunque teologo, per quanto riguarda l'essenza, potrebbe tranquillamente sottoscrivere.' *Galileo e la Chiesa ossia il diritto ad errare,* 195–6.

[63] Fabris, *Galileo Galilei e gli orientamenti esegetici del suo tempo,* 39. Above all, however, 'nell'applicazione di tale criterio ermeneutico [i.e. to discover the literal sense of the Bible] nell'esegesi prevale la prospettiva teologica, acuita dalle preoccupazioni apologetiche e contraversistiche. All'intorno di questa prospettiva appare ancora confusa la linea di demarcazione tra l'affermazione di fede e l'interpretazione storico-culturale della realtà. Alle soglie del metodo e sapere scientifico non appare chiara la distinzione tra concezione ideologica e formula scientifica. Parimenti agli inizi dell'esegesi storico-critica non è distintamente definito il confine tra formulazione storico-culturale del testo biblico e la sua valenza religiosa-teologica.' Ibid. 44.

environment of the Counter-Reformation Church.[64] The Council of
Trent's injunctions concerning the proper reading of Scripture are
accepted by both Galileo and the Inquisition.[65] A crucial feature of
the disputes of the Reformation was the calling into question by the
Reformers of the very criterion of truth by which one resolves
theological questions, namely, the Catholic Church's claim to be
the authentic judge of all such disputes. Although Protestants and
Catholics would disagree about the role of the Church as a criterion
of truth, they could however, and they did, appeal to a common text,
the Bible: a text, which, in a sense, standing alone, served as the only
common ground from which to argue. Both sides, thus, were encouraged to find in the Bible evidence for their respective theological
conclusions. The Bible, therefore, came to be treated as a reservoir of
conflicting theological propositions, of proof-texts to be used in
arguments against one's opponents. As a result of such a 'proposi-
tionalization' of the Bible, Protestants and Catholics tended to treat
the Bible as a theological textbook: a compendium of syllogisms or
dogmatic propositions. One of the obvious dangers in viewing the
Bible as a textbook in theology is a literalistic reading of the text, a

---

[64] Blackwell, *Galileo, Bellarmine, and the Bible*; Arnold Williams, *The Common
Expositor: An Account of the Commentaries on Genesis 1527–1633* (Chapel Hill, NC:
University of North Carolina Press, 1948); Fabris, *Galileo Galilei e gli orientamenti
esegetici del suo tempo*; Leonardi, 'Verità e libertà di ricerca nell'ermeneutica biblica
cattolica dell'epoca galileiana e attuale', 109–47; and Carlo-Maria Martini, 'Gli
esegesis nel tempo di Galileo', in *La Parola di Dio alle origini della chiesa* (Rome:
Biblical Institute Press, 1980), 67–87, are particularly useful in describing the Catholic exegetical tradition at the end of the sixteenth century.

[65] The key passage comes from the fourth session of the Council of Trent: 'The
council further decrees, in order to control those of unbalanced character, that no
one, relying on his personal judgment [*suae prudentiae innixus*] in matters of faith
and morals [*in rebus fidei et morum*] which are linked to the establishment of
Christian doctrine [*ad aedificationem doctrinae christianae pertinentium*], shall dare
to interpret the sacred scriptures either by twisting its text to his individual meaning
[*ad suos sensus contorquens*] in opposition to that which has been and is held by holy
mother church, whose function is to pass judgment on the true meaning and
interpretation of the sacred scriptures [*iudicare de vero sensu et interpretatione
scripturarum sanctarum*]; or by giving it meanings [*interpretari audeat*] contrary to
the unanimous consent of the fathers [*unanimem consensum patrum*], even if interpretations of this kind were never intended for publication.' N. Tanner, (ed. and tr.),
Decrees of the Ecumenical Councils (London: Sheed & Ward, n.d.), ii. 664. Blackwell,
Galileo, Bellarmine, and the Bible, 5–14, offers an excellent analysis of this decree.

literalism which was all too apparent in the Inquisition's reaction to the perceived threat of the new astronomy. Do we not see a similar tendency in Galileo's insistence that we can discover scientific propositions in the Bible? Armed with scientific demonstrations we, or at least wise expositors, possess the key to discover those scientific propositions which are contained in the Bible.

CONCLUSION

Galileo the theologian does not anticipate some modern distinction between the religious character of the Bible and the claims of science; rather, he embraces ancient traditions of Catholic theology and also affirms principles of biblical exegesis characteristic of Counter-Reformation Catholicism. Particular arguments he sets forth in his letters concerning science and Scripture have been used to support what has come to be accepted as a characteristically modern understanding of the autonomy of the natural sciences with respect to the Bible. As he often remarked, in discussing questions of nature one ought not to begin with biblical passages. But he also argues that in the absence of scientific demonstrations one ought to adhere to the knowledge of nature found in the Bible.

It may very well be that the natural sciences today eschew the Aristotelian ideal of knowledge through causes—but Galileo, at least, accepted such a view and is thus, in this sense, more closely connected with his Aristotelian contemporaries and forebears than he is with how today science has come to be seen. Writing, near the end of his life (1640), to Fortunio Liceti in Bologna, Galileo claimed:

against all reason I am impugned as an impugner of the Peripatetic doctrine, whereas I claim (and surely believe) that I observe more religiously the Peripatetic or I should say Aristotelian teaching than do many who wrongfully put me as averse from good Peripatetic philosophy. ... I consider ... that to be truly Peripatetic—that is, an Aristotelian philosopher—consists principally in philosophizing according to Aristotelian teachings, proceeding from those methods and with those true *supposizioni* and principles on which scientific discourse is founded, supposing the kind of general knowledge from which one cannot deviate without the greatest defect. Among these *supposizioni* is everything that Aristotle teaches us in his logic, pertaining to care in avoiding fallacies in discourse, using reason well so as to syllogize properly and deduce from conceded premises the necessary conclusion. ... In this matter, therefore, I am a Peripatetic.[66]

---

[66] Galileo, *Le opere*, xviii. 248.

6

Copernicanism, Jansenism, and Remonstrantism in the Seventeenth-Century Netherlands

Tabitta van Nouhuys

INTRODUCTION

According to the Dutch historian of science Reyer Hooykaas, the Reformation contributed greatly to the rise of modern science. According to the Reformed way of thinking, Man was created by God with the power to scrutinize and understand nature, and had a duty to do so; the idea of the priesthood of all believers was conducive to the idea that both Scripture and nature were to be studied, and could fruitfully be studied, by each individual directly, without the intervention of tradition or interpretation by others. These ideas are of course related to the famous Merton thesis. Not only did Hooykaas devote his energies to explaining the link between Protestantism and science in general; he also wrote specifically on the reception of particular, novel scientific theories. In an article on Copernicanism in England and the Netherlands, he treated the enthusiasm of certain Dutch and English Protestants for the heliocentric theory, and claimed that Catholic contemporaries such as Galileo and Gassendi believed all or most of the Calvinistic scholars in the Netherlands to have been Copernicans.[1] There are, however,

---

[1] Hooykaas, R., 'The reception of Copernicanism in England and the Netherlands', in *The Anglo-Dutch Contribution to the Civilization of Early Modern Society. An Anglo-*

some problems about the evidence he adduces for this claim. It is true that Galileo in his letter to Ingoli wrote that he had heard that the most famous 'heretics' were all Copernicans, but he mentions neither the Dutch Republic nor Calvinism.[2] It seems more likely that he had in mind people such as Kepler, Mästlin, or Rothmann (or just possibly Lansbergen, virtually the only Dutch Copernican at the time, as we shall see shortly). As for Gassendi, during his 1629 visit to the Netherlands he did write to Fabri de Peiresc that 'all these people are for the motion of the earth', as Hooykaas quotes,[3] but looking at the original context it becomes clear that he in fact referred to a group of four people he had met in Breda, two of whom were French (the two Dutchmen being Lansbergen and Issac Beeckman).[4]

We may wonder whether Hooykaas's positive relation between Dutch Calvinism and Copernicanism is not a touch exaggerated. This chapter is an attempt to elucidate the attitude of scholars in both the Protestant Dutch Republic and the Catholic Southern Netherlands to the 'heterodox' scientific theory of Copernicus. If Hooykaas's claim is justified, we would expect the scholars in the North to be more enthusiastic Copernicans than those in the South, especially of course after the condemnation of Galileo, which would have deterred Catholics from being positively inclined towards heliocentrism.

In order to examine this issue, I have selected four figures, two from the North and two from the South, who are interesting both for their religious orthodoxy or heterodoxy, and for their—positive or negative—attitudes to Copernicanism. They are Philip van Lansbergen, a Protestant, possibly Remonstrant, Copernican, and Gisbertus Voetius, a staunchly Calvinistic anti-Copernican, from the North, and Godefridus Wendelinus, an orthodoxly Catholic Copernican, and Libertus Fromondus, a Jansenist anti-Copernican, from the

---

Netherlands Symposium (Oxford: Oxford University Press, 1976), 33–44, at 41–2. See also Hooykaas's preface to his edition of *G. J. Rheticus' Treatise on Holy Scripture and the Motion of the Earth, Verhandelingen der Koninklijke Nederlandse Akademie van Wetenschappen, Afdeling Letterkunde*, NS 124 (Amsterdam: North-Holland, 1984), 182.

[2] Galileo to Francesco Ingoli, in A. Favaro (ed.), *Le opere di Galileo Galilei. Edizione nazionale* VI (Florence: G. Barbèra, 1904), 511.

[3] Hooykaas, 'Reception', 42.

[4] P. Tamizey de Larroque (ed.), *Lettres de Peiresc* (Paris: A. Picard 1893), iv. 201–2.

South. I will examine each in turn, and will touch upon the connections and intellectual contacts between the four, to see whether there are any straightforward relations between their religious stance and their attitude towards Copernicanism. Is there any evidence for Hooykaas's idea, that Protestants were more positively inclined to Copernicanism than Catholics? Were those whose religious ideas were 'orthodox' (either within the Catholic or within the Protestant Church) more averse to the heterodoxy of Copernicus? Were their writings on Copernicanism really about Copernicanism at all, or were they merely weapons in some other, essentially religious, contest? These are the questions I will try and address.

Before I start out, I would like to emphasize that obviously the labels 'orthodox' and 'heterodox' are not by any means fixed. Whether we designate a seventeenth-century author as orthodox or heterodox depends to a large extent on whether we choose to adopt their own, or their contemporaries', definition of orthodoxy. Lansbergen, for instance, may have been regarded as heterodox in the post-1618 Republic (that is, after the purge in which Remonstrants were removed from public office), certainly by someone like Voetius, but he will have regarded himself as perfectly orthodox. Fromondus, the Jansenist, was called a heretic by the Jesuits and the Vatican, but was himself convinced of the orthodoxy of his stance. Similarly, Copernicanism was seen by some as a heterodox doctrine, but obviously not by the Copernicans themselves.

PHILIP VAN LANSBERGEN: A REMONSTRANT COPERNICAN?

The most controversial of the four authors was Philip van Lansbergen. Controversial in his own time, that is, as one of the first realist Copernicans, but also controversial to the historian, because it is difficult to pin down what exactly his religious convictions were. Was he a Remonstrant or not?

Philip van Lansbergen was born in Ghent, in the Southern Netherlands, in 1561, before the onset of the Dutch Revolt, when all the Netherlands were still united under Habsburg rule. His parents were

Reformed, and had to flee after the Iconoclasm of 1566: first to France, then to England, where Philip was educated (probably within the London community of Dutch Reformed exiles, though it is not easy to find any evidence for this). Having studied theology in England, he returned to the Netherlands in 1578 or 1579 to become a minister at Antwerp. When this city succumbed to the army of the Duke of Parma in 1585, all Protestants were forced to convert or leave. Like so many others, Philip left for the Northern Netherlands, studied theology at the newly founded university of Leiden, and, in 1586, was appointed a minister in Goes, in Zeeland. There, he was the subject of a rather mysterious scandal which ultimately led to his expulsion from the ministry.[5]

At a special meeting of the Zeeland Synod in Goes in 1613, Lansbergen and one of his sons, also a minister, were expelled 'because of considerable ill-will towards them among the magistrates of the city of Goes'.[6] There seem to have been several controversies around Lansbergen which led to this outcome. One of these was of a medical nature: Lansbergen, who, despite a prohibition in Goes for ministers to do so, kept a medical practice in addition to his ecclesiastical duties, had administered 'pulvis panchrestus', a medicine concocted by himself containing moschus, to a woman in labour, who had unfortunately died soon afterwards. This incident created a

---

[5] For Lansbergen's life, see A. A. Fokker, 'Philippus Lansbergen en zijne zonen Pieter en Jacob. Bijdrage tot hun leven', in *Archief. Vroegere en latere mededeelingen voornamelijk in betrekking tot Zeeland, uitgegeven door het Zeeuwsch Genootschap der Wetenschappen* I (1856–63), v. 52–100; J. van der Baan, 'Philippus en Petrus Lansbergen. Eene bijdrage, als toevoegsel aan die van Dr. A.A. Fokker', in *Archief. Vroegere en latere mededeelingen voornamelijk in betrekking tot Zeeland, uitgegeven door het Zeeuwsch Genootschap der Wetenschappen* (1869), 205–27; 'Coetus extraordinaris, gehouden binnen der stede Goes, ende begonnen den eersten Octob. 1613, ten overstaan van de Ed. heeren Tenys ende Steengracht, Gedeputeerde Raden der Ed. Mog. heeren Staten van Zeelant, daertoe special. gecommitt. van de voorsz. heeren van den Rade in dato van den 24 Sept. lestleden', in J. Reitsma and S. D. van Veen (eds.), *Acta der provinciale & particuliere Synoden gehouden in de Noordelijke Nederlanden gedurende de jaren 1572–1620 v. Zeeland 1579–1620, Overijssel 1584–1620* (Groningen, 1896), 112–43; Jona Willem te Water (ed.), *Kort verhaal der Reformatie van Zeeland in de zestiende eeuwe; benevens eenige eenige verhandelingen dienende tot ophelderinge van de historie der kerk-hervorminge aldaar: begonnen door den Wel Eerwaarden Heer Willem te Water, in zijn leven Predikant laatst te Axel* (Middelburg, 1766), 278–86; *Nieuw Nederlands Biografisch Woordenboek*, ii. 775–82.

[6] Reitsma and van Veen (eds.), 'Coetus', 130.

controversy among Zeeland physicians, some of whom sided with Lansbergen, while others strongly condemned him. The affair became the subject of a large number of tracts, and made Lansbergen notorious among medics throughout the country.[7]

Fokker, a Dutch historian who has made a detailed study of this affair, is convinced that, despite the medical subject-matter of the dispute, the real reason for its protracted and acerbic nature lay elsewhere. He suggests that Philip Lansbergen was expelled from the ministry because of his religious liberalism, for political reasons, and because of his Copernicanism.[8] During the last few years before his removal from office, Lansbergen had had several quarrels with the Goes city government about the election of a certain Cornelis Zoetwater to the post of mayor; in particular, the government was annoyed at the fact that Lansbergen had, during his sermons, counselled his flock to vote against Zoetwater (allegedly because Zoetwater was a crypto-Catholic). This kind of political question was not to be treated in church, in the magistrates' opinion.[9]

It has further been suggested that there was a link between Lansbergen's disgrace and his Copernican views. There is little concrete, contemporary evidence for this, and Copernicanism is not mentioned in the Acts of the Synod that expelled Lansbergen. However, three quarters of a century later, in 1679, a student at Utrecht defended a disputation in which he stated that 'The Zeeland theologians believed that such a book [Lansbergen's *Uranometria*] could not be published by a member of the church without grave offence. And for this reason the author was at their behest expelled, and his appeal to the Synod of Zeeland was not granted.'[10]

---

[7] See e.g. Cornelis Liens, *Concertatio epistolica cum adversariis Phil. Lansbergii* (Zierikzee, 1614); David Ultralaeus, *Tractatus medicus perbrevis, in quo succincte ac disposite disputatur an puerperae liceat exhibere moschum* (Middelburg, 1613); Cornelius Herls, *Examen tractatus medici de Moscho* (Middelburg, 1613); Jacob van Lansbergen, *Disputatio epistolaris Reverendi viri D. Philippi Lansbergii cum doctissimis medicinae doctoribus Middelburgensibus ... Cum apologia D. Jacobi Lansbergii ...* (Middelburg, 1613); Cornelius Herls, *Responsio ad apologiam Jacobi Lansbergii* (Middelburg, 1613); Hieronymus Smallegange, *Examen quaestionis medicae. An puerperae ... tuto et ex arte possit exhiberi Moschus* (Middelburg, 1613).

[8] Fokker, 'Philippus Lansbergen en zijne zonen', esp. 57–8, 69, and 76.

[9] Ibid. 97–9; see also van der Baan, 'Philippus en Petrus Lansbergen', *passim*.

[10] The student's name was Cornelis Snouk. The sentence from his disputation is quoted in Jona Willem te Water, *Kort verhaal der Reformatie van Zeeland in de zestiende eeuwe* (Middelburg, 1766), 282.

Lansbergen's Copernicanism was very outspokenly realistic: he believed the earth, in reality, revolved round the sun. The Ptolemaic system was physically impossible for a number of reasons, such as the impossibility for the eighth sphere of the fixed stars to move at such a high speed as would be required, given the true dimensions of the universe, in a geocentric scheme.[11]

Lansbergen believed any biblical arguments against heliocentrism to be spurious, because Scripture did not pronounce on matters that were not relevant to salvation.[12] Here, Lansbergen shows himself an adherent of the theory of accommodation, which held that the Holy Spirit had not written the Bible in order to teach mankind about nature, and that scientific theories ought not therefore to be judged by reference to Scripture. This was an old theory: it is to be found in St Augustine and in Calvin, and Kepler and Galileo used it to justify their own Copernicanism. However, in Lansbergen's work, it gained additional significance because of the contemporary religious debates in the Netherlands.

There was a strong religious aspect to Lansbergen's Copernicanism. He believed that the dimensions of the Copernican universe, with its harmonious proportions, had been created by God in order to reveal his power and majesty to man. Lansbergen's universe was divided into three 'heavens', with the sun at their centre: the first was the heaven of the sun, with the planets, including earth, revolving round it; the second was the heaven of the fixed stars, which was immensely bigger than the first, the first being nothing but a point in relation to the second; the third was the throne of God, the abode of the blessed after death. It was the highest and invisible heaven; yet it was intimately connected with the other two, as 'the energies of all three heavens are directed at the same work, in order to perfect it'.[13]

The sun had been placed at the centre for a purpose: not only to illuminate the entire first heaven, but also to enable all the planets to partake of its 'life-giving power' (*vivifica vis*), which was needed for generation. As Hermes Trismegistus said, 'the sun is the visible image of an invisible God'.[14] Moreover, the heavens also contained

---

[11] Philippus Lansbergius, *Commentationes in motum terrae diurnum & annuum* (Middelburg, 1630), 3–6.
[12] Ibid. 11 ff.   [13] Ibid. 32–3.   [14] Ibid. 38.

an image of the Holy Trinity (see St John's 'Three that bear record in heaven, the Father, the Word, and the Holy Ghost, and these three are one'). There were three bodies in heaven that illumined the earth: the sun, the moon, and the air around the earth, and their light was one and the same.[15] The sun was 'a seipso', like the Father: contained by itself, it brought forth its own light. In the same way as the Son proceeded from the Father, so the moon proceeded from the sun, as its light derived from the sun. The air, with its luminous qualities, derived from sun and moon together. The sun had been placed in the centre so that all those who did not possess the written Word of God might nonetheless get to know him and worship him, by seeing the sun.[16]

Earth was in the middle between the three lower and the three higher planets. If it had been placed in the middle of the first heaven, it would have been too far removed from the throne of God; also in its actual position it was able to receive the influences of all the other planets. The earth's daily movement had been created by God in order to allow man to share in the light, warmth, and life-giving power of the sun, while its annual motion existed for us to be able to admire God's works. In particular, it allowed man to measure the heavenly dimensions accurately, which was essential as they reflected God and his Wisdom. Also, seeing the heavens in their full glory showed man that after this life, he was to possess the heavens.[17]

The fact that the exact dimensions of the heavens were recently revealed to man, through the Copernican theory, was a sign of the impending Second Coming of Christ, in the same way that the revelation of the dimensions of the temple in Ezekiel's dream was a sign of its rebuilding.[18]

The vast space between the sphere of Saturn and the second heaven of the fixed stars was peopled with all kinds of creatures of a spiritual or demonic nature. These were the devil and the fallen angels, as well as good angels who had descended from the third heaven. There was continuous strife between the good and the bad angels, both in the second and in the first heaven, and on earth itself.[19]

---

[15] Ibid. 39.   [16] Ibid.   [17] Ibid. 41–4.   [18] Ibid. 45.
[19] Ibid. 53–5.

It is interesting to note Lansbergen's interpretation of the famous passage in Joshua 10, where Joshua commands the sun and moon to stand still in order to prolong the day. This passage was, of course, often quoted in support of a moving sun, the argument being that if it does not move, it cannot be commanded to stand still. Lansbergen, without elaborating, simply quotes the passage as evidence of the fact that God can command the *stars* to stand still if he so wishes.[20]

It will have become clear from this selection from Lansbergen's ideas that his Copernicanism was to a large extent religiously inspired. Virtually all the above ideas are supported in his book by ample references to the Bible, which the author took literally (such as the devils and angels, the location of the third heaven, etc.). He was certainly not averse to the literal interpretation of biblical passages, but his literalism is of a particular sort. It is very reminiscent of Kepler's kind of Copernicanism, with its theological implications, such as the deduction of the existence of the Trinity from the constitution of the heavens, and the endowing of the sun with a life-giving force which is essential to the harmony of the heavens. Much of it was inspired by Neoplatonist and Hermetic ideas. We shall see that Wendelin's 'Catholic Copernicanism' was of a very different, indeed, much more level-headed nature; much more reminiscent of Galileo's style of reasoning.

There is a possibility that Lansbergen's religious convictions were regarded as unorthodox by the faction within the Dutch Reformed Church that became dominant after 1618 and usurped for itself the epithet of 'orthodox'. More particularly, there are some indications that he may have been a Remonstrant or have had Remonstrant sympathies. 'Remonstrantism' referred to the set of beliefs espoused by the Remonstrants, the followers of the theology of Arminius, one of the protagonists of a theological dispute at the university of Leiden. In brief, Arminius held that, despite the Fall, man had retained his responsibility for his actions and could make a free choice between salvation and damnation, while his opponent Gomarus adhered to a strictly interpreted doctrine of predestination. The quarrel over predestination became tied up with political issues as well: Arminianism, or Remonstrantism, affiliated itself with

[20] Philippus Lansbergius, *Commentationes in motum terrae diurnum & annuum* (Middelburg, 1630), 58.

tolerance in religious matters and the right of civil authority to oversee the Church, while the Gomarists or Counter-Remonstrants upheld the idea that the authorities were not to exercise any power in religious matters. By 1617, Dutch society had become deeply divided by these issues.

The conflict ended in the defeat of the Remonstrants. In the autumn of 1618 a National Synod assembled in Dordrecht, the vast majority of whose participants were Counter-Remonstrants. In May 1619, they condemned the Remonstrants as heretics and disturbers of state and Church. Those Arminian preachers prepared to recant were required to subscribe to a formula of submission pledging adherence to the Netherlands Confession and the Heidelberg Catechism, and acceptance of the Acts of the National Synod. Most Remonstrants refused to sign; they were banished from the Republic and settled at Antwerp.[21]

As we have seen, Lansbergen was expelled from the ministry in 1613, five years before the Synod—which would explain why he did not fall victim to the purge if he really was a Remonstrant—but at a time when the quarrels were already well underway. We do not possess much evidence as to Lansbergen's stance in the controversy. Yet we know that two of his close relatives (his brother Franciscus and his nephew Samuel) were Remonstrant ministers in Rotterdam, one of the strongholds of Arminianism. Franciscus was deposed in the purges of 1619 and remained 'unemployed' until 1626, when the tide had turned somewhat and it once again became possible for Remonstrants to hold office.[22] Samuel, interestingly, was one of the ten Remonstrant ministers who held what was dubbed an 'Anti-Synod' in Dordt in 1619, intended to promote the unity of the Remonstrant brethren.[23] The leaders of the Synod were not amused,

---

[21] On the strife between Arminians and Gomarists, see A. Th. van Deursen, *Bavianen en Slijkgeuzen* (Assen: van Gorcum, 1974); Jonathan Israel, *The Dutch Republic. Its Rise, Greatness, and Fall 1477–1806* (Oxford: Oxford University Press, 1995), 411–63; I. Schöffer, 'De Republiek der Verenigde Nederlanden 1609–1702', in I. Schöffer, H. van der Wee, and J. A. Bornewasser (eds.), *De Lage Landen van 1500 tot 1780* (Amsterdam: Elsevier, 1978), 167–267.

[22] See *Nieuw Nederlands Biografisch Woordenboek*, ii, s.v. 'Franciscus van Lansbergen' and 'Samuel Lansbergen'.

[23] See Johannes Tideman, *De Remonstrantsche Broederschap. Biographische naamlijst van hare Professoren, Predikanten en Proponenten, met historische aanteekeningen omtrent hare kweekschool en gemeenten* (Haarlem, 1847), 29–31 and 50.

and all ten were banished; however, they vowed that they would continue to preach, and they refused to sign the 'Akte van Stilstand'. Samuel preached in secret until the 1630s, when he returned to his Rotterdam parish. In addition to his regular duties, he started organizing conventicles or 'colleges', modelled on those of the Rijnsburger Collegianten, a sect which was associated by orthodox Calvinists with Socinianism and heresy.[24]

There is no hard evidence linking Philip's persuasions with those of his brother and nephew, but it is interesting material all the same. Moreover, there are certain marked similarities between Philip's 'theory of accommodation' and the beliefs of the Remonstrants. In his 'Confession of the Remonstrant Ministers', their leader Simon Episcopius stressed the central importance of distinguishing between truths necessary to salvation, and what he called 'unnecessary truths'. The former were very few in number, while concerning the latter, each individual was to be left free to decide what to believe. Thus, those who felt inclined to expound the Scriptures according to their own mind, were not to be convicted of heterodoxy, let alone heresy.[25] Episcopius held that the authority of Scripture was not to be questioned *in matters necessary unto Salvation*, 'by which we only understand those things, without which it is utterly impossible for any Man either to obey the Commandments of Jesus Christ aright and as he ought, or firmly to believe his Divine Promises'.[26] Thus, 'the best interpretation of Scripture is that which most faithfully expresseth the native and literal sence [*sic*] therof, or at least cometh nearest to it, as that alone which is the true and living Word of God ... Now we call the native and literal sence, not so much that, which the words properly taken hold forth ... as that, which though the words rigidly taken do not insinuate or hint it, yet is most agreeable

---

[24] See W. J. Kühler, 'Remonstranten en Socinianen', in G. J. Heering (ed.), *De Remonstranten. Gedenkboek bij het 300-jarig bestaan der Remonstrantsche Broederschap* (Leiden: Lijthoff, [1919]), 137–59 at 148. See also Andrew Fix, 'Radical Reformation and Second Reformation in Holland: The Intellectual Consequences of the Sixteenth-Century Religious Upheaval and the Coming of the Rational World View', *Sixteenth Century Journal*, 18 (1987), 63–80 at 68.

[25] [Simon Episcopius], *The Confession or Declaration of the Ministers or Pastors, which in the United Provinces are called Remonstrants, concerning the chief points of Christian Religion* (London, 1676), 28–31.

[26] Ibid. 72.

to right reason, and the very mind and intention of him that uttered the words, whether it were expressed properly or figuratively'.[27] In 1612, both Franciscus and Samuel Lansbergen published tracts to the same effect.[28]

It is not hard to see the similarities between these ideas and Lansbergen's enunciation of the accommodation theory. The Bible was authoritative, but it was not necessarily its literal interpretation that lent it such authority. It contained many *adiaphora*, matters which were beside the direct purpose of the divine author, and which could therefore safely be interpreted according to right reason. On the other hand, this may not mean anything. We have no direct evidence of Lansbergen's Remonstrantism, and against it can be said that his treatise on the movement of the earth was prefaced with a laudatory poem by Daniel Heinsius, Leiden professor and Counter-Remonstrant. Then again, Gomarus himself remained on friendly terms with Remonstrants such as Gerardus Johannes Vossius throughout his life.

Be this as it may, what *is* clear is that at least one person strove to establish a strong connection between Lansbergen's Copernicanism and the Remonstrant heterodoxy. That person was Gisbertus Voetius.

VOETIUS: ORTHODOX CALVINIST
AND ANTI-COPERNICAN

Voetius was a remarkable figure. He personified the struggle against Remonstrantism, Socinianism, Pelagianism, atheism, scepticism, Epicureanism, libertinism, Cartesianism, Enthusiasm, Catholicism, and in general any other 'heresy' that diverged from his own strictly

---

[27] Ibid. 75.

[28] Samuel Lansbergius, *Christelijcke aenleydinghe tot vrede ende onderlinge verdraechsaemheyt over de huydensdaechsche verschillen* ... (Rotterdam, 1612); Franciscus Lansbergius, *Kort ende christelijck Examen over de Leerpoincten die ten huydighen daghe in gheschil ghetrocken werden ofte het fondament der saligheyt raken ofte niet? Hoe weynich datse importeren ende hoe men dezelfde zonder quetsinghe van fondamentele waerheyt d'een met den anderen kan vereenighen ofte ten minste verdraghen* (Rotterdam, 1612).

defined kind of Calvinist orthodoxy. For, it has to be said, he was a Calvinist of a particular kind, and is probably not representative of the views of many within the Republic whose orthodoxy, by the standards of the Synod of Dort, was beyond doubt.

Voetius, born in 1589, taught at Leiden by Gomarus, was a Counter-Remonstrant and a prominent member of the Synod of Dordt. After an early career as a minister, he was appointed to the Utrecht chair of theology and Hebrew in 1634, which he retained till he died. There, he became the founder and tireless propagator of a movement within the Calvinist church known as the Further Reformation. This movement has been characterized as the Dutch Reformed mode of Pietism.[29] It strove to achieve the personal sanctification of each believer, as well as the radical and total sanctification of all areas of life, and placed great emphasis on true piety, personal self-examination for the marks of the works of the Holy Spirit and the temptations of the devil, and a life in strict agreement with biblical commandments. Ministers were to maintain strict discipline among their flocks.[30] All this earned Voetius the nickname of 'Papa Ultrajectinus', the Utrecht Pope.[31]

During Voetius's professorship at Utrecht, the spirit of the times was not too conducive of such ideas. The repression of Remonstrantism had virtually ended, and other dissenting voices, such as those of the Rijnsburg Collegiants, began to be heard. Also, Voetius objected

[29] Fred A. van Lieburg, 'From Pure Church to Pious Culture: The Further Reformation in the Seventeenth-Century Dutch Republic', in W. F. Graham (ed.), *Later Calvinism. International Perspectives* (Kirksville, Mo.: Sixteenth-Century Journal Publishers, 1994), 409–29 at 413.

[30] On the Further Reformation, see van Lieburg, 'Pure Church to Pious Culture'; Willem J. Op 't Hof, 'Die Nähere Reformation und der Niederländische reformierte Pietismus und ihr Verhältnis zum deutschen Pietismus', *Nederlands Archief voor Kerkgeschiedenis*, 78 (1998), 161–83; Fred A. van Lieburg, *De Nadere Reformatie in Utrecht ten tijde van Voetius. Sporen in de gereformeerde kerkeraadsacta* (Rotterdam: Lindenberg, 1989); C. J. Meeuse, *De toekomstverwachting van de Nadere Reformatie in het licht van haar tijd* (Kampen: de Groot Goudriaan, 1990); Willem J. Op 't Hof, 'Het culturele gehalte van de Nadere Reformatie', *De zeventiende eeuw*, 5 (1989), 129–40.

[31] Nickname coined by Pierre du Moulin, *Papa Ultrajectinus* (Utrecht, 1668). On Voetius's life, see A. C. Duker, *Gisbertus Voetius* (Leiden: Brill, 1897–1915); and the essays in J. van Oort, C. Graafland, A. de Groot, and O. J. de Jong (eds.), *De onbekende Voetius. Voordrachten wetenschappelijk symposium Utrecht 3 maart 1989* (Kampen: Kok, 1989), esp. Aart de Groot, 'Voetius' biografie', at 84–91.

to what he considered the laxity of the public authorities, who failed adequately to repress such ungodliness. Finally, and most importantly, he abhorred the rise of the Cocceians (so named after Voetius' rival Johannes Cocceius), who embraced the new philosophy of Descartes, and whom Voetius was quick to denounce as the 'new Arminians'.[32]

Voetius's efforts to eradicate Cartesianism are probably the best known aspect of his campaign against ungodliness. In a protracted series of acerbic exchanges duing the 1640s, he accused Descartes of being an atheist, not because he denied God's existence, but because his ideas implied that God did not exist (a charge he also levelled at the Remonstrants). Descartes strove to attain the kind of knowledge that was unattainable for human beings, whose knowledge could only be based upon belief in divine revelation on the one hand, and sense experience on the other. Descartes's efforts to divorce philosophy from these two anchors, and base it on reason alone, were bound to fail, according to Voetius.[33]

It has been maintained that Voetius became interested in refuting Copernicanism because heliocentrism was an integral part of Cartesianism, against which he was waging a bitter campaign. There is certainly a lot of truth to this: some of the anti-Copernican works by Voetius and especially by his pupil Maarten Schoock were certainly designed to reinforce the battle against Descartes. It is, however,

---

[32] On Voetius and the Cocceians, see Ernestine van der Wall, 'Orthodoxy and Scepticism in the Early Dutch Enlightenment', in Richard H. Popkin and Arjo Vanderjagt (eds.), *Scepticism and Irreligion in the Seventeenth and Eighteenth Centuries* (Leiden: Brill, 1993), 121–41; E. van der Wall, 'Cartesianism and Cocceianism: A Natural Alliance?', in M. Magdelaine et al. (eds.), *De l'humanisme aux Lumières. Bayle et le protestantisme* (Paris/Oxford: Universitas/Voltaire Foundation, 1996), 445–55.

[33] On Voetius's attacks on Cartesianism, see Theo Verbeek, 'From "Learned Ignorance" to Scepticism: Descartes and Calvinist Orthodoxy', in Popkin and Vanderjagt (eds.), *Scepticism and Irreligion*, 31–45, esp. 37; Th. Verbeek, 'Descartes and the Problem of Atheism: The Utrecht Crisis', *Nederlands Archief voor Kerkgeschiedenis*, 71 (1991), 211–23; T. A. McGahagan, 'Cartesianism in the Netherlands 1639–1676: The New Science and the Calvinist Counter-Reformation' (Ph.D., Pennsylvania, University Microfilms 1976); Th. Verbeek, 'Tradition and Novelty: Descartes and some Cartesians', in Tom Sorell (ed.), *The Rise of Modern Philosophy* (Oxford: Oxford University Press, 1993); Ernst Bizer, 'Reformed Orthodoxy and Cartesianism', *Journal for Theology and the Church*, 2 (1965), 20–82; Theo Verbeek, *Descartes and the Dutch. Early Reactions to Cartesian Philosophy 1637–1650* (Carbondale: Southern Illinois University Press, 1992).

arguable that there was a different and equally important reason why Voetius became interested in blackening Copernicus's reputation; and that this reason was precisely the similarity between the Copernicans' theory of accommodation and the theology of the Remonstrants.

In 1635, Voetius published a work entitled *Thersites Heautontimoroumenos.*[34] This work was a reply to a book by the Remonstrant minister Jacobus Johannes Batelier (the 'Thersites' of the title) who had in the previous year published an *Examen* of Voetius's inaugural lecture, held in Utrecht that same year; a work, moreover, highly praised by the Remonstrant leaders Wtenbogaert and Episcopius.[35] Batelier had resigned his ministry in 1618 and had been formally deposed by the Synod of Dordt in 1619; since then, he had made his living by teaching privately, and was in close touch with the Rijnsburg Collegiants. From 1633, he was a Remonstrant minister in The Hague.[36]

Voetius had felt it necessary to reply to the 'insults' which Batelier had levelled at him in his *Examen*. He compiled a list of 'Novelties, Paradoxes and Heterodoxies' espoused by Batelier.[37] Chief among these was the idea that the words of Scripture were not to be taken in their accurate, literal sense in so far as they did not deal with the essential elements of religion.[38] In this context, Voetius went on to consider the Copernican theory. After a brief overview of the many theologians who had held that the earth was stationary, and after pointing out that the Copernican observations were not guaranteed to be better than those of Ptolemy and Tycho, Voetius came to his main point: the connection between Remonstrantism and Copernicanism, both of which he considered to be forms of atheism. 'I hold

---

[34] Gisbertus Voetius, *Thersites Heautontimoroumenos. Hoc est, Remonstrantium Hyperaspistes, catechesi, et liturgiae Germanicae, Gallicae, & Belgicae denuo insultans, retusus . . .* (Utrecht, 1635).

[35] [Jacobus Johannes Batelier], *Examen accuratum disputationis primae & quasi inauguralis D. Gisberti Voetii, quam proposuit in illustri gymnasio Ultrajecti die 3. Sept. stylo vet. Anno 1634* (s.l. 1634).

[36] On Batelier, see *Nieuw Nederlands Biografisch Woordenboek*, vi, s.v. 'Batelier, Jacobus Johannes of Watelier'; and P. T. van Rooden, 'Het beleid van de Waalse synode tijdens de Remonstrantse twisten', *Nederlands Archief voor Kerkgeschiedenis*, 62 (1982), 180–200.

[37] Voetius, *Thersites*, 44 ff.   [38] Ibid. 44–5.

that the motion of the earth is in flagrant contradiction of the Sacred Scriptures, and therefore I accuse whomsoever adheres to this theory, such as Philip van Lansbergen, of impiety.'[39] Like the Copernicans, he went on, so also have the Remonstrants, and in particular Arminius himself, held ideas that contradict the Scriptures. However, Voetius denied that Lansbergen had been foremost in his mind when he denounced Copernicanism in his lecture, which was not a direct attack on Lansbergen, as Batelier believed. However, Voetius did point out that the Remonstrants had from the beginning supported and shielded Lansbergen.[40]

Clearly, then, in Voetius's mind (as well as, presumably, in that of Batelier) Remonstrantism and Copernicanism were closely related. The rest of his chapter on Copernicanism is in fact a refutation of the Remonstrant theology, reiterating the point that if the whole Bible is not to be taken literally, and if the Holy Spirit is regarded as a liar, there is no way of knowing which bits are true and which are false. For how is it to be established what is pertinent to salvation and what is not? This will undermine the authority of Scripture and open the door wide to atheism and libertinism. The Copernicans are hypocritical, moreover: they themselves quote Scripture, in its literal interpretation, whenever it is convenient to them, while they refute the bits that do not accord with their ideas. In fact, the Copernicans have to rely on a multitude of false hypotheses in order to claim their theory is true: that the Holy Ghost not only does not tell the truth, but even tells blatant falsehoods; that the Holy Ghost does not care about human sciences such as chronology, astronomy, and geography, and does not care whether he makes Moses, David, and Solomon speak falsehoods in these fields, while at the same time, he has granted Copernicus and Kepler the illuminating grace to know the truth in these matters; that the prophets, patriarchs, kings, and priests were so stupid as not to be able to discover the truth, etc. etc.[41]

Thus, as early as 1635, just after his arrival in Utrecht and long before the Cartesian controversy broke out, Voetius was already vigorously opposed to Copernicanism, because it relied on the same atheistical principles as the Remonstrantism he had spent decades of his life combating. A few years later, in 1638, Batelier

[39] Ibid. 262.   [40] Ibid. 263–4.   [41] Ibid. 265–83.

replied to Voetius's accusations; in this reply, Copernicanism was again a prominent topic of dispute, with Batelier defending the Copernicans against Voetius's detractions. Here, Batelier expressly stated his belief that Voetius's sudden interest in Copernicanism was simply another way of attacking and libelling the Remonstrants.[42]

It is interesting to note that Voetius's dislike of scientific theories he considered to be heterodox did not confine itself to Copernicanism. In his huge collection of theological disputations, a recurrent theme is the absurdity and impiety of mystical ideas like those of the Lullists, Hermeticists, and Rosicrucians, as well as an intense mistrust of Paracelsism. These ideas, to Voetius, were just as likely to lead to enthusiasm and atheism as those of the Copernicans. For example, the idea that the stars and planets are moved by intelligences or souls is denounced as absurd,[43] as is the existence of occult powers of the stars and planets,[44] and the idea of the correpondence of microcosm and macrocosm.[45] Given the fact that these are recurrent themes in Voetius's work, we may wonder if one of the reasons for his dislike of Copernicanism, which he associated for the most part with Lansbergen and Kepler, may not have been the propensity of those authors for speculating about the occult influence of the sun on planetary motions, and their idea of finding the Trinity depicted in the arrangement of the heavens and the like. It seems likely that the kind of Copernicanism espoused by our third protagonist, Wendelinus, would have agreed much better with Voetius's ideas.

WENDELINUS: CATHOLIC COPERNICAN

Godefridus Wendelinus was born in Herk, a small town in the present-day Belgian province of Limburg, in 1580. He attended the Jesuit College at Tournai, after which he studied the arts, and later

---

[42] [Jacobus Johannes Batelier], *Gymnasium Ultrajectinum, seu Disputationis Theologicae, quae omnium prima Ultrajecti publice in Illustri tunc Gymnasio, nunc Academia, proposita fuit, Examen accuratum* (Utrecht, 1638), 351–84, esp. 354.

[43] Gisbertus Voetius, *Selectarum Disputationum Theologicarum Pars Prima* (Utrecht, 1648), 693.

[44] Ibid. 709.   [45] Ibid. 713–17.

Hebrew, at Louvain. From there, he embarked on a journey to Prague with one of his fellow students, probably in order to meet the great Tycho Brahe there. Unfortunately, the young Wendelin was afflicted with dysentery when they had got no further than Nuremberg, and decided to return home rather than travel on. He was not to stay at home for long: in 1599, still aged only 19, he travelled to France and Rome in order to obtain an indulgence for the Jubilee of 1600. On his way back, he settled in Provence, in the town of Digne, where he became a teacher. A few years later he became preceptor of the Arnaud family in Forcalquier, and as such he became acquainted with Fabri de Peiresc and Duvair, as well as Gassendi (whom he is said to have taught). Throughout this period, Wendelin made regular celestial observations, with a special interest in lunar eclipses.[46]

In 1612, he returned to the Southern Netherlands, where he was ordained and became a priest in several small parishes, before obtaining a prestigious canonry at Tournai cathedral. It seems that he was entirely orthodox in his religious beliefs; these seem to have been wholly uncontroversial, despite the fact that he lived in a country that was fiercely Counter-Reformed and quick to denounce any form of heterodoxy. He appears to have lived a quiet life of study and pastoral care. And yet, he was a convinced Copernican. Nor does it seem that he needed to be secretive about his astronomical beliefs. According to Mersenne, Wendelin defended the Copernican theory in front of the papal nuncio in the Southern Netherlands, Guido di Bagno.[47]

---

[46] On the life and works of Wendelin, see J. Vandikkelen, 'Bij de vierhonderdste verjaardag van de geboorte van Govaart Wendelen (1580–1667)', *Het Oude Land van Loon*, 35 (1980), 5–33; T. Dethier, 'G. Wendelen, de astronoom', *Het Oude Land van Loon*, 35 (1980), 35–41; Émile Jacques, 'Les Dernières Années de Godefroid Wendelen (Wendelinus) (died 1667)', *Lias*, 10 (1983), 253–71; Florent Silverijser, 'Godefroid Wendelen (1580–1667)', *Bulletin de Institut archéologique liégeois*, 58 (1934), 91–158, and 60 (1936), 137–90; Florent Silverijser, 'Een groot Limburger. Govaart Wendelen', *Limburg*, 3 (1921–2), 82 ff.; R. van Laere, 'Godfried Wendelen 1580–1667', *Spiegel Historiael*, 15 (1980), 544–9; Georges Monchamp, *Galilée et la Belgique. Essai historique sur les vicissitudes du système de Copernic en Belgique* (Saint-Trond: Moreau-Schouberechts, 1892); Constantin Le Paige, 'Un astronome belge du 17e siècle, Godefroid Wendelin', *Bulletin de l'Académie royale de Belgique*, ser. 3, 20 (1890), 709–27.

[47] Marin Mersenne, *Correspondance*, ed. P. Tannery and C. De Waard (17 vols.; Paris: Presses Universitaires de France, 1932–88), iii. 73 and 433.

Moreover, he published several books in which he made no secret of his adherence to heliocentrism.[48]

However, his reasons for espousing the theory were more purely astronomical than those of Lansbergen. In Wendelin's work, we find no trace of speculation about the abode of the blessed, the Trinity, or the presence of angelic intelligences in the heavens. His reasons for rejecting Ptolemy were those of a very scrupulous and level-headed observer, who discovered that what he saw could not be reconciled with the theories he had been taught. Several times in his astronomical works, he expressly stated that, although it was true that the Copernican universe was endowed with harmonic proportions, this was not the reason why he came to adhere to heliocentrism, as nothing would be more abhorrent to a mathematician. Rather, he arrived at his hypotheses on the basis of detailed and numerous observations, and was then pleasantly surprised to discover the harmony of the end result. It just happened to be the case that without the movement of the earth, not a single hypothesis could be framed that was consistent with the observations.[49]

In one of his works, Wendelin explicitly addressed the fact that Copernicanism was considered by many to be a heresy. He believed that Galileo had not dared to call the moon a second earth in his *Sidereus Nuncius* for fear of being declared a heretic. Later, of course, he had been condemned anyway, for expounding the heliocentric theory; yet, claimed Wendelin, he would have been considered even more heretical if he had also explicitly said the moon was a second earth (i.e. equally prone to generation and corruption). However, it was obvious not only that the earth moved, but also that the moon was another earth. In what way was such an opinion detrimental to religion? It had nothing to do with religion, but was neither more nor less than a necessary assumption in order to explain the way the earth and the moon moved. They must be of the same material, as they were both magnets capable of attracting and repelling each other, as Gilbert and Kepler had pointed out. Thus, the idea that the moon was a second earth was nothing more than common sense.[50]

---

[48] Notably his *Diluvium* (Antwerp, 1629); his *Tetralogia Cometica* (Tournai, 1653); and his *Loxias, seu de obliquitate Solis diatriba* (Antwerp, 1626).

[49] Manuscript published by Florent Silverijser, *Les Autographes inédits de Wendelin à la Bibliothèque de Bruges* (Louvain: Ceuterick, 1932), 149.

[50] Ibid. 160–1.

FROMONDUS: JANSENIST ANTI-COPERNICAN

One person who clearly saw a marked difference between Wendelin's commonsensical Copernicanism and Lansbergen's more religiously inspired version was Libertus Fromondus. Born in 1587 in the small village of Haccourt, in the prince-bishopric of Liège, he attended the Jesuit college in Liège, and went on to Louvain in 1604 to study the arts there. Shortly after his arrival at the university, he met and befriended Cornelius Jansenius, the man who unwittingly stood at the cradle of Jansenism, and who was later to play a great role in Fromondus's life. After graduating in 1606, Fromondus went on to teach philosophy at Louvain; from 1617 he also studied theology under Jansenius, with whom he shared a house. In 1628 Fromondus became doctor of theology, and in 1631, on the recommendation of Jansenius, he obtained one of the Louvain chairs in this subject. However, he maintained a life-long interest in natural philosophy and wrote several books on the subject, among which were two bulky works attacking Lansbergen's Copernicanism.[51]

Although, as a young man, Fromondus was quite well disposed towards Copernicanism, and very interested in Galileo's telescopic observations, the promulgation of the anti-Copernican decrees of 1616 and 1633 made him change his mind.[52] In a work he wrote on the comet of 1618, he retreated from his more overtly Copernican

[51] On Fromondus's life and works, see *Biographie nationale de Belgique* (28 vols. + suppl.; Brussels: H. Thiry-van Buggenhoudt (1866–1944), vii. cols. 312–17; L. Ceyssens, 'Le Janséniste Libert Froidmont (1587–1653)', *Bulletin de la société d'Art et d'Histoire du Diocèse de Liège*, 43 (1963), 1–46; H. Demaret, *Notice historique sur Libert Froidmont de Haccourt, Docteur en Théologie, Professeur de l'Université de Louvain etc., et son Mémorial* (Liège: H. Thiry-van Buggenhoudt, 1925); Georges Monchamp, *Galilée et la Belgique. Essai historique sur les vicissitudes du système de Copernic en Belgique* (Saint-Trond: F. Hayez, 1892), 34–53, 72–112; Georges Monchamp, *Histoire du cartésianisme en Belgique* (Brussels, 1886); and the collection of essays in Anne-Catherine Bernès (ed.), *Libert Froidmont et les résistances aux révolutions scientifiques. Actes du Colloque Château d'Oupeye, 26 et 27 septembre 1987* (Haccourt: Association des vieilles familles de Haccourt, 1988).

[52] See T. van Nouhuys, *The Age of Two-Faced Janus. The Comets of 1577 and 1618 and the Decline of the Aristotelian World View in the Netherlands* (Leiden: Brill, 1998), 240–7. Fromondus's youthful sympathy for the Copernican theory can be seen in Libertus Fromondus, *Saturnalitiae Caenae, Variatae Somnio, sive Peregrinatio Caelestis* (Louvain, 1616).

sympathies,[53] and in his two polemical attacks on Philip Lansbergen's Copernicanism, published in 1631 and 1634 respectively, he staunchly defended the anti-Copernican stance.[54] Whereas, in 1631, he did not yet declare Copernicanism a heresy, given the fact that those decrees which deal with dogmas of the faith need to be judged by the pope himself, and not just the cardinals,[55] by 1634 he had learned of the condemnation of Galileo, being in fact the first person to promulgate it in the Southern Netherlands, and the heresy of Copernicanism could no longer be called into question.[56]

However, Fromondus's main reason for writing his books against Lansbergen was religious in nature. He objected strongly to what he regarded as the Protestant character of Lansbergen's Copernicanism.[57] Accusing his opponent of trying, by means of his pious but senseless arguments, to prevent simple and uneducated people from returning to the Catholic Church, Fromondus attacked Lansbergen's defence of the freedom of believers to interpret the Bible for themselves.[58] To Fromondus, this Calvinistic idea was unacceptable: 'Although all can read the Scriptures, not everyone can understand

---

[53] See Libertus Fromondus, *Dissertatio de Cometa Anni 1618* in *De Cometa anni 1618, Dissertationes Thomae Fieni in Academia Lovaniensi Medicinae et Liberti Fromondi Philosophiae Professorum. In quibus tum istius motus, tum aliorum omnium essentia, effectus, & praesagiendi facultas declarantur* (Antwerp, 1619), 79–140, esp. 122–31.

[54] Libertus Fromondus, *Ant-Aristarchus, sive orbis Terrae immobilis liber unicus. In quo decretum S. Congregationis S.R.E. Cardinalium an. 1616 adversus Pythagorico-Copernicanos editum defenditur* (Antwerp, 1631); and Libertus Fromondus, *Vesta, sive Ant-Aristarchi Vindex, Adversus Iac. Lansbergium Philippi F. Medicum Middelburgensem* (Antwerp, 1634).

[55] Fromondus, *Ant-Aristarchus*, 27–9.

[56] Fromondus, *Vesta*, 'Ad Lectorem', where he denies ever having had any sympathy for the Copernican philosophy and publishes the literal text of the letter in which the papal nuntius in Brussels announced to Cornelius Jansenius, professor of theology at Louvain, that the Copernican theory had been condemned by the cardinals.

[57] See for example ch. IV of the *Ant-Aristarchus*, where Fromondus defends the authority of the pope to pronounce on natural philosophical issues against its Protestant detractors; or p. 164 in the *Vesta*, where Fromondus chides the Calvinists for telling lies to the common people and thus deterring them from returning to the 'orthodox' [Catholic] Church.

[58] Fromondus, *Vesta*, 169: 'Vos in sensu vestro pertinaces eritis, nos etiam SS. Patrum doctrinam non deseremus. An ad Spiritus Sancti privatum instinctum (ita enim vestri fere solent) decurret is, & in capitello potius vestro, quam in Ecclesiae Catholicae Capite, & SS. Patribus habitare eum existimavis?'

them,'[59] he said, strongly defending the idea of papal authority: one judge is needed, who alone can decide [on the Bible's interpretation], with the aid of the Holy Spirit. Without such a judge, there are as many opinions as there are people.[60] Moreover, Lansbergen's idea of possessing the heavens by being able to measure them, is totally unfounded: there is no authority for it anywhere in Holy Writ.[61] Fromondus strongly urges Lansbergen to return to the Catholic church, and to do away with his 'ridiculous Copernican theology'.[62]

Why, after having been a cautious but fairly enthusiastic supporter of Copernicanism, did Fromondus subsequently choose to write hundreds of pages of anti-Copernican polemic? Obviously, the most straightforward answer would be, because of the condemnation of Galileo. However, the first book against Lansbergen was written before that condemnation (though, admittedly, after the decree of 1616 which put Copernicus on the Index). Moreover, if the papal decrees had been the true reason for Fromondus's zeal, he would presumably not have continued to refer favourably to the ideas of his friend, the Copernican Wendelin. Yet he did: on several occasions in his *Vesta*, he mentioned 'our most learned friend Wendelin', who, 'though in his philosophy a Copernican',[63] derided certain aspects of Lansbergen's Copernicanism, such as the idea that the earth magnetically attracts the air around it. 'How much more careful and prudent than you are certain other Copernicans, prominent among whom is our famous Wendelin, who has deduced, from Holy Scripture, a most true chronology from the present back to the Deluge, and most consistent with the heavens, and who continues

---

[59] Ibid. 168: 'Quippe etsi omnes legere, non omnes tamen intelligere sacram Scripturam possunt.'

[60] Ibid. 169: 'Cernis ergo iam, si oculos non amisisti, omnem Ecclesiae christianae doctrinam in fluctum dari, & dum unum Capitis Ecclesiae tribunal declinatis, tot tribunalia condere, quot sunt crania in vestris capitibus.'

[61] Ibid. 160–2. On p. 162, Fromondus says: 'In imaginario etiam motus terrae fundo aedificata, imaginaria caelorum spatia, imaginarias siderum moles, denique imaginarium Nic. Copernici mundum, non illum divini Opificis a Moyse nobis descriptum, metitur [Lansbergius].'

[62] See the title of ch. XIX of the *Ant-Aristarchus*: 'Ridicula theologia Copernicana Lansbergij.'

[63] Fromondus, *Vesta*, 57: 'Eamdem virtutem magneticam telluri inculcat eruditissimus Wendelinus noster, qui etsi Philosophiâ Copernicanus, Lansbergium tamen ridet, miratur Keplerum.'

daily to uncover the secrets of nature!'[64] exclaims Fromondus at one point, while elsewhere, he describes Wendelin's exasperated reaction on first learning the details of Lansbergen's ideas. According to Fromondus, Wendelin, after reading Lansbergen's book, came running down to his friend in a rage, saying: 'For whom does this man write, for people, or for dolts? Truly it seems that along with the light of the orthodox faith, they have also rejected the natural light of reason. Where are the instruments, where the experiments, with which they claim to affirm the new theories?'[65]

Thus, it was not so much Copernicanism itself that aroused Fromondus's indignation; it was Lansbergen's 'Calvinist', heretical, kind of Copernicanism. It is important to bear in mind that at roughly the same time Fromondus wrote his anti-Copernican works, he was also engaged in a dispute with none other than Voetius and his pupil Maarten Schoock about which church was the true Church of Christ.[66] Combating Calvinism was clearly foremost in his mind at the time; it is ironic that he should have chosen, as one of the means of ridiculing Calvinism, to attack Copernicanism, whilst one

[64] Ibid. 78: 'Quanto circumspectiores & prudentiores vobis alij Copernicani, & inter eos primus Clarissimus Wendelinus noster, qui ex Scripturâ sacrâ verissimam & caelo consentientem Chronologiam hinc usque ad Diluvium deducit, plurimaque cottidie naturae arcana indidem eruere non cessat.'

[65] Ibid. 156: 'Et sane iudicium Clar. D. Wendelini nostri (Copernicanus etiam hactenus est, ne adversarum partium favore peccare existimes) de parentis tui Astronomiâ, vix est ut audeam tibi perscribere. Cum primum enim in eam incidisset, iratus & despuens domum nostram accurrit. "Et quibusdam illi homines scribunt," inquit, "hominibusne, an fungis? Profecto cum lumine orthodoxae Fidei, videntur naturale lumen intellectûs amisisse. Ubi instrumenta, ubi experimenta, quibus nova ista paradoxa, destructis veterum sententiis, oportebat struere & firmare?" '.

[66] The debate with Voetius had initially been entered into by Jansenius himself; see his *Alexipharmacum pro civibus Sylvae-Ducensibus adversus ministrorum suorum fascinum, seu Responsio brevis ad libellum eorum provocatorium* (Louvain, 1630), to which Voetius reacted with his *Philorium Romanum correctum. Hoc est, Notae & castigationes in declamatiunculam C. Jansenij, titulo Alexipharmaci civibus Buscodu-censibus propinati, &c. editam* (Dordrecht, 1630). Jansenius replied in his *Notarum Spongia quibus Alexipharmacum civibus Sylvae-Ducensibus nuper propinatum aspersit Gisbertus Voetius* (Louvain, 1631), to which Voetius retorted in his *Desperata causa papatus, novissime prodita a C. Iansenio [in Notarum Spongia]* (Amsterdam, 1635). At this point, Fromondus took over from Jansenius, writing a *Causae desperatae Gisb. Voetij ... adversus Spongiam ... Corn. Iansenij ... crisis* (Louvain, 1636), and a *Sycophanta, epistola ad G. Voetium* (Louvain, 1640) to which Voetius's pupil Martin Schoock replied in his *Auctarium ad Desperatissimam causam papatus, sive Responsio ad epistolam Liberti Fromondi ... quam inscripsit Sycophantam* (Utrecht, 1645).

of the very Calvinists he was disputing with had chosen the same means to ridicule, not Calvinism, but Remonstrantism.

Yet Fromondus himself was soon to be declared a heretic. When, in 1640, his close friend Jansenius died before having been able to see his life's work, the *Augustinus*, through the press, he in his will entrusted Fromondus with the publication of the monumental book. In it, Jansenius had expounded what he believed to be the true doctrine of Saint Augustine concerning divine grace and human free will. He hoped and trusted that his book would make a decisive contribution towards solving, in a historically accurate manner, what had long been the hottest issue in Counter-Reformation theology: the question of grace. Jansenius believed he had finally exposed the pure doctrine of Augustine, stripped of any subsequent accretions.[67]

However, the Jesuits, whose position on grace was radically different from that of Jansenius, got wind of the fact that Fromondus was printing a book on the subject. Calling upon a papal decree of 1625 by which it had been forbidden to discuss the question of grace, they demanded that printing be discontinued. Fromondus mounted a firm resistance in the face of his Jesuit opponents, who enjoyed the support of the Holy See.[68] He maintained that the decree of 1625 had never been promulgated in the Netherlands, and that he did not, therefore, consider himself bound by it. Even after the papal condemnation, in 1641, of both the *Augustinus* itself and all the writings that had appeared attacking or defending it, which included all of the apologies Fromondus himself had written for Jansenius, he remained an ardent defender of the irreproachability of the contents of his friend's book. All in all, Fromondus's name came to be mentioned eight times on the Index of Prohibited Books; several times, attempts were made to remove him from his Louvain chair of theology; and his candidature to the bishopric of Tournai was successfully

---

[67] On the papal concern over the question of grace, and the prehistory of Jansenius's involvement with Saint Augustine, see L. Ceyssens, 'Diepere gronden van het Jansenisme', *Tijdschrift voor theologie*, 6 (1966), 395–420 and L. Ceyssens, 'Le Drame de conscience augustinien des premiers jansénistes', in *Augustinus magister. Communications du congrès international augustinien* (Paris: Études Augustinennes, 1954), ii. 1069–76.

[68] Ceyssens, 'Diepere gronden', 408–16.

suppressed.[69] Yet, in spite of these hardships, and in spite of the papal condemnation of Jansenism on two occasions during his lifetime (in the 1642 bull *In eminenti* and the 1653 bull *Cum occasione*) Fromondus never wavered from his standpoint, that the *Augustinus* did not contain anything offensive, let alone heretical.

CONCLUSION

We can conclude that Hooykaas's thesis on the favourable attitude of Calvinists towards Copernicanism is less than accurate. Things were much less straightforward than that. It seems that neither Catholics nor Protestants were very concerned about Copernicanism as a heterodox theory. On those occasions when heliocentrism did become the subject of controversy, this happened in the context of other, essentially religious disputes, and was used as an additional way of blackening the reputation of the various opponents in these disputes. Nor is there any clear-cut relationship between heterodoxy in science and heterodoxy in religion: at times, they coincided (Lansbergen), at times they did not (Fromondus, Wendelin). On the whole it seems that in terms of scientific ideas themselves, religious disputes aside, Catholics and Protestants had much more in common than they themselves, at the time, would have wanted to admit.

[69] Ceyssens, 'Janséniste Libert Froidmont', 35–6.

7

When Did Pierre Gassendi Become a Libertine?

Margaret J. Osler

THE PROBLEM

Pierre Gassendi (1592–1655) is best known as the thinker who baptized the philosophy of Epicurus, hoping to provide a theologically acceptable alternative to Aristotelianism for seventeenth-century thinkers who were searching for a new philosophy of nature. Natural philosophers in the latter half of the seventeenth century regarded Gassendi as one of the founders of the new, mechanical philosophy of nature. Gassendi was a Catholic priest and canon of the cathedral at Digne in the south of France. During his lifetime, he had a reputation as a person of moderate habits who shared the Epicurean values of a quiet life that provided opportunities for the freedom to philosophize and the joys of friendship.[1] Despite his loyalty to his

I am grateful to Sarah Hutton who helped me plan the strategy for this chapter. Margaret Cook contributed useful research.

[1] Lisa Tunick Sarasohn, 'Epicureanism and the Creation of a Privatist Ethic in Early Seventeenth-Century France', in Margaret J. Osler (ed.), *Atoms, Pneuma, and Tranquillity: Epicurean and Stoic Themes in European Thought* (Cambridge: Cambridge University Press, 1991), 175–95. Gassendi's friend, the physician Guy Patin, described Gassendi as follows: 'They make a debauch, but God knows what a debauch. M. Naudé drinks nothing but water, and has never liked wine. M. Gassendi is so delicate that he would not dare to drink it, and imagines that his body would burn up if he had drunk of it.' Patin to Charles Falconet, 27 August 1648, in *Guy Patin and the Medical Profession in Paris in the XVIIth Century*, tr. Francis R. Packard (New York: Paul B. Hoeber, 1924; repr. New York: Augustus M. Kelley, 1970), 95.

ecclesiastical duties and the hundreds of pages he devoted to theological subjects, some twentieth-century scholars have described him
as a clandestine freethinker, one of the *libertins érudits* active in
France during the first half of the seventeenth century. How can
this apparent contradiction be resolved?

LIBERTINISM AND *LE CAS GASSENDI*

In the words of Ian Maclean, 'The word "*libertine*" emerged in the
late sixteenth century as a term of abuse directed at those who were
thought to have rejected traditional authority and were indifferent or
irreverent in matters of religion.'[2] In an influential scholarly study,[3]
René Pintard introduced the term '*libertins érudits*' to denote a
learned group of freethinkers, 'those who exhibit an excess of liberty
in the matter of morality and religion, by relation to that which
dogmas, traditions, customs, and perhaps politics define or recom-
mend'.[4] Because of the constraints of ecclesiastical and political
authority, these *libertins érudits* frequently wrote clandestine works
in an enigmatic style. For this reason, the attribution of libertinism to
a particular writer can involve acrobatic feats of interpretation. For
example, criticism of Aristotelianism or the endorsement of Epicureanism might be read as veiled attacks on theology and religion.
Discussion of such philosophies—even if explicitly disavowed by
their authors—is sometimes taken as evidence of subversive or
heterodox intent.[5]

---

[2] Ian Maclean, 'Libertins', in Edward Craig (ed.), *The Routledge Encyclopedia of Philosophy* (10 vols.; London: Routledge, 1998), v. 620.

[3] René Pintard, *Le Libertinage érudit dans la première moitié du XVIIe siècle* (2 vols.; Paris: Boivin, 1943).

[4] René Pintard, 'Les Problèmes et l'histoire du libertinage, notes et réflexions', *XVIIe Siècle*, 32 (1980), 132–3 and 138.

[5] It is worth noting that the term '*libertin érudit*' was not used in the seventeenth century and was not a term by which Pintard's cast of characters described them-selves. They did use such terms as '*esprits forts*' which they contrasted with the '*vulgaire*'. See Françoise Charles-Daubert, *Les Libertines érudits en France au XVIIe siècle* (Paris: Presses Universitaires de France, 1998), 5–14.

Such interpretative manœuvres have plagued *le cas Gassendi*. Since the publication of Pintard's massive study, many scholars have argued that despite his priestly vocation and the extensive theological discussion found in his writings, Gassendi was in fact a libertine or at least a fellow traveller. The allegation of libertinism has hinged on how commentators have interpreted his first published work, *Exercitationes paradoxicæ adversus Aristoteleos* (1624), a sceptical critique of Aristotelianism, and how they have construed the relationship between the *Exercitationes* and his later Epicurean project.

Pintard interpreted the apparent contradiction between the scepticism of the *Exercitationes* and the Christian Epicureanism of the *Syntagma Philosophicum* as the expression of a dual sensibility. In the early work, according to Pintard, Gassendi followed Pierre Charron (1541–1603) and espoused a complete scepticism, rejecting not only Aristotelian dialectic, physics, and ethics, but all dialectic, physics, and ethics. He adopted *nihil sciri* as his motto and denied the possibility of human knowledge.[6] But, as Pintard continued, Gassendi was of two minds: On the one hand, he did not want to offend the Church and risk suffering the fate of the heterodox thinkers, Giordano Bruno (1548–1600) and Giulio Cesare Vanini (1585–1619), both of whom had met their ends at the stake, or of Galileo Galilei (1564–1642), who had been hauled before the Inquisition and condemned for his endorsement of Copernican astronomy.[7] On the other hand, he did not want to limit his own intellectual freedom.[8] Thus, in the *Syntagma Philosophicum*, Gassendi cloaked his Epicureanism in a theological disguise. As evidence for Gassendi's libertinism, Pintard cited his close association with the well-known group of libertines in France,[9] noting that these sceptical writers found it necessary to assume a mask of orthodoxy. In order to read Gassendi as an advocate of Epicurean materialism, Pintard dismissed Gassendi's lengthy arguments for the immortality of the soul as the

---

[6] Pintard, *Le Libertinage érudit*, 479.

[7] Gassendi and his colleagues were less alarmed by Galileo's condemnation than is commonly thought. See Lisa T. Sarasohn, 'French Reaction to the Condemnation of Galileo: 1632–1642', *The Catholic Historical Review*, 74 (1988), 34–54.

[8] Pintard, *Le Libertinage érudit*, 155.

[9] Especially Elie Diodati (1576–1661), François de La Mothe le Vayer (1588–1672), Gabriel Naudé (1600–53), François Luillier (*c.*1600–51), and the physician, Guy Patin (1599–1672). Ibid. 125–208.

'*subterfuge d'un hérésiarche abois*' and claimed that Gassendi actually believed that 'the soul is material with no difference between man and beast'.[10] Although Pintard thought that Gassendi's youthful scepticism evolved into a kind of positivism in his mature philosophy, he interpreted Gassendi's theology as a mask adopted to ensure his freedom to philosophize. In addition, Pintard claimed that Gassendi's ethics, following Epicurus, was egoist, pagan, and independent of religion.[11]

Pintard's ideas have become received wisdom. In the decades following the publication of his book, several influential commentators adopted his interpretation of Gassendi as a libertine, suggesting various ways to explain away apparently anomalous evidence.

Olivier René Bloch, himself a materialist with an interest in clandestine literature,[12] regards Gassendi's theological objections to his opponents, both ancient and modern, as 'the seasoning of a polemic whose point was purely secular and scientific'.[13] Bloch sees Gassendi as a closet materialist who used methods of dissimulation similar to those employed by Bayle and the Encyclopedists and argues that Gassendi used the language of orthodoxy in a superficial way to

---

[10] Ibid. 487.

[11] Ibid. 490–2. There is an extensive literature discussing and extending Pintard's work. See e.g. G. Spini, *Ricerca dei libertine. La teoria dell'impostura delle religione nel Seicento italiano* (Rome: Editrice Universale de Roma, 1950); J. S. Spink, *French Free-Thought from Gassendi to Voltaire* (London: Athlone, 1960); Antoine Adam, *Les Libertines au XVIIe siècle* (Paris: Buchet Chastel, 1964); *Aspects du libertinisme au XVIe siècle. Actes du Colloque International de Sommières* (Paris: Vrin, 1974); T. Gregory, G. Paganinni, G. Canziani, O. Pompeo Faracovi, and D. Pastini (eds.), *Ricerche su littérature libertina e letteratura clandestine nel seicento* (Florence: La Nuova Italia, 1981); and two special issues of the journal *XVIIe Siècle*—32/127 (April/June 1980) (*Apects et countours du libertinage*) and 37/149 (October/December 1985) (*Libertinage, literature et philosophie au XVIIe siècle*). More recent studies of *libertinage érudit* tend to exclude Gassendi from discussion. See Louise Godard de Donville, *Le Libertin des origines à 1665: un produit des apologétes* (Paris: Papers on French Seventeenth Century Literature, 1989). Charles-Daubert, in *Les Libertines érudits*, criticizes Pintard's sociological and psychological approach to the question of *libertinage érudit* and prefers an analysis of their ideas. Significantly, she does not include Gassendi among the libertines she discusses.

[12] Olivier René Bloch, *Le Matérialisme* (Paris: Presses Universitaires de France, 1985), 124–5, and id. (ed.), *Le Matérialisme et la littérature clandestine* (Paris: La Nuova Italia Editrice, 1982).

[13] Olivier René Bloch, *La Philosophie de Gassendi: Nominalisme, matérialisme, et métaphysique* (The Hague: Martinus Nijhoff, 1971), 312; my translation.

mask the profane materialism that he really espoused. To support this contention, Bloch cites what he interprets as various anomalies and juxtapositions of contradictory theses within Gassendi's writings. Since Gassendi the priest could not openly endorse materialism, the tensions in his thought must, according to Bloch, be interpreted as evidence of deliberate dissimulation.[14] Bloch defends this claim by insisting that Gassendi interpolated the abundant theological material into the section of the *Syntagma Philosophicum* called 'Physics' in the early 1640s, and then only in order to hide his materialism of which he was becoming increasingly aware.[15] Like Pintard, Bloch regards Gassendi's arguments for the existence of God, his providential concern with the creation, finality in the natural world, and the immateriality and immortality of the human soul as window dressing, designed to disguise the actual materialism of his enterprise.[16]

Tullio Gregory, who wrote a book on Gassendi's scepticism forty years ago,[17] has recently included Gassendi among the sceptics and libertines because of his constant appeal to nature and history rather than faith or revelation.[18] According to Gregory, Gassendi shared these naturalist views with François de La Mothe le Vayer, Gabriel Naudé, and other notorious libertines.[19]

---

[14] Ibid. chs. 9–11.　　[15] Ibid. 476–81.　　[16] Ibid. 369 and 374.

[17] Tullio Gregory, *Scetticismo ed empirismo: Studio su Gassendi* (Bari: Laterza, 1961).

[18] Gregory enumerates the following criteria for libertinism: 'First, an erudition that recovers and makes use of classical antiquity well beyond Renaissance humanist traditions concerned with reconciling pagan and Christian. Second, a detached scepticism that rejects the dogmatic, finding in the critical exercise of reason its proper task ... Third, a radical relativism strengthened by the experience of the diverse that denies universal values and reduces ethical norms and religious practices to historical origins. Fourth, an elitist understanding of culture and wisdom as the possession of the 'esprit fort', the free person, and not therefore communicable to the common man ... Fifth and last, a continual appeal to nature as the area within which every natural phenomenon can be located, and as the zone proper to humankind.' Tullio Gregory, ' "Libertinisme Érudit" in Seventeenth-Century France and Italy: The Critique of Ethics and Religion', *British Journal for the History of Philosophy,* 6 (1998), 329.

[19] 'First the stars, then heroes and emperors, were turned into divine entities— with the construction of a pantheon similar to human kingdoms—followed by legislators determined to repress men's wicked passions. These inculcated the belief that a divine nature permeated all creation and observed the most hidden crimes. The result was that men would be punished, if not in this life, then in the next, in an

Did Gassendi, in fact, share the views of his libertine friends, or has he suffered from guilt by association? My reading of Gassendi's writings does not support the view that he was either a sceptic, a materialist, or a libertine. On the contrary, his ideas were deeply informed by his particular theological views that he discussed repeatedly throughout his lifetime.

GASSENDI'S EPICUREAN PROJECT

Examination of Gassendi's writings and the nature of his Epicurean project contradicts the claim that he was a sceptic, a materialist, or a libertine. All of the claims to the contrary rest on the assumption that the various contradictions within his writings are evidence of subterfuge. I am more inclined to interpret them as signs of change and development, and, at a deeper level, to see an underlying consistency and unity in his thought. His fundamental principles—a voluntarist theology, an empiricist epistemology, a nominalist or conceptualist account of universals, and an anti-essentialist metaphysics—remained constant throughout his writings. These are the themes that bind his various works together, and they belie the accusation of libertinism.

Gassendi's first published work, the *Exercitationes paradoxicae adversus Aristoteleos*, was an outgrowth of his lectures on Aristotelian philosophy during his six years of teaching at the University of Aix.[20] Influenced by his reading of the works of various anti-Aristotelian and sceptical writers, Gassendi became very critical of—not to say impatient with—Aristotelian philosophy.[21] Rather than teach

underworld where torments are prepared. Then came philosophers who refined this primitive idea of God, attributing to Him whatever they held to be most appropriate to illustrate his majesty.' Ibid. 333.

[20] Pierre Gassendi, *Dissertations en forme de paradoxes contres les Aristotéliciens* (*Exercitationes paradoxicae adversus Aristoteleos*), bks. I and II, tr. Bernard Rochot (Paris: J. Vrin, 1959), 6–7; in Pierre Gassendi, *Opera Omnia* (6 vols.; Lyons, 1658; facsimile repr. Stuttgart-Bad Canstatt: Friedrich Frommann, 1964), iii. 99–100.

[21] Among those he cited are Spanish humanist Juan Luis Vives (1492–1540), the anti-Aristotelian philosopher Gianfrancesco Pico della Mirandola (1469–1533), the logician and educational reformer Peter Ramus (1515–72), and Montaigne's disciple in scepticism Pierre Charron (1541–1603).

Aristotle, he taught against Aristotle: 'I always made sure that my auditors could defend Aristotle perfectly; but ... I also presented them the principles by which the teachings of Aristotle could be completely destroyed.'[22]

Although he published only Book I of the *Exercitationes* in 1624 and then suppressed Book II in 1625 until it finally saw the light of day in 1649, he had originally planned to write seven books, systematically refuting every aspect of Aristotelian philosophy.[23] The extant books indicate just how thoroughly he intended to demolish Aristotelian philosophy. Gassendi not only claimed that it was full of contradictions and empty of meaning, but also that it was useless as a method for natural philosophy. He repeatedly criticized Aristotelianism for providing no insight into the structure or function of things in the natural world. Mocking Aristotelian science, which was based on the concepts of matter, form, and privation, he asked what those concepts teach us about the real world known by observation—things like the minute organs of the mite, which the recently invented microscope had revealed.[24] As his correspondence with Nicolas-Claude Fabri de Peiresc (1580–1637) and other natural philosophers demonstrates, Gassendi was deeply interested in the astronomy and natural philosophy of his day. The ability of a philosophy to describe a method suitable for the pursuit of knowledge of the world was of critical importance to him. Although he criticized Aristotelianism on sceptical grounds, Gassendi's conclusions were not sceptical. He

---

[22] Gassendi, *Exercitationes*, 6–7, in *Opera Omnia*, iii. 99–100.

[23] Although Rochot identifies Gassendi's reference to 'Mirandulanus' in the Preface of the *Exercitationes* as Gianfrancesco's more famous uncle, the Renaissance humanist and cabbalist Giovanni Pico della Mirandola (1463–94), Schmitt makes a compelling argument that the reference is to the nephew Gianfrancesco, who had made an 'extensive critique of the philosophy of Aristotle using a sceptical approach' in his *Examen vanitatis doctrinae gentium* (1520). Basing his argument on a close comparison of Pico's *Examen vanitatis* and Gassendi's *Exercitationes*, Schmitt demonstrates a resemblance so close that it is convincing of filiation. See Gassendi, *Exercitationes*, 6–7, 11 n. (in *Opera Omnia*, iii. 100); Bernard Rochot, *Les Travaux de Gassendi sur Epicure et sur l'atomisme, 1619–1658* (Paris: J. Vrin, 1944); and Charles B. Schmitt, *Gianfrancesco Pico della Mirandola (1469–1533) and His Critique of Aristotle* (The Hague: Martinus Nijhoff, 1967), 175–8. Gregory also notes the relationship between the two texts. See Gregory, *Setticismo ed empirismo*, 24–5, 33, 40–1.

[24] Gassendi, *Exercitationes*, 488–91, in *Opera Omnia*, iii. 203–4.

sought a method for pursuing an empirically based natural philosophy that he already conceived in Epicurean terms.

In the *Exercitationes*, Gassendi used the methods of the sceptics, especially the arguments of Sextus Empiricus (AD *c*.200), to argue that science in the Aristotelian sense is impossible. In the course of this demonstration, Gassendi enunciated a new definition of 'science', laid the foundations of his empiricist epistemology, denied the independent existence of universals, and articulated his anti-essentialist metaphysics. According to Gassendi, the Aristotelians had regarded science as consisting of certain and evident knowledge, obtained by means of syllogistic demonstrations about necessary causes. Gassendi argued that syllogisms alone do not generate knowledge of the world. They yield true conclusions only if their premises are true. The premises, then, must be known on some independent basis. Aristotle himself had maintained that the principles on which demonstration is based must be tested against 'sensation ... a kind of tribunal before which one makes appeal.'[25]

Gassendi questioned whether sensory knowledge could serve as the basis of demonstrable, certain science.[26] Gassendi's sceptical critique of the senses in the *Exercitationes* followed Sextus Empiricus quite closely.[27] Not satisfied with the suspension of judgement advocated by the ancient sceptics, however, Gassendi sought a middle way, which Richard Popkin has called 'mitigated skepticism.'[28]

We would do best to hold some middle way between the Sceptics ... and the dogmatics. For the dogmatics do not really know everything they believe

---

[25] Ibid. 388–9, in *Opera Omnia*, iii. 182.   [26] Ibid.

[27] See Sextus Empiricus, *Outlines of Pyrrhonism*, bk. I, ch. XIV, tr. R. G. Bury (4 vols.; Cambridge, Mass.: Harvard University Press, 1976), i. 25–94. See Gassendi, *Exercitationes*, 388–93, in *Opera Omnia*, iii. 182–3.

[28] For the revival of the sceptical texts and Gassendi's use of the sceptical arguments see Richard H. Popkin, *The History of Skepticism from Erasmus to Spinoza* (Berkeley: University of California Press, 1979), 18–41, 101–9, and 129–50; and Charles B. Schmitt, *Cicero Scepticus: A Study of the Influence of the Academica in the Renaissance* (The Hague: Martinus Nijhoff, 1972). While Popkin emphasizes the influence of Sextus Empiricus and Pyrrhonian scepticism, Schmitt emphasizes the influence of Cicero and Academic scepticism in the Renaissance. See also Henri Berr, *Du scepticisme de Gassendi*, tr. Bernard Rochot (Paris: Albin Michel, 1960; first published in Latin in 1898); Gregory, *Scetticismo ed empirismo*; and Robert Walker, 'Gassendi and Scepticism', in *The Sceptical Tradition*, ed. Miles Burnyeat (Berkeley and Los Angeles: University of California Press, 1983), 319–36.

they know, nor do they have the appropriate criteria to determine it; but neither does everything that the Sceptics turn into the subject of debate seem to be so completely unknown that no criteria can be found for determining it.[29]

Accepting the force of the sceptical arguments but not content with sceptical conclusions, Gassendi redefined the epistemic goal of science so that certainty is no longer its necessary characteristic. Instead, 'knowledge', for Gassendi, consists of probable statements based on our experience of the phenomena. Probability is the most we can attain.[30] He did not consider accepting probability to be a terrible compromise. Rather, it is an acknowledgement of our own limitations.

Gassendi's theory of knowledge began from a classic statement of empiricism. 'All the ideas that are contained in the mind derive their origin from the senses. ... The intellect or mind is a *tabula rasa* in which nothing is engraved [prior to sensation].'[31] Despite the sceptical critique of the senses, Gassendi argued that sense, properly understood, never fails.[32] For example, the statement that honey tastes sweet to me cannot be challenged by the sceptical arguments. However, the statement that honey *is* sweet is a fallible judgement about the world and is therefore subject to empirical test. Sceptical arguments about round towers, bent oars, and the varying experiences of different individuals and kinds of animals in different circumstances are meaningful when applied to the judgements we make on the basis of our sensations.[33] They do not apply to

---

[29] Gassendi, *Syntagma philosophicum*, in *Opera Omnia*, i. 79 (*Selected Works of Pierre Gassendi*, tr. Craig Brush (New York: Johnson Reprint), 326–7).

[30] Ibid. Bloch, *La Philosophie de Gassendi*, 26.

[31] Gassendi, *Syntagma philosophicum*, in *Opera Omnia*, i. 92. For the history of earlier views of this statement of the empiricist credo, see Paul F. Cranefield, 'On the Origin of the Phrase "*Nihil est in intellectu quod non prius fuerit in sensu*" ', *Journal of the History of Medicine*, 25 (1970), 77–80.

[32] 'It is not the senses themselves but the intellect which makes the error; and when it makes a mistake, it is not the fault of the senses but of the intellect whose responsibility it is as the higher and dominant faculty before it pronounced what a thing is like to inquire which of the different appearances produced in the senses (each one of them is the result of a necessity that produces them as they are) is in conformity with the thing.' Ibid. i. 85 (Brush, *Selected Works of Pierre Gassendi*, 345–6).

[33] Gassendi, *Exercitationes*, 486–7, in *Opera Omnia*, iii. 203.

sensations taken in themselves. These sensations, which Gassendi called the 'appearances', provide the basis for our knowledge of the world, a knowledge that cannot penetrate to the inner natures of things precisely because it is knowledge only of how they appear to us.

Gassendi's mitigated scepticism led him to maintain that even if we cannot have science in the Aristotelian sense of demonstrative knowledge about real essences, we can achieve a science of appearances.[34] On the basis of the appearances, it is possible to seek causal explanations, with the understanding that such reasoning is always conjectural, to be judged by how well these causes explain other effects too.[35] This science of appearances can never achieve certainty.[36] It can, however, attain a measure of probability that is not an unhappy compromise: 'As it is certain that probability is neighbour enough of truth, the danger of error ... is the same when, in seeking the truth you turn away from probability as it is for him who, on his way from Paris to Holland, takes the road which leads to Marseilles.'[37] Gassendi thus redefined the goal of natural philosophy, replacing the traditional search for demonstrative knowledge of real essences with probable knowledge of the appearances. This redefinition of the epistemic goal is not scepticism. It is a recognition of human limitations, but not sceptical despair. This epistemology remained constant throughout Gassendi's writings and is closely connected with the theological views he enunciated in his later writings.

Pintard's assertion to the contrary notwithstanding, Gassendi's Epicurean project was not at odds with the ideas he espoused in the *Exercitationes*. Rather, it embodied his efforts to create a replacement for Aristotelianism, a plan which he had outlined in connection with the *Exercitationes*, and was founded on an epistemology, developed in that work, that he continued to hold throughout his life.

---

[34] He claimed that 'the conditions for science exist, but always an experimental science ... based on appearances.... [A]ll that we are denying is that one can penetrate to the intimate natures of things.' Gassendi, *Exercitationes*, 504–5, in *Opera Omnia*, iii. 207.

[35] Ibid.   [36] Ibid. 498–501, in *Opera Omnia*, iii. 206.

[37] Pierre Gassendi, *Disquisitio metaphysica seu dubitationes et instantiae adversus Renati Cartesii metaphysicam et responsa*, tr. Bernard Rochot (Paris: J. Vrin, 1962), 54–5, in *Opera Omnia*, iii. 283.

In his sketch of projected but unwritten parts of the *Exercitationes*, Gassendi described his intention of replacing Aristotelianism with a philosophy more amenable to the new natural philosophy. He would replace the Aristotelian physics of forms and natural motion with a physics incorporating the void and a non-Aristotelian definition of time. He would attack Aristotle's books on simple corporeal substances, his theory of the elements, his theory of mixed bodies, and his psychology. He would replace Aristotelian metaphysics with a defence of the existence and attributes of God. Finally, he intended to replace Aristotelian ethics with 'the Epicurean doctrine of pleasure'. Recognizing the monolithic character of Aristotelianism, Gassendi concluded his summary of intentions by stating that it is not necessary to refute every detail of Aristotelian philosophy, because once the foundations are removed, the whole structure will crumble.[38] Although Gassendi never completed the *Exercitationes* as outlined in 1624, the Epicurean project on which he embarked full tilt by the late 1620s ultimately fulfilled these goals.

In 1631, Gassendi sent an outline of the project to Peiresc. Contrary to Bloch's claim that theology was a late addition to Gassendi's Epicurean project, this early sketch includes all the rubrics under which Gassendi later discussed theological subjects. These include the existence of the divine nature, its form, its immortality; the cause that produced the world; providence, fate, and fortune; the end of the world; and the immortality of the soul.[39]

[38] Gassendi, *Exercitationes*, 14–15, in *Opera Omnia*, iii. 103. On the continuing influence of Aristotelianiam on Gassendi's physics, see Margaret J. Osler, 'New Wine in Old Bottles: Gassendi and the Aristotelian Origin of Early Modern Physics', *Midwest Studies in Philosophy*, 26, special issue on *Renaissance and Early Modern Philosophy* (2002), 167–84.

[39] See Gassendi to Peiresc, 28 April 1631, in Fabri de Peiresc, *Lettres de Peiresc*, Philippe Tamizey de Larroque (ed.), in *Documents inédits sur l'histoire de France* (7 vols.; Paris: Imprimerie Nationale, 1888), iv. 250–2; repr. in Margaret J. Osler, *Divine Will and the Mechanical Philosophy: Gassendi and Descartes on Contingency and Necessity in the Created World* (Cambridge: Cambridge University Press, 1994), 78–9. Key aspects of the 'Ethics' are not present in this sketch. Sarasohn, following Bloch's analysis of the manuscript evidence, argues that the 'Ethics' was 'written and rewritten' after 1641 when Gassendi met Hobbes. Lisa T. Sarasohn, *Gassendi's Ethics: Freedom in a Mechanistic Universe* (Ithaca: Cornell University Press, 1996), 208–14. For a more recent discussion of the development of Gassendi's project, see Carla Rita Palmerino, 'Pierre Gassendi's *De Philosophia Epicuri Universa* Rediscovered: New Perspectives on the Genesis of the *Syntagma Philosophicum*', *Nuncius*, 14 (1999), 263–94.

Gassendi produced several versions of his Epicurean project of which the *Syntagma Philosophicum*, published posthumously in 1658, was the culmination.[40] Consisting of the traditional three parts of philosophy entitled 'Logic', 'Physics', and 'Ethics', the *Syntagma Philosophicum* contains a complete exposition of philosophy and the history of philosophy.[41] It is a reworking of Epicureanism in terms compatible with orthodox Christian theology.

In order to make Epicureanism an acceptable alternative to Aristotelianism, Gassendi had to confront its theologically objectionable components: polytheism, a corporeal conception of the divine nature, the negation of all providence, the denial of creation ex nihilo, the infinitude and eternity of atoms and the universe, the plurality of worlds, the attribution of the cause of the world to chance, a materialistic cosmogony, the denial of all finality in biology, and the corporeality and mortality of the human soul.[42]

Topics that we consider theological formed an intrinsic part of Gassendi's revision of Epicureanism. Gassendi's account of God, his nature, and his role in the world occurs within the context of arguments against Epicurus's materialistic view of a universe run by chance. In a fifty-page section of the *Syntagma Philosophicum*, 'On the Efficient Principle or Causes of Things', Gassendi undertook to explicate his concept of causality, particularly in relation to God's role in the Creation. He identified cause with the efficient principle, explicitly reducing all causality to Aristotle's efficient cause and demonstrating how the three other Aristotelian causes can be eliminated in favour of the efficient cause.[43] Although elsewhere he

---

[40] Rochot, *Les Travaux de Gassendi sur Épicure*, 191–2.

[41] For one interpretation of the historical aspect of Gassendi's work, see Lynn Joy, *Gassendi the Atomist: Advocate of History in an Age of Science* (Cambridge: Cambridge University Press, 1987). For Gassendi's ethical and political views, see esp. Sarasohn, *Gassendi's Ethics*; see also Marco Messeri, *Causa e spiegazione: La fisica di Pierre Gassendi* (Milan: Franco Angeli, 1985); and Howard Jones, *Pierre Gassendi, 1592–1655: An Intellectual Biography* (Nieuwkoop: B. de Graaf, 1981). For a general historiographical overview of scholarship on Gassendi, see Barry Brundell, *Pierre Gassendi: From Aristotelianism to a New Natural Philosophy* (Dordrecht: Reidel, 1987), 5–15. See also Palmerino, 'Pierre Gassendi's *De Philosophia Epicuri Universe* Rediscovered'.

[42] Bloch, *La Philosophie de Gassendi*, 300.

[43] Gassendi, *Syntagma philosophicum*, in *Opera Omnia*, i. 283–7. Brundell finds Gassendi's reduction of the four Aristotelian causes to the efficient cause significant evidence of his overriding anti-Aristotelian concerns. Brundell, *Pierre Gassendi*, 69–76.

explicitly argued for the existence of final causes in nature and for the fact that they are an appropriate and important part of the subject matter of natural philosophy, he rejected any kind of immanent finality in the Aristotelian sense.[44] What Gassendi called final causes are actually divine intentions imparted to the design of the creation. Thus, God, for Gassendi, externally imposes the purposiveness found in nature. The natural order itself is ruled only by efficient causes, including divine action.

Gassendi interpreted the causal order of nature and the evident fact that various parts of things—particularly plants and animals—are designed for certain ends as evidence of the intelligence of the Creator. Just as the clockmaker applies his intelligence to efficient causes to produce an elegant timepiece, so God utilizes efficient causes in designing the world.[45] God, who creates the second causes he uses, however, differs from the clockmaker, who makes use of materials found in the world. Having introduced the Deity into his discussion of causality, Gassendi proceeded to establish the existence of God and to describe his attributes. On this matter, he explicitly opposed Epicurus. 'Let it be said that Epicurus erred in his description of the nature of the divine; but he seems to have committed the lapse not from malice, but from ignorance.'[46]

Knowledge of God, according to Gassendi, like all knowledge, comes from the senses. God revealed himself directly to Adam and Eve, who thus experienced him immediately and received his gift of faith. Their knowledge has been conveyed to succeeding generations through teachers, prophets, and further revelations.[47] Although our knowledge of God is empirical, we do not have a sensory image of God as Epicurus had thought.[48] Instead Gassendi claimed that things comprehended through the senses are occasions that lead us to form an anticipation or mental image of God. Such occasions can occur from any of the senses—for example, the sense of hearing, as in the

---

[44] See Gassendi, *Disquisitio metaphysica,* 396–9, in *Opera Omnia,* iii. 359. See also Margaret J. Osler, 'Whose Ends? Teleology in Early Modern Natural Philosophy', *Osiris,* 16 (2001), 151–68.

[45] Gassendi, *Disquisitio Metaphysica,* i. 285. [46] Ibid. i. 290.

[47] Ibid. i. 293.

[48] On this difficult point, see A. A. Long and D. N. Sedley, *The Hellenistic Philosophers* (2 vols.; Cambridge University Press, 1987), i. 144–9.

experience of Adam and Eve to whom God spoke directly, or the sense of sight, which reveals God's intelligent design in the world.[49]

The argument from design played a central role in Gassendi's thought, largely providing evidence for God's providential relationship to the creation.[50] Whereas the 'Sacred Faith' informs us of God's existence, observation of his wisdom in the Creation teaches us that the world was created by an intelligent designer: 'The paths of the stars, the vicissitudes of storms, the succession of generations, the order and use of parts—everything, in a word, that is in the world—announces order and declares that the world is a most orderly system.'[51] Epicurean chance or fortune cannot be the source of that order, for 'chance and fortune are indeed nothing'. They are blind, 'not sharing in the plans, not understanding the order'.[52] The harmony and elegance of the world—especially evident in the parts of animals and their generation—indicate that hands other than fortune created it.[53] Similarly, the world's order cannot be innate or immanent. The order observed in the world is the work of 'reason and planning', but the world cannot design itself. It has an external cause, 'what we call God and what can be called the first cause, prime mover, fount of all being and origin of all perfection, the highest being and prince of the world'.[54]

God knows all things: the present, the past, the future, and the concourse of causes. He knows not only all that he has created, but also the infinite other possibilities that he did not create.[55] Gassendi interpreted God's omnipotence as freedom from any necessity or limits. 'There is nothing in the universe that God cannot destroy, nothing that he cannot produce; nothing that he cannot change, even into its opposite qualities.'[56] God's absolute power is in no way constrained by the creation, which contains no necessary relations that might limit God's power or will. Even the laws of nature lack

---

[49] Gassendi, *Syntagma philosophicum*, in *Opera Omnia*, i. 293.

[50] I disagree with Brundell who speaks of Gassendi's 'perfunctory use of the argument from design'. Brundell, *Pierre Gassendi*, 71. Gassendi appeals to design repeatedly, usually to support a providential creationism.

[51] Gassendi, *Syntagma philosophicum*, in *Opera Omnia*, i. 294.

[52] Ibid.   [53] Ibid. i. 312–16.   [54] Ibid. i. 295.

[55] Ibid. i. 307.   [56] Ibid. i. 308.

necessity. God can negate them, just as he can destroy everything else he created. 'He is free from the laws of nature, which he constituted by his own free will.'[57] Indeed, God can do anything short of violating the law of non-contradiction.[58] God was totally free in choosing to create the world: He could have abstained from creating it just as freely as he chose to create it.[59] Moreover, God could have created an entirely different natural order, had it pleased him to do so.[60] That is to say, God could have created black snow, and he could have created a cold, fiery substance just as he can raise the dead and heal the crippled. Even though he has chosen to create this universe—the one containing white snow and hot fire—he has created nothing in it that he cannot change at will. An implicit assumption here (one that Gassendi makes explicit elsewhere) is that there are no essences in the world God created. There are no necessary connections linking fire and heat or whiteness and snow. God could not have made white snow black or hot fire cold, for such combinations of attributes are contradictory.[61] But he could create them with different properties from those that they now possess.

Within the stipulation that nothing God creates can impede his absolute power, he makes use of second causes to carry out the ordinary course of nature.[62] Second causes, as part of the created order, do not restrict God's freedom, because he can dispense with second causes altogether if he chooses.[63] The natural order, which God created by his absolute power, is utterly contingent on his will.

Divine providence and human freedom were fundamental components of Gassendi's conception of the world. Agreeing with Epicurus that the ultimate goal of natural philosophy is to produce tranquillity by giving naturalistic explanations of phenomena, Gassendi disagreed with the ancient atomist's materialistic and antiprovidential outlook. Rather, Gassendi argued, natural philosophy leads to true religion.[64] This religion teaches that 'God is the cause that

---

[57] Ibid. i. 381; also 234.   [58] Ibid. i. 309.   [59] Ibid. i. 318.
[60] Ibid. ii. 851.   [61] Ibid. i. 308.   [62] Ibid. i. 326.
[63] Ibid. i. 317. 'He is free, since he neither is confined by anything nor imposes any laws on himself which he cannot violate if he pleases.... Therefore, God ... is the most free; and he is not bound as he can do whatever ... he wishes.' Ibid. i. 309.
[64] 'Natural philosophy [*Physiologia*] is the contemplation of the natural universe of things from the magnitude, variety, disposition, and beauty of its wonders. ... Our natural reason deduces from it that there exists a most wise, powerful, and good,

created the world and that he rules it with general providence and also special providence for humanity.'[65] Gassendi believed that Epicurus committed his gravest error in asserting that chance, not God, is the cause of the world.[66]

Another aspect of Epicureanism troubling to Gassendi was its denial of the immortality of the soul. 'Here was the error of Epicurus, not that he called void an incorporeal nature, but that he admitted no other incorporeal things, such as those we endorse, like the divine, the angelic, and the human soul.'[67] Epicurus had considered fear of death and anxiety about punishment and reward in the afterlife as the main enemies of tranquillity. By asserting that the soul is material and mortal and thus eliminating the possibility of life after death, he believed that these fears could be allayed. Epicurus had considered the soul, like everything else in the cosmos, to be composed of atoms and the void.[68] In order to legitimate his Christian adaptation of Epicurean atomism, Gassendi insisted on the existence of an immortal, incorporeal human soul. In the process of arguing for the incorporeality of the soul, he spelled out the limits of his mechanization of nature. Bloch's claim to the contrary notwithstanding, Gassendi was not a materialist.[69] Even as he reconstructed Epicurean atomism, he insisted that limits be imposed on what could be explained by the motions of material atoms. God, angels, and the immortal human soul were deliberately excluded from his mechanical philosophy.

Gassendi did not object to the corporeality of the Epicurean *anima*, which he equated with the animal soul.[70] 'The soul [of animals],' he said, 'seems to be a very tenuous substance, just like the flower of matter (*florem materiae*) with a special disposition, condition, and symmetry holding among the crasser mass of the

divine will [*Numen*] by which it is governed ... so that we acknowledge this divine will for the greatness of his excellence and beneficence. And reverence, which is the true religion, must be cultivated.' Gassendi, *Syntagma Philosophicum*, in *Opera Omnia*, i. 294 i. 128.

[65] Ibid. i. 311.   [66] Ibid. i. 320–1.

[67] Gassendi to Valois, November 1642, ibid. vi. 157.

[68] Epicurus, 'Letter to Herodotus', 63–7, in Long and Sedley, *The Hellenistic Philosophers*, i. 65–6. See also J. M. Rist, *Epicurus: An Introduction* (Cambridge: Cambridge University Press, 1972), ch. 5.

[69] See Bloch, *La Philosophie de Gassendi*, esp. 285.

[70] For an extensive discussion of Gassendi's views on the animal soul, see Sylvia Murr, 'L'Âme des bêtes chez Gassendi', *Corpus*, 16/17 (1991), 37–63.

parts of the body.[71] The *anima* is the principle of organization and activity for the organism. It is the source of the animal's vital heat, a phenomenon that can be explained by the subtlety and activity of its constituent atoms. Ever since the initial creation, the souls of animals have been transmitted from one generation to the next by the biological process of reproduction.

But the animal soul is only one part of the human soul. It is with regard to the *animus* or rational soul that man was made in the image of God.[72] The rational soul is very different from the sensitive soul because it is incorporeal and directly created by God. 'In agreement with the Holy Faith, we say that the mind, or that superior part of the soul (which is appropriately rational and unique to man) is an incorporeal substance, which is created by God, and infused into the body ... it is like an informing form.'[73]

Gassendi's discussion shifted, at this point, from assertion of faith to philosophical argument. He defended the incorporeality of the soul on three grounds: that 'the intellect is distinct from the imagination';[74] that the intellect can know itself; and that not only do we form concepts of universals, but we also perceive the reason for their universality.[75]

Having established the incorporeality of the soul to his own satisfaction, Gassendi finally addressed the question of the soul's

---

[71] Gassendi, *Syntagma Philosophicum*, in *Opera Omnia*, ii. 250. Gassendi had used very similar language in talking about the principle of motion in individual objects such as boys or atoms: 'For when a boy runs to an apple offered to him, what is needed to account for the apple's attraction to the boy is not just a metaphorical motion, but also most of all there must be a physical, or natural, power inside the boy by which he is directed and impelled toward the apple. Hence it may apparently be said most plainly that since the principle of action and motion in each object is the most mobile and active of its parts, a sort of bloom of every material thing (*quasi flos totius materiae*) and which is the same thing that used to be called form, and may be thought of as a kind of rarefied tissue of the most subtile and mobile atoms—it may therefore be said that the prime cause of motion in natural things is the atoms, for they provide motion for all things when they move themselves through their own agency and in accord with the power they received from their author in the beginning; and they are consequently the origin, and principle, and cause of all the motion that exists in nature.' Ibid. i. 337, tr. Brush, in *The Selected Works of Pierre Gassendi*, 421–2. Bloch interprets Gassendi's talk of the *flos materiae* as an unacknowledged influence of the animism of Telesio and Campanella. See Bloch, *La Philosophie de Gassendi*, 228–30.

[72] Gassendi, *Syntagma Philosophicum*, in *Opera Omnia*, ii. 255.

[73] Ibid. ii. 440.   [74] Ibid.   [75] Ibid.

immortality. He called this proof the 'crown of the treatise' and the 'last touch of universal physics'.[76] His strategy was to prove the immortality of the soul from faith, physics, and morality. As a statement of faith, Gassendi declared: '[The rational soul] survives after death or remains immortal; and as it bore itself in the body, either it will be admitted to future happiness in Heaven, or it will be thrust down unhappy into Hell, and it will regain its own body in the general resurrection, just as it was in itself and will receive its good or evil.'[77] Although 'the divine light shines for us from this Sacred Faith', theologians have been accustomed to discuss arguments for and against the immortality of the soul.[78] His support of an article of faith with philosophical and physical arguments was Gassendi's response to the Fifth Lateran Council's call on philosophers to 'use all their powers', including natural reason, to defend the immortality of the soul.[79]

Gassendi invoked what he called an argument from physics— commonly used in seventeenth-century discussions about the soul[80]—that 'the rational soul is immaterial; therefore it is immortal'. An immaterial thing is also immortal or incorruptible because, 'lacking matter, it also lacks mass and parts into which it can be divided and analysed. Indeed, this kind of thing neither has dissolution in itself nor fears [it] from another.'[81]

---

[76] Gassendi, *Syntagma Philosophicum*, in *Opera Omnia*, ii. 620
[77] Ibid. ii. 627.
[78] Ibid. On Gassendi's attitude toward the relationship between truths of reason and truths of faith, see Sylvia Murr, 'Foi religieuse et *libertas philosophandi* chez Gassendi', *Revue des sciences philosophiques et théologiques*, 76 (1992), 85–100.
[79] Fred S. Michael and Emily Michael, 'Two Early Modern Concepts of Mind: Reflecting Substance vs. Thinking Substance', *Journal of the History of Philosophy*, 27 (1989), 31.
[80] See Kenelm Digby, *Two Treatizes in One of which The Nature of Bodies; in the other The Nature of Mans Soule; is looked into: in Way of Discovering, of the Immortality of Reasonable Soules* (Paris: Gilles Blaizot, 1644; facsimile repr., New York: Garland, 1978), 350, and Henry More, *The Immortality of the Soul, So Farre Forth As It Is Demonstrable from the Knowledge of Nature and the Light of Reason* (London: 1662); facsimile repr. in Henry More, *A Collection of Several Philosophical Writings* (1662) (2 vols.; New York: Garland, 1978), 21. See also Ben Lazare Mijuskovic, *The Achilles of Rationalist Arguments: The Simplicity, Unity and Identity of Thought and the Soul from the Cambridge Platonists to Kant. A Study in the History of an Argument* (The Hague: Martinus Nijhoff, 1974). I am grateful to James E. Force for providing this reference.
[81] Gassendi, *Syntagma Philosophicum*, in *Opera Omnia*, ii. 628.

Gassendi based his third, moral line of argument for the immortality of the soul on an assumption that might be called the principle of the conservation of justice: 'To the extent that it is certain that God exists, so it is certain that he is just. It is appropriate to the justice of God that good happens to the good and evil to the wicked.' But in this life, anyway, rewards and punishments are not so justly apportioned. Consequently, 'there must be another life in which rewards for the good and punishments for the evil are distributed'.[82]

Gassendi completed his Epicurean project in the 'Ethics', the third and final part of the *Syntagma Philosophicum*. Epicurean ethics was founded on the principle that maximizing pleasure is the goal of life. Pleasure, according to Epicurus, consists of mental tranquillity and freedom from bodily pain. Gassendi reinterpreted the concepts of pleasure and human action in specifically Christian terms, thereby creating a Christian hedonism that found a natural place in his providential world-view.[83] He claimed that God has instilled in humans a natural desire for pleasure and a natural aversion to pain. In this way, God guides human choices, without negating free will. The prudent pursuit of pleasure will ultimately lead to the greatest pleasure of all, the beatific vision of God in heaven.[84] This conception of hedonism is a far cry from the decadence and immorality that Pintard and others ascribed to the libertines.

Gassendi's extensive treatment of theological issues and his determination to treat them were present from the early stages of his project, making it impossible to support the claim that he was a sceptic, a materialist, or a *libertin érudit*. On the contrary, I would argue that he was a rather typical seventeenth-century natural philosopher who considered topics such as divine providence, finality, and the immortality of the soul as central components of his attempt to create a new philosophy. His views on these matters were intricately and intimately connected to his views about how the world works and what we can know about it. There was no separation between theology and philosophy in his thought, and he did not use theological arguments simply to protect himself against a repressive

---

[82] Ibid. ii. 632
[83] The only major study of Gassendi's 'Ethics' is Sarasohn, *Gassendi's Ethics*.
[84] Sarasohn, *Gassendi's Ethics*, ch. 3.

church. How, then, did twentieth-century scholars come to consider him to be a libertine?

WHEN DID GASSENDI BECOME A LIBERTINE?

This question can be approached by asking, 'When did Gassendi become a libertine?' The short answer is 1943, the year when Pintard published his seminal book, for no one had labelled Gassendi a libertine during the preceding three centuries.

Natural philosophers in the seventeenth century did not consider Gassendi to be a dangerous freethinker (such as Thomas Hobbes, whom they reviled for alleged atheism and materialism). The pious Robert Boyle (1627–91), for example, rejected the Epicureans who denied divine providence and design and explained the origin of the world in terms of chance, but he always considered Gassendi to be an exception.[85]

In succeeding decades, commentators acknowledged Gassendi's revival of Epicureanism, but they tended not to include him in the same category as the libertines or materialists. For example, Pierre Bayle (1647–1706) frequently mentioned Gassendi in his *Diction-naire historique et critique*, but most often as a respected philosopher, paired with Descartes. Although Bayle defined 'libertinism' in a lengthy note, he did not include Gassendi on his list of libertines, which included Pierre Charron, François de La Mothe le Vayer, and Jean-Louis Guez de Balzac.[86] In a note in the entry on 'Rodon (David de) or rather DERODON (David)', Bayle wrote, 'It is an absurd thing to

---

[85] For example, in the preface to his treatise on final causes Boyle stated, 'For *Epicurus* and *most* of his Followers (for I except some few late ones, especially the Learned *Gassendus*) Banish the Consideration of the ends of things; because the World being, according to them, made by Chance, no Ends of any Thing can be suppos'd to have been intended.' Robert Boyle, *A Disquisition about the Final Causes of Things: Wherein it is Inquir'd Whether, And (if at all) with what Cautions, a Naturalist should admit Them?* (1688) in *The Works of Robert Boyle*, ed. Michael Hunter and Edward B. Davis (14 vols.; London: Pickering & Chatto, 2000), xi. 81.

[86] In a note in the article on Des-Barreaux, Bayle described what he meant by 'libertines': 'he was afraid of being rallied for quitting the title of a Free-thinker, if he did not continue to talk as a libertine. It is probable enough that those who, in Company, affect to oppose the most common Truths of Religion, say more than they

say, with Gassendus and Derodon, that God contributes to the preservation of creatures by preventing their destruction.'[87] Bayle's *Dictionnaire* contains other references to Gassendi, but most of them refer to him in connection with astronomy. Nowhere did Bayle include him among the libertines or materialists. Similarly in the *Encyclopédie*, Diderot and d'Alembert did not link Gassendi to the libertines. They described Gassendi as the restorer of Epicureanism but did not number him among the freethinkers.

Many later histories of philosophy follow the same pattern. Most writers mention Gassendi's piety and his project to Christianize Epicureanism. Usually they focus on his debate with Descartes in the *Objections and Replies*. In the middle of the nineteenth century, Jean-Philibert Damiron affirmed Gassendi's orthodoxy and found it in each of his published works.[88] At the turn of the twentieth century, Harald Höffding included a two-page chapter on Gassendi in his *History of Modern Philosophy*, focusing on Gassendi's differences from Descartes. Although he attributed Gassendi's spiritualistic conclusions to his need to conform to the demands of the Church, nevertheless, he did not suggest that there was any dissimulation on Gassendi's part, and he credits him with making it no longer necessary to 'regard atomism as an absolutely godless doctrine.

---

think. Vanity has a greater share than Conscience in their Disputes: they imagine the singularity or boldness of the Sentiments they maintain will pronounce them the reputation of great Wits. Thus they are tempted, against their own Perswasion, to expose the difficulties to which the Doctrines of *Providence* and the Gospel are subject. By little and little, they get a habit of impious Talk, and, if their Vanity is attended with a sensual Life, they make a Swift Progress in Wickedness. This ill habit contradicted on one hand under the guidance of Pride, and on the other prompted by Sensuality, deadens the Impressions of Education. I meant that it suppresses the sense of those Truths they learnt in their Infancy concerning the Deity, Heaven, and Hell. But it is not a Faith quite extinguisht; it is only Fire concealed in the Ashes. They perceive the Activity of it, as soon as they reflect within themselves, and particularly on the approach of any Danger. They are even more afraid than other men, nay, they grow superstitious.' Pierre Bayle, *The Dictionary Historical and Critical of Mr. Pierre Bayle*, 2nd edn. (London: 1734–8; facsimile repr., London: Routledge/Thoemmes, 1997), ii. 648.

[87] Ibid. iv. 886.

[88] 'Si vous y joignez un trait caractéristique de sa manière de penser, qui au reste, paraît en lui aussi sincere qu'invariable, je veux dire son orthodoxie avouée et rappelé hautement dans chacune de ses œuvres.' Jean-Philibert Damiron, *Essai sur l'histoire de la philosophie en France au XVIIe siècle* (2 vols.; Paris: Hachette, 1846), i. 385.

Natural Science might now undisturbedly avail herself of the atom-
istic hypothesis.'[89] As late as 1938, Émile Bréhier wrote about Gassendi in similar terms, criticizing his inconsistency in imposing God
and the immaterial, immortal soul on Epicurean atomism but not
questioning the sincerity of his stated views.[90] In a similar vein,
Frederick Albert Lange, in his massive *History of Materialism*, argued
that although Gassendi introduced the theological elements into his
philosophy, his philosophy could be considered independent of
them.[91]

It was not until Pintard published *Le Libertinage érudit* in 1943
that Gassendi's purported libertinism was widely accepted. Why was
Pintard so determined to label Gassendi a freethinker? At this point,
the lack of biographical information about Pintard forces me to
speculate, but my speculation is not entirely without grounds. René
Pintard was a scholar living in occupied France during World War II.
Could it be that his focus on freethinking and clandestine literature
was a subtle way of engaging in resistance to the oppressive regime
within which he was living? His writings contain a few very suggestive comments that give credence to this speculation. In the preface to
Le Libertinage érudit, he thanked various colleagues for helping him
publish the book that '*les circonstances rendaient particulièrement*

---

[89] Harold Höffding, *A History of Modern Philosophy: A Sketch of the History of
Philosophy from the Close of the Renaissance to Our Own Day*, tr. B. E. Meyer (2 vols.;
London: Macmillan, 1900), i. 255–6.

[90] Émile Bréhier, *The History of Philosophy: The Seventeenth Century*, tr. Wade
Baskin (Chicago: University of Chicago Press, 1966; first published Paris: Presses
Universitaires de France, 1938), 12–13.

[91] 'Gassendi stands widely apart from Lucretius in accepting an immortal and
incorporeal spirit; and yet this spirit, like Gassendi's God, stands so entirely out of
relation to his system, that we can very conveniently leave it out of sight. Nor is
Gassendi led to adopt it for the sake of this unity; he does so because religion
demands it.' Lange placed Gassendi, along with Hobbes, at the root of modern
materialism. Frederick Albert Lange, *The History of Materialism and Criticism of
Its Present Importance*, 3rd edn. (3 vols in 1), tr. Ernest Chester Thomas (London:
Routledge and Kegan Paul, 1877, 1890, and 1892; first published in German, 1865), i.
267–8. Further, in a dissertation originally published in Latin in 1898, Henri Berr
argued that scepticism was the unifying theme of Gassendi's philosophy, from the
early *Exercitationes* to the posthumous *Syntagma Philosophicum*. Although Berr
mentioned other sceptics in passing, his interpretation of Gassendi rests on a close
analysis of his philosophical works. Berr, *Du scepticisme de Gassendi*.

malaisée.[92] He described Gassendi in a way that may be revealing of his own circumstances: '*Mais où trouver un refuge contre la tyrannie de la pensée officielle, sinon dans le vieux scepticisme des philosophes grecs.*'[93] He spoke of his circumstances more explicitly during a ceremony, under the auspices of the Centre de Philologie et de Littératures Romanes de Strasbourg in 1975 honouring his contributions to scholarship and teaching. In an autobiographical statement, he wrote about the War and the Occupation:

My nomination to the Faculty of Poitiers would have been a happier promotion if it had not been at the same moment as Munich, and after that the 'phoney war' [*la drôle de guerre*] and the occupation. ... One would have been ashamed to lose courage before a man such as our dean, the philosopher Jean-Raoul Carré, who, in the work of Fontenelle, had plucked 'the smile of reason'. ... Powerful, jovial, overflowing with life, he had— during the two wars—united to his striking bravery a flawless lucidity. The trial of our country was for him a torture, and he knew that for him the end would be deportation.[94]

Perhaps the thought of Gassendi's freethinking provided Pintard himself with a refuge from the tyranny under which he was living.

CONCLUSION: HISTORICAL ACTORS AND HISTORIANS' ACTORS

This tale of Gassendi's libertinism raises a troublesome historiographical question: by what criteria can we distinguish genuine from feigned belief? Articulating some absolute criterion is probably impossible, and so we must do what historians normally do, construct stories that are consistent with as much of the evidence as possible. I believe that, in the absence of evidence to the contrary, we must take historical actors and their documents at face value.

---

[92] Pintard, *Le Libertinage érudit*, i. xi.   [93] Ibid. 150.
[94] René Pintard, in *Remise de mélange de littérature française* (Strasbourg, 1975), 13. For an account of scholarly life during the Occupation, see Natalie Zemon Davis, 'Censorship, Silence and Resistance: The *Annales* during the German Occupation of France', *Historical Reflections/Réflexions*, 24 (1998), 351–74.

Discerning dissimulation, like proving conspiracy theories, is very difficult if we lack corroborating evidence. Gassendi's writings are laced with theology, and I have found no hint—in either his published works, his letters, or in his reputation—that he was feigning belief. My position rests on the assumption that people mean what they say, an assumption that can be mistaken because people sometimes lie or hide their true beliefs for self-protection or for political ends. If one were determined to argue for dissimulation, any evidence to the contrary could be dismissed as ... well ... dissimulation. In the case at hand, I have argued that Gassendi's accusers have either ignored or misread important parts of his writings. So, although historical reasoning cannot achieve certainty and the possibility of error remains, I think it makes more sense to follow the evidence than to force it into a procrustean bed.

What can we learn about writing the history of philosophy from this episode? As historians we have learned to understand the thinking of historical actors in terms of their own context. Perhaps we have to take the same approach to ourselves as historians, understanding that we bring assumptions to our endeavour, just as our actors brought assumptions to theirs. Although it is not possible for us to escape our own assumptions, we can become aware of them and understand their sources. The 'true story' about historical actors may remain as elusive as metaphysical certainty about the physical world. But consciousness of our own intellectual baggage may help us avoid the crudest sort of projections back onto the historical figures that we study.

8

Hobbes, Heresy, and Corporeal Deity

Cees Leijenhorst

INTRODUCTION

The Great Fire of London of 1666 occurred amidst an atmosphere of mounting religious hysteria in England. The irate souls wasted little time in finding a suitable scapegoat in Thomas Hobbes, as his *Leviathan* of 1651 was considered by many to be the very epitome of heresy and atheism. The House of Commons set up a committee to consider a 'Bill against Atheisme Prophaneness and Swearing impowered to receive Informacion toucheing such bookes as tend to Atheisme Blasphemy or Prophaneness or against the Essence or Attributes of God. And in particular ... the booke of Mr Hobbs called the Leviathan'.[1] A more salient version of these events is to be found in the *Brief Lives* by John Aubrey, who was not only an incurable gossip, but also a friend and admirer of his fellow Wiltshireman. According to Aubrey, some of the bishops made a motion in Parliament 'to have the good old gentleman burnt for a heretic'.[2] Fortunately for Hobbes, the order to set up a committee was countered by his protector, the Secretary of State Henry Bennet, Baron of Arlington.[3] Nevertheless, the wave of controversy sparked off by the

---

[1] N. Malcolm, *The Correspondence of Thomas Hobbes*, i (Oxford: Oxford University Press, 1994), p. xxv. This article is an elaborated version of my 'Hobbes and Corporeal Deity', *Rivista Critica di Storia della Filosofia*, 21 (2004), 73–96.

[2] J. Aubrey, *Brief Lives, Chiefly of Contemporaries, Set Down by John Aubrey, Between the Years 1669 and 1696*, ed. A. Clark (Oxford, 1898), 339.

[3] Similar bills, were, however reintroduced in 1674, 1675, and 1680.

Leviathan and Hobbes's other works failed to die down. Although the stubborn old gentleman was not bodily committed to the flames, his books were. In 1683, John Fell, dean of Christ Church College and later bishop of Oxford, managed to have *Leviathan* and *De Cive* formally banned by Hobbes's old university. In addition, Hobbes's works were publicly burnt in the Bodleian quadrangle. Hobbes luckily did not have to witness this humiliating and frightening experience: he had already died in 1679, a good 90 years of age. Nonetheless, in the final decades of his life he had responded to all the various charges of atheism and heresy made against him. He did so in a number of works, only a few of which appeared in print during his lifetime.[4]

In these works, Hobbes addresses the issue of heresy in a threefold manner. First, using subtle juridical arguments, Hobbes concludes that contemporary English law had neither the legal framework nor the proper juridical authorities for a formal charge of heresy. In his manuscript on the law of heresy, Hobbes argues that Elizabeth's statute of 1559 had repealed the earlier heresy statutes and had made legal prosecution of heresy impossible. According to Hobbes, the High Commission, the Ecclesiastical Court installed by Elizabeth, had not declared anything to be heretical, so that 'as at this day there is noe Statute in force, nor any Law in England whereby to punish any man for any matter of Doctrine in Religion, nor ground for any Writ to autorise such punishment but only the Ordinaries have still power to excommunicate such as they had in the year of our Lord

---

[4] (1) 'Hobbes and the Law of Heresy', *Journal of the History of Ideas*, 29 (1968), 409–14. This is a manuscript (Hardwick MS 145, no. 18), ed. by Samuel Minz. According to Franck Lessay, the text should be dated between 1666 and 1668 (*Thomas Hobbes. Textes sur l'hérésie et sur l'histoire* (Paris: Vrin, 1993), 61). According to Schuhmann, Review of Y. C. Zarka (ed.), *Thomas Hobbes. Œuvres*, *British Journal for the History of Philosophy*, 4 (1996), 161, it is 'a more detailed alternative version to the last part of *A Narration*, written in the wake of Williamson's criticism of (at least part of) this text'. (2) *Appendix ad Leviathan Latine*, in *Opera Omnia* (Amsterdam, 1668). (3) *An Answer to a Book Published by Dr Bramhall* ... (London, 1682). According to F. Lessay, *Thomas Hobbes. De la liberté et de la nécessité* (Paris: Vrin, 1993), 121, Hobbes wrote this book in 1668. (4) *An Historical Narration concerning Heresie, and the Punishment thereof* (London, 1682). Again, according to Lessay, *Hérésie*, 17, this work was written around 1668. Also of interest is *Mr Hobbes Considered in His Loyalty, Religion, Reputation, and Manners. By Way of a Letter to Dr Wallis* (London, 1662).

1639 which is granted them by the Statute made in the 13th year of this present King, which they may doe according to the Canons set forth in the first year of King James, but upon their Excommunication there follows no Writ for imprisoning the Excommunicate, nor for burning of a Heretick'.[5] Moreover, in the *Appendix* to the Latin *Leviathan* and elsewhere, Hobbes refers to the fact that according to Elizabeth's statute, the High Commission may not condemn as heretic any doctrine that is not expressly deemed so by the first four church councils, which according to Hobbes nullifies any attempt to prosecute his alleged heresies.[6] In his *Narration concerning Heresy*, Hobbes adds that in no way had this criterion been made the basis for an officially legal prosecution of heresies.[7] Finally, with the abolition of the High Commission by Charles I, there was no longer any authority that could deal with charges of heresy.

Whether or not these arguments are convincing is of no concern to us here.[8] What is more interesting is the second strategy Hobbes uses to combat allegations of heresy, which is to trace the history of the concept of heresy. According to Hobbes, the term 'heresy' originally meant nothing other than simply a private opinion, especially an opinion held by one of the various Greek sects (Academics, Peripatetics, Epicureans, and the like). However, Greek philosophy

[5] Minz, 'Hobbes and the Law of Heresy', 414.

[6] *App. ad LL* (*OL* iii. 555). References to Hobbes's works are given according to the Molesworth edition (London, 1839; repr. Aalen, 1966), except for *De Corpore*, which is cited after the critical edition by Karl Schuhmann (Paris: Vrin, 1999). *EW* designates the *English Works*, *OL* the *Opera Latina*. Volume numbers are in roman, page numbers in arabic numerals. The following abbreviations are used: *DCo* = *De Corpore* (followed by the chapter in roman and the article in arabic numerals); *DHo* = *De Homine* (followed by the chapter in roman and the article in arabic numerals); *DCi* = *De Cive* (followed by the chapter in roman and the article in arabic numerals); *EL* = *Elements of Law* (followed by the chapter in roman and the article in arabic numerals); *L* = *Leviathan*; *DM* = *De Motu*. By *De Motu*, I refer to the manuscript still known under the misleading title of *Anti-White*. On the title *De Motu*, see K. Schuhmann, 'Hobbes dans les publications de Mersenne en 1644', 4–5. *OMC* = *Objectiones ad Cartesii Meditationes*; *HN* = *An Historical Narration concerning Heresy*; *ABB* = *An Answer to Bishop Bramhall*; *App. ad LL* = *Appendix ad Leviathan Latine*; *Dialogus* = *Dialogus Physicus de Natura Aeris*; *DP* = *Decameron Physiologicum*; *CRL* = *Mr Hobbes Considered in His Loyalty, Religion, Reputation, and Manners*, *HE* = *Historia Ecclesiastica*.

[7] *HN* (*EW* iv. 405–6).

[8] For a rather negative judgement, see R. Wilman, 'Hobbes on the Law of Heresy', *Journal of the History of Ideas*, 31 (1970), 610–13.

colonized the early Church, giving the concept of heresy a different meaning. Heresy came to stand for an unpermitted, false belief held by a minority, as opposed to 'catholic' orthodoxy. In fact, Hobbes argues that the introduction of the Greek philosophers' 'heresies' had a pernicious effect on the early Church:

Most of the pastors of the primitive church were ... chosen out of the number of these philosophers; who retaining still many doctrines which they had taken up on the authority of their former masters, whom they had in reverence, endeavoured many of them to draw the Scriptures every one to his own heresy. ... And this dissension amongst themselves, was a great scandal to the unbelievers, and which not only obstructed the way of the Gospel, but also drew scorn and greater persecution upon the church.[9]

In this sense, Hobbes's history of heresy stands in the context of his massive critique on the infusion of pagan sophistry in unadulterated primitive Christianity, as it can be found in the fourth part of the *Leviathan*. As is well known, Hobbes mounts a massive attack there on the incorporeal soul and other nonsensical and dangerous concepts that have entered the Church through its unhappy marriage with pagan learning.

One of the main functions of Hobbist histories is to illustrate a philosophical doctrine.[10] In this case, the history of heresy teaches us two lessons. First, as Patricia Springborg has aptly demonstrated, Hobbes shows that heresy is 'an essentially historical problem and the creation of pagan philosophers'.[11] In this way, Hobbes tries to distract attention from his own 'heresies'. The second lesson is a point that this chapter will discuss extensively, namely that reason and faith should be kept separate at all cost.

The third way in which Hobbes defends himself against accusations of heresy is to demonstrate that even if a proper legal framework had been in place, the charge of heresy would still lack a real basis. Especially in his *Appendix* to the Latin *Leviathan*, Hobbes shows that the alleged heresies of the *Leviathan* are in fact confirmed

[9] *HN* (*EW* iv. 389).

[10] See J. P. Sommerville, 'Hobbes, Selden, Erastianism, and the History of the Jews', in G. A. J. Rogers and T. Sorell (eds.), *Hobbes and History* (London: Routledge, 2000), 180: 'Hobbes found in history what theory had already proved.'

[11] P. Springborg, 'Hobbes, Heresy, and the *Historia Ecclesiastica*', *Journal of the History of Ideas*, 55 (1994), 558.

not only by natural reason but also by Scripture, the early Church fathers, the first four Church Councils and the Nicene Creed. The last two references are of special relevance, as they constitute the standard of orthodoxy as defined by Elizabeth's High Commission. Hobbes actually heavily criticized these first councils in his *Historia Ecclesiastica* for combining Greek philosophy with Christian faith, where he also found fault with Emperor Constantine for allowing ecclesiastical authorities too much freedom.[12] The fact that Hobbes combines this critique with his diligent submission to the decrees of the early Church is only one of the many reasons why doubts have been raised concerning the sincerity of Hobbes's professed orthodoxy.[13]

The most interesting doctrine that Hobbes describes as perfectly orthodox is that of the corporeal nature of God. In fact, the *Leviathan* had not expressly stated that God was a body. What Hobbes did do was to reject the notion of an incorporeal substance as a contradiction *in adjecto*: all substances are bodies, hence to accept the existence of incorporeal substances would be identical to affirming the existence of an incorporeal body, which is absurd. The *Leviathan*, however, does not extensively deal with the question of what this means for God, who was traditionally conceived to be an incorporeal substance. Bishop John Bramhall, however, one of Hobbes's staunchest opponents, was quick to draw the obvious conclusion:

By the same reason, to say that God is an incorporeal spirit, is to say there is no God at all. Either God is incorporeal, or he is finite and consists of parts, and consequently is no God. This, that there is no incorporeal spirit, is that main root of Atheisme, from which so many lesser branches are daily sprouting up.[14]

So, faced with Bramhall's criticisms, Hobbes decided that to attack is the best defence: in the 1668 *Appendix*, he explicitly acknowledged God's corporeal nature, something that had only been an implicit

---

[12] *HE* (*OL* v. 380).

[13] See Springborg, 'Hobbes, Heresy, and the *Historia Ecclesiastica*', 563. For a defence of Hobbes's orthodoxy, see A. P. Martinich, *The Two Gods of Leviathan. Thomas Hobbes on Religion and Politics* (Cambridge: Cambridge University Press, 1992).

[14] John Bramhall, *The Catching of Leviathan or the Great Whale* (London, 1658; repr. New York: Garland, 1977), 471.

conclusion in the *Leviathan*. At the same time, he defended the orthodoxy of this astounding doctrine.

Much can be said about the effectiveness of this defence. For example, the only Church father who in some sense does confirm Hobbes's position is Tertullian, whose Stoic conception of God's corporeal nature is nevertheless a very lonely voice among the *Patres*. Moreover, Hobbes does not tire of saying that the first four Church Councils and the Nicean Creed never explicitly acknowledge God's incorporeal nature, which, nonetheless, is not the same as admitting that God is indeed corporeal. A full discussion of the merits of Hobbes's attempt to find theological support for his daring doctrines will, however, have to be deferred to another occasion. What we will deal with here is the question to what extent Hobbes's 'heresy' is linked to his philosophical views. We can break down this overall question into two specific ones. First, given that Hobbes's explicit affirmation of God's corporeal nature comes very late in his publishing career, is his position consistent throughout all his works? Second, given that God is corporeal, how does he fit Hobbes's natural philosophy, i.e. the study of corporeal nature? We will start, however, with a discussion of Hobbes's general views on the relation between religion and science, which are of paramount importance not only for understanding Hobbes's concept of heresy, but also his views on God's corporeal nature.

THE SEPARATION OF REASON AND FAITH

Hobbes offers several explanations for why reason and faith should be kept separate.[15] The first might be called an external one. Reason and faith, philosophy and religion are two different practices, each with its own sets of rules. Philosophy is the domain of private

---

[15] There is an abundant literature on Hobbes's views on religion. For a good overview and useful references, see P. Springborg, 'Hobbes on Religion', in T. Sorell (ed.), *The Cambridge Companion to Hobbes* (Cambridge: Cambridge University Press, 1992), 346–80. See also K. Schuhmann, 'La Question de Dieu dans la philosophie de Hobbes', in D. Weber (ed.), *Hobbes, Descartes et la Métaphysique* (Paris: Vrin, 2005).

opinion and of debate between these opinions. Religion, by contrast, is neither a set of articles that can be demonstrated rationally, nor a supernatural source of truth. As is known, in the *Leviathan* Hobbes demonstrates on scriptural grounds that all spiritual authority ultimately lies in the hands of the sovereign, since the prophetic age in which God revealed himself directly to humankind lies in the past. Religion is basically a set of laws, promulgated by the sovereign, with which all citizens have to comply. Faith is thus essentially a matter of law and common public conduct, while philosophy belongs to the sphere of private opinion.[16] Hobbes distinguishes between practices that should not be confused: one does not play rugby on a tennis court.

Hobbes, however, does not just offer an external but also an internal, epistemological criterion for the separation of reason and faith. Philosophy deals with things that are conceivable to us. Since God is incomprehensible, he can never be the object of scientific demonstration. We find in Hobbes's work several specifications of why God is incomprehensible.[17] The most important for our purposes is exemplified by a passage from the *Leviathan*, in which Hobbes explains that philosophy deals with what has first been in the senses.[18] The only things that are accessible to our sense

---

[16] See *DCo*, Ep. Ded.: 'Contra hanc Empusam [sc. scholasticam dictam θεολογίαν exorcismus (credo) melior excogitari non potest, quam ut Religionis, id est, Dei honorandi colendique regulae a legibus petendae, a Philosophiae regulis, id est, a privatorum hominum dogmatibus distinguantur, quaeque Religionis sunt, Scripturae Sacrae, quae Philosophiae sunt, rationi naturali tribuantur.'

[17] See *DM* 149, 317, 319, 384; *L* 12 (*EW* iii. 97); *EL* xi. 1 (*EW* iv. 59); *OMC* (*OL* v. 259–60); *DCi* xvii. 28 (*OL* ii. 412–13), *DCi* xviii. 4 (*OL* ii. 420).

[18] *L* 3 (*EW* iii. 17): 'Whatsoever we imagine is finite. Therefore there is no idea or conception of any thing we call infinite. No man can have in his mind an image of infinite magnitude; nor conceive infinite swiftness, infinite time, or infinite force, or infinite power. When we say any thing is infinite, we signify only, that we are not able to conceive the ends and bounds of the things named; having no conception of the thing, but of our own inability. And therefore the name of God is used, not to make us conceive him; (for he is incomprehensible; and his greatness and power are unconceivable;) but that we may honour him. Also because whatsoever (as I said before,) we conceive, has been perceived first by sense, either all at once, or by parts; a man can have no thought, representing any thing, not subject to sense. No man therefore can conceive any thing, but he must conceive it in some place; and indued with some determinate magnitude; and which may be divided into parts; nor that any thing is all in this place, and all in another place at the same time; nor that two, or more things can be in one, and the same place at once: for none of these things ever

perception are bodies that have a finite, determinate magnitude, and hence a determinate place. Moreover, bodies with finite magnitude are divisible into parts. Now, according to all canonical texts (Scripture, the Nicene Creed, etc.), God has no parts, he has no circumscribed place but is omnipresent, and he is infinite. Hence, we can have no idea of God's essence.

All in all, human reason can only infer *that* God exists, not *what* he is.[19] In this context, Hobbes uses one of the traditional proofs for the existence of God, namely the causal one. By postulating the existence of a first cause, an infinite regress of causes is prevented. One of the most interesting formulations of this argument is found in the *Objections to Descartes' Meditations*, where Hobbes compares the finding of God as the first cause with a blind man, who upon feeling the heat of the fire concludes that there actually is something that causes the heat, but which he cannot see and which we call 'a fire'.[20] Similarly, we postulate that there must be a cause of our ideas, which again must have a cause, until finally we arrive at the supposition of an eternal cause that has no further cause. Just like in the case of the blind man, we infer that there must be a cause, but we have no positive idea or conception of it.

In all contexts, the basic idea is the same: in Hobbes's mechanistic universe bodies can only be put in motion by other bodies. These, in turn, also need an external cause of their motion. In order to prevent an infinite regress of external causes, we need to postulate a First Mover. In *De Corpore* Hobbes adds that unlike the Aristotelian First

---

have, or can be incident to sense; but are absurd speeches, taken upon credit (without any signification at all,) from deceived philosophers, and deceived, or deceiving schoolmen.'

[19] DM 319, 384, 395–6; EL xi. 2 (*EW* iv. 59); *OMC* (*OL* v. 260); L 34 (*EW* iii. 383).

[20] *OMC* (*OL* v. 260): 'Videtur ergo nullam esse in nobis Dei ideam. Sed sicut caecus natus, saepius igni admotus, et sentiens se calere, agnoscit esse aliquid a quo calefactus est, audiensque illud appellari ignem, concludit ignem existere, nec tamen qualis figurae aut coloris ignis sit cognoscit, vel ullam omnino ignis ideam vel imaginem animo obversantem habet: itaque homo cognoscens debere esse causam aliquam suarum imaginum vel idearum, et causae illius aliam causam priorem, et sic continuo, deducitur tandem ad finem sive suppositionem alicujus causae aeternae, quae quia nunquam coepit esse, causam se habere priorem non potest, necessario aliquid aeternum existere concludit: nec tamen ideam ullam habet, quam possit dicere esse ideam aeterni illius, sed rem creditam vel agnitam nominat vel appellat *Deum*'. Same metaphor in *EW* iv. 60; *OL* v. 260; *EW* iii. 92 en *OL* iii. 83.

Mover, the one he postulates should also move itself, the reason being that bodies can only be moved by other bodies if those are themselves in motion.[21]

As Arrigo Pacchi has shown, Hobbes uses here a traditional proof for the existence of God, but adapts it to his own, non-traditional, purposes. Its function is not to demonstrate rationally an article of faith and defend it against the infidels, as had been the case, for instance, for Thomas Aquinas. Rather, it gives 'some kind of reassurance that a conception of Nature and of man—as part of a mechanically regarded Nature—grounded on a deterministic principle or causal necessity, is really well grounded'.[22] As Pacchi rightly points out, in Hobbes's case the traditional *via* is not a proof or formal demonstration at all, but rather some kind of hypothesis at which we arrive by carefully considering the natural world. In the passage from the *Objections*, Hobbes indeed speaks about the 'supposition of an eternal cause' (*suppositionem alicujus causae aeternae*). Karl Schuhmann has demonstrated that Hobbes's version of the argument is rather a description of the psychological process by which people come to *believe* that there is a first cause or a first mover.[23] As, for instance, *Leviathan* states, 'it is impossible to make any profound inquiry into natural causes, without being inclined thereby to believe there is one God eternal', and that we 'shall at last come to this, that there must be . . . one first mover'.[24] Hobbes thus wholly relegates this kind of quasi-proof to the religious sphere, which has nothing to do with scientific inquiry.

Thus, against Descartes's notion of innate ideas, Hobbes makes it clear that even if we can infer God's existence, we still do not have a positive idea of his essence. This means that all the names that we give to God cannot be seen as cognitive statements concerning his nature, but only as a non-cognitive or performative expression of our wish to honour him. This is shown by the fact that we largely use

[21] *DCo* xxvi. 1 (*OL* i. 336).

[22] A. Pacchi, 'Hobbes and the Problem of God', in G. A. J. Rogers and A. Ryan (eds.), *Perspectives on Thomas Hobbes* (Oxford: Clarendon, 1988), 181. See also A. Pacchi, 'Hobbes e il Dio delle cause', in *La storia della filosofia come sapere critico. Studi offerti a Mario dal Pra* (Milan: Franco Angeli, 1984), 303.

[23] Karl Schuhmann, 'La Question de Dieu'.

[24] *L* 11 (*EW* iii. 92) and *L* 12 (*EW* iii. 96).

negative expressions: God is in-finite, in-comprehensible, etc. God
clearly transcends our rational categories. This does not mean that
according to Hobbes God can be reached through some kind of
ecstatic *unio mystica*. Rather, to return to our athletic metaphor:
speaking of God is not the task of science or philosophy, but part
of the ballgame of religion, a matter of public conduct regulated by
the sovereign and those that are appointed by him as the official
interpreters of Scripture. The only characteristic of God that is
the prerogative of the philosopher is to speak of his bare existence
('Deus est').[25]

From this short summary, it should be clear that according to
Hobbes nothing good could come from mixing the domains of faith
and reason. Hobbes not just warns against confounding the two
practices of religion and philosophy, but he also criticizes transgressions of the epistemological boundaries between religion and philosophy. His best-known attacks are found in the fourth part of the
Leviathan ('The Kingdom of Darkness'), especially in its chapter 46,
'Of Darkness from Vain Philosophy and Fabulous Traditions'.[26]
Hobbes discards scholastic metaphysics and theology as a combination of Christian faith and heathen philosophy. By trying to philosophize on matters of faith, which should have been founded upon
belief and submission, the scholastics were inevitably reduced to
using meaningless expressions or 'insignificant speech', as Hobbes
calls it.

In the end, it is not just scholastic theology that Hobbes rejects but
any theology that presents itself as a science of the divine. Traditionally, theology was defined as the doctrine concerning the nature and
attributes of God. However, in the beginning of *De Corpore*, Hobbes
excludes from the sciences precisely this form of theology, namely

---

[25] *DM* 395–6: 'Ego vero, dum considero Dei naturam esse inconceptibilem,
propositiones autem esse orationes quasdam, quibus Conceptus nostros de naturis
rerum pronuntiamus, in eam opinionem propendeo nullam propositionem veram
esse posse circa naturam Dei praeter hanc unam: Deus est, neque ullam appellationem naturae Dei convenire praeter unicum nomen *Ens*, caetera omnia tribui non ad
veritatem philosophicam explicandam, sed ad affectus nostros, quibus Deum
magnificare laudare et honorare volumus declarandos.'

[26] On Hobbes's critique of scholastic metaphysics, see C. Leijenhorst, *The Mechanisation of Aristotelianism. The Late Aristotelian Setting of Thomas Hobbes's Natural
Philosophy* (Leiden: Brill, 2002), 27–34 and 38–50.

'the doctrine concerning the nature and attributes of the eternal, ingenerable and incomprehensible God' (*doctrinam de natura et attributis Dei aeterni, ingenerabilis, incomprehensibilis*).[27] Philosophy has to do with how causes generate effects and how effects are generated by their causes. God, however, is ungenerated. To use Hobbes's terminology: in God there is no 'composition and division'. Hence, he cannot be the object of scientific demonstration.

The only 'theology' that remains is the interpretation of Scripture, which is an inherently practical discipline. It interprets the revealed word of God not as a means of getting to know his nature, but in order to teach the subjects of a commonwealth the right kind of submission to their lawful sovereign. However, if we look at the way Hobbes himself interprets Scripture, especially in the extensive third and fourth parts of the *Leviathan*, we may instead witness a heavy use of philosophy. Pacchi rightly says that Hobbes is among the first to develop a historical-critical and rational method of biblical interpretation on the basis of his philosophy.[28] In this sense, Hobbes himself seems to trespass on the premises to which he had denied access to all philosophers. Nevertheless, his trespassing is less paradoxical than it may appear at first sight. For Hobbes only permits the use of reason and hence of philosophy in the interpretation of Scripture as long as it does not pretend to give speculative insight into that which will always remain inaccessible to it, namely the nature and attributes of God.[29] Thus, despite his use of reason in the interpretation of Scripture, Hobbes maintains the distinction

---

[27] *DCo* i. 8 (*OL* i. 9).

[28] A. Pacchi, *Scritti Hobbesiani* (Milan: Franco Angeli, 1998), 98.

[29] See the famous beginning of part 3 of the *Leviathan* (*L* 32; *EW* iii. 359–60): 'Nevertheless, we are not to renounce our senses, and experience; nor (that which is the undoubted word of God) our natural reason. For they are the talents which he hath put into our hands to negotiate, till the coming again of our blessed Saviour; and therefore not to be folded up in the napkin of an implicit faith, but employed in the purchase of justice, peace, and true religion. For though there be many things in God's word above reason; that is to say, which cannot by natural reason be either demonstrated or confuted; yet there is nothing contrary to it; but when it seemeth so, the fault is either in our unskilful interpretation or erroneous ratiocination. Therefore, when any thing therein written is too hard for our examination, we are bidden to captivate our understanding to the words; and not to labour in sifting out a philosophical truth by logic, of such mysteries as are not comprehensible, nor fall under any rule of natural science. For it is with the mysteries of our religion, as with

between philosophy and religion first of all in an epistemological sense. The divine mysteries remain hidden from the philosophical mind. As for the pragmatical sense of the distinction, Hobbes's position is a bit more complicated. By interpreting Scripture by means of philosophy, he seems to break his own code in formulating a private opinion in a realm in which obedience is due. However, Hobbes defended himself by saying that at the time of writing there was no established political and ecclesiastical authority to which he could have submitted his interpretation, but instead his *Leviathan* defends the very concept of obedience to the lawful authorities.

Pacchi has also underlined the fact that Hobbes's use of his materialist and determinist philosophy in the interpretation of Scripture does not in principle clash with his separation of science and faith.[30] Nevertheless, according to Pacchi, in another sense Hobbes does venture a few 'illegal' philosophical excursions into the religious realm. As one example of these transgressions, Pacchi mentions precisely Hobbes's digressions about God's corporeal nature in the *Appendix* to the Latin *Leviathan* and other works of the 1660s.[31] Nonetheless, as will become clear, these digressions do not violate the 'no access signs' posted by Hobbes himself.

2. THE CONSISTENCY OF HOBBES'S NOTION OF CORPOREAL DEITY

In two important articles, Edwin Curley has argued that Hobbes was fundamentally inconsistent with respect to the corporeal character of God.[32] According to Curley, the Latin *Leviathan* of 1668 is more or

---

wholesome pills for the sick, which swallowed whole, have the virtue to cure; but chewed, are for the most part cast up again without effect. But by the captivity of our understanding, is not meant a submission of the intellectual faculty, to the opinion of any other man; but of the will to obedience, where obedience is due.'

[30] Pacchi, 'Hobbes and the Problem of God', 186; and id. *Scritti Hobbesiani*, 99.

[31] Pacchi, *Scritti Hobbesiani*, 105.

[32] E. Curley, '*I Durst not Write so Boldly* or How to Read Hobbes's Theological-Political Treatise', in P. Bostrenghi (ed.), *Scienza e Politica* (Naples: Bibliopolis, 1992), 497–593; and E. Curley, 'Hobbes versus Descartes', in R. Ariew and M. Grene (eds.), *Descartes and his Contemporaries. Meditations, Objections and Replies* (Chicago: Chicago University Press, 1995), 97–109.

less the only publication in which Hobbes unequivocally claims that God is a body. In his earlier works, he had defended a range of different, but mutually contradicting, positions. According to *De Motu*, for instance, we should trust Scripture, which tells us that God is an incorporeal substance. Curley states that Hobbes was not inconsistent for a lack of philosophical subtlety, but for reasons of prudence. According to Curley, Hobbes was in his heart of hearts a downright atheist. Given that a defence of this view in public would have been sheer suicide, Hobbes played a hide-and-seek game: in different works, he tried different positions, none of which represented his true convictions about God. The publication that comes closest to his hidden atheism is the Latin *Leviathan*. This work, however, was published overseas and in what Curley considers a foreign language. Moreover, by then, he was at a very advanced age, which probably subdued any fear of persecution. Curley thinks that this work propounds what Hobbes himself calls 'atheism by consequence', which is defined as defending a position that is so contradictory to all established descriptions of God, that it practically entails atheism.[33] According to Curley, upholding the corporeality of God is in fact an example of such a position: 'But if God were corporeal, he would not be God, for well-known reasons. Therefore, God does not exist.'[34] In this respect, Curley finds himself in the good company of Bishop Bramhall, who equally thought that affirming the corporeal character of God amounted to denying his very existence.

Let us review Curley's thesis point by point, starting with the alleged 'fideism' of *De Motu*. This fideism emerges from Hobbes's rejection of White's contention that natural reason can prove the existence of God.[35] Curley thinks that this contradicts Hobbes's causal proof for the existence of God.[36] Martinich, by contrast, has pointed out that what Hobbes rejects here is White's claim of having offered a formal *demonstration* of God's existence.[37] As we have seen above, Hobbes thinks that we can arrive at only the *hypothesis* of God's existence. Just as the blind man has no conception of the fire

---

[33] For Hobbes's definition of 'atheism by consequence', see *ABB* (*EW* iv. 383–4).
[34] Curley, 'Hobbes versus Descartes', 108.   [35] See *DM* 308–9f.
[36] Curley, 'I Durst Not Write So Boldly', 580.
[37] Martinich, *The Two Gods of Leviathan*, 348.

that warms him, we do not have a conception of God. This precludes any formal demonstration of God's existence, because demonstrations apply only to what we actually conceive.[38] In other words, *De Motu* is not more or less fideistic than the works that propound Hobbes's causal hypothesis of God's existence. In fact, *De Motu* itself quite specifically states that the only true philosophical proposition concerning God is that he exists.[39] Again, this is perfectly in line with Hobbes's general view that philosophy can only state *that* God exists, not *what* he is.[40]

But also with respect to God's corporeality, *De Motu* constitutes much less of a fideistic anomaly than Curley makes it out to be. Curley actually makes a distinction between three different positions Hobbes is supposed to have defended throughout his works. In Curley's words, the *Leviathan* and the *Elements of Law* say that 'God exists, but we cannot know his nature; so, we cannot know whether he is corporeal or not.'[41] *De Motu* says that 'reason cannot instruct us on this subject, either one way or the other; therefore, it is necessary to recur to Sacred Scripture, which tells us that God is immaterial'.[42] Finally, in the 1660s Hobbes states that 'God exists, and he is corporeal, and there is no theological problem with that position.'[43]

In order to judge the validity of this claim, let us first examine *Leviathan* and *Elements of Law*. The *Leviathan* starts with the familiar assertion that philosophy can conceive only of bodies, i.e. entities with determinate dimensions and a determinate place. Given this restriction, Hobbes strongly suggests that we might as well simply equate the concept of being and the concept of body: 'the universe, that is, the whole mass of all things that are, is corporeal ... and because the universe is all, that which is no part of it, is nothing; and

---

[38] *DM* 308–9.

[39] *DM* 396: 'Propendeo nullam propositionem veram esse posse circa naturam Dei praeter hanc unam: Deus est, neque ullam appellationem naturae Dei convenire praeter unicum nomen *Ens*.'

[40] Neither Curley nor Martinich refer to the earlier article by Pacchi that resolves the seeming contradiction between *De Motu* and Hobbes's other works with respect to the causal proof of God's existence (see Pacchi, 'Hobbes e il Dio delle Cause', 306).

[41] Curley, 'Hobbes versus Descartes', 108.   [42] Ibid. 109.

[43] Ibid.

consequently no where'.[44] Subsequently, Hobbes examines what this restriction implies for diverse kinds of beings. As for finite spirits, such as human souls, Hobbes is very clear. We cannot conceive of them otherwise than as bodies, i.e. as entities with determinate dimensions.[45] The fact that they are not visible does not make any difference. As is well known, Hobbes devotes a lot of space in the *Leviathan* to prove that Scripture does not state that souls and other spirits are incorporeal substances, but rather that they are beings with determinate dimensions. God, however, is a different issue: 'But for spirits, they call them incorporeal; which is a name of more honour, and may therefore with more piety be attributed to God himself; in whom we consider not what attribute expresseth best his nature, which is incomprehensible; but what best expresseth our desire to honour Him'.[46]

God is infinite, omnipresent and indivisible. In other words, he does not share any of the defining characteristics of natural bodies. In that sense, it is not unwarranted to call him incorporeal. Paradoxically, however, philosophy can also state (though not formally demonstrate) that God exists. Since philosophy teaches us that everything that exists is a body, God would actually be a body, something that Hobbes implies but does not explicitly admit in the *Leviathan*. The result of these considerations would be that God is in fact an incorporeal substance, a notion that, as said, in Hobbes's eyes contains a contradiction *in adjecto*. Although Hobbes himself prefers to call God an incomprehensible substance rather than an incorporeal substance, he does not object to this qualification for honour's sake.[47] The only condition is that we make clear that we do not speak 'dogmatically, with intention to make the divine nature understood; but piously, to honour him with attributes, of significations, as remote as they can from the grossness of bodies visible'.[48] By using

---

[44] *L* 46 (*EW* iii. 672).   [45] Ibid.   [46] Ibid.

[47] See also *L* 34 (*EW* iii. 383–4), where Hobbes uses the label 'incorporeal substance' without further qualification: '*The Spirit of God moved upon the face of the waters.* Here if by the Spirit of God be meant God himself, then is motion attributed to God, and consequently place, which are intelligible only of bodies, and not of substances incorporeal; and so the place is above our understanding, that can conceive nothing moved that changes not place, or that has not dimension; and whatsoever has dimension, is body.'

[48] *L* 12 (*EW* iii. 97).

this philosophically absurd notion, we only emphasize our inability to grasp his nature. Thus, when we speak of God as an incorporeal substance, we are playing a religious ballgame, not a philosophical one: we speak 'piously', not 'dogmatically'. Paradoxical as it may seem, God is thus both a body and an incorporeal substance. When we speak as philosophers, we say that God exists, which philosophically speaking means that he is a body. However, he is a body whose nature transcends our rational categories. So, if we switch to a religious discourse, we may actually also call him an incorporeal substance.

Exactly the same position is found in the *Elements of Law*. Throughout the *Elements*, the same identification of 'being' and 'body' is operative. Here, Hobbes also claims that finite spirits such as angels and human souls are fine, imperceptibly thin, bodies. He also states that this is more in line with Scripture than the view that they are incorporeal substances.[49] Likewise, the *Elements* make the same distinction between finite bodies and the infinite, incomprehensible substance of God. Just as in the *Leviathan*, Hobbes allows also in the *Elements* for the use of the non-philosophical, non-biblical term 'incorporeal substance', as long as we make clear that 'When we attribute the name of spirit unto God, we attribute it not as the name of anything we conceive, no more than when we ascribe unto him sense and understanding; but as a signification of our reverence, who desire to abstract from him all corporal grossness.'[50] In other words, Hobbes again refers to the distinction between philosophical and religious discourse, between things that we 'conceive', and things that command our 'reverence'.

Curley suggests that the real difference is between *Elements of Law* and *Leviathan*, on the one hand, and *De Motu* on the other. *De Motu* is more 'fideistic' than the other works in that it lets Scripture decide that God is indeed an immaterial substance. In reality, however, Hobbes defends the same position, albeit phrased somewhat differently than in the *Leviathan* and *Elements of Law*. Hobbes repeats that the human mind can only conceive of substances with finite, determinate dimensions and with a determinate place. Hobbes therefore

---

[49] *EL* xi. 5 (*EW* iv. 62).   [50] *EL* xi. 4 (*EW* iv. 61).

explicitly equates the concepts of being (*ens*) and body (*corpus*).[51] On account of his infinite dimensions, God is incomprehensible. Philosophy, however, can sustain the proposition that God is a being (*ens*), with the implicit consequence that he is a body. However, he is a substance whose nature goes beyond our philosophical understanding. In religious terms, Christians have called God an incorporeal substance, inspired by Scripture.[52] Although Hobbes in this context does not explicitly reject the claim that the notion of incorporeal substance is biblical, he emphasizes again that it is a philosophically absurd notion. It may, however, be used in religious discourse, where we do not employ language that expresses our knowledge of God, but our sole wish to praise and honour him.[53]

In sum, *De Motu* propounds the same 'fideism' as Hobbes's two main English political works. What Curley fails to note is that the 'materialist' description of God's corporeality and the 'fideist' label of incorporeal substance do not mutually exclude each other. I agree with Curley that in the *Elements* Hobbes suggests that 'God is a subtle corporeal substance'.[54] Philosophically speaking, God is a corporeal substance for the same reason that he is a being. This however, does not prevent the *Elements* from simultaneously affirming that we may perfectly well name God an incorporeal substance in a religious context. This seeming paradox is not the mark of a bad philosopher, or, for that matter, of one who tries to play desperate hide-and-seek games. It is simply the result of Hobbes's basic distinction between philosophical and religious discourse, which he consistently applies in all three works discussed.

The same distinction is at work in Hobbes's later works, where he unequivocally admits God's corporeity. Let us look at a passage from Hobbes's acrimonious polemics with John Wallis: 'Is not Mr Hobbes his way of attributing to God, that only which the Scriptures attribute to him, or what is never any where taken but for honour, much better than this bold undertaking of yours, to consider and decipher God's nature to us?'[55] In other words, Hobbes clearly states that his admission that God is a 'a most pure, simple, invisible spirit

---

[51] *DM* 312. [52] *DM* 127.
[53] *DM* 396: 'Caetera omnia tribui non ad veritatem philosophicam explicandam, sed ad affectos nostros, quibus Deum magnificare et honorare volumus declarandos.'
[54] Curley, 'I Durst Not Write So Boldly', 582. [55] *CRL* (*EW* iv. 426).

corporeal'[56] does not pretend to give any insight into God's nature, which remains as hidden as it had been in his earlier works. Hobbes emphasizes that in describing God as a subtle, corporeal spirit that is moreover infinite, he is not speaking philosophically about the nature of God, which is in fact what he accuses Wallis of doing. The notion of an infinite, simple spirit is as 'incomprehensible' as that of an incorporeal substance. For, as said, the human mind can only conceive of bodies that have a finite and determinate magnitude and a determinate and circumscribed place.

The only difference between this position and the earlier one of *De Motu, Elements of Law,* and *Leviathan* is that in the *Appendix* to the Latin *Leviathan* and other works of the 1660s, Hobbes explicitly rejects the notion of incorporeal substance as a suitable name for God. In his earlier works, Hobbes had already indicated that the notion of incorporeal substance is unbiblical—a claim which by the way has a good deal of truth in it—and that he himself had rather not use this philosophically absurd notion. However, in principle he did not have any objections to it, as long as it was made clear that one was speaking 'piously' and not 'dogmatically' about God. In his later works, however, Hobbes took a stricter position on the use of what he considered non-biblical vocabulary. We can only guess at the reasons behind this change of mind. One reason could be that Hobbes had witnessed how in the intense polemics surrounding the *Leviathan,* his opponents had used the notion of an incorporeal substance in a non-religious, philosophical way, pretending thereby to provide an insight into God's nature. This may have led Hobbes to dissociate himself completely from the non-biblical vocabulary that he had only hesitantly accepted anyway.

In sum, Curley's claim that through the years Hobbes offered a whole range of different, even contradictory conceptions of God's (non-)corporeality is wrong. On the contrary, there is a remarkable structural consistency of Hobbes's position on this issue, despite the minor changes that did occur. There is thus no evidence for Curley's contention that for strategic reasons Hobbes tried out different positions, which, however, did not represent his true convictions.

---

[56] *ABB* (*EW* iv. 313). See also *App. ad LL* (*OL* iii. 561).

For Curley, the position that comes closes to Hobbes's hidden atheism lies in the public admission of the 1660s that God is a corporeal spirit, which was already foreshadowed by the famous lost *London Letter* of 1640 that also unequivocally spoke of a corporeal Deity.[57] According to Curley, on the logic of Hobbes's own philosophy, this assumption leads to the inevitable conclusion that God does not exist. In other words, the notion of a corporeal deity would be Hobbes's most explicit signal that in reality he did not believe in God's existence at all. In order to buttress this claim, Curley patches together arguments gathered from several of Hobbes's works:[58]

1. God is corporeal.
2. The universe is the aggregate of all bodies.
3. Therefore, God is identical either with the whole of the universe or with a part of it (an inference from (1) and (2), but accepted by Hobbes at *EW* iv. 349).
4. To hold that God is identical with the whole of the universe is equivalent to atheism, since it denies that the universe has a cause.
5. If God is identical with a part of the universe, he is finite, since no part of any whole can be infinite.
6. To hold that God is finite is equivalent to atheism, since God, by definition, is infinite.
7. Therefore, to affirm (3) is to embrace atheism.

Martinich has rejected this argument by contending that it is patched together from works that span three decades. Moreover, according to Martinich, Hobbes's 'ability to see the consequences of his premises was surely flawed'.[59] This is not a very effective counter-argument. Hobbes is known as a thinker whose philosophy underwent very few major transformations. In that sense, it is not a priori wrong to quote from works that were written at such large intervals of time. However, contrary to what Curley claims, Hobbes's text does not necessarily lead to supposedly atheist consequences. Therefore, the question of whether or not Hobbes foresaw the consequences of his own premises is irrelevant for this issue.

---

[57] On the London Letter, see Malcolm, *Correspondence*, p. liii.
[58] Curley, 'I Durst Not Write So Boldly', 587.
[59] Martinich, *The Two Gods of Leviathan*, 350.

The crucial step in the argument is (3). The statement Curley refers to occurs in Hobbes's discussion with Bramhall. It responds to an objection that the Bishop had already voiced on other occasions. If, as Hobbes says in the *Leviathan*, the universe is the aggregate of all bodies, and whatever is not a body is nothing, God is either a finite body or nothing, both of which leads straight to atheism. Against this, Hobbes repeats that God is a 'corporeal, but yet a pure spirit'.[60] Moreover, Hobbes says that by universe he means 'the aggregate of all things that have being in themselves'. Since God has being, 'it follows that he is either the whole universe, or part of it'. In his *Answer*, Hobbes does not specify whether God is the whole or just a part. If, however, we look at the *Leviathan*, it becomes quite clear what answer Hobbes would have given to the Bishop. As Curley rightly stresses, the *Leviathan* explicitly rejects any form of pantheism, because it implies that the world has no cause.[61] This leaves no other choice than to admit that God is a part of the universe. Indeed, in the passage Bramhall criticizes, Hobbes suggests that this is in fact the case. As already mentioned, after having claimed that 'the universe, that is, the whole mass of all things that are, is corporeal',[62] Hobbes discusses the different 'regions' of the universe: finite bodies, finite spirits, and God, which implies that he is a part of the universe.

Since God is a being, he is necessarily a 'part' of the universe as Hobbes defines it, namely the 'aggregate of all being'. But, according to Curley, this in turn must lead to the atheist conclusion that God is finite, given that *De Motu* unequivocally states that no part of a whole can be infinite.[63] Although this is correct, Curley omits another crucial tenet of Hobbes's mereology: the notions of whole (*totum*) and part cannot be meaningfully applied to infinite entities.[64] Since our finite minds cannot conceive of parts other than as finite, the whole that is composed of parts will inevitably also remain finite. Since God is infinite, this means that he cannot in any meaningful way be called either a whole or a part. Now, this does not contradict Hobbes's own statement from his *Answer to Bishop Bramhall*. What we have here is simply the above-mentioned distinction between

---

[60] *ABB* (*EW* iv. 349).   [61] *L* 31 (*EW* iii. 351).   [62] *L* 46 (*EW* iii. 672).
[63] *DM* 111.   [64] *DCo* vii. 12 (*OL* i. 88).

philosophical and religious discourse about God only in another guise. Since God is a being, he is a 'part' of the universe, and since the universe is corporeal, he is corporeal too. However, as we have seen, he is a body that does not have any of the characteristics of normal bodies, but instead infinity, omnipresence, and indivisibility. Hence, we might as well call him an incorporeal body, or in any case a body whose nature transcends our understanding. Likewise God is a part of the universe that does not have the normal characteristic of parts, namely finitude.[65] In other words, God is a part of the corporeal universe of which we can have no conception. The application of the concept of part thus runs completely parallel to that of the concept of body. There is therefore no reason to assume that by calling God either the whole of the universe or its part, Hobbes is giving covert atheistic signals to his readers. Hobbes only implies that the notion of part, if applied to God, is meaningless. Similarly, in *De Corpore*, Hobbes states that the question whether the world is finite or infinite is a matter of religion, not of philosophy.[66]

While Curley's interpretation of Hobbes's corporeal deity is not tenable, the one by Zarka that he criticizes is not completely convincing either. Zarka claims that Hobbes only affirms the corporeal nature of God, when his opponents press him.[67] This statement should therefore not be taken literally. If we have to say something about God's nature, the best we can do is to say that he is corporeal, because we do not have any other concept of substance. However, in itself this label does not have any validity. It is 'the blasphemy of a reason that wants to pass beyond the limits of the knowable'.[68] Hobbes's strict position is that God exists, but that His nature is not conceivable by us. Only when his opponents put pressure on him, does he relinquish this position.

In answer to this, Curley in fact rightly points to the lost *London Letter* of November 1640 to Mersenne, which criticizes Descartes's

---

[65] See *DCi* xv. 14 (*OL* ii. 341) where Hobbes says that it is wrong to say that God himself 'habeat partes, aut quod sit totum aliquid'.

[66] *DCo xxvi.* 1 (*OL* i. 335).

[67] Y-Ch. Zarka, *La Décision métaphysique de Hobbes* (Paris: Vrin, 1987), 148.

[68] Y-Ch. Zarka, 'Espace et représentation chez Hobbes', *Recherches sur le XVIIe siècle*, 7 (1984), 175: 'C'est bien plutôt un blasphème, le blasphème d'une raison qui veut sortir des limites du connaissable.'

Dioptrique.[69] We have only Descartes's reply to this letter, but on the basis of this reply and the epistolary exchanges between Mersenne, Descartes, Hobbes, and Charles Cavendish we can actually reconstruct what Hobbes must have said. Descartes there mentions Hobbes's affirmation of the corporeal character of the human soul and of God, to which he does not wish to answer.[70] It is thus not strictly true that Hobbes only affirms the corporeal character of God when his opponents press him to do so. I would like to add that despite what Zarka says, 'God is a body' should be taken literally, because it is equivalent to saying 'God exists' which is all a philosopher can say 'dogmatically' about God. Contrary to what Zarka implies, Hobbes makes it quite clear that the thesis 'God is an infinite, simple corporeal spirit' is not meant as a 'dogmatic' insight into his nature, but as a 'pious' way of honouring him. It is as incomprehensible and non-blasphemous a title as that of 'incorporeal substance', which Hobbes had acknowledged with hesitation in his earlier works. In his polemics with Bramhall and others Hobbes did not pass beyond 'the limits of the knowable' that he had himself stipulated. I agree thus with Zarka *contra* Curley that Hobbes's strict position is indeed that God exists, but that we do not know his nature. I disagree, however, that Hobbes's notion of corporeal deity is in conflict with this position.

By way of conclusion, we can say that Hobbes's position on God's corporeal nature may be blatantly heterodox, but it is neither inconsistent nor implicitly atheistic. But another problem still remains. God's nature may be incomprehensible, he is still a body and as such a topic for Hobbes's natural philosophy, the doctrine that studies corporeal nature. How, then, should we understand the relation between God and Hobbes's physics?

GOD, *PRIMUM FLUIDUM* AND ETHER

Agostino Lupoli has recently given a highly interesting analysis of the problem of how to square God with Hobbes's

---

[69] Curley, 'Hobbes versus Descartes', 107.

[70] Descartes to Mersenne, for Hobbes, 21 January 1641, in *Correspondance du P. Marin Mersenne* (Paris: Beauchesne, 1967), 427.

physics.[71] He shows that Hobbes defines God as a subtle spirit, i.e. as a fine, fluid body. The question Lupoli asks is how this fluid body relates to the other fluids Hobbes lists in his physics, where a kind of ether is mentioned that pervades all solid bodies and where prime matter is described as a *primum fluidum* created by God. Lupoli argues that these descriptions of different fluids cannot be squared with each other and explains this in terms of an inner conflict in Hobbes's account of creation. On the one hand, he declares that all questions about the beginning of the world are non-philosophical and the prerogative of those that are appointed by the sovereign to interpret Scripture. On the other hand, he is tempted to give a more detailed, physical description of the corporeal deity and his relation to the physical cosmos. In the end, according to Lupoli, he preferred his account to remain sketchy and paradoxical, rather than transgressing the boundaries of the philosophically knowable as he had himself defined them.

To begin with, the notion of *primum fluidum* remains vague. In order to understand this concept, one should keep in mind Hobbes's distinction between *fluidum* and *durum*. A fluid body is defined by him as a body, whose parts are easily separable.[72] According to Hobbes, this separability is due to the fact that the parts of a fluid body have little motion. In his kinetic universe a phenomenon such as cohesion has to be explained in terms of actual motion. To cohere or to resist pressure is an action, and all action is motion. Therefore, in contradiction to Descartes, Hobbes explains the hardness or strong cohesion of a body as the result of the swift motion of its constituent particles. Conversely, fluid bodies easily yield to pressure on account of the slow motion of their parts.[73]

Now, in some passages Hobbes suggests that fluids had been created before solid bodies.[74] According to Lupoli, Hobbes thought that the first matter out of which the universe was created was an

---

[71] A. Lupoli, '*Fluidismo e Corporeal Deity* nella filosofia naturale di Thomas Hobbes: a proposito dell'Hobbesiano *Dio delle Cause*', *Rivista di Storia della Filosofia*, 54 (1999), 573–609.

[72] *DM* 185: 'Fluidum appellare omnes solent id cujus partes a se invicem facile separantur.'

[73] *Dialogus* (*OL* iv. 285).

[74] Ibid. See Lupoli, '*Fluidismo e Corporeal Deity*', 595.

absolute, motionless fluid. Through some kind of compression, God
then created solid atoms that subsequently constituted solid natural
bodies. This notion of a primary fluid is difficult to square with
another concept of fluid found in Hobbes's work, namely that of the
fluid ether. This subtle body is said to fill all voids in the universe and
also plays an important role in the transmission of light. In contrast
to the motionless *primum fluidum*, Hobbes describes this ether as a
very mobile body.[75] This description by itself makes it difficult to
identify the two notions of fluid. To make matters even more per-
plexing, Hobbes qualifies the ether as prime matter (*materia
prima*).[76] The latter, however, is also said to be simply a name
(*merum nomen*).[77] It is a term that refers to body in general, not to
any specific body or component of material reality. There thus
appears to be a tension between the metaphysical concept of prime
matter as non-entity and the physical description of prime matter as
an absolutely fluid body. This tension is amplified by the fact that
strictly speaking the creation of solid bodies out of the *primum
fluidum* should have led to the disappearance of the latter, because
if the parts of the motionless fluid are compressed and hence set in
motion, they lose their status of fluid body.[78] How then can Hobbes
still speak of a fluid ether that obviously fills all voids in the universe?

Things become even less transparent if we turn to the third notion
of fluid, namely God himself. According to Lupoli, Hobbes enter-
tains several models of creation (or, for that matter, of non-creation)
without making a definitive choice for any of them.[79] Hobbes pays
lip-service to the Christian notion of a *creatio ex nihilo*, implying that
God created the primary fluid, out of which he subsequently formed
the universe. But in other contexts, Hobbes presents a weaker concept of creation according to which God acts as a kind of Platonic
Demiurge on a pre-existent fluid. Finally, one also finds traces of a
possible pantheist identification of God with the fluid ether and
possibly even with the primary fluid. Lupoli states that, in the end,
Hobbes possibly shied away from all the heterodox consequences of

[75] *DCo* xxvi. 5 (*OL* i. 348).
[76] *DCo* xxvii. 1 (*OL* i. 364). See Lupoli, '*Fluidismo* e *Corporeal Deity*', 588.
[77] *DCo* viii. 24 (*OL* i. 105).
[78] Lupoli, '*Fluidismo* e *Corporeal Deity*', 597.
[79] Ibid. 606–7.

his various models and chose the option of agnosticism. Although, despite his own warnings, Hobbes did speculate about various forms of divine creation, his final answer remained that the notion of creation cannot be grasped by our finite human mind, and that hence all problems about the beginning of the world and its relation to God are religious questions that are the prerogative of the sovereign and those appointed by him as interpreters of Scripture. Hobbes chose to remain undecided on these matters, rather than adopting what Lupoli deems the most obvious solution: an identification of the *primum fluidum* with God, attributing 'self-moving powers to a unique primary matter'.[80]

Although Hobbes's account of the relation between the Creator and his creation is indeed complicated, the picture that emerges from it is clearer than Lupoli suggests. First of all, the relation between the primary fluid and the subtle ether is not as paradoxical as it may seem at first sight. Most of the paradoxes that arise according to Lupoli have to do with the fact that Hobbes appears to identify the ether with prime matter. If, however, we look at the passage that according to Lupoli propounds this identification, we have to reach a different conclusion: 'And lastly, I suppose, that the parts of the pure aether (as if it were the First Matter) have no motion at all but what they receive from bodies which float in them, and are not themselves fluid.'[81] Hobbes evidently *compares* the parts of the ether with prime matter, but does not *identify* them. Moreover, Hobbes does not refer here to his own notion of prime matter but to the classical scholastic notion. In the Aristotelian-scholastic tradition prime matter is the inert, homogeneous 'stuff' that receives the form and hence also its principle of mobility. As said, Hobbes no longer maintains this notion of matter as a material constituent but simply defines prime matter as body in general or body, taken in a universal sense, omitting all particular characteristics of individual bodies.[82] Just as

---

[80] Ibid. 609: 'Mai prende corpo nei suoi scritti una chiara e univoca ipotesi che attribuisca a un'unica materia originaria un potere autocinetico.'

[81] *EW* i. 448; *DCo* xxvi. 1 (*OL* i. 364): 'Denique in partibus puri aetheris (tanquam in materia prima) motum praeter illum, quem habet ab innatantibus sibi corporibus non liquidis, suppono esse nullum.'

[82] On the relation between Aristotelian accounts and Hobbes's concept of matter, see Leijenhorst, *Mechanising Aristotelianism*, 150–5.

prime matter in the classical, non-Hobbesian sense is itself motion-less and receives motion from God, the parts of the pure ether have no proper motion but are moved by the solid bodies that float in it. This implies that contrary to what Lupoli claims, Hobbes does not confound the metaphysical notion of prime matter and the physical notion of pure ether.

This passage also solves another problem noted by Lupoli, namely that the primary fluid is motionless, while the pure ether is described as inherently mobile. In the passage quoted above, Hobbes does not say that the ether as a whole is in rest, but only that its parts do not have their own motion. This is in line with Hobbes's general notion of fluid. As he explains in his *Dialogus Physicus*, a fluid as a whole may move, while its parts are in relative rest.[83] As said, the parts of a fluid have no or only a minimal power of resistance. In Hobbes's vocabulary, they have no proper *conatus*, the *conatus* being defined as the smallest conceivable motion. Rather, the parts merely touch but do not press each other. It is precisely this lack of *conatus* of the *parts* of the ether that explains why they can so easily be moved by solid bodies that float in it. From the lack of motion of the parts of the primary fluid, Lupoli appears to infer that the primary fluid is motionless as a whole, just like prime matter, which according to Hobbes has no motion.[84] Apart from the fact that Hobbes does not identify the primary fluid and prime matter, the inference from the parts to the whole is also wrong: the parts of a fluid may be in relative rest, while the fluid as a whole is mobile. In sum, contrary to what Lupoli states, there is no reason for refraining from an identification of the supposedly immobile primary fluid with the inherently mobile subtle ether. Parts of this mobile ether may have been compressed into solid bodies, whose particles move very swiftly. This, however, does not mean that the ether completely goes out of existence, as Lupoli suggests. Nor will it lose its motion as a whole.

According to Lupoli, the real problems only start when we try to fathom the relation between the physical fluid(s) and God. In some passages, Hobbes appears to hint at an identification of the subtle

---

[83] *Dialogus* (*OL* iv. 284): 'Per quietem intelligo duarum partium inter se quietem, cum se mutuo tangunt quidem, sed non premunt. Nam et fluida moveri tota possunt, retenta fluiditate; et dura quiescere, ut tamen partes eorum moveantur.'

[84] Lupoli, '*Fluidismo* e *Corporeal Deity*', 597.

ether and God. The most convincing passage Lupoli adduces is: 'Because He that created them [sc. natural bodies] is not a fancy, but the most real substance that is, who being infinite, there can be no place empty where He is, nor full where He is not.'[85] If we recall that Hobbes describes the task of the subtle ether as having to fill all empty places of the universe, this description of God does indeed come very close to that of the subtle ether. Nevertheless, according to Lupoli, a full identification of the two entities not only remains paradoxical for theological reasons, but certainly also for philosophical reasons. Lupoli thinks that the absolute lack of motion of the *primum fluidum* cannot be squared with God being the eternally moved source of motion of all bodies.[86] Given that Lupoli's attribution of absolute rest to the *primum fluidum* is incorrect, this argument cannot be valid either. There is, however, a more convincing reason for why Hobbes did not pantheistically identify God and the subtle ether or the *primum fluidum* that is the same. In *De Motu*, Hobbes unequivocally mentions the ether as an example of a *spiritus* that can be conceived by human reason.[87] In other words, Hobbes clearly considers the ether to be a finite, created body and not the infinite corporeal Deity. The pantheist solution to the problem of the relation between supranatural and natural fluid(s) therefore appears to be ruled out by Hobbes himself.

According to Lupoli, there still remain two possible scenarios: either God created the primary fluid and subsequently the whole universe or God acted as a kind of Demiurge on a pre-existent fluid. Lupoli notes that Hobbes has a certain preference for what he calls a 'weak version' of creation out of pre-existent matter.[88] However, the two passages that Lupoli quotes in order to substantiate this claim are not conclusive. The first passage is taken from the Dedicatory Epistle to *De Corpore*, which compares the construction of a coherent philosophy with God's creation of the world. Hobbes describes this creation as an ordering of a confused chaos. However, first of all he is not making a philosophical point here, but uses metaphorical

---

[85] *DP* (*EW* iv. 89).

[86] Lupoli, '*Fluidismo e Corporeal Deity*', 605.

[87] *DM* 312: "Spiritus itaque, si entia sint, quae concipi possunt, ut aer, aether, spiritus animalis vel aliud tenuius, corpora sunt."

[88] Lupoli, '*Fluidismo e Corporeal Deity*', 607.

language befitting the rhetorical context of a dedication. Secondly, God's ordering of a confused chaos does not necessarily imply that this chaos pre-existed. In many alchemical accounts of creation, for instance, God is supposed to impose order on a chaos that he himself had first created.[89] The second passage is from the beginning of *De Homine*, where Hobbes explicitly summarizes a view of creation held by others, adding that we can have no knowledge about the creation of the world and have to rely on the authority of Scripture instead.[90] Therefore, this passage does not give us any indication as to Hobbes's preference for a given version of creation. In sum, there does not appear to exist any reason for doubting Hobbes's sincerity with respect to his outspoken endorsement of the orthodox Christian *creatio ex nihilo*.[91]

But there still remain a number of problems. Hobbes describes the universe as a plenum, in which all potentially empty spots are filled by the subtle ether. It appears, then, that there is no room left for the subtlest fluid of all, namely God himself. This, however, is hard to square with passages such as the one mentioned above in which Hobbes speaks of a direct intervention of God in the material world on account of his omnipresence, which he compares with the mixture of water with a saline solution, producing a substance that looks milky. The parts of the water and the solution do not merge, since two bodies cannot simultaneously be in one place. Instead, the mixture is the result of 'the activity of the mineral water, changing it [sc. the water] every where to the sense, and yet not being every where, and in every part of the water'.[92] In the same way, God 'who is an infinitely fine Spirit, and withal intelligent, can make and change all species and kinds of body as he pleaseth'. This comparison does not solve the problem of God's location. In the case of the two liquids, we have to suppose that their parts occupy distinct, finite places. God, however, is a different story: as said, no place is full unless he is present. But does this not mean that the divine, corporeal fluid violates the fundamental principle of natural philosophy that

---

[89] See H. Holzhey and W. Schmidt-Biggeman (eds.), *Grundriss der Geschichte der Philosophie. Die Philosophie des 17. Jahrhunderts, 4/1: Das Heilige Römische Reich Deutscher Nation. Nord- und Ostmitteleuropa* (Basle: Schwabe, 2001), 13.
[90] *DHo* i. 1 (*OL* ii. 2).   [91] *App. ad LL* (*OL* iii. 513).
[92] *ABB* (*EW* iv. 310).

bodies cannot coincide? Hobbes again gives his standard agnostic answer: 'the way by which God Almighty worketh [...] is past my apprehension'.[93]

As Lupoli rightly remarks, the fact that Hobbes draws God into the material cosmos creates problems not only of a theological nature, but also of a physical nature. In this sense, Hobbes's usual agnostic answer is far from satisfactory. Nonetheless, it has become clear that his account of the relation between divine and mundane fluids is less incoherent than Lupoli claims it to be. Hobbes appears to favour the notion of one single fluid, both subtle ether and *primum fluidum*, out of which solid bodies were created. In line with his general rejection of pantheism, Hobbes repudiates the identification of subtle ether and corporeal Deity. The question of how we should *conceive* of the creation of the mundane fluid by the divine one remains, however. Hobbes gives a simple, if not simplistic, answer: don't. The notion of creation cannot be conceived by philosophers who can safely leave this kind of question in the hands of the religious authorities appointed by the sovereign.

CONCLUSION

We have studied Hobbes's strict distinction between reason and faith as it emerges from his history of heresy. Furthermore, we have concluded that Hobbes consistently applies this distinction to the topic of God's corporeal nature, one of the other central issues in Hobbes's writings on heresy. Nevertheless, we have also seen that tensions between his 'theology' and physics still remain, although at this point Hobbes is more consistent than he is often made out to be. Now, Hobbes holds that his views are perfectly orthodox. Hobbes would have thought that it was rather the scholastic manuals of metaphysics contained in the Bodleian which deserved to be burnt in its quadrangle, and not his own works. Is this really convincing? This volume gives ample demonstration of the fact that notions of orthodoxy, heterodoxy, and heresy are extremely complicated with

---

[93] Ibid.

respect to seventeenth-century science and religion. With the head of the Church of England being a closet Catholic and a range of Protestant sects that outstrips that of a typical Southern Mississippi town, seventeenth-century England was certainly no exception to this. Aloysius Martinich has tried to solve this problem by making a distinction between the orthodox view and standard/non-standard views. The first is a normative notion whereas the second consists of sociological ones. According to Martinich, Hobbes is orthodox, since he conforms to the Christian creeds of the first four Church Councils, which, as said, is Hobbes's own criterion.[94] Thus, Martinich holds that Hobbes has some non-standard opinions, but no unorthodox ones. It is of course not particularly difficult to stick to one's own criterion of orthodoxy, especially if one is to interpret this criterion oneself. Martinich's defence of Hobbes's orthodoxy is impressive, but it is a historical fact that all the various sects, as well as most of the leading scientists in seventeenth-century England, including Wallis and Boyle, agreed that Hobbes was either a heretic or an atheist. Hobbes's distinction between philosophy and religion may have been consistent, but it failed to convince his contemporaries. If Hobbes's philosophy led him to the conclusion that God is a corporeal spirit, either 'dogmatically' or 'piously', this meant that his philosophy was wrong. For Cambridge Platonists such as More, Cudworth, and Stillingfleet, Hobbes's philosophy became the epitome of the dangerous materialism that the 'new philosophy' must get rid of if it was to avoid heresy and atheism.

---

[94] Martinich, *Two Gods of the Leviathan*, 1.

9

'The true frame of Nature': Isaac Newton, Heresy, and the Reformation of Natural Philosophy

Stephen D. Snobelen

> So then 'twas one designe of the first institution of the true
> religion to propose to mankind by the frame of the ancient
> Temples, the study of the frame of the world as the true Temple
> of the great God they worshipped. And thence it was that the
> Priests anciently were above other men well skilled in the
> knowledge of the true frame of Nature & accounted it a great
> part of their Theology.
>
> Isaac Newton[1]

Some of the ideas developed in this chapter formed part of my seminar at All Souls in
February 2001. I am grateful to the seminar participants for their helpful comments.
An earlier draft of this chapter was presented as a paper in May 2003 at the meeting of
the Canadian Society for the History and Philosophy of Science in Halifax, Nova
Scotia. I am likewise grateful to those attending this event for their useful feedback
and advice. For permission to quote from manuscripts in their archives, I would like
to acknowledge the Syndics of the Cambridge University Library; the Jewish National
and University Library, Jerusalem; and the Provost and Fellows of King's College,
Cambridge. Except in a few select examples, transcriptions from Newton's manuscripts are presented in 'clean text' format, with abbreviations expanded, deletions
omitted and insertion markers removed. Original capitalization and spelling have
been retained. In addition to my own transcriptions, I utilized some of the growing
collection of transcriptions being produced by the Newton Project (www.newton-
project.ic.ac.uk, accessed 13 April 2005).

[1] Isaac Newton, Jewish National and University Library, Jerusalem, Yahuda MS 41,
fo. 7r.

NEWTON AND THE DUAL REFORMATION

In his notes for his projected biography of Isaac Newton, John Conduitt suggests that Newton had been engaged in the reform of both natural philosophy and theology—a dual reformation:

The only thing he was heard to say with pleasure of his work: was when he died he should have the satisfaction of leaving Philosophy less mischievous than he found it—Those who will consider his Irenicum & Creed might allow him to have said the same of revealed religion—If there be any of so narrow principles as not to bear with his not going into one point of the highest orthodoxy let them reflect what an advantage it is to Christianity in general in this age of infidelity to have a Layman such a Philosopher &c. have spent so much study upon divinity & so publick & strenuous an advocate for it.[2]

The first claim, that Newton believed his labours would contribute to the improvement of natural philosophy, is presumably based on oral testimony to which Conduitt, who had married Newton's half-niece Catherine Barton in 1717, was privy. The second claim, that Newton may as well have said as much with respect to theology, appears to be based on an extrapolation from the contents of Newton's vast collection of religious papers, which fell into Conduitt's hands when the former died in 1727. But this is not all. As Conduitt hints in the second half of this passage, Newton's theological manuscripts reveal that the author of the *Principia* and the *Opticks* had veered into religious heterodoxy. Although this fact troubled the orthodox Anglican Conduitt, he was too familiar with Newton's private theological writings to deny it.

William Whiston, who was a convert both to Newton's natural philosophy and his unorthodox religion, had no such misgivings about the great man's denial of the Trinity. For him, it was reason for celebration. When writing about 'the invention of the wonderful *Newtonian* philosophy', Whiston declares:

I look upon [it] in an higher light than others, and as an eminent prelude and preparation to those happy *times of the restitution of all things, which*

---

[2] Conduitt, King's College, Cambridge, Keynes MS 130.7, fo. 2v.

God has spoken of by the mouth of all his holy prophets, since the world began, Acts iii. 21. To which purpose see his excellent corollaries relating to religion ... Nor can I forbear to wish, that my own most important discoveries concerning true religion, and primitive christianity, may succeed in the *second* place to his surprizing discoveries; and may together have such a divine blessing upon them, that the *kingdoms of this world*, as I firmly expect they will, may soon *become the kingdoms of our Lord, and of his Christ, and he may reign for ever and ever!* Amen. Amen.[3]

Whiston, too, thus argued for something like a dual reformation in natural philosophy and theology.[4] The premillenarianism that Whiston inherited in part from Newton also shines through his first claim. Newton's 'surprizing discoveries' were to help prepare the way for the coming Millennium. And Whiston claims the same for his own discoveries concerning the primitive truth of Christianity. What he does not make explicit here is the fact that a great deal of his own heterodox theology owed much to Newton. Consciously or unconsciously, Whiston is thus arguing that this dual reformation is inherently a *Newtonian* dual reformation. The link between the renewal in natural philosophy and the recovery of the true religion is also hinted at in Whiston's reference to Newton's 'excellent corollaries relating to religion'—an allusion to the natural theological and theological material Newton added to the conclusions of the later editions of his *Principia* and *Opticks*.

Few men knew Newton better than these two. As a relation, Conduitt was part of Newton's domestic circle. He also had unparalleled access to Newton's literary remains. As for Whiston, he enjoyed a twenty-year friendship with Newton that lasted until sometime around 1714. During these years he was given privileged access to Newton's thoughts on religion. Thus the statements of Conduitt and Whiston merit serious evaluation. I want to argue that they should not be taken as merely rhetorical, but that they instead reflect ideals and agendas to which Newton himself consciously adhered. This chapter has four main aims. First, by

---

[3] William Whiston, *Memoirs of the Life and Writings of Mr. William Whiston*, 2nd edn. (London, 1753), 34.

[4] In a work on natural theology, Whiston explicitly links advances in natural philosophy with progress in scriptural interpretation (William Whiston, *Astronomical Principles of Religion, Natural and Reveal'd* (London, 1717), 259, 272–7).

exploring Newton's belief that the ancient forms of both natural philosophy and religion had been corrupted and were therefore in need of purification, it will determine the degree to which Newton himself saw his work in terms of a 'dual reformation', that is to say, that he was consciously promoting two reformations. Second, it will show that these reformations in Newton's conception were fundamentally linked even if he wanted to preserve some distinctions between natural philosophy and religion. Third, this chapter will assess the relationship between Newton's published texts on natural philosophy and religion on the one hand, and draft material he composed on the *prisca sapientia* (ancient wisdom) and *prisca theologia* (ancient theology) on the other. Finally, it will be important to consider the role played by the pivotal dynamic of Newton's theological heresy and how this coloured his dual reformation as a whole.[5]

NEWTON'S DUAL REFORMATION IN HISTORY AND HISTORIOGRAPHY

A spirit of reform was in the air during the period in which Newton came of age. The early sixteenth-century Magisterial Reformation of Luther and Calvin unleashed a reformist impulse that in turn led to a series of subsequent religious reform movements, including the Radical Reformation's Anabaptists and Socinians, who went much further than Luther and Calvin in seeking the renewal of Christianity. The central driving force behind all these movements was a primitivist impulse and the concomitant belief that the Medieval Church

[5] I earlier explored the Newtonian religious reformation in Snobelen, 'Isaac Newton, Heretic: The Strategies of a Nicodemite', *The British Journal for the History of Science*, 32 (1999), 381–419 (where I suggest (p. 418) that Newton was participating in a dual reformation) and id., 'Caution, Conscience and the Newtonian Reformation: The Public and Private Heresies of Newton, Clarke and Whiston', *Enlightenment and Dissent*, 16 (1997), 151–84. I also treat aspects (mainly those not dealt with in this present chapter) of the relationship between Newton's heresy and his natural philosophy in Snobelen, 'To Discourse of God: Isaac Newton's Heterodox Theology and His Natural Philosophy', in Paul B. Wood (ed.), *Science and Dissent in England, 1688–1945* (Aldershot, Hants.: Ashgate, 2004), 39–65.

had become corrupt. This generally diffused primitivist impulse had been partly fed at the beginning of the Reformation by Renaissance humanism and philology. And it continued in Newton's own period. At the very moment when Newton came into the world in 1642 English Calvinists were clamouring for religious reform in England. As their name implies, one goal of the Puritans was to create a purer form of Christianity than that seen in High-Church Anglicanism, which was viewed as spiritually corrupt, excessively ritualistic, and over-institutionalized. This ideal is also seen in many of the Protestant dissenting movements of Newton's more mature years. But the Church of England itself also deployed the rhetoric of reform in its self-affirming characterizations of the Church of Rome as doctrinally, politically, and morally corrupt.

A reformation was also under way in natural philosophy. A century before Newton's birth Nicholas Copernicus and Andreas Vesalius, inspired in part by the same humanistic currents that helped motivate the religious reformers, helped initiate the period of the quickening of natural philosophical innovation and discovery that we now with hindsight refer to as the Scientific Revolution. This began shortly after the Protestant Reformation and was signalled by the 1543 publication of both Copernicus's *De revolutionibus* and Vesalius's *De fabrica*, works that transformed, respectively, astronomy and anatomy. The excitement generated by these works and those that followed from other innovating natural philosophers did not subside in the subsequent one hundred years. Yet neither Copernicus nor Vesalius championed a radical break with the past. Both were men of the Renaissance and both loosely subscribed to the Renaissance topos of the *prisca sapientia*, namely, that one of the highest goals of scholarship was to recover lost ancient wisdom. Copernicus saw his astronomical reformation as fulfilling the ideals of the ancient astronomers and modelled his *De revolutionibus* after Ptolemy's *Almagest*. Similarly, Vesalius was inspired by Galen when composing his *De fabrica*. Both men sought to perfect the work of their ancient exemplars. In other words, as we would say, they thought in terms of reformation rather than revolution.[6] The irony

---

[6] Peter Dear has recently spoken about a 'Scientific Renaissance' in the sixteenth century that focused on the reformation of knowledge and has distinguished this period from the 'Scientific Revolution' of the seventeenth century, which sought a

in this is that although both men played down their break with the past, in important and far-reaching ways they did this very thing.

Nearer to Newton's time in the seventeenth century, scholars began to think increasingly in terms of leaving the ancients behind. Thus, the French philosopher René Descartes self-consciously set out to reform, from the ground up, philosophy and natural philosophy, which he wanted to free from the stagnation and misdirection of Scholastic thought. Although in his rhetoric he claimed that he was making a decisive break with the past, there are many examples in Descartes's thought of continuity with the past. In a sense, Cartesianism amounted to a new Scholasticism. Still, Descartes's intellectual project served to stimulate a much more radical spirit of reform in natural philosophy.[7] Another relevant example from the seventeenth century is Francis Bacon, who appealed for the systematic reform of philosophy and natural philosophy in such works as the *Advancement of Learning* and the *Instauratio magna* (*The Great Instauration*). At the end of the seventeenth century and the beginning of the eighteenth century the legacies of the humanistic reform movements of the sixteenth century and the more recent radical reforming approaches clashed in the so-called 'Battle of the Books'.[8] Curiously, Newton exemplifies both traditions, although it is clear that his heart was with those who wanted to recover ancient knowledge.

Some early modern intellectuals saw links between the religious and natural philosophical reformations, a phenomenon treated in some recent historiography. John Hedley Brooke speaks about the seventeenth-century Protestant conception of two related reformations in his 1991 monograph on science and religion:

For some Protestant thinkers, experimental science promised a way of reversing the effects of the original curse, a way of making a better world that might in some small way mirror the perfection of God's heavenly kingdom, a way of restoring the world to a condition fit for Christ's earthly rule. Affirmations of a strong parallel between religion and scientific reform are not difficult to find. Thomas Culpeper remarked in 1655 that, as Reformed theology rejected a pope in religion, so a reformed science rejected a pope in philosophy. It was easy to claim, as did Thomas Sprat in his

---

more radical break with the past. For more on this, and how Copernicus and Vesalius exemplify this humanist tradition, see Dear, *Revolutionizing the Sciences: European Knowledge and Its Ambitions* (Houndmills: Palgrave, 2001), 8, 30–48.

[7] Cf. Dear, *Revolutionizing the Sciences*, 48.   [8] Ibid.

History of the Royal Society (1667), that the two reformations had this in common: Each prized the original copies of God's two books, nature and the Bible, bypassing the corrupting influence of scholars and priests.[9]

As will be seen, these ideas resonate with those Newton himself held. In his 1998 work on Protestantism and early modern natural philosophy, Peter Harrison not only eloquently details the scholarly conception of two reformations, but provides a considerable number of examples of the relationship between the shift in biblical hermeneutics from the allegorical modes of the Medieval period to the literal-historical methods characteristic of Protestantism, and the movement away from the emblematic view of nature to a more empirical approach.[10] This particular link is germane to Newton's own thought. Another dynamic, that of millenarian aspirations, is evinced in the well-known frontispiece of Francis Bacon's *Instauratio magna*, which depicts ships of learning transgressing the limits of human knowledge represented by the Pillars of Hercules.[11] The epigram on this frontispiece, *'Multi pertransibunt et augebitur scientia'* ('Many shall run to and fro, and knowledge shall increase'), reflects Bacon's conviction that the quickening of knowledge we now call the Scientific Revolution was a fulfilment of biblical prophecy.[12]

Several studies in the past two decades have, in various ways, pointed to the dynamic of a dual reformation in Newton's thought. In his 1982 study of Newton's 'Origines', Richard Westfall argued that Newton, Whiston, and the English Cartesian Thomas Burnet all linked the restoration of true natural philosophy with the restoration of true natural religion.[13] John Gascoigne has also come to a similar conclusion about these three figures.[14] Newton's desire to use his

[9] John Hedley Brooke, *Science and Religion: Some Historical Perspectives* (Cambridge: Cambridge University Press, 1991), 111.

[10] Peter Harrison, *The Bible, Protestantism and the Rise of Natural Science* (Cambridge: Cambridge University Press, 1998), esp. 64–120.

[11] A reproduction of this image can be found in Steven Shapin, *The Scientific Revolution* (Chicago: Chicago University Press, 1996), 21.

[12] The epigram is a quotation of Daniel 12: 4.

[13] Richard Westfall, 'Isaac Newton's *Theologiae gentilis origines philosophicae*', in W. Warren Wagar (ed.), *The Secular Mind: Transformations of Faith in Modern Europe* (New York: Holmes & Meier, 1982), 26.

[14] John Gascoigne, ' "The Wisdom of the Egyptians" and the Secularization of History in the Age of Newton', in Stephen Gaukroger (ed.), *The Uses of Antiquity: The Scientific Revolution and the Classical Tradition* (Dordrecht: Kluwer, 1991), 188–9.

Principia to aid in the reinstatement of the *prisca theologia* is one of
the themes of Simon Schaffer's 1987 essay on the providentialist
aspects of Newton's cometography.[15] Similar themes are presented
by Betty Jo Teeter Dobbs in her second monograph on Newton's
alchemy, in which she set out the view that Newton believed the
reformation of the true religion had been enhanced by the demonstrable successes of his *Principia*.[16] Kenneth Knoespel's 1999 essay on
Newton's 'Origines' carefully considers the relationship between
Newton's goals for the *Principia* and his efforts to recover the true
religion, concluding that '[i]t is possible that Newton found in his
own work the creation of a new interpretative instauration that
would lay a foundation for a reformed religion integrating the
moral teachings of Jesus with a knowledge of the coherence of
creation', and that we gain much by drawing together 'Newton's
interpretative work as a natural philosopher' and his 'interpretative
work in history and religion'.[17] Building on the insights of these and
other scholars, I will now turn to consider Newton's dual reformation
in detail.

THE EARLY FOUNDATIONS OF NEWTON'S DUAL
REFORMATION

Newton's religious awareness began before his interest in natural
philosophy manifested itself, although both began early. He grew
up in a Protestant world that saw the Bible as a chief focus; the
Protestant faith and the Word of God were also central to his
education at grammar school in the 1650s. It is also possible that
early on he began to read through the two to three hundred

---

[15] Simon Schaffer, 'Newton's Comets and the Transformation of Astrology', in
Patrick Curry (ed.), *Astrology, Science and Society* (Woodbridge: Boydell, 1987),
219–43.

[16] Betty Jo Dobbs, *The Janus Faces of Genius: The Role of Alchemy in Newton's
Thought* (Cambridge: Cambridge University Press, 1991), 170.

[17] Kenneth Knoespel, 'Interpretative Strategies in Newton's *Theologicae gentilis
origines philosophiae*', in James E. Force and Richard H. Popkin (eds.), *Newton and
Religion: Context, Nature, and Influence* (Dordrecht: Kluwer, 1999), 179–202 (quotations from pp. 200 and 201).

theological books his stepfather the Reverend Barnabas Smith left behind at his death in 1653.[18] Four of ten books he is known to have bought in 1661, the year of his matriculation at Trinity College, Cambridge, were on theology.[19] A list of the sins of his youth that he compiled in 1662 attests to austere religious sensibilities.[20] But none of this is particularly exceptional for the time.

What was exceptional was his rapid move from the normal Scholastically based curriculum to an energetic and impassioned exploration of the new philosophy shortly after arriving at Cambridge. Partway through his four years of undergraduate studies, Newton left behind Aristotle and began a voyage of discovery into the new mechanical philosophy, imbibing the works of Descartes, Walter Charleton, Galileo, Robert Boyle, Thomas Hobbes, Henry More, and others.[21] Evidence of this extra-curricular reading and dramatic reorientation of his studies comes in part from a blank notebook he purchased the year he arrived at Trinity College. But already in his undergraduate days Newton also began to exhibit an interest in *ancient* alternatives to Aristotle, for Epicurean atomism and the Epicurean Lucretius also figure in these notes.[22] Moreover, these notes include matters theological. While it is true, as McGuire and Tamny point out, that Newton left a large gap between the headings relating to natural philosophy and the final two relating more overtly to theology ('Of the Creation' and 'Of the Soul'),[23] which may reflect some sort of intention to keep natural philosophy and theology separate in his notebook, it is nonetheless the case that theological topics occur in the natural philosophical section as well, including discussions of God, creation, the soul, and biblical exegesis.[24] This notebook suggests that Newton was already at this

---

[18] Richard Westfall, *Never at Rest: A Biography of Isaac Newton* (Cambridge: Cambridge University Press, 1980), 58.

[19] Ibid. 83, 309–10.

[20] Richard Westfall, 'Short-Writing and the State of Newton's Conscience, 1662', *Notes and Records of the Royal Society of London*, 18 (1963), 10–16.

[21] Westfall, *Never at Rest*, 89.

[22] Newton in J. E. McGuire and Martin Tamny (eds.), *Certain Philosophical Questions: Newton's Trinity Notebook* (Cambridge: Cambridge University Press, 1983), 49–54, 119–20, 337–45, 421–5, 393.

[23] Ibid. 447–53.   [24] Ibid. 337–9, 356–7, 374–7, 406–9.

young age beginning to ponder how questions natural philosophical might relate to questions theological.

While Newton's 'Certain Philosophical Questions' reveals a period of natural philosophical discovery, other manuscripts demonstrate that the period from 1664 to 1666 also saw the blossoming of a brilliant mathematician, for it was during these years, the *anni mirabiles*, that Newton developed his method of fluxions (calculus), began his experiments on optics, and started work on his mathematical physics.[25] Towards the end of his *anni mirabiles*, probably by 1666, Newton added to his research programme the study of chemistry/alchemy (the distinction between the two being a more recent one). By the end of the decade, Newton had begun not only serious reading in alchemy, but had obtained two furnaces, initiated his own experimental programme, and also insinuated himself into secret alchemical networks.[26] Soon Newton would obtain from alchemy cognitive ingredients that would lead him away from mechanical philosophical orthodoxy. Newton's 'Certain Philosophical Questions' and his early exploration of alchemy provide ample evidence of an inquisitive and ranging mind, a mind that knew few intellectual boundaries. But they do not offer obvious signs of religious heresy.

These came in the early 1670s. Whether it was because his wide-ranging mind led him to move on to conquer theology, or whether it was because a 1675 ordination deadline spurred him on, Newton began a massive study of Church history and doctrine in the early 1670s, hot on the heels of his election to the Lucasian Professorship in 1669. This study became a consuming passion. As Westfall put it, 'there can be no reasonable question that at least part of the time, when Newton expressed impatience at the interruptions caused by optical and mathematical correspondence during the 1670s, it was theology that preoccupied him'.[27] Central to his new theological research project was a thorough examination (or re-examination) of the Word of God.[28] This intense study of the Scriptures quickly led him to conclude that the Trinity, the central tenet of Christian

---

[25] An excellent account of Newton's *anni mirabiles* can be found in Westfall, *Never at Rest*, 140–75.
[26] Ibid. 96, 281–8.   [27] Ibid. 310. The other study was alchemy (ibid. 281).
[28] On this, see ibid. 310–25.

orthodoxy, was a post-biblical corruption. He was determined to bypass doctrinal innovation and recover the original faith of the first Christians. By the middle of the decade, he had arrived at a view of God akin to that of the ancient heresy of Arianism.

Central to his antitrinitarian, biblicist theology was the belief that only the Father is truly God. In the second in a list of twelve antitrinitarian statements he wrote out in the early 1670s, he asserted: 'The word God put absolutly without particular restriction to the Son or Holy ghost doth always signify the Father from one end of the scriptures to the other.'[29] The union between the Father and the Son is not one of substance, but a moral union of will.[30] In these early conclusions Newton believed he had recovered some of the original purity of primitive Christianity. From the perspective of his Trinitarian Anglican confrères, these conclusions constituted the deepest heresy. Newton could have publicized his new-found heresy, but this would have brought legal sanction and transformed him into a social pariah. Instead, he embraced a policy of secrecy much like that followed by the practice of alchemy with which he had become engaged less than a decade earlier. With some minor exceptions that will be examined below, Newton hid his heresy from the public and adopted the stance of a secret heretic—a Nicodemite.[31] But unpublished works like 'Paradoxical Questions concerning the morals and actions of Athanasius and his followers',[32] and his 'An historical account of two notable corruptions of Scripture in a Letter to a Friend',[33] both of which date from the years immediately after the publication of the *Principia*, reveal that Newton's theological agendas were both reformist and heretical. Although few knew in his lifetime, he shared similar radical aims to the late seventeenth and early eighteenth-century Unitarian opponents of the Church of England.

---

[29] Newton, Yahuda MS 14, fo. 25r. For a transcription of these twelve statements, see Westfall, *Never at Rest*, 315–16.

[30] Newton, Yahuda MS 14, fo. 25r.

[31] For more on Newton's Nicodemism, see Snobelen, 'Isaac Newton, Heretic'.

[32] William Andrews Clark Library (UCLA), MS **N563M3 P222. A shorter and later draft is Keynes MS 10; see also Keynes MS 11.

[33] Newton to John Locke, 14 November 1690, *The Correspondence of Isaac Newton*, ed. H. W. Turnbull, J. F. Scott, A. Rupert Hall, and Laura Tilling (7 vols.; Cambridge: Cambridge University Press, 1959–77), iii. 82. For the text of the 'Two Notable Corruptions', see ibid. iii. 83–144.

The most extensive manuscript Newton penned before writing the *Principia* was a 600-folio commentary on the Apocalypse. This early prophetic treatise, written when Newton was in his early thirties and still fresh with the exuberance of discovery, hints at associations between the study of God's Word and the study of God's Works. Because Newton believed that the same God who inspired the Scriptures also created the world, he was convinced that there were fundamental linkages between the Book of Scripture and the Book of Nature:

As the world, which to the naked eye exhibits the greatest variety of objects, appears very simple in its internall constitution when surveyed by a philosophic understanding, and so much the simpler by how much the better it is understood, so it is in these visions. It is the perfection of God's works that they are all done with the greatest simplicity. He is the God of order and not confusion. And therefore as they that would understand the frame of the world must indeavour to reduce their knowledg to all possible simplicity, so it must be in seeking to understand these visions.[34]

Not only should one expect a common simplicity in the Two Books, but, as each Book was written by the same Author, one should be able to use similar methods in the study of both.

THE *PRISCA SAPIENTIA* AND THE *PRINCIPIA MATHEMATICA*

Newton's burgeoning interest in early Christianity and biblical prophecy in the early to mid-1670s formed an important part of a broader research agenda with which he became passionately engaged in this period. It is around this time that Newton began an extensive survey of ancient writers in a quest to restore the ancient wisdom that had been lost through corruption. This ancient wisdom had originally been given to Noah after the Flood and, crucially, embraced both religion and the philosophy of nature. His literal acceptance of the *prisca sapientia* tradition was both reformist and wide-ranging. As Niccolò Guicciardini notes, Newton's enthusiasm for the ancients extended to his alchemy, theology, and mathematics: 'It is striking that in the same years Newton began attributing to Jews,

[34] Newton, Yahuda MS 1.1a, fo. 14r.

Egyptians and Pythagoreans a lost knowledge concerning alchemy, God *and* mathematics. It is plausible that in Newton's mind the restoration of the lost books of the ancient geometers of Alexandria was linked to his attempt to re-establish a *prisca sapientia*.[35] As Guicciardini demonstrates so well, Newton's classical turn in the 1670s and the emergence of his commitment to a *prisca geometria* provide illuminating backdrops for the writing of the *Principia* in the 1680s. In short, these dynamics reveal that he was trying to recover the methods of the ancients. This goes a long way to explaining the 'classical façade' of the *Principia*, which, as it happens, is not merely a façade.[36] Once again, this is not just rhetorical window-dressing; Newton's method is directly informed and shaped by the ancients.[37] Newton's commitment to the *prisca* tradition is one important context for the composition of the *Principia mathematica*. Another is his theological view of physics.

Sometime before the publication of the *Principia*, Newton wrote a treatise on natural philosophy in which he makes his break with Cartesianism explicit. This untitled treatise is now known by its initial words, 'De gravitatione et aequilibrium fluidorum' ('On the gravity and equilibrium of fluids'),[38] which some scholars now think dates to the years immediately prior to the composition of the *Principia*.[39] Perhaps more than any other document that

[35] Niccolò Guicciardini, *Reading the* Principia: *The Debate on Newton's Mathematical Methods for Natural Philosophy from 1687 to 1736* (Cambridge: Cambridge University Press, 1999), 31.

[36] Yet the mathematics deployed in the *Principia* are not completely isomorphic with ancient geometry (see ibid. 99–117; I. Bernard Cohen, 'A Guide to Newton's *Principia*', in Newton, *The* Principia: *Mathematical Principles of Natural Philosophy*, tr. I. Bernard Cohen and Anne Whitman, assisted by Julia Budenz (Berkeley: University of California Press, 1999), 114–17, 122–7). As is often the case with his thought, Newton's *Principia* looks forward even as it looks to the past.

[37] For more on Newton's classicism, see Guicciardini, *Reading the* Principia, 27–38, 101–6. See also my review of Guicciardini, Snobelen, 'Mathematicians, Historians and Newton's *Principia*', *Annals of Science*, 58 (2001), 75–84.

[38] A transcription and English translation can be found in A. Rupert Hall and Marie Boas Hall (eds.), *Unpublished Scientific Papers of Isaac Newton* (Cambridge: Cambridge University Press, 1962), 89–156.

[39] Dobbs, *The Janus Faces of Genius*, 138–44; J. E. McGuire, 'The Fate of the Date: The Theology of Newton's *Principia* Revisited', in Margaret J. Osler (ed.), *Rethinking the Scientific Revolution* (Cambridge: Cambridge University Press, 2000), 271–95. The Halls dated the manuscript to the period 1664–8 (Hall and Hall, *Unpublished Papers*, 89–90).

came from his hand, this manuscript demonstrates that Newton's natural philosophy was tightly bound up with a theistic understanding of the world. Not only is God a recurring and pivotal theme in 'De gravitatione', but Newton is at pains therein to develop an understanding of nature that is unambiguously and incontrovertibly dependent on God as a precondition. In this manuscript he also attacks the Cartesian natural philosophy as a system that encourages atheism. 'De gravitatione' forms an important theological backdrop to the first edition of the *Principia*, which, with its single reference to God and natural theology, appears misleadingly secular.[40]

The same is true of Newton's conception of the *prisca sapientia*, which is hinted at from the very first line of Newton's great work. The opening sentence of his preface to the first edition of the *Principia* reads:

SINCE THE ANCIENTS (according to Pappus) considered mechanics to be of the greatest importance in the investigation of nature and science and since the moderns—rejecting substantial forms and occult qualities—have undertaken to reduce the phenomena of nature to mathematical laws, it has seemed best in this treatise to concentrate on *mathematics* as it relates to natural philosophy.[41]

On the face of it, this programmatic statement appears to signal a bringing together of ancient mechanics and modern mathematics, and it is clear that the *Principia* at least does this. From the perspective of the history of science, Newton's *Mathematical Principles of Natural Philosophy* represents the culmination of the rise in status of mathematical realism in natural philosophy that is commonly traced from Copernicus's *De revolutionibus* of 1543 through the works of such natural philosophers as Kepler, Galileo, and Descartes on to Newton. As with Kepler and some others, however, Newton's conviction that matter and geometry go hand in hand comes in good measure from his commitment to the number mysticism of the ancient pre-Socratic Pythagoreans. After his opening sentence,

[40] For more on the theological backdrop to the first edition of the *Principia*, see I. Bernard Cohen, 'Isaac Newton's *Principia*, the Scriptures, and the Divine Providence', in Sidney Morgenbesser, Patrick Suppes, and Morton White (eds.), *Philosophy, Science, and Method: Essays in Honor of Ernest Nagel* (New York: St Martin's, 1969), 523–48.

[41] Newton, *Principia* (Cohen-Whitman), 381.

Newton goes on in his preface to praise mathematics and in particular *geometry,* that powerful science of numbers that came to maturity three centuries before the time of Christ in the works of Euclid.

These are brief and obscure hints at Newton's commitments to the *prisca* tradition in the *Principia.* But he had considered publishing more explicit declarations. In the preface to book III of the *Principia,* Newton reveals that his original composition of book III was a less intensely mathematical affair than what he was publishing in 1687:

On this subject I composed an earlier version of book 3 in popular form, so that it might be more widely read. But those who have not sufficiently grasped the principles set down here will certainly not perceive the force of the conclusions, nor will they lay aside the preconceptions to which they have become accustomed over many years; and therefore, to avoid lengthy disputations, I have translated the substance of the earlier version into propositions in a mathematical style, so that they may be read only by those who have first mastered the principles.[42]

From what we know of Newton, this explanation for the suppression of original *System of the world (De mundi systemate)* rings true.[43] But in addition to the general difference in style, the presence of nine hypotheses at the beginning (later converted into the four rules of reasoning and the six phenomena) and a more elaborate account of comets, the published version of book III differs from the original version in one more important respect: the *System of the World* is prefaced with an account of the views of the ancients on cosmology that reinforces Newton's commitment to the *prisca* tradition.[44]

This prefatory material opens with an explicit assertion that many of the earliest philosophers understood the universe to be heliocentric.[45] This heliocentric philosophy of nature, Newton elaborates, was taught 'of old' by Philolaus, Aristarchus of Samos, Plato 'in his riper years', the Pythagoreans, Anaximander ('more ancient still'), and

[42] Ibid. 795.

[43] An English translation of *De mundi systemate* can be found in Newton, *Sir Isaac Newton's Mathematical Principles of Natural Philosophy and His System of the World,* tr. Andrew Motte and rev. Florian Cajori (Berkeley, 1962; first pub. 1934), ii.

[44] For an English translation of a manuscript draft of this material (Cambridge University Library (hereinafter CUL) MS Add. 3990, fo. 1), see Westfall, *Never at Rest,* 434–5.

[45] Newton, *Principia* (Motte-Cajori), 549.

Numa Pompilius, the latter of whom Newton records as erecting a circular temple to honour Vesta with a 'perpetual fire' kept burning in its centre to present the sun.[46] Never mind that the Pythagorean system was not technically heliocentric in that it posited a central fire about which both the sun and earth revolved; it is enough that Newton believed it to be heliocentric. He is on firmer ground with Aristarchus of Samos, now sometimes referred to as the 'Copernicus of antiquity'. What is important here is that Newton is seeking an ancient, mainly pre-Socratic tradition of philosophy that upheld heliocentrism.

While acknowledging that some early philosophers such as Anaxagoras and Democritus believed 'that the earth possessed the centre of the world', Newton contends that the ancient heliocentrists and geocentrists alike held that 'the motions of the celestial bodies were performed in spaces altogether free and void of resistance'.[47] This, Newton implies, was the most ancient view. 'The whim of solid orbs', he continues, 'was of a later date, introduced by *Eudoxus, Calippus,* and *Aristotle*; when the ancient philosophy began to decline, and to give place to the new prevailing fictions of the *Greeks*'.[48] For Newton, early equals better. The doctrine of crystalline spheres (which held sway in some quarters into the early seventeenth century) is labelled a novelty and a fiction.

Newton next turns to comets, which he treats in both versions of book III, and points out that 'the phenomena of comets can by no means tolerate the idea of solid orbits'. The ancient Chaldeans, Newton adds, viewed comets as a species of planet that revolved around the sun. But with the introduction of solid orbits, comets were confined to the sublunary sphere and were only 'restored ... to their ancient places in the higher heavens' by the observations of more recent astronomers.[49] With these observations, the crystalline spheres evaporated. It is important for Newton that this knowledge came through empirical rather than speculative means. It is also instructive that he uses the language of restoration.

---

[46] Newton, *Principia* (Motte-Cajori), 549.   [47] Ibid.   [48] Ibid. 549–50.
[49] Ibid. 550. Here Newton is thinking of developments in astronomy beginning with the late sixteenth century.

Newton suggests that the difficulty of explaining how a planet that otherwise would move away in a straight line from the body it is orbiting could be held within a circular orbit led the ancients to posit the notion of solid spheres. With the disappearance of these spheres, the moderns proposed other mechanical solutions, such as the vortical theories of Kepler and Descartes, or the mechanism of 'impulse or attraction', as with Borelli and Hooke. Newton rejects these hypotheses and states instead that his method is the 'mathematical way' of describing the phenomena, a way that avoids 'all questions about the nature or quality of this force'.[50] Although he suppressed this prefatory material along with the entire treatise, Newton would return to these themes again and again in his private writings, the later drafts of the *Principia* and *Opticks* and even in the published versions of these texts.

THE CLASSICAL SCHOLIA

The introductory paragraphs of Newton's suppressed *System of the World* confirm that he saw his mathematical physics as a recovery of ancient lost knowledge in terms of the *prisca sapientia*. By the early 1690s, when he was planning a second edition of the *Principia*, he was actively considering introducing bolder and more extensive affirmations of his commitment to the *prisca* tradition in additions to a revised version of his *magnum opus*. These intentions were relayed by Newton to David Gregory in his visit to Cambridge in May 1694.[51] Amongst notes taken after his meetings on 5, 6 and 7 May, Gregory records: 'He will spread himself in exhibiting the agreement of this philosophy with that of the Ancients and principally that of Thales. The philosophy of Epicurus and Lucretius is true and old, but was wrongly interpreted by the ancients as atheism'.[52] Written in Latin and Greek with copious references to ancient sources, the additions were meant to supplement

---

[50] Ibid.
[51] For Gregory's memoranda on this visit, see *Correspondence of Newton*, iii. 334–55, 384–9.
[52] Gregory in *Correspondence of Newton*, iii. 335, 338.

propositions IV–IX of book III and are now known collectively as 'the Classical Scholia'.[53]

In the six scholia Newton outlines several natural philosophical truths that he believed were anciently held by the ancient Egyptians, Greek pre-Socratics, and Epicureans. In the scholium meant to complement proposition IV, Newton writes:

That the earth's moon is a ~~dense~~ body made of earth, and that it is heavy and would fall toward our earth due to the force of gravity if it were not prevented from doing so ~~and held in suspension on its path of rotation~~ due to the force of its circular motion, is an old view, since one school of philosophy taught namely that the earth's moon is an earth floating up above ... This view appears to be taken from Ionic philosophy. This is what was passed on from Thales through Anaximander and Anaximenes to Anaxagoras.[54]

Later in this scholium, Newton not only contends that Anaxagoras believed that the moon was heavy, like the earth, but that '[t]hrough the fiction of the lion falling from the earth's moon and the stone falling from the sun he taught the gravity of the bodies of the sun and the earth's moon; through the figment of ascending stones he taught the force opposite to gravity, that of rotation.' To this he adds: 'This is not meant to be taken literally. The mystic philosophers usually hid their tenets behind such figments and mystical language.'[55]

---

[53] Newton's original autograph is Royal Society MS 247, fos. 6–14. The transcription in the hand of David Gregory is Royal Society MS 210. On the Classical Scholia, see J. E. McGuire and P. M. Rattansi, 'Newton and the "Pipes of Pan" ', *Notes and Record of the Royal Society*, 21 (1966), 108–42; Paolo Casini, 'Newton: the Classical Scholia', *History of Science*, 22 (1984), 1–58; Volkmar Schüller, *Newtons Scholia aus David Gregorys Nachlaß zu den Propositionen IV–IX Buch III seiner* Principia (Berlin: Max-Planck-Institut für Wissenschaftsgeschichte, 2000); Schüller, 'Newton's *Scholia* from David Gregory's Estate on the Propositions IV through IX Book III of his *Principia*', in *Between Leibniz, Newton, and Kant: Philosophy and Science in the Eighteenth Century*, ed. Wolfgang Lefèvre (Dordrecht: Kluwer, 2001), 213–65; Alexandre Koyré and I. Bernard Cohen (eds.), *Isaac Newton, Isaac Newton's* Philosophiae Naturalis Principia Mathematica: *The Third Edition (1726) with Variant Readings* (Cambridge: Cambridge University Press, 1972), ii. 803–7. I use Schüller's translation below.

[54] Newton, 'Newton's *Scholia*', 219 (transcription style as in Schüller's original). Proposition IV reads: 'The moon gravitates toward the earth and by the force of gravity is always drawn back from rectilinear motion and kept in its orbit' (Newton, *Principia* (Cohen-Whitman), 803).

[55] Newton, 'Newton's *Scholia*', 221.

At the beginning of his scholium on proposition vi, Newton asserts: 'That all bodies located around the earth, air and fire as well as the others, are heavy toward the earth and that their gravity is proportional to the quantity of matter of which they consist, was known to the ancients,' and then goes on to quote from Lucretius's arguments for the existence of a void.[56] The first two sentences of the scholium on proposition viii state:

The ratio with which gravity decreases as the distance from the planet increases was not sufficiently explained by the ancients. They appear to have concealed this ratio using the harmony of the celestial spheres, whereby they portrayed the sun and the remaining six planets Mercury, Venus, Earth ~~Jupiter~~, Saturn as Apollo with the seven-stringed lyre and measured the intervals between the spheres through tone intervals.

And, after citing the testimony of Pliny, the Pythagoreans, Macrobius, Proclus, Aeschylus, and Eusebius, Newton concludes that '[t]hrough this symbol they indicated that the sun acts on the planets with its force in the same harmonic ratio to the different distances as that of the tensile force to strings of different length, i.e., in a duplicate inverse ratio to the distances.'[57] In other words, the ancients had understood the Inverse-Square Law of gravity, but as with the heaviness of the moon had concealed it in a figure.

In a variant draft of the scholium on proposition ix, Newton offers a hint about the cause of universal gravitation that adumbrates arguments that later found their way into the General Scholium of 1713. The opening lines of this variant draft read: 'Up to this point I have explained the properties of gravity. I have not made the slightest consideration about its cause. However, I would like to relate what the ancients thought about this ... Quite apparently the heavens are nearly free of bodies, but nevertheless filled everywhere with a certain infinite *spiritus*, which they called God.'[58]

---

[56] Ibid. 225. Proposition vi reads: 'All bodies gravitate toward each of the planets, and at any given distance from the center of any one planet the weight of any body whatever toward that planet is proportional to the quantity of matter which the body contains' (Newton, *Principia* (Cohen-Whitman), 806).

[57] Newton, 'Newton's *Scholia*', 235. Proposition viii reads: 'Gravity exists in all bodies universally and is proportional to the quantity of matter in each' (Newton, *Principia* (Cohen-Whitman), 810).

[58] Newton, 'Newton's *Scholia*', 241. Proposition ix reads: 'In going inward from the surfaces of the planets, gravity decreases very nearly in the ratio of the distances from the planets' (Newton, *Principia* (Cohen-Whitman), 815).

Thus, even Newton's surmise that universal gravitation was in some way grounded in the omnipresence of God, something he spoke about openly in private and later hinted at in the General Scholium, is provided with an ancient antecedent. Near the end of the variant draft, Newton also claims that the ancient philosophers 'believed that this one God lives in all bodies as its temple, and thus they fashioned the old temples following the example of the heavens ~~the fire in the center of the temple for the sun~~ by portraying the sun as a fire in the center of the hall and the planets as the people walking around it, which they called the microcosm'.[59] It is likely that when Newton wrote '*unum Deum*' he was thinking of the one true God of the heretical antitrinitarian theology he had already espoused for two decades. Whether or not this is so, it is clear that he believed that the sages of deepest antiquity had a heliocentric conception of the solar system.

One can only speculate as to what the reaction would have been had the Classical Scholia been published in the second edition of the *Principia*, rather than having to wait until the mid-1960s to be revealed to the scholarly world. As it was, Newton did manage to insert some hints of his adherence to the *prisca* tradition in the General Scholium of the second edition when it was finally published in 1713. Published or not, Newton argues in the Classical Scholia that his mathematical physics represent a reformation of natural philosophy in that they are a revival of the lost *prisca sapientia*. And this does not need to be seen as mere rhetoric. After all, the mechanical philosophy of the seventeenth century itself emerged in part as a revival of ancient Epicureanism. It is possible that Newton actually obtained insights from his study of ancient natural philosophy.

THE DUAL REFORMATION IN THE 'ORIGINES'

The *Principia* was not the only treatise Newton laboured on in the mid- to late 1680s. During the same years that saw the composition of the *Philosophiae naturalis principia mathematica*, Newton

----

[59] Newton, 'Newton's *Scholia*', 243.

produced a monumental manuscript bearing the title 'Theologiae gentilis origines philosophicae' ('The Philosophical Origins of Gentile Theology').[60] During Gregory's visit to Newton at Cambridge in May 1694, shortly after this manuscript was completed, Newton either summarized its contents or allowed Gregory to peruse the document. It is difficult to improve on Gregory's pithy synopsis:

He has written a tract on the origin of the Gentiles [*gens*]. Religion is the same at all times, but that which was received pure by Noah and the first men, the Nations [*Ethnicus*] corrupted by their own inventions; Moses initiated a reformation [*reformatio*] but retained the indifferent things [*adiaphora*] of the Egyptians (it was the Egyptians who most of all corrupted religion with superstition and from them it spread to other Gentiles [*gens*]). Christ reformed [*reformō*] the religion of Moses.[61]

As Gregory's notes insinuate, the themes of corruption and reformation are central to the 'Origines'. A disordered and inchoate document, scholarship on the 'Origines' is still in its early stages.[62] Westfall, one of the first to study the 'Origines', recognized that one of its central messages was that 'true natural philosophy supports true religion'.[63]

In the 'Origines' Newton's primitivism became more ambitious as his study of religious corruption expanded to include a recovery of the Ur-religion of the Noachides. This was the ultimate goal, because this religion was the post-Diluvial restoration of the original religion

---

[60] Newton, Yahuda MSS 16.1 and 16.2; related material can be found in Newton, Yahuda MSS 17.1, 17.2, and 17.3. A later (*c.* early 1690s), shorter draft in English can be found in Yahuda MS 41. Sections of Yahuda MS 16 are written in the hand of Humphrey Newton, who was Isaac Newton's amanuensis from *c.*1685 to 1690. Humphrey Newton also copied out *De motu*, Newton's Lucasian Lectures for 1685 and 1686, *De mundi systemate*, and the fair copy of the first edition of the *Principia* (I. Bernard Cohen, *Introduction to Newton's 'Principia'* (Cambridge: Cambridge University Press, 1971), 299).

[61] Gregory in *Correspondence of Newton*, iii. 336, 338. I have adapted the translation given in the *Correspondence*.

[62] On the 'Origines', see Westfall, 'Newton's *Theologiae Gentilis Origines Philosophicae*', 15–34; id. *Never at Rest*, 351–6. Westfall's thesis in his article that Newton was a proto-deist is untenable on several grounds, including the fact that he was a biblicist and a believer in scriptural prophecy. See the corrective provided in James E. Force, 'Newton and Deism', *Science and Religion/Wissenschaft und Religion*, ed. Änne Bäumer and Manfred Büttner (Bochum: Brockmeyer, 1989), 120–32.

[63] Westfall, *Never at Rest*, 407.

of humanity, as practised by Cain and Abel. This faith was simple, ethical, and monotheistic. It also involved the study of God's creation. Newton initiated this massive study of religious ethnography, ancient mythology, pagan idolatry, and Gentile theology not only to identify the features of the first religion and trace its subsequent corruption, but also to distill the original, true understanding of nature. It is instructive that this project began not in Newton's declining years, but around the same time he composed and published the first edition of the *Principia*—a book that he believed revealed the true understanding of nature that had been lost centuries before. Newton begins a draft of chapter one by arguing that 'the Gentile theology was philosophical and above all looked to the astronomical and physical knowledge of the system of the world'.[64] Adding to this, he asserts that the ancients 'practised a two-fold philosophy, sacred and vulgar: the Philosophers handed down the sacred to their disciples through types and riddles, while the Orators recorded the vulgar openly and in a popular style'.[65] Newton goes on to say that this original 'sacred philosophy flourished above all in Egypt and was founded on the knowledge of the stars'.[66] As Westfall points out, Newton often referred to this original philosophy as 'astronomical theology'.[67]

The slightly later and more orderly English draft of this material helps reveal the main contours of Newton's arguments. He begins this draft: 'The religion most ancient and most generally received by the nations in the first ages was that of the Prytanea or Vestal Temples'.[68] These Temples were built around a central fire, which Newton believed was meant to represent the sun in the heliocentric view of the solar system. Later in this manuscript he states:

[64] Newton, Yahuda MS 16.2, fo. 1r (my translation). The original Latin is: 'Quod Theologia Gentilis Philosophica erat, et ad scientiam Astronomicam & Physicam systematis mundani apprimè spectabat'.

[65] Newton, Yahuda MS 16.2, fo. 1r (my translation). The original Latin is: 'Philosophiam antiquam duplicem coluere, sacram et vulgarem, sacram Philosophi per typos et ænigmata discipulis suis tradidere: vulgarem Oratores aperte et stylo populari scripserunt'. Newton's use of the verb *colō* is noteworthy, as this word, from which *cultus* is derived, not only can have the senses 'practise', 'cultivate', or 'study', but can also refer to religious worship.

[66] Newton, Yahuda MS 16.2, fo. 1r (my translation). The original Latin is: 'Philosophia sacra in Ægypto apprimè floruit et in scientia syderum fundata fuit'.

[67] Westfall, *Never at Rest*, 353.   [68] Newton, Yahuda MS 41, fo. 1r.

as the Tabernacle was contrived by Moses to be a symbol of the heavens (as St. Paul & Josephus teach) so were the Prytanæa amongst the nations ... The whole heavens they recconed to be the true & real Temple of God & therefore that a Prytanæum might deserve the name of his Temple they framed it so as in the fittest manner to represent the whole systeme of the heavens. A point of religion then which nothing can be more rational.[69]

The Jewish Tabernacle and Temple were pure representations of the system of the heavens. Other ancient nations corrupted their Temples and worship with idolatry and polytheism.

Shortly afterward, Newton extends his discussion about the purpose of ancient temples to elaborate the role of the ancient priests:

So then 'twas one designe of the ~~true systeme of the~~ first institution of the true religion to propose to mankind by the frame of the ancient Temples, the study of the frame of the world as the true Temple of the great God they worshipped. And thence it was that the Priests anciently were above other men well skilled in the knowledge of the true frame of Nature & accounted it a great part of their Theology ... The learning of the Indians lay in the Brachmans who were their Priests, that of the Persians in the Magi who were their Priests, that of the Babylonians in the Chaldeans who were their Priests ... So then the first religion was the most rational of all others till the nations corrupted it. For there is no way <(without revelation)> to come to the knowledge of a Deity but by the frame of nature.[70]

Newton thus believed the ancients saw a link between earthly temples and the heavenly temple and thus between theology and cosmology. The ideal of a physico-theology, which involved an empirical study of nature and was championed by many natural philosophers in the late seventeenth and early eighteenth centuries, Newton saw prefigured in the ancient prytanaeum. And, because one could discover knowledge about God in nature (as one could also discover knowledge about God in the Scriptures), a pure and correct method for the study of nature was required. Newton's use of the expression 'system of the world' in his *Principia* takes on added meaning against the backdrop of the synonymous expressions 'system of the heavens', 'frame of the world', 'true frame of nature', and 'frame of nature' used in this private manuscript. What is more, the claim that natural philosophy

---

[69] Ibid. fos. 5r–6r.
[70] Ibid. fo. 7r. One deletion and one set of insertion markers retained.

was a *part* of the original religion's theology, and thus perhaps subordinate to it, is reminiscent of the Medieval commonplace that natural philosophy was a handmaid (*ancilla*) to theology, the queen of the sciences. Whatever Newton is saying about the relationship of natural philosophy to theology, it is clear that he believed the roles of theologian and natural philosopher converged in the role of the priests in the original religion.

There is evidence to suggest a reflexive dynamic in these commitments. In 1692 the young Cambridge clergyman Richard Bentley preached the first Boyle Lectures in defence of Christianity. When revising these lectures for publication, Bentley sought Newton's help in bolstering the apologetics of the seventh and eighth sermons with the physics of the *Principia*.[71] In all, Newton wrote four letters in reply to Bentley.[72] The opening sentence of his first epistolary reply is now famous: 'When I wrote my treatise about our Systeme I had an eye upon such Principles as might work wth considering men for the beleife of a Deity & nothing can rejoyce me more then to find it usefull for that purpose'.[73] Newton went on in this first letter and the three that followed to sketch out a series of arguments from his physics and astronomy for design in nature. Newton's letters to Bentley are too well known to require further comment. But Newton's testimony, even though it is found in a letter to a clergyman, provides additional evidence that the author of the *Principia* also had theological aims in mind for his great work.

Another example is a manuscript on place, time, and God that dates from the early 1690s.[74] Written in Latin and bereft of a title (I

---

[71] The first six lectures were issued as separate volumes in 1692; the final two were issued in 1693, both bearing the title *A Confutation of Atheism from the Origin and Frame of the World*. These two volumes are reproduced in facsimile in I. Bernard Cohen and Robert E. Schofield (eds.), *Isaac Newton's Papers and Letters on Natural Philosophy* (Cambridge: Cambridge University Press, 1958), 313–94.

[72] Newton to Bentley, 10 December 1692, 17 January 1693, 11 February 1693, 25 February 1693, *Correspondence of Newton*, iii. 233–6, 238–40, 244–5, 253–6; the 1756 printed edition of these letters appears in Cohen and Schofield (eds.), *Newton's Papers and Letters on Natural Philosophy*, 279–312.

[73] Newton to Bentley, 10 December 1692, *Correspondence of Newton*, iii. 233.

[74] CUL MS Add. 3965, section 13, fos. 541r–542r, 545r–546r; J. E. McGuire, 'Newton on Place, Time, and God: An Unpublished Source', *British Journal for the History of Science*, 11/38 (1978), 114–29; a transcription of the original Latin and an English translation can be found on pp. 116–23.

will refer to it by its first three words, 'Tempus et locus'), this manuscript consists of eight numbered paragraphs. Not only is 'Tempus et locus' based in part on 'De gravitatione', but it overlaps in content with the Scholium on the Definitions,[75] thus further revealing and establishing the theological context of Newton's conception of space and time in the *Principia*. In paragraph four, after mentioning the eternity and infinity of space, Newton articulates the argument from plenitude, asserting that 'God … will be demonstrated to be more powerful, wiser, better, and in every way more perfect from the eternal succession and infinite number of his works, than He would be from works merely finite.' At some point after penning this paragraph, he added the statement: 'Nam Deus ex operibus cognoscitur' ('For God is known from his works').[76] In this terse five-word sentence, Newton sums up his entire empirical natural theology.

THE DUAL REFORMATION IN THE *OPTICKS*

In his memoranda on his visit to Cambridge in May 1694—the visit during which Newton discussed his 'Origines' and revealed to him the 'Classical Scholia'—David Gregory also reported seeing 'Three Books of Opticks'.[77] Whatever the reason for the delay (some speculate that Newton was waiting for the death of his critic Robert Hooke), it would be another decade before the *Opticks* appeared. Like the first edition of the *Principia*, the first edition of the *Opticks* contained few hints that Newton was engaged in a dual reformation. But also as with the *Principia*, Newton both contemplated including bold statements in the first edition of the *Opticks* and added such in later editions.

Included in a series of manuscripts that relate to Newton's final revisions and additions to the first edition of the *Opticks*, including the original sixteen Queries, is a draft preface and an associated

---

[75] McGuire, 'Newton on Place, Time, and God', 124.
[76] Newton, ibid. 119.
[77] Gregory in *Correspondence of Newton*, iii. 338.

fragment that treat, among other things, Newton's natural philosophical method and natural theology. They can confidently be dated to the three or four years immediately prior to the 1704 publication of the *Opticks*. J. E. McGuire gave the title 'Principles of Philosophy' to the first document and published transcriptions of both in 1970.[78] In the first document Newton seeks to outline his empirical natural philosophical method and he does this by listing four examples of the method. The first comes straight from natural theology: 'One principle in Philosophy is ye being of a God or Spirit infinite eternal omniscient omnipotent, & the best argument for such a being is the frame of nature & chiefly the contrivance of ye bodies of living creatures.' Once again we see Newton using the crucial expression 'the frame of nature'—an expression found in his 'Original of Religions'. It is also instructive that Newton states that the being of God is a principle in natural philosophy. One can find evidence of God's creative hand at work in the frame or structure of nature and Newton goes on to expostulate about the symmetry in the structure of the bodies of animals: 'All the great land animals have two eyes in the forehead, a nose between them a mouth under the nose, two ears on ye sides of ye head, two arms or two fore leggs or two wings on the sholders & two leggs behind & this symmetry in ye several species could not proceed from chance there being an equall chance for one eye or for three or four eyes as for two, & so of the other members'.[79] After elaborating on this argument, Newton concludes:

& therefore ye first formation of every species of creatures must be ascribed to an intelligent being such a being as we call God. These & such like considerations are the most convincing arguments for such a being & have convinced mankind in all ages that ye world & all the species of things therein were originally framed by his power & wisdom. And to lay aside this argum^t is very unphilosophical.[80]

---

[78] J. E. McGuire, ' "Newton's Principles of Philosophy": An Intended Preface for the 1704 *Opticks* and a Related Draft Fragment', *The British Journal for the History of Science*, 5 (1970), 178–86. The manuscript reference is CUL MS Add. 3970.3. fo. 479r–v and 480v. I have corrected McGuire's transcriptions against the original, removing deleted material, but including Newton's assertions.

[79] Newton in McGuire, 'Newton's "Principles of Philosophy" ', 183.

[80] Newton, ibid. I have retained one of Newton's deletions.

Thus, Newton argues, an empirical examination of the 'frame of nature' will lead one directly to God.[81]

Although they did not form part of the first edition of 1704, some of the natural theological arguments of the 'Principles of Philosophy' made an appearance in modified and attenuated forms at the end of Queries 28 and 31 in the later editions of the *Opticks*.[82] This happened first when Newton added these and other Queries to the first Latin edition of 1706.[83] They first appeared in English in the second English edition of 1717, and then in the English editions of 1721 and 1730.[84] Query 28 opens with an attack on Descartes's impulse theory of light and concludes with an inductive argument from design. At the end of the penultimate paragraph of this Query, Newton rejects the aetherial medium required for the Cartesian theory of light and then commences the final paragraph as follows: 'And for rejecting such a Medium, we have the Authority of those the oldest and most celebrated Philosophers of *Greece* and *Phœnicia*, who made a *Vacuum*, and Atoms, and the Gravity of Atoms, the first Principles of their Philosophy; tacitly attributing Gravity to some other cause than dense Matter.'[85] In these words, which first appeared in the Latin edition of 1706, we see a hint at the arguments about the ancients he presented in much more detail in the suppressed Classical Scholia finally making it into a public text.

---

[81] Another example of Newton's use of the expression 'frame of the world' (a term Bentley used in the title of his Boyle Lectures) as part of a natural theological argument can be found in Sotheby's 1936 Lot 255.1 (Sotheby's 2004 Lot 511.i; private collection), where Newton wrote: 'The wisdom and power which appears in the frame of the world and its various parts is sufficient to convince men that they were framed by a wise and powerful being' (transcription courtesy of Jean-François Baillon).

[82] McGuire recognized this in a note to his 1970 transcription (McGuire, 'Newton's "Principles of Philosophy" ', 183 n. 19).

[83] Newton, *Optice: sive de reflexionibus, refractionibus, inflexionibus & coloribus lucis libri tres* (London, 1706), 314–15, 345–6. Newton added Queries numbered 17–23 to the 1706 edition. The Latin edition was translated by Newton's associate Samuel Clarke.

[84] For their form in the final, fourth edn., see Newton, *Opticks*, 369–70, 402–3. Newton inserted eight new Queries in the English edition of 1717 immediately after the original sixteen (as Queries 17–24), and renumbered the seven Queries added to the Latin edition 1706 as 25–31. Thus, Queries 28 and 31 in the later English editions correspond to Queries 20 and 23 in the 1706 edition (see A. Rupert Hall, *All Was Light: An Introduction to Newton's* Opticks (Oxford: Clarendon, 1993), 238).

[85] Newton, *Opticks*, 369.

But there is more. He continues his argument by attacking the hypothetical-deductive method:

Later Philosophers banish the Consideration of such a Cause out of natural Philosophy, feigning Hypotheses for explaining all things mechanically, and referring other Causes to Metaphysicks: Whereas the main Business of natural Philosophy is to argue from Phænomena without feigning Hypotheses, and to deduce Causes from Effects, till we come to the very first Cause, which certainly is not mechanical; and not only to unfold the Mechanism of the World, but chiefly to resolve these and such like Questions.[86]

Not only is this a stinging critique of the excesses of the mechanical philosophy, but it also contends that an inductive study of nature will lead to the conclusion that nature is ultimately contingent on the Creator. Additionally, it is this inductive method—not the failed method of Descartes—that will reveal the 'Mechanism of the World'. Newton bolsters these arguments with a list of natural phenomena that he believes attest to the existence of a divine designer, including the motions of comets and planets, the placement of the stars and the bodies of animals. He concludes this Query with another apologetic statement: 'And though every true Step made in this Philosophy brings us not immediately to the Knowledge of the first Cause, yet it brings us nearer to it, and on that account is to be highly valued.'[87] It is precisely because it leads to a knowledge of God that Newton believes his method is superior.

The sanitized statements on natural theology found in the published editions of the *Opticks* amount to what he allowed to slip through his own self-censorship. But as is often the case with his public documents, these cautious statements can be illuminated by the frank language of his unpublished manuscripts. The best example of this is an English draft of Query 23 (31) that dates to around the time of the publication of the Latin edition of 1706.[88] This draft opens with a more explicit articulation of the argument about the

---

[86] Newton, *Optics*, 369.   [87] Ibid. 370.

[88] Westfall suggests that this draft dates to around 1705 (*Never at Rest*, 647). Given the use of the number '23' for the Query, it certainly cannot date more than a year earlier than this. The same consideration shows that it must date to before 1717, when the second English edition was published complete with its renumbered Queries.

ancients and the vacuum that appeared near the end of Query 28 (20):

> Qu 23. By what means do bodies act on one another at a distance. The ancient Philosophers who held Atoms & Vacuum attributed gravity to Atoms without telling us the means unless perhaps in figures: as by calling God Harmony & representing him & matter by the God Pan & his Pipe, or by calling the Sun the prison of Jupiter because he keeps the Planets in their orbs. Whence it seems to have been an ancient opinion that matter depends upon a Deity for its laws of motion as well as for its existence.[89]

Thus Newton not only contemplated opening a window on the contents of the Classical Scholia, but also considered running an argument that supported his belief that the laws of motion were contingent on the existence of God and that this belief had an ancient precedent. Two paragraphs later he launches into an attack on the hypothetical method:

> A man may argue plausibly for blind fate against final causes but I find by experience that ... I am constantly aiming at something. Were it not for experience I should not know that matter is heavy or impenetrable or moveable or that I think or am or that there is matter or any thing else. And therefore to affirm any thing more then I know by experience & reasoning upon it is precarious. Even arguments for a Deity if not taken from Phænomena are slippery & serve only for ostentation.[90]

In these lines Newton makes it clear that one of the chief defects of the hypothetical method of Descartes is that it does not offer secure arguments for the existence of God. At this point he raises the spectre of atheism, suggesting that 'An Atheist will allow that there is a Being absolutely perfect, necessarily existing & the author of mankind & call it Nature'.[91] Moreover, Newton adds that the atheist 'may tell you further that the Author of mankind was destitute of wisdome & designe because there are no final causes & and that matter is space & therefore necessarily existing & having always the same quantity of motion, would in infinite time run through all variety of forms one of which is that of man'.[92]

---

[89] CUL MS Add. 3970 (B), fo. 619r.
[90] Ibid. A pointed dig at Descartes's *cogito* and rationalist methodology can be detected in the fourth line of this excerpt.
[91] Ibid.   [92] Ibid. fos. 619r–v.

For Newton, it is God who is necessarily existing in that nature is dependent on his existence:

We see the effects of a Deity in the creation & thence gather the cause & therefore the proof of a Deity & what are his properties belongs to experimental Philosophy. 'Tis the business of this Philosophy to argue from the effects to their causes till we come at the first cause & not to argue from any cause to the effect till the cause as to its being & quality is sufficiently discovered.[93]

Thus, although Newton uses the more polite term 'unphilosophical' in his draft 'Principles of Philosophy' and in the published Query 31, his private papers show that what he really meant is that such arguments incline to atheism.[94] In contrast, he believed that his method leads straight in the opposite direction. What these arguments show is that Newton believed the same inductive method that yielded such spectacular results in natural philosophy would also lead to the pious conclusion that there was and is a creative hand at work behind the 'frame of nature'.

THE DUAL REFORMATION IN THE GENERAL SCHOLIUM

When Newton published the second edition of his *Principia* in 1713 he added a concluding General Scholium.[95] In this short document he made explicit some of his views about the *prisca sapientia* and *prisca theologia* to which he had subscribed at the time of the

[93] CUL MS Add. 3970 (B), fo. 619r.

[94] Cf. Newton, Keynes MS 7, fo. 1, where he also openly attacks atheism at the beginning of another articulation of the argument from design based on the bilateral symmetry of structure in animal bodies.

[95] On the General Scholium, see James E. Force, 'Newton's God of Dominion: The Unity of Newton's Theological, Scientific and Political Thought', in J. E. Force and Richard H. Popkin, *Essays on the Context, Nature and Influence of Isaac Newton's Theology* (Dordrecht: Kluwer, 1990), 75–102; R. De Smet and K. Verelst, 'Newton's Scholium Generale: The Platonic and Stoic Legacy—Philo, Justus Lipsius and the Cambridge Platonists', *History of Science*, 39 (2001), 1–30; Stephen Snobelen, ' "God of Gods, and Lord of Lords": The Theology of Isaac Newton's General Scholium to the *Principia*', *Osiris*, 16 (2001), 169–208; Larry Stewart, 'Seeing Through the Scholium: Religion and Reading Newton in the Eighteenth Century', *History of Science*, 34 (1996), 123–65.

publication of the first edition of the *Principia*, but had cautiously withheld from public scrutiny. This document is laced with explicit and not-so-explicit clues to Newton's natural philosophical and theological agendas. The natural philosophical apologetics of the General Scholium are made evident from its very first line: 'The hypothesis of vortices is beset with many difficulties.'[96] In the paragraph headed by this declaration Newton rids the universe of vortices using the empirical evidence that came from the eccentric motion of comets.[97] Without lingering on this point, Newton moves quickly to eliminate the subtle aether on which the Cartesian vortical system depended. The celestial spaces are instead like the vacuum in Boyle's airpump: 'All bodies must move very freely in these spaces, and therefore planets and comets must revolve continually in orbits given in kind and in position, according to the laws set forth above' (i.e. in the *Principia*).[98]

Newton next describes how the six primary planets revolve in the same direction on a near plane and concludes: 'And all these regular motions do not have their origin in mechanical causes, since comets go freely in very eccentric orbits and into all parts of the heavens.'[99] The cause, which is certainly not mechanical, is God himself: 'This most elegant system of the sun, planets, and comets could not have arisen without the design and dominion of an intelligent and powerful being.'[100] Not only is this beautiful system contingent on the dominion of God, but the unity of natural phenomena is grounded in, and guaranteed by, his unity: 'And if the fixed stars are the centers of similar systems, they will all be constructed according to a similar design and subject to the dominion of *One*, especially since the light of the fixed stars is of the same nature as the light of the sun, and all the systems send light into all the others'.[101]

Having introduced his God, Newton goes on to describe him: 'He rules all things, not as the world soul but as the lord of all. And because of his dominion he is called Lord God *Pantokrator*.'[102] This use of a biblical name of God initiates a string of biblical titles and attributes for God, including 'my God', 'your God', 'the God of Israel', 'God of Gods', and 'Lord of Lords'.[103] All these titles are

[96] Newton, *Principia* (Cohen-Whitman), 939.
[97] Ibid.   [98] Ibid. 940.   [99] Ibid.   [100] Ibid.
[101] Ibid.   [102] Ibid.   [103] Ibid. 940–1.

meant to emphasize that the true God is not an abstract perfection remote from the physical world. Instead, he is a God of dominion, the meaning of whose names and the reality of whose sovereignty derive from his standing in relation to all that is contingent on him, whether his creation or his creatures. This God of dominion is the God of Newton's faith *and* his natural philosophy. This is also the God of Newton's absolute space and time:

He is eternal and infinite, omnipotent and omniscient, that is, he endures from eternity to eternity, and he is present from infinity to infinity; he rules all things, and he knows all things that happen or can happen. He is not eternity and infinity, but eternal and infinite; he is not duration and space, but he endures always and is present everywhere, and by existing always and everywhere he constitutes duration and space.[104]

God comes first, and hence absolute space and time are predicates of God's infinite extension and eternal duration.

What may appear at first glance to be only a partially relevant excursus on the nature of God is in fact much more than this: it is an argument that also hints at an alternative for the mechanical aether of Descartes that he has summarily dismissed in the introduction of the General Scholium. This alternative is the omnipresence of God. Having determined that gravity is universal, Newton hints that an explanation for the universality and immediacy of gravity can be found in the infinite extension of God's presence through his Spirit: 'In him all things are contained and move, but he does not act on them nor they on him. God experiences nothing from the motions of bodies; the bodies feel no resistance from God's omnipresence.'[105] The line 'in him all things are contained and move' is taken from Acts 17: 28, which records its use by the Apostle Paul. Paul, in turn, as Newton knew, was citing the Stoic writer Aratus's *Phaenomena*. This is stressed in a footnote on this statement, which begins: 'This opinion was held by the ancients.' Newton then lists Pythagoras, Cicero, Thales, Virgil, Philo Judaeus, and Aratus as ancient authors who also espoused this view. He adds to these names Paul, John, Moses, David, Solomon, and Jeremiah as biblical authors who likewise believed in God's omnipresence and that creation is contained

---

[104] Newton, *Principia* (Cohen-Whitman), 941.   [105] Ibid. 941–2.

within this divine omnipresence.[106] Thus, although he aborted his plans to include the Classical Scholia in the second edition of the *Principia*, an element of the argument contained therein appears in the footnote on God and space.

Newton is also at pains to emphasize that these truths about the Deity do not derive from direct experience, inner light, Platonic forms, or Cartesian distinct ideas: 'But there is no direct sense and there are no indirect reflected actions by which we know innermost substances; much less do we have an idea of the substance of God. We know him only by his properties and attributes and by the wisest and best construction of things and their final causes, and we admire him because of his perfections; but we venerate and worship him because of his dominion.'[107] Once again, Newton articulates his belief in a nature that is utterly contingent on the existence of God: 'All the diversity of created things, each in its place and time, could only have arisen from the ideas and the will of a necessarily existing being'. He draws the theological portion of the General Scholium to a close with the positive declaration: 'This concludes the discussion of God, and to treat of God from phenomena is certainly a part of natural philosophy.'[108]

But there is more. In using biblical titles of God that Newton believed were restricted to the Father,[109] and in arguing that the term 'God' is a relative term, denoting dominion and rule rather than essence and substance as in the Trinitarian conception,[110] he is revealing his heretical hand to those with eyes to see.[111] In stating that we 'have ideas of [God's] attributes', but that we do not 'have an idea of the substance of God'[112] he is not only championing an empirical understanding of God, but is also probably attacking the Trinitarian proclivity to articulate the relationship between the Father and Christ in metaphysical terms resting on notions of substance. Newton's presentation in the General Scholium of an

---

[106] Ibid. 941–2 n. j.   [107] Ibid. 942.

[108] Ibid. 943. The 1713 edition reads 'experimental philosophy'.

[109] Snobelen, ' "God of Gods, and Lord of Lords" ', 181.

[110] Ibid. 183–4.

[111] That some contemporary observers recognized oblique antitrinitarianism in the General Scholium is shown in Stewart, 'Seeing Through the Scholium'.

[112] Newton, *Principia* (Cohen-Whitman), 942.

omnipresent God not only connects with his belief that absolute space is a predicate of God's spatial ubiquity, but has an antitrinitarian corollary, since in his private manuscripts Newton is adamant that it is only the Father, and not the Son, who possesses the attribute of immovability.[113] In the third edition of 1726, he strengthened his antitrinitarian argument by adding a footnote on the term 'God' in which he argues that the Bible allows for beings other than the True God to be called God, as in Psalm 82 where the Hebrew magistrates are called 'gods' (Hebrew *'elohim*) due to their role representing the True God.[114] As any astute contemporary theologian would have known, this was a standard argument of antitrinitarian exegetes. Another insertion in the 1726 edition further bolstered the antitrinitarian argumentation of the General Scholium. In following the statement 'Every sentient soul, at different times and in different organs of senses and motions, is the same indivisible person' a few lines later with the declaration 'God is one and the same God always and everywhere',[115] Newton both manages to enshrine the Jewish and unitarian Christian expression of faith 'God is one' ('*Deus est unus*') in the *Principia*, and imply the unipersonality of God—a heretical tenet. Viewed in this antitrinitarian light, Newton's earlier insinuation about the unity of creation being founded on the unity of God takes on an added significance.

After concluding the overtly theological portion of the General Scholium, Newton turns to natural philosophical method. In acknowledging that he has 'not yet assigned a cause to gravity', he argues that it is enough that he can describe it mathematically. Although he does not mention Descartes directly, it is clear that the French natural philosopher is one of his targets when he avers that he will not resort to vain hypothesizing in his famous declaration: '*hypotheses non fingo*' ('I do not feign hypotheses'). He adds: 'For whatever is not deduced from the phenomena must be called a

---

[113] Newton, Keynes MS 8. Newton's unitarian conception of space can be contrasted with the Lutheran Johannes Kepler's Trinitarian conception of the universe, in which the Father is associated with the Sun, the Son with the fixed stars, and the Holy Spirit with the intervening space (Robert S. Westman, 'The Copernicans and the Churches', in David C. Lindberg and Ronald L. Numbers (eds.), *God and Nature: Historical Essays on the Encounter Between Christianity and Science* (Berkeley: University of California Press, 1986), 97).

[114] Newton, *Principia* (Cohen-Whitman), 941 n. g.   [115] Ibid. 941.

hypothesis; and hypotheses, whether metaphysical or physical, or based on occult qualities, or mechanical, have no place in experimental philosophy'.[116] Finally, Newton concludes the General Scholium with a short paragraph on 'a certain very subtle spirit pervading gross bodies and lying hidden in them'. Newton is certain of the existence of this spirit and, although he is not certain of the nature of its operations, he wants to suggest that it can explain the forces of attraction between both small and large bodies. It is his antidote to excessive mechanism. Its inclusion in a document that also speaks openly about God's omnipresence is also more than suggestive. This spirit must be taken as an integral element of his natural philosophy, which, as is sketched out in the General Scholium, has God as its focal point.

The General Scholium serves as public testament to Newton's agendas for natural philosophy and theology, even though these agendas are accessible only to the highly adept reader. Not only is Newton at pains to champion an inductive natural philosophy and to stress that 'to treat God from phenomena is certainly part of natural philosophy', but he implies that a correct understanding of God will jettison Trinitological formulations. Ultimately for him, hypotheses in natural philosophy and religion lead to corruption. Newton's natural philosophy and his heretical theology are also linked by this methodology. Just as a humble and inductive reading of the Book of Nature leads one to the Creator, so a humble and inductive reading of the Book of Scripture leads one to the One True God of the Bible. The two reformations come together in the General Scholium.

THE TRUE RELIGION AND 'NATURAL PHILOSOPHY IN ALL ITS PARTS'

Even after the publication of the General Scholium in 1713 Newton continued to toy with additional revelations in print. In one of the unpublished draft prefaces of the *Principia* composed in the years after the release of the second edition, Newton outlines his natural philosophical method and summarizes some of the content of his

---

[116] Ibid. 943.

magnum opus. As Cohen notes, this draft preface 'is of special interest because it sets forth clearly what Newton considered to be the goals and achievements of the *Principia*'.[117] One passage not only provides a synopsis of the Classical Scholia, but explicitly states that Newton believed he was merely reviving the lost philosophy of the ancients:

> The Chaldeans long ago believed that the planets revolve in nearly concentric orbits around the sun and that the comets do so in extremely eccentric orbits, and the Pythagoreans introduced this philosophy into Greece. But it was also known to the ancients that the moon is heavy toward the earth, and that the stars are heavy toward one another, and that all bodies in a vacuum fall to the earth with equal velocity and thus are heavy in proportion to the quantity of matter in each of them. Because of lack of demonstrations, this philosophy fell into disuse, and I did not invent it but have only tried to use the force of demonstrations to revive it.[118]

Thus, while the *Principia* was to provide the demonstrations that the ancients had not been able to provide, its philosophy was not new, but rather a restoration of the original philosophy that had been lost.

But it was not only the ancient natural philosophy that had been lost and corrupted and thus required restoration. Moral philosophy was also in need of reformation. And this reformation was related to the reformation in natural philosophy, as Newton concludes in the final paragraph of Query 31:

> And if natural Philosophy in all its Parts, by pursuing this Method, shall at length be perfected, the Bounds of Moral Philosophy will be also enlarged. For so far as we can know by natural Philosophy what is the first Cause, what Power he has over us, and what Benefits we receive from him, so far our Duty towards him, as well as that towards one another, will appear to us by the Light of Nature.[119]

Since the pure natural philosophy led inductively to an understanding of the Creator, this reformation is in turn related to one in religion—which would be an undoing of the corruption and idolatry of the Gentiles who had departed from the original religion of the Noachides:

---

[117] Cohen, 'Guide', in Newton *Principia* (Cohen-Whitman) 49.

[118] Newton in Cohen, 'Guide', ibid. 49.

[119] Newton, *Opticks*, 405. The wording is the same in the 1717 edn.

And no doubt, if the Worship of false Gods had not blinded the Heathen, their moral Philosophy would have gone farther than to the four Cardinal Virtues; and instead of teaching the Transmigration of Souls, and to worship the Sun and Moon, and dead Heroes, they would have taught us to worship our true Author and Benefactor, as their Ancestors did under the Government of Noah and his Sons before they corrupted themselves.[120]

And the worship of 'our true Author and Benefactor' was the ultimate purpose of Newton's natural philosophy.

In the introduction to a collection of essays that treat several of the themes outlined above, McGuire eloquently outlines the importance of the ancients to Newton's intellectual project:

For Newton, the incorporation of ancient wisdom into his vision of nature is more than a ritualistic deference to tradition: it constitutes an active appropriation of tradition into the structure of his understanding of nature. As Newton construes it, understanding comprises more than sets of propositions linked together into chains of argument, or the active comprehension of the content either of propositions or occurrent mental states. For him, it is an event dynamically poised at the cognitive interface between historical patterns emerging from those embodiments. Indeed, for Newton, tradition is a cultural appropriation that both enables and limits innovative thought. It does not exist passively in an objectified past, but actively in the very interstices of intellectual life. Thus, the transformation of *renovatio* into *innovatio* involves an active interrogation of a living past by a mind at liberty to think.[121]

For McGuire, then, it is not merely the case that Newton believed the thought of the ancients adumbrated his own understanding of nature, but that there is a very real intellectual relationship between Newton's reading of ancient natural philosophy and the cognitive content of his own natural philosophy. Thus McGuire claims both a weak relationship between ancient wisdom and Newton's natural philosophy (that the *prisca* tradition was a part of the *context* of Newton's mathematics, optics, and physics), as well as a strong relationship (that the *content* of Newton's mathematics, optics, and

---

[120] Ibid. 405–6. The concluding statement 'as their Ancestors did under the Government of Noah and his Sons before they corrupted themselves' was added to the 1721 edn.

[121] J. E. McGuire, *Tradition and Innovation: Newton's Metaphysics of Nature* (Dordrecht: Kluwer, 1996), pp. xi–xii.

physics was in part shaped by his reading of the ancients). This chapter has added weight to these conclusions.

Throughout much of his adult life, Newton pursued two reformations, one in natural philosophy and one in religion. The results of the natural philosophical reformation have long been known to the world due to their publication in the *Principia* and the *Opticks*. Because his theological reformation involved the deepest heresy, he chose not to bring the results of this reformation to the public—at least not openly. In both reformations, the ancients were his constant guide. And, just as he believed the ancient Babylonian magi integrated religion with their study of nature, so, too, Newton believed that the ideal for his age was a unified philosophy that brought together the studies of the Book of Nature and the Book of Scripture. Although neither the initial editions of the *Principia* nor the *Opticks* made explicit his programme to recover the *prisca sapientia* and the *prisca theologia*, he had become committed to these twin goals, and the close relationship between them, before he began to compose the first of them. It is now known that he considered releasing more explicit affirmations with the first edition of the *Principia* (in the suppressed *System of the World*) and in the first edition of the *Opticks* (in the unused draft preface). Shortly after the publication of the *Principia* he composed the Classical Scholia for a projected second edition. Although this material remained unpublished, brief hints of the arguments contained therein, and much else besides, including a forceful affirmation of natural theology and the centrality of God to natural philosophy, did make their way into the General Scholium of 1713. As for the *Opticks*, only two years after the first edition was released, the natural theology and the *prisca sapientia* were displayed in the new Queries of the *Optice* of 1706. The presence of these commitments in Newton's private writings long before his great works went through the press shows that they are not merely *post factum* rhetorical ornamentation. Queries 28 and 31 and the General Scholium, found at the conclusions of his books and thus helping to establish their overall purpose, open a window on his private thoughts, even if the window is open only a crack and the hidden meaning still partially obscured by a veil of oblique phrases meant to restrict the meaning to the worthy.

It was Newton's desire to construct a natural philosophy that demonstrated that nature was contingent on the existence of God, whether this be the beauty and symmetry seen in creation or the grounding of absolute space and time in God's omnipresence and eternal duration. Newton's God of dominion and his view of nature as dependent on God are two halves of a whole. And the correct understanding of each was the result of a right reading of the Books of Nature and Scripture respectively. Athanasius and the Homoousians had brought about an apostasy in religion by infusing metaphysics and doctrinal novelties into religion. Descartes and other mechanical philosophers had taken the wrong path in natural philosophy, a way of corruption and human pride that would yield philosophical romances in place of the truth of nature. Hypotheses had yielded substance talk and the abomination of the Trinity in religion, just as it had led to solid orbs and vortices in natural philosophy. Both were forms of idolatry. Furthermore, a pure natural philosophy and method led to the First Cause—not as a foundational axiom or initial hypothesis as in the a priori reasoning of Cartesianism or as the conclusion of purely thought-based reasoning as in the Platonized ontological arguments of Anselm, but in the inductive a posteriori reading of nature inspired in part by the Hebraic-biblical intuition that works backwards from the beauty, order, and unity of nature to the One true God. Descartes's method was the inverse of the method that resulted in truth about nature and God. Newton was intent on developing a physics for all time for which God was not merely a pious overlay, but that demonstrated that he was the personal power and source behind all nature. That Newton believed his radical theology was thoroughly bound up with this natural philosophy is made plain by the juxtaposition of his covert attack on the Trinity and his natural philosophical apologetics in the General Scholium.

There is one remaining curiosity. Why the asymmetry between the release of the results of the natural philosophical reformation and the secrecy enshrouding the religious reformation? While his publication of the *Principia* and the *Opticks* suggests that he felt that the time was ripe to bring the reformation of natural philosophy to the wider world, Newton did not believe the original Gospel or pure monotheism would be preached openly and successfully for two centuries or more after his passing.[122] And yet he was sure that this day would eventually arrive. Perhaps this is one reason why he risked exposure by heretic-hunters and embedded his heretical theology in the General Scholium to await the time to come when they would be understood.

[122] Snobelen, 'Isaac Newton, Heretic', 391–3.

10

The Heterodox Career of Nicolas Fatio de Duillier

Scott Mandelbrote

A MAN IN WHOM THERE WAS NO GUILE

There never was a better Man, than Mr Facio: His whole Life, like that of his blessed Master, was spent in doing good: And it might be as truly said of him, as some Person said of Nathaniel; *he was a Man in whom there was no guile*. As to his Learning: He had few, if any equals: He had read more than almost any other Man; and had the Happiness of remember[ing] every thing he had ever read. But, great as his Learning was; his Modesty and Humility was still greater: He could bare contradiction from Children in Knowledge; and that, too in things that were plain and evident to him even to a Demonstration.[1]

In the early 1760s, the Genevan natural philosopher George-Louis Le Sage (1724–1803) tried to discover more about one of his intellectual predecessors, Nicolas Fatio de Duillier (1664–1753), who had shared

I should like to thank the following for their help in the preparation of this essay: Michael Heyd, Peter Jones, Anita McConnell, Fritz Nagel, Tabitta van Nouhuys, Maria-Cristina Pitassi, Michael Screech. A draft was completed during my term as a Visiting Fellow in Abteilung II of the Max-Planck-Institut für Wissenschaftsgeschichte in Berlin. I am grateful to all my colleagues there for many helpful conversations, and am particularly indebted to the comments and suggestions of Lorraine Daston, Volkmar Schüller, and Andrew Sparling.

[1] Bibliothèque Publique et Universitaire, Geneva [hereafter, BPU], MS Fr. 2064, fo. 111; on Nathaniel, cf. Christ's words in John 1: 47.

his interest in a mechanical theory of gravitation.[2] Le Sage initially found out about Fatio from surviving members of his family and from Gabriel Cramer, Professor first of Mathematics and then of Natural Philosophy at the Academy of Geneva.[3] Cramer, together with his student Jean Jallabert, had once developed a mechanical interpretation of gravity of his own, under the influence of copies of some of Fatio's manuscripts that his brother, Jean-Christophe Fatio (1659–1720), had made and that had remained in Geneva.[4] With the assistance of François Calandrini, a descendant of Fatio, Le Sage made contact with the rector of Madresfield, Worcestershire, Corfield Clare, with whom Nicolas Fatio had lodged during his last years in England. Clare had acted as Fatio's executor and had inherited a share of his books and papers, in payment for debt. Another share had been left to the widow of Jean Allut, one of Fatio's closest friends and a fellow disciple of the French Prophets, whose apocalyptic teachings had caused considerable disturbance during the years immediately following their arrival in England in 1706.[5] On 26 August 1761, Clare replied to Calandrini, sending an encomium to Fatio's innocence and learning, a catalogue of his surviving manuscripts, and critical comments on 'the old Woman [Mrs Allut, who] would sell all the Manuscripts in her hands (and wich are the greatest share of them) unknown to me, if any body offered her enough for them'.[6] Despite such encouragement, Le Sage struggled to obtain Fatio's

---

[2] On Le Sage, see Michael Heyd, *'Be Sober and Reasonable': The Critique of Enthusiasm in the Seventeenth and Early Eighteenth Centuries* (Leiden: Brill, 1995), 261–73; Matthew R. Edwards (ed.), *Pushing Gravity: New Perspectives on Le Sage's Theory of Gravitation* (Montreal: Apeiron, 2002).

[3] See BPU, MS 2050.

[4] On Cramer, see Isaac Benguigni, *Gabriel Cramer. Illustre mathématicien, 1704–1752* (Geneva: Cramer, 1998), and BPU, MS Fr. 2017; on Jean-Christophe Fatio's work as a copyist, see BPU, MS Fr. 603, fos. 64, 97–100. For parts of Fatio's work that reached Le Sage in 1758, see the pages copied by Firmin Abauzit of Rouen from a manuscript provided by Christophe Fatio, now added to BPU, MS Fr. 603. For the ordering of this manuscript, see Horst Zehe, *Die Gravitationstheorie des Nicolas Fatio de Duillier* (Hildesheim: Gerstenberg, 1980), 293–306.

[5] See Hillel Schwartz, *The French Prophets. The History of a Millenarian Group in Eighteenth-Century England* (Berkeley: the University of California Press, 1980) and id., *Knaves, Fools, Madmen and that Subtle Effluvium. A Study of the Opposition to the French Prophets in England, 1706–1710* (Gainesville: University Presses of Florida, 1978).

[6] BPU, MS Fr. 2064, fo. 111; see also MS Fr. 602, fo. 262.

papers from England over the next four years, finally succeeding in purchasing those that Clare had given as a settlement to one of his own creditors, John Ingram. This was achieved through the intervention of Lord and Lady Stanhope, to whose son, Charles, Le Sage had acted as tutor during the family's stay at Geneva in 1764, and with the help of several Swiss intermediaries resident in London. In April 1765, Le Sage bought the majority of Fatio's manuscripts for £8, but the death of Ingram seems to have frustrated the transfer of some of the papers that remained at Worcester. The manuscripts reached Stanhope in London in February 1766 and thence made their way to Geneva.[7]

Once he had obtained these papers, Le Sage was able to begin to reconstruct the theory of gravity on which Fatio had worked intermittently for fifty years, from the late 1680s until at least the early 1740s.[8] Apart from their antiquarian and patriotic interest, Fatio's manuscripts were an important element in the history of ideas of gravity that Le Sage was himself composing. They provided a critical link between the analysis of ancient theories of gravity, which he described in his 'Lucrèce Newtonien', and his writings on the ideas of Newton and his eighteenth-century interpreters.[9] Partly through his study of Fatio, Le Sage was aware of the complexity and uncertainty of some of Newton's theories regarding the cause of gravity.[10] He shared a lack of confidence in the solutions that the Englishman had found with earlier commentators on Newton's work, particularly

[7] BPU, MS Fr. 602, fos. 204–5, 255–65; MS Fr. 2043; MS Fr. 2050; MS Fr. 2064, fos. 104–17; some of Fatio's books and papers remained at Worcester and in the hands of Clare's descendants, see Royal Society, London, MS 64, fos. 1–2r. See also Bernard Gagnebin, 'De la Cause de la pesanteur. Mémoire de Nicolas Fatio de Duillier présenté à la Royal Society le 26 février 1690', *Notes and Records of the Royal Society of London*, 6 (1949), 105–60, esp. 118–24.

[8] Fatio's own account of the chronology of his work on gravity is at BPU, MS Fr. 603, fos. 65–8; see also MS D.O. Autogr. Newton (Papiers Fatio).

[9] BPU, MSS Fr. 2011–17, esp. 2015; for an early realization of the similarities between Fatio's theory of gravity and the ideas of Lucretius, see the comments of David Gregory in March 1703, Royal Society, London, MS 247, fo. 87[a]r.

[10] For consideration of the problems faced by Newton and his contemporaries in this context, see I. Bernard Cohen, *The Newtonian Revolution* (Cambridge: Cambridge University Press, 1980); Betty Jo Teeter Dobbs, *The Janus Faces of Genius* (Cambridge: Cambridge University Press, 1991), 122–249; Rudolf de Smet and Karin Verelst, 'Newton's Scholium Generale: The Platonic and Stoic Legacy—Philo, Justus Lipsius and the Cambridge Platonists', *History of Science*, 39 (2001), 1–30.

Daniel and Johann Bernoulli, and to some extent with Fatio him-self.[11] Le Sage distinguished between 'les Newtoniens moderés & les *Newtonolatres*', suggesting that for most contemporary English philo-sophers Newtonian ideas had assumed the status once reserved for the work of Aristotle. He was also worried by the theological direc-tion taken by many who had commentated on Newton's work, in which it seemed that the self-sufficiency of the operations of natural laws might displace awareness of and reverence for a divine creator.[12] As a result, he showed an interest in the ideas of John Hutchinson and his followers, who had proposed a mechanical system of nature based on circulation promoted in a universal aether through the agency of fire, light, and air. This trinity of material agents mirrored the transcendent divine Trinity, which had created the system of the world. Hutchinson and his followers were extremely critical of what they took to be the idolatry of Newton's descriptions of God, for example, in the account of God's substance in the 'General Scholium' that Newton added to the second edition of the *Principia* in 1713.[13]

Le Sage was not, however, a follower of Hutchinson, any more than Fatio had been: neither Le Sage nor Fatio subscribed to Hutch-inson's idiosyncratic system for reading Hebrew without reference to the Masoretic vowel points, which ultimately provided the theo-logical underpinning both for his description of the Trinity and for his account of the working of the natural order. Fatio had put

[11] E. A. Fellman, 'The *Principia* and Continental Mathematicians', *Notes and Records of the Royal Society of London*, 42 (1988), 13–34; Niccolò Guicciardini, *Reading the* Principia. *The Debate on Newton's Mathematical Methods for Natural Philosophy from 1687 to 1736* (Cambridge: Cambridge University Press, 1999), 250–60.

[12] BPU, MS Fr. 2043 (it was necessary to consult this manuscript on microfilm, where it proved impossible to determine whether or how it had been foliated); cf. P. M. Heimann and J. E. McGuire, 'Newtonian Forces and Lockean Powers: Concepts of Matter in Eighteenth-Century Thought', *Historical Studies in the Physical Sciences*, 3 (1971), 233–306; Heimann, ' "Nature is a Perpetual Worker": Newton's Aether and Eighteenth-Century Natural Philosophy', *Ambix*, 20 (1973), 1–25.

[13] See G. N. Cantor, 'Revelation and the Cyclical Cosmos of John Hutchinson', in L. J. Jordanova and Roy Porter (eds.), *Images of the Earth* (Chalfont St Giles: BSHS, 1979), 3–22; C. B. Wilde, 'Hutchinsonianism, Natural Philosophy and Religious Controversy in Eighteenth Century Britain', *History of Science*, 18 (1980), 1–24; cf. Isaac Newton, *The Principia*, tr. I. Bernard Cohen, Anne Whitman, and Julia Budenz (Berkeley: University of California Press, 1999), 939–44. Le Sage had been reading J[ohn] H[utchinson], *A Treatise of Power, Essential and Mechanical* (London, 1732).

forward original ideas of his own about the metre of Hebrew poetry, and the proper way of translating the Bible, but these owed something to the contemporary debate over the work of biblical critics such as Francis Hare and François Masclef that also informed Hutchinson's writings, rather than being derived from Hutchinson himself.[14] Le Sage dismissed even Fatio's efforts in this field. He offered to pay Clare one shilling for every thousand words of Fatio's loose papers on gravity but was uninterested in his theological manuscripts, which included translations of Job as well as of the Psalms. These Le Sage rejected as 'useless'.[15]

Le Sage believed that Fatio's writings on gravity were useful because they offered a way of demonstrating the providential activity of God in nature. This was the explanation for his interest in mechanical theories of gravity and for his rejection of Newtonian concepts that might appear to make force inhere as a power in matter. For similar reasons, many eighteenth-century English readers also preferred to assimilate Newton's ideas to mechanical theories of the aether, although they usually did so without reference to the work of Fatio.[16] Le Sage regarded Fatio's work on the mechanical theory of gravity as a mark of scientific orthodoxy. It offered a way to preserve the advances that Continental natural philosophers had made during the seventeenth century towards a new physics that gave concrete

---

[14] Fatio's publications on Hebrew poetry may be found in *The Present State of the Republick of Letters*, 17 (1736), 236–53; cf. the discussion in *The Gentleman's Magazine*, 6 (1736), 609–10, 642–6; 7 (1737), 9–10, where Fatio asserted that he had not ignored the Hebrew vowel points and accents in his work. See also François Masclef, *Grammatica Hebraica a punctis aliisque inventis Massorethicis libera* (Paris, 1716); Francis Hare, *Psalmorum liber, in versiculos metrice divisus* (London, 1736); James L. Kugel, *The Idea of Biblical Poetry* (New Haven: Yale University Press, 1981), 264–6. Fatio compared his own work explicitly to Hare's, see BPU, MS Fr. 602, fo. 170; William Whiston forwarded Fatio's letter on the metre of Hebrew poetry to Hare in 1734 because of its similarity to his theories, see BPU, MS Fr. 601, fos. 270–1. For evidence that Fatio's interest in Hebrew poetry was of long standing, see H. W. Turnbull et al. (eds.), *The Correspondence of Isaac Newton* (7 vols.; Cambridge: Cambridge University Press, 1959–77), iii. 242–3 (Fatio to Newton, 30 January 1693).

[15] BPU, MS Fr. 2064, fos. 107–8, 112v: Le Sage offered Clare a crown for any page bearing the signature of Newton, Halley, or Huygens; £2 for every thousand words of Fatio's poetry on the subject of gravity, and 1s. for every letter belonging to Fatio.

[16] G. N. Cantor, *Optics after Newton* (Manchester: Manchester University Press, 1983), 91–113; Arnold Thackray, *Atoms and Powers* (Cambridge, Mass.: Harvard University Press, 1970), esp. 26–32, 135–40. Newton himself denied that gravity was inherent in matter, see Turnbull et al. (eds.), *Correspondence of Isaac Newton*, iii. 240.

proof of the activity of God and of the nature of the soul, without recourse to revelation and the confessional disputes that it provoked.[17] At a simple level, therefore, two eighteenth-century commentators on Fatio's life and work provide a solution to the problem of the heterodox career of Nicolas Fatio. In different ways, the responses of Corfield Clare and George-Louis Le Sage were that Fatio was not heterodox.

For Clare, Fatio was a good man and an apostolic, perhaps even Christlike, figure. Clare was not unique in making an implicit comparison at this level. When he learned that Fatio and two advocates of the French Prophets had been tried for publishing seditious pamphlets and that as a punishment they had been publicly paraded at the scaffold at the start of December 1707, Gottfried Wilhelm Leibniz wrote that 'the affair of the French Prophets has had a bad ending, and that angers me out of affection for Monsieur Fatio: since, as he is an excellent mathematician, I do not rightly understand how he could have embarked on such an affair. The Judges were against the men from the Cévennes, and if anything could have swayed people, it was his reputation.'[18] Leibniz's concern was certainly not the product of sympathy for the doctrines that Fatio and his friends were preaching. It derived from respect for Fatio's intellectual ability, rather than from close personal friendship. Moreover, Leibniz's regard for Fatio was sustained despite philosophical disagreement and irrespective of

---

[17] See Stephen Gaukroger, *Descartes' System of Natural Philosophy* (Cambridge: Cambridge University Press, 2002); Jean-Robert Armogathe, 'Proofs of the Existence of God'; Alan Gabbey, 'New Doctrines of Motion', both in Daniel Garber and Michael Ayers (eds.), *Cambridge History of Seventeenth-Century Philosophy* (2 vols.; Cambridge: Cambridge University Press, 1998), i. 305–30, 649–79; for the background to these developments, see Charles H. Lohr, 'The Sixteenth-Century Transformation of the Aristotelian Division of the Speculative Sciences', in D. R. Kelley and R. H. Popkin (eds.), *The Shapes of Knowledge from the Renaissance to the Enlightenment* (Dordrecht: Kluwer, 1991), 49–58, and id., 'Metaphysics', in Charles B. Schmitt, Quentin Skinner, Eckhard Kessler, and Jill Kraye (eds.), *The Cambridge History of Renaissance Philosophy* (Cambridge: Cambridge University Press, 1988), 537–638.

[18] Leibniz to Thomas Burnet, 16 March 1708, in Gottfried Wilhelm Leibniz, *Die philosophischen Schriften*, ed. C. J. Gerhardt (7 vols.; Berlin, 1875–90), iii. 316–18. ['L'affaire des Prophetes Cevennois a eu une mechante catastrophe, et j'en suis faché pour l'amour de M. Fatio: car comme c'est un homme excellent dans les Mathematiques, je ne comprehends pas bien comment il a pû estre embarqué dans une telle affaire. Les Juges ont esté contre les Cevennois, et si quelque chose a pû balancer les gens, c'a esté sa reputation.']

Fatio's role in promoting dispute over Leibniz's role in the invention of the calculus.[19] Clare, on the other hand, knew Fatio well and appears to have been on friendly terms with a number of the followers of the French Prophets.

Clare may have minimized Fatio's heterodoxy for personal reasons or may even have sympathized with the piety that it represented. Le Sage, in contrast, was worried by Fatio's religious disposition and his prophetic writings. He was therefore concerned 'to examine what precisely that error of judgement was that Fatio had, in order to delude himself that he was able to perform miracles'.[20] By rationalizing heterodoxy in this way, Le Sage could rehabilitate Fatio's natural philosophy for the purposes of his own pious natural theology. Yet these were not the standard responses to Fatio's religious enthusiasm, nor did most commentators consider that his religious heterodoxy cast no aspersions on the plausibility of his natural philosophy.

THE INVENTION OF A RELIGIOUS ENTHUSIAST

The Oxford diarist and future nonjuror, Thomas Hearne, perhaps unsurprisingly characterized Fatio in these terms: 'a Man of strong natural parts ... a most excellent Mathematician, & has no mean skill in several other Parts of Learning; but it has always been observ'd of him that he is a sceptick in Religion, a Person of no virtue, but a meer Debauchee'.[21] Edward Calamy, a leading London Presbyterian minister, who would have disagreed with Hearne about many other matters, nevertheless commented about Fatio that 'a mathematician's

---

[19] See e.g. Gottfried Wilhelm Leibniz, *Sämtliche Schriften und Briefe. Dritte Reihe: Mathematischer naturwissenschaftlicher und technischer Briefwechsel*, v, ed. Heinz-Jürgen Hess and James G. O'Hara (Berlin: Akademie-Verlag, 2003), 181–9; cf. Nicolas Fatio de Duillier, *Lineae brevissimi descensus investigatio geometrica duplex* (London, 1699); *Acta eruditorum* (November 1699), 510–16; (May 1700), 198–208; (March 1701), 134–6.

[20] BPU, MS Le Sage 43a, sachet 29, card 1 ['examiner en quoi précisement consistoit cet Ecart de jugement qui avoit Fatio, à se flater de pouvoir opérer des miracles'].

[21] *Remarks and Collections of Thomas Hearne*, ed. C. E. Doble et al. (11 vols.; Oxford, 1884–1918), ii. 243–4.

on a sudden turning an enthusiast, and to see one that discovered no great regard to the Revelations made by the real apostles of our Saviour, so zealous to promote the reception of those which the Camisars pretended to, had but an odd aspect'.[22] The Basle mathematician, Johann Bernoulli, wrote contemptuously of Fatio the 'visionary' and commented that, in his mathematical disputes, 'it would therefore be best if I were to send him as a fanatic to the pillory, where he has already stood, and leave him standing there until his prophetic spirit inspires him that I am right and that he really is wrong'.[23] The most damning view of the consequences of Fatio's heterodoxy, however, came from his brother, Jean-Christophe (1659–1720). With the age-old charity of the first-born son, Jean-Christophe lamented that Nicolas's behaviour would lose him his reputation and despaired of what his father would have said, had he still been alive. In his opinion, the men whom Nicolas Fatio followed were charlatans rather than visionaries: 'How can it be that your pretended prophets, having predicted that a dead man should be brought back to life on a particular day, given that the dead man remains in the tomb, are not false prophets, and by consequence Impostors?'[24] For

---

[22] Edmund Calamy, *An Historical Account of My Own Life*, ed. John Towill Rutt (2 vols.; London, 1829), ii. 74; Calamy also suspected Fatio of being a Spinozist, *Historical Account*, i. 190.

[23] Johann I Bernoulli to Nicolaus I Bernoulli, 23 November 1712, Öffentliche Bibliothek der Universität Basel, MS L Ia 22, 9 ['Es wird also das beste seyn wan ich ihn alss einen Fanaticum nach der pilory woran er schon gestanden schicke, und ihn daran stehen lasse biss ihm seyn prophetischer geist eingiebet dass ich recht, er aber unrecht habe.'].

[24] BPU, MS Fr. 601, fos. 145–58; quotation at 152r ['Comment se peut il, que vos pretendus prophetes, ayant predit, qu'un mort devoit resusciter à un Jour marqué, et que le mort resté dans le tombeau, ne soient pas des faux prophetes, et par consequent des Imposteurs']. Jean-Christophe Fatio referred particularly to his brother's belief in a prophecy relating to the resurrection of Thomas Emes; some context for his hostility may be provided by the comments of Gilbert Burnet, bishop of Salisbury, about the French Prophets in his correspondence with the Genevan theologian, Jean-Alphonse Turrettini, see BPU, MS Fr. 485, especially fos. 211–12. For Nicolas Fatio's conversation about Emes, see Edinburgh University Library, MS Dk.1.2.1, number 65; BPU, MS Fr. 602, fos. 19–21. Fatio's belief in the resurrection of Emes continued to be a focus for mockery later in the eighteenth century, see Voltaire, *L'Homme aux quarante écus*, ed. Brenda M. Bloesch, in *The Complete Works of Voltaire*, lxvi (Oxford: Voltaire Foundation, 1999), 345; Voltaire, *Dieu et les hommes*, ed. Roland Mortier, in *The Complete Works of Voltaire*, lxix (Oxford: Voltaire Foundation, 1994), 447–8; see also Schwartz, *The French Prophets*, 113–25.

Jean-Christophe Fatio, heterodoxy threatened the honour and live-
lihood not only of Nicolas Fatio but also of his family and was the
result of both philosophical and religious error.

Nicolas Fatio de Duillier thus presents a case study in the interaction of religious and scientific heterodoxy, in the relationship
between knowledge and belief. The differing reactions towards his
heterodoxy among Fatio's contemporaries and his successors demonstrate the impossibility of assuming that there was any simple
dynamic between science and heterodoxy. For some writers, particularly those who were concerned primarily with contemporary moral
and ecclesiastical values, Fatio's unreasonable religious position was
the only aspect of his career that was more than a curiosity. To his
natural philosophical peers, the apparent derailment of Fatio's intellectual career by involvement with religious enthusiasm seemed at
best distressing, at worst evidence that any failings that he might have
as a mathematician could be attributed to psychological or intellectual disturbance. Fatio's friends, on the other hand, saw evidence in
his religious comportment of the humility and understanding that
they believed to be appropriate in a pious student of nature. His
intellectual heirs, however, were worried that the enthusiasm of his
religious stance threatened the credibility of his natural philosophy,
despite its compatibility with true religion. To a considerable extent,
these eighteenth-century positions have continued to colour modern
assessments of the ideas and beliefs of Fatio. More recent commentators have also been concerned with the closeness of Fatio's relationship with Isaac Newton, particularly during the early 1690s,
shortly after his arrival in England.[25] As a consequence, they have
tended to interpret Fatio's heterodoxy in the light of Newton's own
religious beliefs. In doing so, they have hardly advanced on the
position of Voltaire, who, writing in 1742, juxtaposed Fatio's involvement with the French Prophets and Newton's interest in the

---

[25] In particular, Frank E. Manuel, *A Portrait of Isaac Newton* (Cambridge, Mass.:
Belknap Press of Harvard University Press, 1968), 191–212; Charles Andrew Dom-
son, *Nicolas Fatio de Duillier and the Prophets of London* (New York: Arno, 1981);
Margaret C. Jacob, 'Newton and the French Prophets: New Evidence', *History of
Science*, 16 (1978), 134–42.

fulfilment of prophecy.[26] Although some eighteenth-century writers did wonder whether Newton had shared Fatio's commitment to the French Prophets, the evidence provided by contemporary exchanges within Newton's small circle of close acquaintances suggests that his interest was limited to curiosity and concern for the position of his friend.[27] Newton's prophetical writings show none of the concern with the immediate fulfilment of prophecy that dominated Fatio's conversation; moreover Newton's interest was exclusively in the exposition of biblical prophecy, rather than in the prophesying of his contemporaries. Although Newton did share Fatio's desire for the peace of the Church, he interpreted this in a context that reached back to the fourth century, as well as into the future.[28] Moreover, the whole of Newton's activity as a biblical interpreter was overshadowed by his own heterodox denial of the doctrine of the Trinity. Despite the mystical tone of much of Fatio's language about God, there is no evidence that he shared this heresy with Newton: 'I am convinced that the doctrine of the Unitarians is less close to the Truth than the common doctrine of the Trinity, when it is well understood.'[29]

---

[26] Voltaire, *Œuvres complètes* (54 vols.; Paris, 1829–31), xxxiii. 44–5; cf. Isaac Newton, *Observations upon the Prophecies of Daniel, and the Apocalypse of St. John* (London, 1733). This point has been made persuasively by Michael Heyd, *"Be Sober and Reasonable"*, 255–6.

[27] Joseph Spence, *Observations, Anecdotes, and Characters of Books and Men*, ed. James M. Osborn (2 vols.; Oxford: Clarendon, 1966), i. 283; cf. Edinburgh University Library, MS D.1.61, fo. 707.

[28] For example, Newton's writings on prophecy, dating from the 1670s onwards, now in Jewish National and University Library, Jerusalem, MS Yahuda Var. 1/ [hereafter Yah. MS] 1. Newton's ideas about the peace of the Church were made clearest in King's College, Cambridge, MS Keynes 3, although see also Yah. MS 15; Fondation Martin Bodmer, Geneva, MS 'Of the Church'; William Andrews Clark Memorial Library, University of California Los Angeles, MS 'Paradoxical Quaestions concerning [th]e morals & actions of Athanasius and his followers'. Cf. the remarks of Fatio reported in Royal Society, London, MS 247, fo. 63[c]v.

[29] For Newton's attitude to the Trinity, see in particular New College, Oxford, MS 361.4, fos. 2–41; printed in Turnbull et al. (eds.), *Correspondence of Isaac Newton*, iii. 83–122; see also Richard S. Westfall, *Never at Rest. A Biography of Isaac Newton* (Cambridge: Cambridge University Press, 1980), 311–18. Cf. the position of Fatio expressed in BPU, MS Fr. 603, fos. 227–37, and particularly in MS Fr. 602, fos. 22r–24v, Nicolas Fatio to Jean-Christophe Fatio, 19 December 1707, at fo. 24r ['Je suis convaincu: Que la Doctrine des Unitaires, approche moins de la Vérité; que ne fait la Doctrine commune sur la Trinité, quand elle est bien entenduë'].

Fatio's heterodoxy, therefore, cannot be explained by the influence of another's heresy. Nor are contemporary suggestions that it might represent some form of madness entirely convincing.[30] It is necessary to take seriously, however, the extent of dismay at or lack of understanding of Fatio's religious and intellectual development. In the process, it may be possible to reintroduce an element of coherence into Fatio's behaviour that struck neither his English nor his Continental, particularly his Genevan, contemporaries. This is not to explain away Fatio's heterodoxy; rather it is an attempt to comprehend why he made certain choices and how he lived with their unexpected consequences. Since it is almost certain that Nicolas Fatio de Duillier did not set out to be regarded as heterodox, either as a natural philosopher or as a Christian, to trace his career should also provide a means of reflecting on the ways in which orthodoxy and heterodoxy shade into one another.

CHARM: INTELLECT, EMOTION, AND THE LIMITS OF PATRONAGE

To begin at the beginning, Fatio was born at Basle on 16 February 1664, the second son and seventh child of Jean-Baptiste Fatio (1625–1708) and his wife, Catherine Barbaud (d. 1692). His paternal ancestors had been attracted to the reformed religion and left Italy, Fatio later suggested, in search of religious liberty. Jean-Baptiste Fatio inherited a considerable fortune, built up through his father's success in iron and silver mining, which he invested in the 1670s in the purchase of an estate at Duillier, fourteen miles from Geneva. Nicolas's mother was a Lutheran, who opposed his father's intentions that he should study for the ministry and wanted him instead to find employment with a Protestant court in Germany.[31] He learned Latin

---

[30] On the relationship between enthusiasm and insanity, see Schwartz, *Knaves, Fools, Madmen*; Michael MacDonald, 'Religion, Social Change, and Psychological Healing in England, 1600–1800', *Studies in Church History*, 19 (1982), 101–25.

[31] On Fatio's birth, ancestry, and early life, see his letter to Edward Chapeau, 26 January 1732, printed in William Seward (ed.), *Anecdotes of Some Distinguished Persons, Chiefly of the Present and Two Preceding Centuries*, 2nd edn. (4 vols.; London, 1795–6), iv. 420–42; on his parents, see J.-A. Galiffe, *Notices généalogiques sur les familles genevoises*, iv, 2nd edn., ed. Aymon Galiffe (Geneva: A. Julien, 1908), 193–4.

and Greek at home, and enrolled at the Academy in Geneva, from 1678. There, he also acquired some Hebrew and followed courses in philosophy, mathematics, and astronomy, particularly those offered by Jean-Robert Chouet.[32] Fatio recorded the content of lectures on natural philosophy that Chouet delivered, beginning on 24 May 1678, and continuing to take notes in 1679 and 1680. Chouet began with logic, proceeded through metaphysics (the nature of various types of being), and moved on to physics (the science of natural bodies), which he regarded as the theoretical part of philosophy and which included the various disciplines of mathematics (arithmetic, geometry, music, and astronomy), as well as pneumatology, or the study of spirits.[33] The disagreement of Fatio's parents over his future perhaps helped him to determine his own path, although his activities in later life reflected both his father's concern for right religion and his mother's sense that further social and material advancement was most likely to come from the hand of a wealthy and powerful patron. In any case, Fatio was a precocious student and before his eighteenth birthday he had written to the astronomer, Giandomenico Cassini, at the Observatory in Paris about the rings of Saturn, the size of the sun and the moon, and their distance from the earth.

With the help of Chouet and of the Abbé Nicaise, Fatio travelled to Paris in order to work with Cassini. He stayed there between spring 1682 and October 1683, and witnessed Cassini's first observations of zodiacal light. After his return to Geneva, Fatio carried out further work on this phenomenon, which would later have a central role to play in his mature natural philosophy. He was able to locate its

---

[32] *Le Livre du Recteur: Catalogue des étudiants de l'Académie de Genève* (Geneva, 1860), 170. On Chouet's teaching, see Michael Heyd, *Between Orthodoxy and the Enlightenment* (The Hague: Nijhoff, 1982).

[33] The first half of Fatio's compendium of Chouet's lectures is now BPU, MS Lat. 221; Chouet's own texts can be found at MSS Lat. 220 and 292. Readers who are intrigued by coincidences might wish to know that the flyleaf of MS Lat. 221 bears the inscription 'Amicus Plato, Amicus Ar[istote]les: sed Magis Amica Veritas', the same epigraph that Isaac Newton (along with perhaps hundreds of others) used some fourteen years earlier at the start of his undergraduate notebook, now Cambridge University Library, MS Add. 3996, at fo. 88r. See also J. E. McGuire and Martin Tamny (eds.), *Certain Philosophical Questions: Newton's Trinity Notebook* (Cambridge: Cambridge University Press, 1983), 336–7.

position in the plane of the ecliptic.[34] Chouet first reported his modifications to Cassini's discoveries in *Les Nouvelles de la république des lettres* in March 1685 and Fatio published them in full in 1686. He was keen to point out that the light that he and Cassini had observed need not be a transient phenomenon, but might be as old as creation. He was also aware at this stage of the difficulty of resolving his findings about the refraction of the light of the sun with Cartesian theories of astronomy and the aether.[35]

Fatio's notebooks from this period demonstrate an extraordinary range of interests in astronomy, mathematics, optics, fortification, and medicine. They reveal his awareness of the work of Galileo and Descartes and show him designing observatories, scientific instruments, and machines, studying the anatomy of the eye, describing insects, and devising remedies. They anticipate some of the philosophical concerns that continued to occupy him for much of the rest of his life, but indicate his desire at this stage to place the study of nature within an orthodox and rational theological framework. Although the extent of Fatio's orthodoxy and even his rationality would later be questioned, his notebooks show the close relationship from the inception of his study of nature between a mechanical natural philosophy and a reformed scholastic theology.[36]

Fatio expanded the range of his scientific investigations between July and September 1685, when he undertook a survey of Mont Blanc with his elder brother, Jean-Christophe.[37] It is clear from his correspondence, however, that he had already begun to explore the possibility that discovery and theoretical innovation in the study of nature might provide him with his route to financial and social advancement.[38] While he was staying on his father's estate, the opportunity

---

[34] BPU, MS D.O. Autogr. Rilliet (Fatio to Nicaise, 25 December 1681); MS Fr. 602, fos. 2–4, 6–7; MSS Jallabert, 41/1–3.

[35] *Lettre de Mr. N. Fatio de Duillier a Monsieur Cassini … Touchant une lumiere extraordinaire qui paroît dans le ciel depuis quelques années* (Amsterdam, 1686), esp. 11, 22, 28–9. See also Bibliothèque de l'Observatoire, Paris, MSS B.4.1 and B.4.10; BPU, MS Fr. 601, fos. 29–44; Jean Le Clerc, *Epistolario*, ed. Maria Grazia and Mario Sina (4 vols.; Florence: Olschki, 1987–97), i. 347–9.

[36] BPU, MSS Jallabert 41, 47, esp. 47/1, fos. 78–9; 47/2, fo. 28.

[37] Sir Gavin de Beer, 'The History of the Altimetry of Mont Blanc', *Annals of Science*, 12 (1956), 3–29; BPU, MS Fr. 606/1.

[38] BPU, MS Fr. 601, fos. 46–7 (Abbé de Catelan to Fatio, 20 July 1684).

that he was seeking appeared to have materialized. He learned of the plans of a guest of his father's, a renegade Piedmontese count called Fenil, to win the favour of Louis XIV by seizing William, Prince of Orange, in a raid on the beach at Scheveningen, where the prince habitually took the sea air without a guard. Fenil intended to kidnap him and spirit him away in a boat to Dunkirk. When Fatio retold the story of this plot later in his life, he was keen to stress that his reaction to Fenil's plan was to fear for the life of the Protestant prince. He was, however, unable to resist the opportunity to boast of the connections that he had made in Paris, who included Louis XIV's minister, Louvois. The willingness of Fenil to reveal the details of his scheme to Fatio also suggests that Fatio initially shared his acquaintance's desire to ingratiate himself at the French court. In betraying Fenil's confidences, however, Fatio was able to exploit the networks of contacts provided with the rival court of William of Orange by another visitor to Geneva, the exiled Gilbert Burnet, future bishop of Salisbury.[39]

In spring 1686, Fatio travelled to Holland in Burnet's company, in order to give warning about Fenil's scheme. Between them, Burnet and Fatio duly convinced William and the States of Holland of the reality of the threat, so that a permanent guard was placed around the prince. Concrete rewards for Fatio's action were, however, slow in coming, although his name was canvassed for a post at the University of Leiden and in connection with a planned mathematical professorship for the instruction of the nobility and gentry of Holland.[40] Fatio's journey was not without fruit, despite such disappointments. While he was in the Netherlands, he oversaw the publication of his letter to Cassini, and cultivated the friendship of an even more distinguished natural philosopher, Christiaan Huygens. Prompted by the receipt of several publications by Ehrenfried von Tschirnhaus, Huygens encouraged Fatio to begin work on the problem of calculating the tangents of curved lines. Fatio published an article on this

---

[39] Seward (ed.), *Anecdotes*, iv. 427–36; Gilbert Burnet, *History in His Own Time*, ed. Thomas Burnet (4 vols.; London, 1753), ii. 388–9.
[40] Le Clerc, *Epistolario*, i. 449.

subject in the *Bibliothèque universelle et historique* in April 1687, initiating an exchange with Tschirnhaus.[41]

At the end of the spring, Fatio left for England, where, in June 1687, he attended a number of meetings of the Royal Society, to which he was introduced on the authority of Henri Justel. There he picked up rumours of a new book, Isaac Newton's *Philosophia naturalis principia mathematica* (1687), which he soon communicated to Huygens, remarking that 'they have reproached me with being too Cartesian, and made me to understand that, following the meditations of their author, all physics has been completely altered'.[42] Fatio's original aim in London had been to make the acquaintance of Robert Boyle, whom Burnet had known since 1663, and seek his help in finding employment. He did indeed make contact with Boyle, but he noted ominously that that natural philosopher was in no better health than Huygens.[43] Although he quickly offended Robert Hooke, who described him disparagingly as the 'Perpet[ual] Motion man', Fatio quickly added to his circle of influential friends.[44] During the winter of 1687, he retreated to Oxford and collaborated with Edward Bernard, Savilian Professor of Astronomy, for whom he wrote an account of the molten bronze sea that had been located in the Temple of Solomon (1 Kings 7: 23–6).[45] Although he was

[41] Christiaan Huygens, *Œuvres complètes* (22 vols.; The Hague: Nijhoff, 1888–1950), ix. 117–20, 154–8, 174–5, 181; xx, 491–504; xxii, 734–8; *Bibliothèque universelle et historique*, 5 (1687), 25–33; 13 (1689), 46–76; see also Manfred Kracht, 'E.W. von Tschirnhaus: His Role in Early Calculus and His Work and Impact on Algebra', *Historia Mathematica*, 17 (1990), 16–35.

[42] Royal Society, London, MS Journal Book VII (1686–90), 42, 45; Huygens, *Œuvres complètes*, ix. 167–71, 190; Petrus Joannes Uylenbroek (ed.), *Christiani Hugenii aliorumque seculi XVII virorum celibrium exercitationes mathematicae et philosophicae ex manuscriptis in Bibliotheca Academiae Lugduno-Batavae* (2 vols.; The Hague, 1833), ii. 99 ['ils m'ont reproché que j'étois trop Cartesien, et m'en fait entendre que, depuis les meditations de leur auteur, toute la physique étoit bien changée'].

[43] Le Clerc, *Epistolario*, i. 458–9; Huygens, *Œuvres complètes*, ix. 167–71; Bibliothèque nationale de France, Paris, MS N.A.F. 4218, fos. 26–7; cf. Fatio's later correspondence with Boyle, Royal Society, MS Boyle Letters, vol. 3, fos. 1–2. For Burnet's links with Boyle, see Michael Hunter (ed.), *Robert Boyle by Himself and his Friends* (London: Pickering, 1994), pp. xxii–xxv; for his continuing assistance to Fatio after the Glorious Revolution, see BPU, MS Fr. 601, fo. 62r.

[44] R. T. Gunther (ed.), *Early Science in Oxford*, x (Oxford: Clarendon, 1935), 191; see also 176, 190.

[45] Edward Bernard, *De mensuris et ponderibus antiquiis libri tres*, 2nd edn. (Oxford, 1688), sig. Nn2v–Qq1v.

admitted as a Fellow of the Royal Society on 2 May 1688, Fatio was disappointed in his hopes of gaining a pension from the tutoring that he undertook in England. After the Glorious Revolution he did, however, strengthen his reputation with the English virtuosi when Huygens visited London in summer 1689. His services to the House of Orange also led at this time to limited patronage from several leading Whig politicians, notably John Hampden. With Hampden and his allies, Fatio worked to secure the employment of Swiss guardsmen, formerly in the pay of Louis XIV, for English, and later for Dutch, service. For a while, Fatio continued to regard Huygens as his principal intellectual patron, helping to distribute presentation copies of his *Traité de la Lumière* (Leiden, 1690), which included an account of the working of gravity. However, when he returned to England in autumn 1691, after a stay in the Netherlands as a tutor to Hampden's nephew, his friendship with Newton came to predominate.[46]

Fatio was Newton's closest friend in the period immediately prior to the latter's apparent breakdown in the summer of 1693. Although it is unlikely that Newton's strange behaviour at that time was provoked by the intensity of his relationship with Fatio, it certainly coincided with a cooling between them.[47] For eighteen months, the two men collaborated extensively, particularly on alchemical investigations. Here, Fatio was able to introduce Newton to a range of literature in French, which he translated for him.[48] Newton was also

---

[46] Huygens, *Œuvres complètes*, ix. 333, 357–8, 361–3, 370–3, 379, 381–8, 391–3, 407–12, 416, 444–5, 464, 516–20; x. 145–6; an example of the presentation copies that Fatio distributed for Huygens may be found at Bodleian Library, Oxford, shelfmark Savile G.10 (John Wallis's copy). For Fatio's activities more generally, see Seward (ed.), *Anecdotes*, iv. 437–42; BPU, MS Fr. 610, fos. 15–16;

[47] Manuel, *Portrait of Isaac Newton*, 191–225; Westfall, *Never at Rest*, 531–41. It should be clear that I see no merit in the suggestion that Newton's behaviour in 1693 might be due to developments in his relationship with Fatio, nor in the view that their friendship was based on sexual attraction, whether consummated or unconsummated: cf. Michael White, *Isaac Newton: The Last Sorcerer* (London, 1997), 235–52, 357. This interpretation is based largely on the exaggeration of Newton's comments in a single letter, see Turnbull et al. (eds.), *Correspondence of Isaac Newton*, iii. 231.

[48] Turnbull et al. (eds.), *Correspondence of Isaac Newton*, iii. 245, 261–3, 265–7; Karin Figala, John Harrison, and Ulrich Petzold, '*De Scriptoribus Chemicis*: Sources for the Establishment of Isaac Newton's (Al)chemical Library', in P. M. Harman and Alan E. Shapiro (eds.), *The Investigation of Difficult Things* (Cambridge: Cambridge University Press, 1992), 135–79, esp. 152–3; for reciprocal evidence of Fatio's reading in the English alchemical tradition, see BPU, MS Fr. 609, fo. 46.

interested in Fatio's ideas about a mechanical cause for gravity, which were first read at the Royal Society on 4 July 1688 and which resurfaced in the context of a discussion of Huygens's ideas at a meeting on 26 February 1690.[49]

According to Fatio, the world contained only a small quantity of solid matter and space itself was almost empty, but there was a subtle and rarefied form of matter that could penetrate the pores in gross bodies. This permeated the universe and was strongly agitated indifferently in all directions, so that individual particles moved at remarkable speed in straight lines. The result of that movement was to create a force around all substantial bodies, for instance carrying heavy objects down towards the earth. On encountering gross bodies, the agitated particles of subtle matter lost some of their force, which, over large distances at least, thus obeyed an inverse square law.[50] Fatio's ideas about gravity developed in part from the observation of a fine celestial matter and its effects that he had described in his work with Cassini. They drew directly on the mechanical theories of Huygens presented in *Traité de la lumière*, but were potentially more compatible with the ideas of force presented in Newton's *Principia*. In their joint alchemical work of the early 1690s, both Fatio and Newton explored the structure of matter, with the intention of developing a better understanding of the way in which gravity and other kinds of force, understood primarily in mechanical terms, might be communicated between bodies.[51] Fatio was convinced that Newton approved of his explanation of gravity and that he was therefore able

---

[49] Bernard Gagnebin, 'De la cause de la pesanteur', Horst Zehe, *Die Gravitationstheorie des Nicolas Fatio de Duillier*, 129–63; Zehe, 'Die Gravitationstheorie des Nicolas Fatio de Duillier', *Archive for History of Exact Sciences*, 28 (1983), 1–23; Royal Society, London, MS Journal Book VII (1686–90), 131, 268.

[50] The simplest account of Fatio's ideas is contained in a letter to Huygens of 24 February 1690, see Huygens, *Œuvres complètes*, ix. 381–9, esp. 384. Fatio developed this work in a number of manuscripts, many of which were collected by Le Sage but are now incomplete; see particularly BPU, MS 603, fos. 62–104, esp. 78–80. The clearest expression of Fatio's ideas about gravity can be found in Öffentliche Bibliothek der Universität Basel, MS L.Ia.755, fos. 36–58, on which see particularly K. Bopp, *Drei Untersuchungen zur Geschichte der Mathematik* (Berlin: W. de Gruyter, 1929), 19–66. The manuscript was copied for Jacob Bernoulli between 1699 and 1701.

[51] *Lettre de Mr. N. Fatio de Duillier*, 25–9. See also Dobbs, *The Janus Faces of Genius*, 170–91; Karin Figala and Ulrich Petzold, 'Alchemy in the Newtonian Circle: Personal Acquaintances and the Problem of the Late Phase of Newton's Alchemy', in

to provide a mechanical solution to the problem of causation that dogged the reception of the first edition of the *Principia*:[52]

It produces gravitation around all the more substantial bodies that exist, without obstructing their different movements. It is very simple and perfectly provides a cause of the diminution of gravity inversely according to the square of distances. Mr Newton and Mr Halley believe that it is true ... It establishes quite a different idea of philosophy from those that one has had up until now; nevertheless all that it makes me [find] conforms to the ideas that Mr Newton has previously had and when it has once been grasped it appears extremely reasonable. This theory opens the way to a variety of researches into the intimate structure of bodies, for which we do not yet have any useful principle.[53]

Newton later disparaged Fatio's work on gravity in conversation with the Scottish mathematician, David Gregory.[54] Even so, Fatio's promise as a mathematician and natural philosopher was sufficient for Newton to have allowed him unparalleled access to his mathematical papers during the early 1690s.[55] As a result of this privilege, Fatio was able to communicate a list of corrections to the *Principia* to Huygens,

---

J. V. Field and Frank A. J. L. James (eds.), *Renaissance and Revolution* (Cambridge: Cambridge University Press, 1993), 173–91; cf. BPU, MS Fr. 610, fo. 17v; Öffentliche Bibliothek der Universität Basel, MS L.Ia.755, fos. 37–8.

[52] Uylenbroek (ed.), *Exercitationes mathematicae et philosophicae*, ii. 113; cf. Roberto de A. Martins, 'Huygens's Reaction to Newton's Gravitational Theory', in Field and James (eds.), *Renaissance and Revolution*, 203–13.

[53] BPU, MS Fr. 610, fo. 17v, Nicolas Fatio to Jean-Christophe Fatio, 9/19 June 1690: 'Elle produit des pesanteurs autour de tous les corps grossiers qui existent, non obstant leurs divers movemens. Elle est tres simple et rend parfaitement raison de la diminution de la pesanteur en la raison reciproque des quarrez des distances. Monsieur Newton et Monsieur Halley croient qu'elle est veritable.... Elle établit toute une autre idée de la Philosophie q[ue] [ce]lles que l'on a eues jusques à present; neanmoins tout ce qu'elle m'a fait [trouver] conforme aux idées que Monsieur Newton avoit auparavant et quand il est une fois conçu il paroit extremement raisonnable. Cette Theorie ouvre l'éntrée à diverses recherches touchant la structure intime des corps, pour laquelles on n'avoit encore aucun principe qui fut de quelque usage.' The manuscript is damaged in several places.

[54] Royal Society, London, MS 247, fo. 71v, cf. fo. 72v; Edinburgh University Library, MS Dc.1.61, fo. 199r–v. Gregory also later reported Huygens's criticisms, Edinburgh University Library, MS Dk.1.2.1, number 4.

[55] See Royal Society, London, MS 64; Edinburgh University Library, MS Dc.1.61, number 64; Uylenbroek (ed.), *Exercitationes mathematicae et philosophicae*, ii. 124–5.

who sent them in turn to Leibniz. Leibniz then allowed Johann Groening to publish them in 1701.[56]

Fatio had been one of the first attentive readers of the *Principia*, and, as early as March 1690, he intended to add corrections from Newton's manuscripts to those that he had himself made in his own copy of the book. By the end of 1691, Fatio despaired of convincing Newton to undertake a new edition of the work but entertained the thought of producing with Newton's help a corrected version, to be printed in folio rather than quarto, over the next two to three years. He appears to have worked extensively to build up his knowledge of the *Principia* with this project in mind between November 1691 and April 1692. At this time, he intended to add a preface to the *Principia* that would explain Newton's system of gravity, perhaps through the application of his own ideas.[57] Despite his skill as a mathematician, however, Fatio seems really to have got to grips with only a relatively small part of the *Principia*.[58] Moreover, Fatio's work on this project was effectively brought to a halt by his need for more remunerative employment and by the increased distance that this and other events put between him and Newton. In part, this distance may have been due to the development of Newton's own ideas about the causes and mechanism of gravity. Fatio was sceptical of Newton's claim to have found evidence that the ancients had understood the Copernican system and had shared his view of gravity. He thus implicitly rejected

---

[56] See D. T. Whiteside (ed.), *The Mathematical Papers of Isaac Newton* (8 vols.; Cambridge: Cambridge University Press, 1967–81), viii. 19; I. Bernard Cohen, *Introduction to Newton's 'Principia'* (Cambridge: Cambridge University Press, 1971), 40–2, 184–7; W. G. Hiscock (ed.), *David Gregory, Isaac Newton and their Circle* (Oxford: printed for the editor, 1937), 26–7, 32–3; Royal Society, London, MS 247, fo. 87.

[57] For these plans, see Fatio's copy of Isaac Newton, *Philosophiae naturalis principia mathematica* (London, 1687), Bodleian Library, Oxford, shelfmark RRW.23 (formerly 4o Z. 23 Art.); Royal Society, London, MS 64; Huygens, *Œuvres complètes*, x. 241, 348–55; xxii. 158–9; Uylenbroek (ed.), *Exercitationes mathematicae et philosophicae*, ii. 124–7; Whiteside (ed.), *Mathematical Papers*, vi. 315–16; Cohen, *Introduction to Newton's 'Principia'*, 179–87; Stephen Peter Rigaud, *Historical Essay on the First Publication of Sir Isaac Newton's Principia* (Oxford, 1838).

[58] Fatio's comments to Huygens at the end of April 1692 suggest that he had at that point worked over only sections 1–5 and 9 of Book One and the final part of Book Three of the *Principia*, see Huygens, *Œuvres complètes*, xxii. 158–9; cf. Rob Iliffe, 'Butter for Parsnips. Authorship, Audience, and the Incomprehensibility of the *Principia*', in Mario Biagioli and Peter Galison (eds.), *Scientific Authorship* (New York: Routledge, 2003), 33–65, esp. 56.

the alternative to a mechanical hypothesis of gravity that Newton was developing in the early to mid-1690s, in which, as Fatio put it, 'the cause of gravity inheres in matter as a result of a direct law imposed by the Creator of the Universe'. He also shared his doubts with Huygens, who identified one of Newton's sources as Plutarch's 'De facie in orbe lunae' but contradicted the suggestions that Newton had made about the extent of the Pythagoreans' knowledge of modern cosmology.[59]

Throughout the period of his closest collaboration with Newton, Fatio continued to seek academic preferment outside England, particularly in Amsterdam.[60] He resisted inducements that would have made him, in effect, Newton's amanuensis. By summer 1694, he had found a different patron and was living at Woburn Abbey as a tutor to the duke of Bedford's son, Wriothesley Russell, a position for which he had sought the backing of another friend, John Locke.[61] He remained in the duke of Bedford's service for some time, accompanying his pupil in his studies at Oxford and, during 1697–8, in Holland.[62] In addition to this position, Fatio continued to pursue business ventures of his own. By 1693, he had begun a long association with the watchmakers, Peter and Jacob Debaufre, and, on

---

[59] For Newton's ideas, see J. E. McGuire and P. M. Rattansi, 'Newton and the "Pipes of Pan" ', *Notes and Records of the Royal Society*, 21 (1966), 108–43; Paolo Cassini, 'Newton: The Classical Scholia', *History of Science*, 22 (1984), 1–58; Volkmar Schüller, 'Newton's *Scholia* from David Gregory's Estate on the Propositions IV through IX Book III of his *Principia*', in Wolfgang Lefèvre (ed.), *Between Leibniz, Newton and Kant*, Boston Studies in the Philosophy of Science 220 (Dordrecht: Kluwer, 2001), 213–65, available in more complete form as *Newtons Scholia aus David Gregorys Nachlass zu den Propositionen IV–IX Buch III seiner* Principia, Max-Planck-Institut für Wissenschaftsgeschichte Preprint 144 (Berlin, 2000); Edinburgh University Library, MS Dk.1.2.2, folio D. Cf. BPU, MS Fr. 610, fos. 21–2, Fatio to M. de Beyrie, 30 March 1694 ['la cause de la Pesanteur soit inherente dans la matiere par une loi immediate du Createur de l'Univers']; and the earlier exchange with Huygens: Uylenbroek (ed.), *Exercitationes mathematicae et philosophicae*, ii. 127; Huygens, *Œuvres complètes*, xxii. 155–7.

[60] See Turnbull et al. (eds.), *Correspondence of Isaac Newton*, iii. 243–5.

[61] E. S. de Beer (ed.), *The Correspondence of John Locke* (8 vols.; Oxford: Clarendon, 1976–89), iv. 792; v. 353; Royal Commission on Historical Manuscripts, *Tenth Report: Appendix. Part VI* (London, 1887), 256–7. This letter from Locke to Fatio on 29 January 1694 appears to have eluded the editors of the Clarendon edition of Locke's writings.

[62] BPU, MS Fr. 602, fos. 96, 100; Bodleian Library, Oxford, MS Rawlinson Letters 109, fos. 28–9.

1 November, he showed a pendulum watch with a spiral spring of their manufacture at the Royal Society. Together with the Debaufres, Fatio pioneered techniques for drilling precious stones, particularly rubies, and applied them to watch and clock mechanisms, winning a patent in 1704. Newton tested the accuracy of one of Fatio's watches, and its susceptibility to cold, in December 1704. The watches were exhibited at the Royal Society in March 1705, and advertised as being accurate enough to determine latitude at sea. Opposition from the Clockmakers' Company, however, prevented the extension of Fatio's patent beyond its initial fourteen years.[63]

Fatio's early activities in England bear on a number of themes that have significance for his later career. During his first years in London, Fatio was largely dependent on a network of acquaintances who had strong links with the French-speaking world. He was supported by Justel; he lodged for a while with the Protestant secretary of the French ambassador and with a French apothecary; his friend Hampden had lived in France between October 1680 and September 1682, and had close contacts with French Protestants. Rather than accept Newton's offer that he come to lodge near him in Cambridge, Fatio preferred to live with a French jeweller in London.[64] Despite the fact that Newton's letters to Fatio display an unusual level of warmth and affection from as early as 10 October 1689, Fatio clearly continued to treat Huygens with equal or greater regard for some time after his arrival in England.[65] On the other hand, his unreliability as a correspondent concerned both Huygens and Newton at this time.[66]

---

[63] See Royal Society, London, MS Journal Book VIII (1690–6), 198–9, 210–11; Sir Henry Ellis (ed.), *Original Letters of Eminent Literary Men*, Camden Society 23 (London, 1843), 315–19; Hiscock (ed.), *David Gregory, Isaac Newton and their Circle*, 21–2; *Reasons of the English Watch and Clockmakers against the Bill to Confirm the Pretended New Invention of Using Precious and Common Stones about Watches, Clocks, and other Engines* ([London, 1704]); *Reasons for an Act Intituled, An Act for the Further Encouragement of a New Art, or Invention, of Working and Applying of Precious and More Common Stones for the Greater Perfection of Watches, Clocks, and other Engines* ([London, 1704]); David Thompson, 'Huguenot Watchmakers in England: With Examples from the British Museum Horological Collections', *Proceedings of the Huguenot Society of Great Britain and Ireland*, 26 (1994–7), 417–30.

[64] See Turnbull et al. (eds.), *Correspondence of Isaac Newton*, iii. 231, 241.

[65] See ibid. 45; vii. 390–1.

[66] Ibid. iii. 79; Huygens, *Œuvres complètes*, ix. 362.

Moreover, the sensitivity of Fatio's health to the effects of the English climate was already apparent in winter 1687.[67]

Fatio was conscious of his ability and eager to sell it at an appropriate rate. At the same time, he was painfully aware of the uncertainty of the financial prospects that awaited him once his father had provided for his seven sisters and for his elder brother.[68] Throughout the late 1680s and early 1690s, Fatio was looking for a way to make his name that would also make him a living. His activities encompassed natural philosophy, mathematics, watchmaking, and the alchemical production of medical remedies.[69] In his relationship with Huygens, Fatio strove to avoid subservience. He used his role as an intermediary both to develop Huygens's reliance on information and services that he might provide and to suggest that his own natural philosophy built on and surpassed that of his mentor.[70] He was assertive in his dealings with Newton and determined not to become the creature of another natural philosopher. He used his knowledge and understanding of the *Principia* and its author to bolster his authority in correspondence with Continental mathematicians, but regarded himself as Newton's teacher as well as his pupil. A hint of Fatio's sense of his own status can be gleaned from the fact that on 10 July 1689, he joined Huygens and Hampden in recommending Newton for the headship of a Cambridge College.[71] Fatio remained a privileged member of Newton's circle after 1693, even though he had successfully defended his intellectual and material independence.

[67] Huygens, *Œuvres complètes*, xxii. 126, where Fatio revealed that he was afraid that he had consumption; cf. Turnbull et al. (eds.), *Correspondence of Isaac Newton*, iii. 229–31, 241–3. Manuel, *Portrait of Isaac Newton*, 199–205, seizes on Fatio's ill-health as a contributor to the supposed psychological strains of his relationship with Newton.

[68] Turnbull et al. (eds.), *Correspondence of Isaac Newton*, iii. 267–8.

[69] On Fatio's financial hopes concerning medical recipes, see ibid. 265–70.

[70] For example, Uylenbroek (ed.), *Exercitationes mathematicae et philosophicae*, ii. 105–22; cf. Fatio to John Wallis, 2 May 1690, bound in Bodleian Library, Oxford, shelfmark Savile G.10.

[71] Huygens, *Œuvres complètes*, ix. 333. Fatio's desire to maintain his independence from Newton may be compared with George Starkey's efforts to distance himself from Robert Boyle, see William R. Newman and Lawrence M. Principe, *Alchemy Tried in the Fire* (Chicago: University of Chicago Press, 2002), 208–72.

FREEDOM: OR NOTHING LEFT TO LOSE

It is hard not to consider Fatio's career after 1693, or perhaps even after 1689, in terms of failure. When he arrived in England, Fatio was an exceptionally promising mathematician who had also recently secured the prospect of serious political patronage.[72] This did not materialize, despite the revolutionary events of 1688 and Fatio's contacts with Hampden and other Whig aristocrats. Perhaps this was because of the extreme politics that his friends espoused, which set them against the direction of the Court, especially in the early 1690s.[73] The reputation of Hampden, in particular, may also have helped to tar Fatio with associations of scepticism and libertinism, of the kind that Hearne later raised.[74] Yet Fatio's religious orthodoxy was not in question at this stage of his career, a fact that he confirmed in his expressions of hostility towards the religious mysticism of Pierre Poiret and Antoinette Bourignon. Their ideas would later appeal to some of those who, like Fatio, were affected by the French Prophets. In June 1687, however, they seemed for Fatio to be the product of 'imagination[s] that were not very well regulated'.[75] When Fatio rushed back to England to make contact with Newton in September 1691, the cause was his desire to press his claim to the Savilian professorship of astronomy at Oxford, recently vacated by his friend Edward Bernard. As part of the doomed case that he mounted, Fatio drew attention to the alleged impiety of Edmond

[72] For Fatio's ability as a mathematician, see Whiteside (ed.), *Mathematical Papers*, vii. 78–9.

[73] On shifts in the politics of this period, see Henry Horwitz, *Parliament, Policy and Politics in the Reign of William III* (Manchester: Manchester Unversity Press, 1977).

[74] Accounts of Hampden's corruption by the critical ideas of the Oratorian Richard Simon circulated widely in England: see British Library, London, MS Sloane 3229, fos. 183–4; MS Stowe 747, p. 35; Nottingham University Library, 2nd Portland Deposit, MSS Pw 2 Hy 227–8. For evidence of Fatio's awareness of and critical attitude to the work of Richard Simon, see Bibliothèque nationale de France, MS N.A.F. 4218, fos. 30–1.

[75] Bibliothèque nationale de France, MS N.A.F. 4218, fos. 26–7, Fatio to Abbé Nicaise, 5 June 1687 ['une certaine Antoinette Bourignon, femme de qui l'imagination n'étoit pas trop bien reglée …']; for an example of someone who was moved both by Bourignon and by the French Prophets, see the diary of Richard Roach, Bodleian Library, Oxford, MS Rawlinson D. 1152, fos. 112, 115.

Halley, another candidate who turned out to be unsuccessful.[76] In 1692, Newton felt that Fatio's allegorical readings of Genesis, the Psalms, and Job 'indulge[d] too much in fansy'. The sense of the imminent threat of the persecutory hand of God that Fatio read into these texts indeed resonated with the later claims of the French Prophets, but it may be possible to see in it also some parallels with the style of scriptural argument and application practised by more obviously rational Genevan theologians.[77] Certainly, Fatio's Genevan contemporaries were intrigued and disturbed by the more literal interpretation of the chronological fulfilment of prophecy, as practised by William Lloyd, who was successively bishop of St Asaph, Coventry and Lichfield, and Worcester between 1680 and his death in 1717. The method of Lloyd's exegesis was closer to that of Newton than of Fatio, although, unlike Newton, Lloyd anticipated that the final events foretold in prophecy were about to be fulfilled in his own time.[78] But irrespective of the origins of Fatio's reading of prophecy, the method of contemporary Genevan theology was clearly apparent in the interest in natural theology that he also stated during the early 1690s.[79]

One of the benefits of Fatio's mechanical theory of gravity was that it had clear implications for natural theology. On 21 February 1690, Fatio informed his elder brother, Jean-Christophe, about the nature of Newton's theories concerning gravity and the shortcomings of

---

[76] Huygens, *Œuvres complètes*, x. 145–6; this is the significance of the haste to bring about a meeting with Newton on Fatio's return, which White, *Isaac Newton*, 240, reads as a sign of sexual attraction.

[77] Turnbull et al. (eds.), *Correspondence of Isaac Newton*, iii. 245; cf. Fatio's letter at 242–3. For a possible Genevan comparison, see a sermon on Gen. 1: 24–6 by Jean-Alphonse Turrettini at BPU, MS C.P. 18. Turrettini was later a critic of the French Prophets, see BPU, MS Fr. 601, fos. 147–8.

[78] On the reception of Lloyd's ideas in Geneva, see BPU, MS Fr. 485, fo. 207r–v (Gilbert Burnet to Jean-Alphonse Turrettini, 2 November 1705); BPU, MSS Archives Tronchin, 44, fos. 103–10 (letters of Lloyd and Louis Tronchin); 82, fo. 200r ('Calcul de William Lloyd ev[eque] de St Asaph' by Louis Tronchin). See also A. Tindal Hart, *William Lloyd, 1627–1717* (London: SPCK, 1952). There are some superficial similarities between the method of Lloyd and Newton and that practised by Fatio at BPU, MS Fr. 605/1, fo. 12r.

[79] For example, BPU, MS Archives Tronchin 119, 'Abrégés de Lecons de Theol-[ogie] de Mr T[urrettini]'. Jean-Alphonse Turrettini met both Fatio and Newton in England in January 1693, see Turnbull et al. (eds.), *Correspondence of Isaac Newton*, iii. 241.

those of Huygens, which, he argued, paid too little attention to the inverse square law. He implied that his own ideas had several further advantages, including the fact that they did not require that there be too many fine particles filling the universe. He went on to indicate that 'it could be that this gravity may be one of the first laws by which the Author of Nature governs the world', although he conceded that this might mean, as Newton suspected, that it could not be described 'in a geometrical manner'. Nevertheless, such speculation led him into further meditation along the natural theological lines indicated by Newton, concerning the way in which gravity held the stars and planets in place and prevented them from collapsing inwards, and suggested that it gave similar structure to plants and animals.[80] Newton's own interest in the possibility that his ideas might have natural theological implications antedated the exchanges that lay behind Richard Bentley's Boyle Lectures of 1692: 'In Mr Newtons opinion a good design of a publick speech (and which may serve well at ane Act) may be to shew that the most simple laws of nature are observed in the structure of a great part of the universe; that the philosophy ought ther to begin, and that the Cosmical Qualities are as much easier as they are more universal than particular ones, and the general contrivance simpler than that of Animals plants &c.'[81] The alchemical study that Fatio undertook in the early 1690s can also be linked to this natural theological impulse, since the prophetic interpretation that Fatio presented of Genesis may have depended on his recognition that 'there are several alchemists who believe that in this chapter [Genesis 1] Moses also had in mind some of their most considerable operations'.[82] Even so, Jean-Christophe Fatio later

---

[80] BPU, MS Fr. 610, fos. 3v–4r ['il pourroit être que cetter pesanteur seroit une des premieres loix par lesquelles l'Auteur de la Nature gouverne le monde et qu'on n'en pourroit rendre aucun conte d'une maniere geometrique']; cf. BPU, MS Fr. 606/4, a later manuscript in which Fatio explained at greater length his interest in the natural theological implications of gravity. See also M. A. Hoskin, 'Newton, Providence and the Universe of Stars', *Journal for the History of Astronomy*, 8 (1977), 77–101.

[81] Royal Society London, MS 247, fo. 71v, probably dating from November or December 1691; cf. Turnbull et al. (eds.), *Correspondence of Isaac Newton*, iii. 233–40.

[82] BPU, MS Fr. 605/1, fo. 12r ['il y a divers Alchimistes q[ui] croient q[ue] dans ce Chap[itre] Moyse a aussi eu en vue q[ue]lq[ue]s unes de leurs operations les plus considerables']; cf. the alchemical and cabbalistic references in the horoscope of creation later drawn up by Fatio, BPU, MS Fr. 603, fo. 34r.

criticized his brother's credulity in trusting the works of Paracelsus and his followers.[83]

The most pressing reason, however, for Fatio's interest in the cause of gravity was also recognized by his elder brother. To prove Descartes's system to be wrong in a significant manner would help to establish Fatio's place in the world, materially as well as intellectually.[84] If Fatio's mechanical theory of gravity won broad acceptance, he would have succeeded where Huygens and even Newton had failed. Huygens's experimental modelling of the Cartesian theory of gravity at the Académie Royale des Sciences in 1669 had shown that a system of circulating subtle matter could explain gravity. The development of these ideas in his *Traité de la lumière*, moreover, brought further experiments with pendula to bear in their support. Fatio's theory, however, proposed significant modifications to the work of Descartes, reinforcing those introduced by Huygens, in particular through its use of inelastic collisions to explain gravity; its apparent compatibility with the inverse square law, and its acceptance of a largely empty universe. At the same time, it promised to overcome some of the aspects of Newton's thought that Continental natural philosophers found most difficult, especially its use of the concept of attraction. In so doing, Fatio's theory would preserve the rational grounds for the analysis of nature that provided an underpinning for contemporary natural philosophy through natural theology.[85] Yet, ultimately, Fatio failed to seize this chance. Although he continued to work on his ideas about gravity for the rest of his life, his inability to sustain the interest of Newton and his closest followers or to develop his notions adequately during the 1690s proved fatal to his ambitions. It forced him back into a life of prospecting and tutoring that

[83] BPU, MS Fr. 601, fo. 146r.

[84] Ibid. fos. 101–2 (Jean-Christophe Fatio to Nicolas Fatio, 15 July 1690).

[85] See E. J. Aiton, *The Vortex Theory of Planetary Motion* (London: Macdonald, 1972), 75–85, 106–14; William R. Shea, 'The Unfinished Revolution: Johann Bernoulli (1667–1748) and the Debate between the Cartesians and the Newtonians', in Shea (ed.), *Revolutions in Science* (Canton, Mass.: Science History Publications, 1988), 70–92; H. J. M. Bos, M. J. S. Rudwick, H. A. M. Snelders, and R. P. W. Visser (eds.), *Studies on Christiaan Huygens* (Lisse: Swets & Zeitlinger, 1980); Gianfranco Mormino, 'Le Rôle de Dieu dans l'œuvre scientifique et philosophique de Christiaan Huygens', *Revue d'histoire des sciences*, 56 (2003), 113–33; cf. the enthusiastic correspondence between Fatio and Jacob Bernoulli, in David Speiser et al. (eds.), *Der Briefwechsel von Jacob Bernoulli* (Basle: Birkhäuser, 1993), 160–200.

perpetuated his position as an outsider and denied him the opportunity of a respectable and orthodox career.

Alongside his activities as a tutor and entrepreneur, Fatio pursued
other natural philosophical and practical endeavours. Influenced by
John Evelyn's translation of the writings of Jean de la Quintinie, he
explored the effects of the use of sloping surfaces to maximize the
heat of the sun for plants growing upon them. He directed the
building of such a sloping wall for fruit-trees at Belvoir Castle, and,
in 1697, composed the text of *Fruit-Walls Improved* (London, 1699),
whose publication he clearly intended to reignite his search for
patronage.[86] In this book, which drew attention to the divine wisdom
that lay behind the variety of creation, Fatio also remarked on
changes in the weather since 1683, which he attributed to a decline
in the incidence of sunspots, and the consequent dispersal of a mist
between the sun and the earth.[87] Fatio's interest in the physical
processes by which the sun's heat could be transmitted was linked
to his earlier explorations of zodiacal light, to his ongoing work on
the cause of gravity, and to his later investigations, in the years
around 1705, of the paths of comets and the nature and prophetic
interpretation of the aurora borealis.[88] For all these phenomena,
Fatio continued to offer a mechanical explanation, in terms of the
motion of tiny particles and their effects, yet he was also influenced
by Newton's ideas about the importance of comets and other celestial
bodies in providing nourishment to the earth. Fatio's own alchemical
work, which drew increasingly on the combinatorial possibilities
provided by the ideas of Ramon Lull, suggested that divine spirit

---

[86] Fatio's extraordinarily detailed plans for the printing, binding, and distribution
of *Fruit-Walls Improved* may be found at Royal Society, London, MS 64, fos. 24v–26r;
cf. Jean de la Quintinie, *The Compleat Gard'ner*, tr. John Evelyn (London, 1693). See
also Peggy Kidwell, 'Nicholas Fatio de Duillier and *Fruit-Walls Improved*: Natural
Philosophy, Solar Radiation, and Gardening in Late Seventeenth Century England',
Agricultural History, 57 (1983), 403–15; Stephen Switzer, *The Practical Fruit-Gardener*
(London, 1724), 295–8.

[87] Nicolas Fatio de Duillier, *Fruit-Walls Improved* (London, 1699), pp. xvii,
114–17.

[88] Hiscock (ed.), *David Gregory, Isaac Newton and their Circle*, 23, 28, 31, 35, 39;
Eric G. Forbes, Lesley Murdin, and Frances Willmoth (eds.), *The Correspondence of
John Flamsteed*, iii (Bristol: Institute of Physics, 2002), 334–6; BPU, MS Fr. 607;
British Library, London, MS Sloane 4055, fo. 27.

might activate matter.[89] Yet, taken together, these aspects of Fatio's natural philosophical work demonstrated his commitment to the notion that God had designed nature as a self-sustaining system, which would demonstrate his general providence. This idea even informed Fatio's work on the reduction of the effects of friction in clock movements, and lay at the heart of his long-standing interest in perpetual motion machines.

As a companion to *Fruit-Walls Improved*, Fatio published *Lineae brevissimi descensus investigatio geometrica duplex* (London, 1699), a discussion of the attempts that had been made to solve the problem of determining the curve linking any two points, not in the same vertical line, along which a body would most quickly descend from the higher to the lower point. The brachistochrone problem had originally been posed in June 1696 by Johann Bernoulli, and was solved almost immediately by Leibniz, the Marquis de l'Hôpital, and, most successfully, Newton. In his book, as well as drawing attention to the significance of his own progress towards the calculus in 1687, Fatio stressed Newton's priority in reaching a full understanding of this technique, thus criticizing the claims of Leibniz. Along with several others, Fatio had pressed Newton to publish his work on the calculus throughout the 1690s. Although Fatio's work can be seen retrospectively as initiating a long-running dispute over priority, at the time his use of Newton's ideas represented part of a strategy to provoke the interest of foreign mathematicians in his own work. The first exchanges took place in the *Acta eruditorum*. There, in 1699, Bernoulli reviewed *Lineae brevissimi* in a hostile manner; the following year, Leibniz attacked Fatio's interpretation of the invention of the calculus; finally, in 1701, the editors printed an abbreviated reply by Fatio to his critics. The debate continued in letters between Fatio and Jacob Bernoulli, which exploited Bernoulli's intellectual rift with his younger brother, Johann. In this correspondence, Fatio also passed ideas about gravity onto Bernoulli. Fatio's final contribution to the controversy came in a letter to his brother, Jean-Christophe,

---

[89] BPU, MS Fr. 603, fos. 34–58, 215–45; MS Fr. 605/6; cf. MS Fr. 605/9. See also Wilhelm Schmidt-Biggemann, *Topica universalis. Eine Modellgeschichte humanistischer und barocker Wissenschaft* (Hamburg: Meiner, 1983), 155–211.

concerning the solid of least resistance, which was published in the
Philosophical Transactions in 1713.[90]

In 1699, Fatio travelled to Switzerland, remaining at Duillier,
where he was reconciled to his father, until 1701. There, he worked
again on his theory of gravity, refining his ideas about the effect that
streams of fast-moving, minute particles might have on larger bodies,
which were largely composed of empty space. He also surveyed the
mountains around Lake Geneva in company with his brother and
deepened his knowledge of the prophetic texts of the Bible.[91] Following his return to England, he lived in London, working as a
mathematical tutor in Spitalfields, where, in summer 1706, he
encountered the Camisard prophets: Durand Farge, Jean Cavalier,
and Elie Marion. Exiled Huguenots who had fled the persecutions in
the Cévennes, these men were inspired with words and visions that
foretold the imminent and dramatic reversal of their situation. In
part this would take place through the fulfilment of events described
in biblical prophecy, but it would also derive from the restoration of
life and health to the community from miracles and acts of divine
intervention that were predicted by the French Prophets themselves.
Fatio soon began to attend the Prophets' assemblies and acted as one
of their scribes, recording during their periods of inspiration words
and actions that carried a millenarian message of impending destruction and judgement.[92] He reported on the motives and activities
of the French Prophets to Newton and introduced David Gregory
to one of their meetings. Gregory recorded his experience in this
manner:

[90] See n. 19 above. See also *Philosophical Transactions*, 28 (1713), 172–6; Speiser
et al. (eds.), *Briefwechsel von Jacob Bernoulli*, 160–200; Speiser et al. (eds.), *Die
Streitschriften von Jacob und Johann Bernoulli* (Basle, 1991), 64, 485; Whiteside
(ed.), *Mathematical Papers*, vi. 466–80; Derek Thomas Whiteside, 'Patterns of Mathematical Thought in the Later Seventeenth Century', *Archive for History of Exact
Sciences*, 1 (1960–2), 179–388, at 380–1; A. Rupert Hall, *Philosophers at War* (Cambridge: Cambridge University Press, 1980), 100–28.

[91] Domson, *Nicolas Fatio de Duillier*, 79–81; cf. BPU, MSS Fr. 601, fos. 1–4, 146r;
602, fo. 102r; 603, fos. 63–4, 77–80; 606/1.

[92] See Dr Williams's Library, London, MSS 24.33–4; Domson, *Nicolas Fatio de
Duillier*; Schwartz, *The French Prophets*, 73–112; Philippe Joutard, *La Légende des
Camisards* (Paris: Gallimard, 1977). See also Daniel Vidal, *Le Malheur et son prophète*
(Paris: Payot, 1983), which discusses the significance of Fatio's dreams for the
interpretation of the situation in Languedoc.

They are exceedingly agitated & moved with violent motions, when they have the fitt of Prophecy ... They told us that some times they know in the morning that they will have the Fitt of Prophecy that day, as in the afternoon; at other times it quite surpprizes them. They read us a Paper giving an account of the beginning of the Commotions in the Cevennes, & of this Gift of Prophecy which is very universal there, & of the carrying on that war, & of the Crueltys & Barbaritys used against them, and of their great successes when they fought by order of those that are inspired, in the time of their Fitt, & of Childrens Raptures ... [93]

Fatio's work with the French Prophets generated considerable criticism of his intentions and confirmed the sense that his sympathies were those of a religious enthusiast rather than a sober mathematician and natural philosopher. He searched for evidence that biblical prophecy was being fulfilled in the work of the Prophets, and also appeared to link his ideas about the origins of gravity to the physical causation of acts of divine punishment. He later recorded Jean Allut speaking of the Devil agitating the sea to cause a deluge that threatened to swamp God's people 'through vortices', in a manner which echoed directly the language of Cartesian cosmology.[94] Jean-Christophe Fatio de Duillier was astonished by his brother's abandonment of sober and rational religion. He recalled Nicolas's interest in Cabbala and in the allegorical interpretation of Job in order to attack what he now saw as an absurd tendency to error in his younger brother. This inclination led him to follow pretended prophets who did not themselves understand what they were saying.[95] In London, the French Prophets aroused even more threatening criticism as a result of the suspicion of the more orthodox refugee churches, which led to various attempts to suppress their activities. These came to a head with the trial on 4 July 1707 at Queen's Bench of Fatio, Marion, and Jean Daudé. On 22 November, a second jury convicted the men

[93] Royal Society, London, MS 247, fo. 63v; cf. Edinburgh University Library, MS Dc.1.61, fo. 707.

[94] See n. 93 above: in the Edinburgh MS Gregory referred to Fatio's claim that 'Lord Napier makes these very years of 1706, 1707, 1708, & 1709, the Critical years for vindicating Religion & good men.' See also [Charles Portalès et al.], *Cri d'alarme, en avertissement aux nations, qu'ils sortent de Babylon, des tenebres, pour entrer dans le repos de Christ* ([Amsterdam], 1712), 271–2: Fatio arranged the publication of this book.

[95] BPU, MS Fr. 601, fos. 145–6.

of publishing a seditious work, and on 1 and 2 December, they were paraded before the mob on the scaffold at Charing Cross. The Duke of Ormonde, to whose brother, the Earl of Arran, Fatio had once been tutor, ensured that guards protected them from excessive injury.[96] In March 1708, Fatio participated in the French Prophets' mission to Colchester, and, in June 1711, he finally left London as one of their emissaries to the Continent, seeking to establish a new series of Protestant alliances and to warn of the coming apocalyptic struggle. Fatio and his accomplices travelled to Berlin, and thence to Halle and Vienna. On a second mission in 1712–13, they visited Stockholm, Prussia, Halle, Constantinople, Smyrna, and Rome.[97]

THE LIFE OF HETERODOXY

After the conclusion of his travels, Fatio remained in Holland for some time. He completed accounts of the missions that he had undertaken with his companions and of the prophecies that had accompanied them. He arranged for the publication of several of these in French and also translated them into Latin.[98] Later, Fatio returned to London, where he continued to communicate material to the Royal Society, and to work on meteorological phenomena that could be assimilated to his prophetic schemes. For example, in 1717, he gave a series of papers on the precession of the equinoxes and on climatic change, which he believed gave support to the physical underpinnings of his theory of gravity.[99] By the spring of 1717,

[96] Schwartz, *The French Prophets*, 110–12; Charles Bost (ed.), 'Mémoires inédits d'Abraham Mazel et d'Élie Marion sur la guerre des Cévennes 1701–1708', *Publications de la Société Huguenote de Londres*, 34 (1931), esp. 165–8.

[97] On these activities, see [Portalès et al.], *Cri d'alarme*; [Charles Portalès et al.], *Plan de la justice de Dieu sur la terre dans ces derniers jours* ([Amsterdam], 1714); [Charles Portalès et al.], *Quand vous aurez saccagé, vous serez saccagés: car la lumiere est apparue dans les tenebres, pour les détruire* ([Amsterdam], 1714); BPU, MSS Fr. 602, fos. 19–21; 605/2 (a manuscript draft of *Plan de la justice*); 605/3; 605/7.

[98] See n. 96 above; [Charles Portalès et al.], *Delineatio justitiae divinae*, tr. N[icolas] F[atio] ([Amsterdam], 1714); [Portalès et al.], *Ubi devastaveritis, devastabimini*, tr. N[icolas] F[atio] ([Amsterdam], 1714).

[99] Royal Society, London, MS Journal Book XI (1714–20), 168–9, 172, 174–5, 179–80.

Fatio had moved to Worcester. He passed the remainder of his life in that city, and at nearby Madresfield. There he continued to work on perpetual motion and to design watches (including one for Richard Bentley), in collaboration with Benjamin Steele.[100] He pursued his interests in alchemy and medicine, in conjunction with Francis Moult. Thus, in 1737, he communicated his discovery of a salt that he hoped would prove to be 'the true Niter of the Ancients' to Francis Hauksbee.[101] He also developed his ideas on the use of jewelled watches to find latitude at sea and hoped to extend his work to longitude. With this in mind, he sought in vain for the royal patronage that would allow him to complete his observations.[102] After Newton's death, Fatio advised his executor, John Conduitt, on the design of the monument that was to be erected in Westminster Abbey. He also composed a Latin poem on Newton and his system that returned to some of the themes of his own theory of gravity. He considered publishing that theory in 1735, but pulled back from doing so. Nevertheless, in his later work, Fatio suggested that his own ideas about gravity, solar parallax, and the relative sizes of the planets of the solar system had corrected and even surpassed the achievement of Newton.[103] Fatio published further fragments of his ideas about astronomy between 1737 and 1738, but otherwise lived in obscurity and relative poverty in Worcester until his death in April 1753.[104]

Fatio maintained contact with surviving members of the group that had formed around the French Prophets until the end of his

---

[100] Turnbull et al. (eds.), *Correspondence of Isaac Newton*, vi. 391–2.

[101] British Library, London, MS Add. 28536, fo. 238.

[102] Nicolas Fatio de Duillier, *Navigation Improv'd. Being chiefly the Method for Finding the Latitude* (London, 1728); BPU, MS Fr. 602, fos. 123–4, 137–62; MS Fr. 609.

[103] See Karin Figala and Ulrich Petzold, 'Physics and Poetry: Fatio de Duillier's *Ecloga* on Newton's *Principia*', *Archives internationales d'histoire des sciences*, 37 (1987), 316–49; cf. the material bound in Fatio's copy of the 3rd edn. of Isaac Newton, *Philosophiae naturalis principia mathematica* (London, 1726), Bodleian Library, Oxford, shelfmark 4o Z. 24 Art. See also BPU, MS Fr. 603, fos. 187–93; MS Fr. 607; MS Fr. 610, fos. 43–4; King's College, Cambridge, MSS Keynes 96 and 131.

[104] *The Gentleman's Magazine*, 7 (1737), 412–14, 440, 490–1, 547–8, 611–15; 8 (1738), 195–6, 305–6, 352–4; a notice of Fatio's death appears in *The Gentleman's Magazine*, 23 (1753), 248. Cf. BPU, MSS Fr. 604; 607.

life.[105] His commitment to their ideas provides striking proof of the extent of his conversion. He assimilated to their teaching his interests in biblical theology and alchemy, and perhaps even his theories about natural theology and philosophy. In later life, Fatio therefore came to resemble William Whiston, with whom he continued to correspond. He appeared to be a natural philosopher whose promise had been destroyed by enthusiasm, despite his conviction that his beliefs would advance understanding 'until we arrive to Angelical Wisdom'.[106] Yet unlike Whiston, who was for a time Lucasian Professor of Mathematics at Cambridge, Fatio's career had developed without any financial or institutional stability. He had established his reputation by a mixture of intellectual rigour and personal charm, and through the judicious apprenticeship of his talents to prominent masters. He had then advanced many of his ideas as an outsider in a country undergoing a political revolution and during a period in which the aggression of Louis XIV seemed to pose a threat to all Protestants. In these circumstances of emotional and political uncertainty, Fatio's choices may seem slightly less bizarre, if no less heterodox. Towards the end of his career, Fatio recognized that he might sometimes have been gullible in his reaction to people who claimed to be messengers from God. He did not, however, interpret his involvement with the French Prophets in that light.[107] The fact that their prophecies had not come true in the manner that had been expected was not in itself proof that they were false. The moral worth and spiritual insight of Fatio's friends provided a demonstration of the trustworthiness of their claims. The failure of prophecy was a challenge to the interpretative skill of the believer, rather than to the authority of God or of those whom he had chosen.

The natural theology to which Fatio returned throughout his career was compatible with the world of prophecy in which he came to dwell. Yet it also continued to display the effects of the intellectual training that had shaped his earlier descriptions of God and gravity. This attempted rationalization of the relationship

[105] For example, see BPU, MS Fr. 601, fos. 209, 239; MS Fr. 602, fos. 123–4, 177.

[106] BPU, MS Fr. 602, fos. 123–4; cf. James E. Force, *William Whiston. Honest Newtonian* (Cambridge: Cambridge University Press, 1985).

[107] BPU, MS Fr. 601, fo. 209v; cf. Fatio's defence of his beliefs in reply to his brother's criticisms, MS Fr. 602, fos. 22–4.

between education, knowledge, and experience in the development of Fatio's beliefs is not one that would have appealed to later readers, such as Le Sage. But Le Sage had his own view of the growth of the intellectual tradition of which the young Fatio formed a part and his own sense of what could and should be known. It is a paradox that, as a result, he excluded as heterodox the ideas of the Englishmen who had been themselves so puzzled by Fatio's conversion to enthusiastic religion.

11

'Claiming Him as Her Son': William Stukeley, Isaac Newton, and the Archaeology of the Trinity

David Boyd Haycock

In 1730 the recently ordained clergyman Dr William Stukeley (1687–1765) declared in a letter to his fellow antiquary Roger Gale that his 'main motive' in pursuing his antiquarian studies into the ancient religion and remains of Celtic Britain was to 'combat the deists from an unexpected quarter'.[1] It was this same motivation that had led him to seek ordination the previous year, when he had told another friend, William Wake, numismatist and Archbishop of Canterbury, that he had 'ever been studious in divinity, especially in the most abstruse & sublime parts of it', and that his 'disquisitions into the history of our Celtic ancestors, & their religion, have ... given me the opportunity of discovering some notions about the Doctrine of the Trinity which I think are not common'. Indeed, Stukeley told the Archbishop that he believed he could 'prove' the Trinity 'to be so far from contrary to, or above, human reason, that 'tis deducible from reason its self. What else can we think, my Lord, of the explicit sentiments the antient Egyptians, Plato, our old Druids, & all the heathen philosophers, had of this divine truth, as I can show in a

[1] Stukeley to Roger Gale, 25 June 1730, in W. C. Lukis (ed.), *The Family Memoirs of the Rev. William Stukeley, M.D.: and the Antiquarian and Other Correspondence of William Stukeley, Roger and Samuel Gale, &c, Vol. 3* (Surtees Society, 80, 1887), 267.

thousand instances?'[2] Wake had replied encouragingly, telling Stukeley, 'Never was there a time in which we wanted all the assistance
we can get against the prevailing infidelity of the present wicked age;
& as our adversaries are men pretending to reason superior to others,
so nothing can abate their pride, & stop their prevalence, than to see
christianity defended by those who are in all respects as eminent in
naturall knowledge, & philosophicall enquiries, as they can pretend
to be.'[3] With Wake's encouragement, Stukeley set out on this course
of study, eventually publishing in 1740 and 1743 two major texts on
the 'Celtic Druid' stone circles at Stonehenge and Avebury.[4] Yet as I
shall show in this chapter, his attempts to use archaeology in a proto-
scientific method against deism, and to defend his great hero Isaac
Newton against accusations of heterodoxy, led him into the very
theories he was attempting to refute.

Principal among the 'men pretending to reason' from whom Wake
felt the Church was so threatened were the Cambridge Arians and
Newtonian scholars William Whiston and Samuel Clarke. It seems
likely that these were the men, along with the Oxford lawyer Matthew
Tindal and (possibly) the Irish pantheist and antiquary John Toland,
whom Stukeley was naming under the blanket term 'deists'. Deism
emerged in later seventeenth-century England and for a time shared
a close link with contemporary scientific thought. It advocated the
argument that the existence of God could be based upon natural
reason alone, without reference to revelation. Deism was also one of
the forms of heterodoxy identified by Robert Boyle to be combated in
the annual sermons established by his will, to prove the truth of
Christianity 'against notorious Infidels, *viz.* Atheists, Deists, Jews and
Mahometans'.[5] In 1692 the first man to deliver these influential

---

[2] Stukeley to Wake, 3 June 1729, in William Stukeley, *The Commentarys, Diary,
and Common-Place Book of William Stukeley* (London: Doppler, 1980), 141–2.

[3] Wake to Stukeley, 10 June 1729, in Stukeley, *The Commentarys*, 144.

[4] *Stonehenge: A Temple Restor'd to the British Druids* (London: printed for W. Innys
and R. Manby, 1740) and *Abury: A Temple of the British Druids* (London: printed for
W. Innys and R. Manby, 1743).

[5] Quoted in Roger L. Emerson, 'Latitudinarianism and the English Deists', in J. A.
Leo Lemay, *Deism, Masonry and the Enlightenment: Essays Honoring Alfred Owen
Aldridge* (London: Associated University Press, 1987), 19–48, 26, from Sampson
Letsome and John Nickell (eds.), *A Defence of Natural and Revealed Religion Being
a Collection of the Sermons* (1739).

'Boyle Lectures' was the young Cambridge graduate and future Master of Trinity College, Cambridge, Richard Bentley. Through a correspondence with Trinity's Lucasian Professor of Mathematics, Isaac Newton, Bentley drew on Newtonian natural philosophy to show the necessary presence of God's hand in the continual operation of nature and hence to confound presumed atheists. Though the first edition of Newton's seminal *Principia Mathematica* (1687) had contained only one reference to God as Creator, Newton told Bentley that when he had written the book, 'I had an eye upon such Principles as might work with considering men for the beliefe of a Deity & nothing can rejoyce me more then to find it usefull for that purpose.'[6] Newton's *Opticks*, published in 1705, added further weight to a scientific proof for the existence of God, whilst the 'General Scholium' which Newton added to the 1713 edition of the *Principia* made his belief in this position even clearer. There he stated: 'This most beautiful System of the Sun, Planets and Comets, could only proceed from the counsel and dominion of an intelligent and powerful being ... He is Eternal and Infinite, Omnipotent and Omniscient; that is, his duration reaches from Eternity to Eternity; his presence from Infinity to Infinity; he governs all things, and knows all things that are or can be done.'[7] The universe was God's almighty creation.

Whilst the so-called 'argument from design', as expounded by churchmen and naturalists such as John Ray in *The Wisdom of God Manifested in the Works of Creation* (1692), had already gone a considerable distance to 'proving' from a natural philosophical position the existence of a deity, the addition to this argument of Newtonian theory added weight and substance of the highest intellectual order. For William Whiston, Newton's sometime protégé and successor as Lucasian Professor of Mathematics at Cambridge, deism was simply what he called the 'last Refuge' of 'some Irreligious Persons' following 'that surprizing and overbearing Light, which

---

[6] Newton to Bentley, 10 December 1692, quoted in Michael Hunter, *Science and Society in Restoration England* (Cambridge: Cambridge University Press, 1981), 184.
[7] Isaac Newton, *The Mathematical Principles of Natural Philosophy. Translated into English by Andrew Motte* (2 vols.; London: printed for Benjamin Motte, 1729), ii. 388–90. See Larry Stewart, 'Seeing Through the Scholium: Religion and Reading Newton in the Eighteenth Century', *History of Science*, 34 (1996), 123–65.

Sir Isaac Newton's wonderful discoveries have afforded; whereby they have perceived that Natural Religion, with its Foundations, were now become too certain to bear any farther Opposition'.[8] Whiston directly dated the origin of what in 1717 he called 'the present gross *Deism*' to Bentley's inaugural Boyle Lectures. Whiston accepted the proven authority of the argument from design, and believed 'he who will now be an *Atheist*, must be an absolute *Ignoramus* in Natural Knowledge; must neither understand the Principles either of Physicks or Astronomy'.[9] Whiston hoped, furthermore, that the scientific discoveries 'produc'd from Modern Astronomy, Mathematicks, and Philosophy' over the previous two centuries could be directly utilized in the support of Scripture.[10]

Whiston was not alone in holding the opinion that atheism had been crushed by Newtonianism. An anonymous author claimed in 1710 that Bentley had in his Lectures proved the 'Being of God' through 'the excellent Sir *Isaac Newton's Principia Mathematica*'. The same author added, 'Have not all Writers upon that Subject Copied after his *Boyle's Lectures*? And have not the Atheists been silent since that time, and shelter'd themselves under Deism?'[11]

But there was a problem. Whilst Newtonianism clearly challenged atheism, it also seemed to render unnecessary the need for revelation; it appeared actually to *strengthen* the deist position: according to Newtonian physics, God could be known from nature alone. Freethinkers such as John Toland thus latched onto Newtonianism as a valuable weapon in their assault on organized religion and what he called 'priestcraft'. Whilst Whiston claimed that 'the Generality of the *Deists*' were known to be 'Superficial in their Learning, about such Matters',[12] this could not be said of Newtonians such as the Royal Society's vice-president Martin Folkes, who went so far as to establish in the early 1720s what Stukeley called 'an infidel Club' where Fellows

[8] William Whiston, *Astronomical Principles of Religion, Natural and Reveal'd* (London: printed for J. Senex and W. Taylor, 1717), 242.

[9] Ibid. 242–3.   [10] Ibid. 274.

[11] Richard Bentley, *The Present State of Trinity College in Cambridg[e], In a Letter from Dr. Bentley, Master of the Said College, to the Right Reverend John Lord Bishop of Ely*, 2nd edn. (London: printed for A. Baldwin, 1710), 'Publisher's Remarks to the Reader'.

[12] Whiston, *Astronomical Principles*, 244.

'of the heathen stamp, assembled'.[13] So although Newton and his supporters had proved to their own satisfaction the existence of God through natural philosophy, what *sort* of God had they proved, exactly? As Whiston himself pointed out, the Newtonian philosophical system did not by itself affirm a *Christian* deity. Whiston and Newton thus sought to validate a strictly Christian God through the fulfilment of Scripture prophecy and miracles.[14] Newton's posthumously published works thus included *The Chronology of Ancient Kingdoms Amended* (1728) and *Observations Upon the Prophecies of Daniel, and the Apocalypse of St. John* (1733). But Newton and Whiston's detailed biblical studies duly led them, as well as their Cambridge colleague Samuel Clarke, into the fourth-century heresy of Arianism, the denial of the Holy Trinity.

Though Newton tried to keep his antitrinitarian opinions hidden, they were openly broadcast by Whiston, who in 1710 was expelled from the University for preaching antitrinitarian doctrines. They could also be deciphered by astute readers of the 'General Scholium', as Larry Stewart has shown. In 1713 the nonjuror bishop George Hickes wrote to a friend expressing his belief that 'It is their Newtonian philosophy wch hath Made Not onely so many Arians but Theists, and that Not onely among ye laity but I fear among our devines.'[15] And the following year John Edwards, a doctor of divinity and former Fellow of St John's College, Cambridge, observed that through the 'General Scholium' Newton 'seems to me to lay open his Heart and Mind, and to tell the World what Cause he espouses at this Day, viz. the very same which Dr. Clarke and Mr. Whiston have

---

[13] W. C. Lukis (ed.), *The Family Memoirs of the Rev. William Stukeley, M.D.: and the Antiquarian and Other Correspondence of William Stukeley, Roger and Samuel Gale, &c*, i (Surtees Society, 73, 1882), 99–100.

[14] Whiston, *Astronomical Principles*, 242. See James E. Force, *William Whiston: Honest Newtonian* (Cambridge: Cambridge University Press, 1985), 66, 70–6; see also Maurizio Mamiani, 'Newton on Prophecy and the Apocalypse', and Scott Mandelbrote, 'Newton and Eighteenth-Century Christianity', both in I. Bernard Cohen and George E. Smith (eds.), *The Cambridge Companion to Newton* (Cambridge: Cambridge University Press, 2002), 387–408, 409–30.

[15] George Hickes to Roger North, quoted in James E. Force and Richard H. Popkin, *Essays on the Context, Nature and Influence of Isaac Newton's Theology* (Dordrecht: Kluwer Academic, 1990), 53.

publickly asserted'.[16] Thus the ironic situation arose that, though Whiston had himself preached against deism, he eventually found himself accused of deism. In 1742 a pamphlet published under the title *A Dissertation on Deistical and Arian Corruption* identified the 'great Enemies of the Christian Faith, in the late and present times' as 'the Arian, Socinian, and other Deists'. The anonymous author explained that since both Arians and Socinians 'deny several *fundamental* Doctrines' of the Holy Scriptures, and 'in so doing, invalidate all Revelation ... the difference between them and avowed Deists, is rather *verbal* than *real*; and therefore, I rank them all under the same common Name of *Deists*.[17] He then identified 'the two most open and avowed Defenders of the Arian Deism' as William Whiston and Samuel Clarke's friend and mouthpiece, the clergyman and antiquary John Jackson.[18]

When Newton died in 1727, Stukeley received a letter from Newton's personal physician, Richard Mead, informing him that their 'great Friend Sr Isaac Newton' was dead. Whilst Mead told Stukeley that he had not heard if Newton before dying 'sayd any thing about a Future State', he took the trouble to add, 'This much I think I know of his Opinions, that he was a Christian, believd Revelation, though not all the Doctrines which our Orthodox Divines have made Articles of Faith.'[19] Stukeley himself later wrote of Newton in his manuscript biography, 'several people of heretical, & unsetled notions, particularly those of Arian principles, have taken great pains to inlist Sr Isaac into th[e]ir party. but *that* with as little justice, as the antichristians. the ch[urch] of England intirely claims him as her son, in faith & in practice.'[20] This reference to men 'of Arian principles'

[16] John Edwards, *Some Animadversions on Dr. Clarke's Scripture-Doctrine, (As he Stiles it) of the Trinity* (London: printed for the author, 1712), 27, and *Some Brief Critical Remarks on Dr. Clarke's Last Papers* ... (London: printed, and sold by Ferdinando Burleigh, 1714), 40, both quoted in Stewart, 'Seeing Through the Scholium', 132.

[17] Anonymous, *A Dissertation on Deistical and Arian Corruption: Or, Plain Proof, that the Principles and Practices of Arians and Deists are Founded Upon Spiritual Blindness, and Resolve into Atheism* (London: printed for G. Strahan, 1742), 1.

[18] Ibid. 8.

[19] Mead to Stukeley, 4 April 1727, Bodleian Library, MS Eng. misc. c. 114, fo. 50.

[20] William Stukeley, 'Memoirs of Sr Isaac Newtons Life', Royal Society of London, MS 142, fo. 67.

undoubtedly indicates Whiston, with whom Stukeley was acquainted between the 1720s and the 1750s.

Stukeley was well placed to understand the permutations of Newtonianism and its potential threat to orthodox religion. He had been an avid student of the 'new science' of Descartes, Locke, Boyle, and Newton whilst reading for his degree in Physic at Corpus Christi College, Cambridge, in the first years of the eighteenth century (where Whiston had been one of his lecturers).[21] In 1718, after a period as a country doctor, he had moved to London and was admitted a Fellow of the Royal Society of London, then under Newton's presidency. Stukeley, like Newton, was a native of Lincolnshire and this, together with his reverence for the great man and his discoveries, led to a period of comparatively close friendship. Stukeley presented papers at the Royal Society defending the Newtonian System and demonstrating how it could be used to verify such biblical events as the Flood, and how anatomy revealed the evidence of a divine maker. He was elected to the Society's Council, discoursed privately with Newton on astronomy and biblical chronology, and stood creditably, though unsuccessfully, to succeed Edmond Halley as the Society's secretary.

Stukeley thus moved within the intimate Newtonian circles of the Royal Society and retained a life-long interest in natural philosophy. Well-educated in the new science, if traditional and sometimes ill-judged in his outlook, he was also a devout and seemingly orthodox Christian who dedicated his life's work as an antiquary to defending Newton from accusations of heterodoxy, and to combating irreligion. Stukeley's great ambition was, he wrote in 1732, to 'protect our most excellent Church against the insolent attacks of atheists, Deists, sceptics, infidels, & all its open & Secret enemys'.[22] To do this, he would study history and antiquities.

The use of historical studies in the pursuit of the proof of Christian doctrine had developed through the seventeenth century in Western

---

[21] For a full account of Stukeley's intellectual career and his relationship with Newton and the Royal Society, see David Boyd Haycock, *William Stukeley: Science, Religion and Archaeology in Eighteenth-Century England* (Woodbridge: The Boydell Press, 2002).

[22] William Stukeley, 'Disquisitio de Deo. Or an Enquiry into the Nature of the DEITY'. Bodleian Library, MS Eng. misc. e. 650.

Europe. In continental Europe the Dutch humanist scholar Hugo Grotius, the Jesuit scholar Athanasius Kircher, and the Dutch theologian Gerard Vossius, had all made important researches into the relationship between ancient history and Christianity. In England similar work had been pursued by a number of important Cambridge Latitudinarian divines, including Edward Stillingfleet, author of *Origines Sacrae: Or, a Rational Account of the Grounds of Natural and Reveal'd Religion* (1662), and the one-time Master of Stukeley's *alma mater*, John Spencer, author of *De Legibus Hebraeorum Earum Rationibus* (1685), a book considered a founding text in the study of comparative religion.

Given this context, not unsurprisingly Newton himself took an interest in ancient history, as did his colleague and collaborator on the publication of the *Principia*, Edmond Halley. As well as Newton's two works on biblical chronology there was a mass of unpublished manuscripts. These included speculations upon the origin of Egyptian hieroglyphs and the belief that Stonehenge was a 'Prytanea', or ancient circular temple with a fire burning at its centre—proof to him of the Ancient's knowledge of the heliocentric system.[23] Stukeley also recorded conversations with Newton on subjects such as Solomon's Temple and the populating of the world after the Flood. Halley, meanwhile, attempted to date Julius Caesar's invasion of Britain by astronomical phenomena, and discussed with Stukeley and other antiquaries the possible origin of Stonehenge.[24] At a time when most commentators believed it to have been built by the Romans or Danes, the Oxford antiquary Thomas Hearne recorded in 1722 that 'Dr Halley hath a strange, odd Notion that Stonhenge is as old, at least almost as old, as Noah's Flood.'[25] Stukeley cleverly used Halley's scientific research into the declension of the compass, suggesting that the Druids had 'us'd a magnetical compass, in laying down their works', and the errors in alignment with the contempor-

[23] See Newton, Jewish and National University Library, Israel, Yahuda MS 41, fos. 3–3v, quoted in Rob Iliffe, '"The Idols of the Temple": Isaac Newton and the Private Life of Anti-idolatry', Ph.D. thesis (Cambridge, 1989), 81.

[24] Edmond Halley, 'A Discourse Tending to Prove at what Time and Place, Julius Caesar Made his first Descent upon Britain', *Philosophical Transactions*, 16 (1691), 495–501.

[25] Hearne, diary, 20 April 1722, in *Remarks and Collections of Thomas Hearne* (11 vols.; Oxford, 1906–21), vii. 350. See Haycock, *William Stukeley*, 124–5.

ary 'quarters of the heavens' was because 'the needle var'd so much, at that time, from the true meridian line'. He recalled in 1740 that 'I open'd this affair, near 20 years ago, to Dr *Halley*, who was of the same sentiment.'[26] This theory, based on contemporary scientific theory, led Stukeley to date the construction of Stonehenge to 460 BC, and of Avebury to 1860 BC. The freethinking Martin Folkes (whom Stukeley described as 'In matters of religion an errant infidel & loud scoffer'[27]) was yet another leading Newtonian scholar and gifted mathematician with a keen interest in antiquarian matters. It seems certain that to all these scholars, the interest in both science and antiquities was not coincidental: the two were profoundly linked.

The work of William Whiston clearly illustrates the way the connection could be developed. He devoted an extensive section of his *Astronomical Principles of Religion, Natural and Reveal'd* (1717)— which he dedicated to Newton and the Royal Society—to the subject of ancient religion. Having carefully developed his argument to show the authenticity of the Newtonian system, and upon this foundation the principles of natural religion, part VIII of the book was used to show that his foregoing inferences were 'the common *Voice of Nature and Reason*', and that this could be proved 'from the *Testimonies* of the most considerable Persons in all Ages'.[28] Which is to say, Whiston believed the intellectual systems of all the ancient philosophies could be reconciled with the scriptural (and Newtonian) account. In Whiston's argument, Scripture was true because everyone in the past (once confusion and errors had been removed) recorded identical accounts of the natural history of the world. After presenting over thirty-five pages of extracts from the Bible to illustrate this, Whiston proceeded to present similar 'Testimonies, from the ancient Heathen Writers'.[29] In the final part of the book, addressed 'especially to the *Scepticks* and *Unbelievers* of our Age', he noted Grotius and Stillingfleet as sources who showed how the 'Sacred Records' were 'evidently' supported by 'those most Ancient, Authentick, and Numerous books and Fragments'.[30] As well as written sources, these also included what we would now term archaeological records. Whiston attested that he believed the Jewish and Christian

---

[26] Stukeley, *Stonehenge*, 57.   [27] Lukis, *Family Memoirs*, i. 99–100.
[28] Whiston, *Astronomical Principles*, 156.   [29] Ibid. 194.
[30] Ibid. 271.

Revelations to be true 'because there have been generally such standing Memorials preserv'd of the Truth of the Principal Facts, as give us
great Assurances they were real. That this is a proper and usual way of
preserving the Memory of past Actions, the Customs, and Medals,
and Pillars, and Inscriptions, and Solemnities, and Sepulchral Monuments of all Nations, do Testify.'[31]

Whiston's evidence is exactly the type of material Stukeley spent
years examining, both in the field and in his library. Whiston's book
appears in Stukeley's library,[32] and it is clear that Stukeley believed he
could develop arguments such as this still further. Indeed, he effectively believed that 'archaeology' could be claimed to warrant the
status of science (more so even than his former profession of medicine, whose claims to being a science he sorely questioned). Stukeley
believed that history, like physics, was ultimately true at all times and
in all places. By the detailed examination of historical sources, the
truth of the past (which was, essentially, the truth of God's Word)
could be studied, unravelled, and exposed to view, countering the
views of atheists, deists, and heathens. Newton himself had effectively
done this when he had shown that the Ancients had both understood
the inverse-square rule of gravity and the heliocentric system—
arguments that the Oxford astronomer David Gregory read and
included in his *Elements of Astronomy, Physical and Geometrical*
(1715), where they were read in turn by Stukeley.[33] For Stukeley,
knowledge of antiquities and Scripture was important in what he
described as the present age 'when men of learning affect to throw off
the restraints of Religion, as they think them, supposing it tis not
capable of bearing the light & the truth, of demonstration & experiment; like mathematics & natural knowledge'.[34] For like mathematics
and natural history, archaeology and theology *could* be open
to scientific-type proofs. Advancing upon the earlier work of the

---

[31] Whiston, *Astronomical Principles*, 277.

[32] See Stuart Piggott (ed.), *Sale Catalogues of Libraries of Eminent Persons*, x.
Antiquaries (London: Mansell Information Publishing, 1974), 439.

[33] See J. E. McGuire and P. M. Rattansi, 'Newton and the "Pipes of Pan" ', *Notes
and Records of the Royal Society*, 21 (1966), 108–43, and Betty Jo Teeter Dobbs, *The
Janus Faces of Genius: The Role of Alchemy in Newton's Thought* (Cambridge: Cambridge University Press, 1991), 196.

[34] Corpus Christi College, Cambridge, MS 617 fo. 37.

Wiltshire antiquary John Aubrey, Stukeley declared 'Truth & reason is my aim.'[35] Yet like Bacon, Stukeley was also aware that his work was beyond the capacity of one man—hence, in part, his enthusiasm for founding societies such as the Antiquaries and the Brazen Nose, as well as his early involvement in Freemasonry in the 1720s. As he wrote, his researches were but 'pregnant materials' for 'future times ... to work upon, & when other of like nature shall be brought in competition therewith, & many monuments of a kind compar'd together [they shall] mutually explain each other'.[36]

One way in which Stukeley hoped to establish his antiquarianism on more scientific grounds was by the rigorous use of the Baconian tenets of measurement, collection, and comparison. Sir Francis Bacon was one of Stukeley's intellectual heroes—his first gift to the newly founded Society of Antiquaries in 1717 was a print of the great philosopher. In his researches into Celtic temples Stukeley was careful to examine and measure as many similar monuments in Britain as he could, and to gather information on those he heard of abroad. In this practice he was surely influenced by his earlier interest in natural history, when as a physic student he had collected plant samples around Cambridgeshire, armed with the botanical works of John Ray and Nehemiah Grew. Stukeley's argument that stone circles were the work of the Celtic Druids, and not the Romans, as the architect Inigo Jones had influentially argued, was thus founded on his detailed mensurations. He used these to establish the 'Druid's cubit', a unit of measurement that seemed to prove a common builder behind all stone circles, and akin to the modern (but controversial) archaeological theory of a 'megalithic yard'.[37]

When *Stonehenge* was finally published in 1740 Stukeley was told by his friend Samuel Gale that it had been 'well received' at the Society of Antiquaries, and 'it is agreed, if you can maintain the truth of your mensurations, the whole must be owned a demonstration'.[38] Roger Gale also wrote declaring: 'Without flattery I think it is a masterpiece, and that for the future no one will dare to dispute the

---

[35] Bodleian Library, MS Eng. misc. c. 323, fo. 37.

[36] Ibid. fo. 173.

[37] See Douglas Heggie, *Megalithic Science* (London: Thames & Hudson, 1981), ch. 3.

[38] Samuel Gale to Stukeley, 14 May 1740, in Lukis, *Family Memoirs*, i. 320.

true founders of that stupendous work.'[39] Like the rest of the Society, Gale considered Stukeley's measurements and his 'Druid's cubit' to be the linchpin of the argument, 'for that is the foundation of all your observations, & being once allowed, your whole superstructure is immoveable'.[40]

But there was a further way in which the study of antiquities could be claimed to have a scientific edge to it: archaeological sources were arguably free from error and corruption. 'Corruption' was a key word in understanding religious history; it was one of the principles upon which the whole Protestant Reformation had been based. As the Anglican Book of Common Prayer declares: 'There was never any thing by the wit of man so well devised, or so sure established, which in continuance of time had not been corrupted.'[41] Thus in the opinion of many theological scholars, that which was the most ancient, was the most true, as it predated corruption. This was perhaps the appeal of 'archaeological' evidence to Whiston. As Stukeley wrote, 'We rightly affirm, Truth is most antient, fable & fiction is new. When fabulous theology is antient, it shows true Religion is more antient.'[42] In comparison to Herodotus, say, the Scriptures were superior historical sources, for 'what Herodotus tells us, is but modern'.[43] In the conclusion to *Opticks*, Newton argued that as the ancients' religious practices had become corrupted, so had their understanding of true natural philosophy been lost. For Newton, the two processes were essentially synonymous.[44] This belief that the ancients had held great knowledge that was subsequently corrupted and lost, was firmly held by Stukeley. As he wrote, 'Science for the most part was carried to its height in old times: & innumerable discoverys & inventions, as we now account them, were formerly

---

[39] Roger Gale to Stukeley, 20 May 1740, ibid. iii. 274.

[40] Roger Gale to Stukeley, 11 December 1741, ibid. i. 329.

[41] 'Concerning the service of the church.'

[42] Fremasons Hall, London, MS 1130 Stu. (4), 'Observations on various matters, 1735', fo. 38.

[43] Freemasons Hall, London, MS 1130 Stu. (7), 'On Egyptian Antiquitys, 1742', fo. 2.

[44] See Isaac Newton, *Opticks: Or, A Treatise of the Reflections, Refractions, Inflections and Colours of Light*, 3rd edn. (London: printed for William and John Innys, 1721), 379. See also Frank E. Manuel, *The Religion of Isaac Newton* (Oxford: Clarendon, 1974), 43.

things well known, & afterwards lost.'[45] Newton was, for Stukeley, 'the Great Restorer of True Philosophy'.[46]

As Stukeley cleverly realized, archaeological remains, like mathematical formulae, were in essence (if not in practice) incorruptible. In his unpublished manuscript of 1732, 'Fasti Evangelici, or Chronological Commentarys of the Life & Actions of Jesus Christ', he wrote that ancient 'coyns, marbles, inscriptions of the Roman Fasti & the like unsuspected monuments' from the first century AD were 'of the utmost service' in detailing Jesus's life, for 'they prove the truth & credibility of a thing beyond any other'. These antiquarian objects overcame the many prejudices of early modern theological arguments because they were

taken from uncorrupted proofs coeval with the matter of fact, & made without any immediate regard to our history. they are witnesses without prejudice, not lyable to the errors & depravations of writings, to slips of the pen, to blunders of transcribers, errors of the press, or combinations of designing men. they are as publick & authentic records, which have preservd their curios form thro' the current of 1700 years, & why should we not teach their artful strokes to speak better things than their authors thought of. Providence seems to have directed them to be made at that time, being then in highest vogue & perfection of art, & buryed them of the most part in the earth, during the succeeding ages of barbarity & ignorance on purpose to restore them to light in these days of learning & curiosity, for this very use.[47]

It was in this way that Stukeley would use his researches at Avebury, which ran parallel to those at Stonehenge, and which were published in 1743. It was in this book, rather than the earlier one, that he would fulfil the promise he had made to Archbishop Wake prior to his ordination. Using physical, archaeological evidence, Stukeley aimed to prove the existence of the Holy Trinity, thus defeating Whiston's claim that Newton was an Arian, and claiming him for the Church of England, 'in faith & in practice'. By proving Stonehenge had been built by the Druids in about 460 BC, he could then easily show how Avebury was even older (the wear on the less-worked sarsen stones showed this), dating it to 1860 BC, about 2,200 years after the

---

[45] Freemasons Hall, MS 1130 Stu. (7), 'On Egyptian Antiquitys, 1742', fo. 1.

[46] Freemasons Hall, MS 1130 Stu (1), fo. 179.

[47] Corpus Christi College, Cambridge, MS 617, 'Fasti Evangelici, or Chronological Commentarys of the Life & Actions of Jesus Christ' (1732), fos. 25–7.

generally accepted date of the Creation of the Earth.[48] Then, by explaining how Avebury was a representation of the Celtic Druid's belief in the Holy Trinity, his evidence predated Athanasius's dictate by well over 2,000 years. The doctrine of the Trinity could thus *not* be considered to be a more modern corruption. It went right back to the earliest years after the Flood, when the sons of Noah had repopulated the Earth.

While the precise form of the argument with its reliance on archaeology seems quite original to Stukeley, it was again based on ideas that were common in early modern thought, reflecting a type of argument and research that Newton himself also used. Newton believed that there had been one original religion, passed directly by God to Adam. This had gradually been corrupted, until God had sent the Flood to wipe out mankind. Only Noah and his children had survived, and they carried with them the true religion of Adam. This in time and in its turn was corrupted; Moses had wrought a return to the true path, as had Jesus in his turn. The Protestant Reformation had paved the way for the next and final Revelation.

Thus in *The Chronology of Ancient Kingdoms Amended* Newton stated that the religion of Moses and the prophets was based on 'The precepts of the sons of Noah, which was the primitive religion of both Jews and Christians'.[49] In other unpublished manuscripts he describes Noah's faith as 'The religion of loving God and our neighbour', and suggested that this ethical system was subsequently taught to 'the heathens by Socrates, Confucius and other philosophers, the Israelites by Moses and the Prophets and the Christians more fully by Christ and his Apostles'.[50] The evidence of ancient temples seemed to show to Newton the vestiges of the ancient truth, corrupted by the

---

[48] In *The Annals of the World* (London: printed by E. Tyler, for J. Crook, 1658), James Ussher computed that Creation had occurred in 4004 BC. This exact date, though disputed, was given official Anglican sanction and was included in the Authorized Version of the Bible from 1701.

[49] Isaac Newton, *The Chronology of Ancient Kingdoms Amended. To Which is Prefix'd, A Short Chronicle from the First Memory of Things in Europe, to the Conquest of Persia by Alexander the Great* (London: printed for J. Tonson, and J. Osborn and T. Longman, 1728).

[50] Newton in the unpublished MS 'Irenicum', quoted in H. McLachlan (ed.), *Sir Isaac Newton: Theological Manuscripts* (Liverpool: Liverpool University Press, 1950), 28, and Newton in the unpublished manuscript 'A Short Scheme of the True Religion', quoted ibid. 52.

pagan priests. Newton's interest in ancient temples thus extended as far afield as Ireland, Egypt, China, India, and Scandinavia, as well as England and Stonehenge.[51]

Yet in his hostility to the antiquity of the doctrine of the Trinity, Newton was taking a position in opposition to that of other prominent Dutch and English writers of the mid- to late seventeenth century. Vossius and Grotius had made detailed studies of pagan religious practices, and claimed to show how they all had their origins in Judaeo-Christian belief. Newton's Cambridge colleagues Ralph Cudworth and Henry More both defended the antiquity of the Trinity. Cudworth's reading of the ancient sources indicated to him that trinitarian theology could be found in Orpheus, Pythagoras, and Plato, and in the arcane theology of the Egyptians, Persians, and Romans.[52]

Nevertheless, there was growing opposition in Newton's day to the authenticity of Trinitarianism. In 1690 in *Vindication of the Unitarians* the Oxford-educated lawyer William Freke had defined the Trinity as 'the stumbling block in Christianity'.[53] Similarly in 1695 the Cambridge-educated theologian Stephen Nye—who had already claimed that Socinianism (an antitrinitarian heresy similar to Arianism) was the heir to pristine monotheistic Christianity—argued in a counter-argument to Cudworth that trinitarian Christianity could claim to have *no* ancient tradition. It was, rather, made up of

---

[51] Newton, Jewish and National University Library, Israel, Yahuda MS 41, fos. 3r–v.

[52] Ralph Cudworth, *The True Intellectual System of the Universe* (London: printed for Richard Royston, 1678), ii. 312; see Peter Harrison *'Religion' and the Religions in the English Enlightenment* (Cambridge: Cambridge University Press, 1990), 33. Theophilus Gale, *The Court of the Gentiles: Or, A Discourse Touching the Original of Human Literature, both Philologie and Philosophie, from the Scriptures and Jewish Church ... Part I* (Oxford, 1669), 346; Henry More, *Conjectura Cabbalistica* (1662) 'Preface', 1, quoted in Iliffe, ' "The Idols of the Temple" ', 30. Gerard Vossius, *De Theologia Gentili et Physiologia Christiana* (1641); see Force and Popkin, *Isaac Newton's Theology* (1990), 10; Grotius, *The Truth of the Christian Religion* (1711), 'Translator's Preface'; John Gascoigne, 'The Wisdom of the Egyptians and the Secularisation of History in the Age of Newton', in Stephen Gaukroger (ed.), *The Uses of Antiquity: The Scientific Revolution and the Classical Tradition* (Dordrecht: Kluwer Academic, 1991), 171–212, 190.

[53] Justin Champion, *The Pillars of Priestcraft Shaken: The Church of England and its Enemies, 1660–1730* (Cambridge: Cambridge University Press, 1992), 109.

'Novelties, corruptions, and depravities of genuine Christianity'.[54] This controversy was largely silenced by the terms of the Blasphemy Act of 1697, but the trinitarian question re-emerged in the second decade of the eighteenth century when Clarke and Whiston both publicly expounded and published antitrinitarian opinions they had learnt from Newton.[55]

In *Abury: A Temple of the British Druids* Stukeley effectively, if not explicitly, offered his services in claiming an orthodox Newton for the Anglican Church. His study of Celtic temples and idolatry in the 1720s had led him to the conclusion that an apparent Druidic knowledge of the Trinity proved Trinitarianism had patriarchal authenticity, and hence pre-existed Athanasius's dictate. His archaeology 'proved' the speculations of Gale, Cudworth, and More. And by proving that Arianism did not—indeed, *could not*—exist, and that the truth and antiquity of the Trinity could be substantiated archaeologically, Stukeley could save his hero Newton from what he considered unfounded accusations of heterodoxy. The same argument would also indicate that a belief in the Trinity was not something necessarily 'beyond reason', a challenge that the deist writer Anthony Collins had levelled against the doctrine in 1707.[56] It was this that Stukeley had specifically claimed to be able to contradict in his 1729 letter to Wake, when he had observed of the Trinity, 'I can prove it to be so far from contrary to, or above, human reason, that 'tis deducible from reason itself.'[57]

Stukeley spent some two decades writing and rewriting his field notes and undertaking his bibliographical researches before their publication in the early 1740s. His reading was wide-ranging, and

---

[54] Stephen Nye, *Letter of Resolution Concerning the Doctrines of the Trinity and Incarnation* (1695), quoted in Champion, *Pillars of Priestcraft* (1992), 109–10. See Martin Greig, 'The Reasonableness of Christianity? Gilbert Burnet and the Trinitarian Controversy of the 1690s', *Journal of Ecclesiastical History*, 44 (1993), 631–51.

[55] See Eamon Duffy, ' "Whiston's Affair": The Trials of a Primitive Christian', *Journal of Ecclesiastical History*, 27 (1976), 129–50; Force, *William Whiston*; Larry Stewart, 'Samuel Clarke, Newtonianism, and the Factions of Post-Revolutionary England', *Journal of the History of Ideas*, 42 (1981), 53–72; see also Thomas Pfizenmaier, 'Was Isaac Newton an Arian?', *Journal of the History of Ideas*, 58 (1997), 57–80.

[56] In his *Essay Concerning the Use of Reason in Propositions*. See Hening Graf Reventlow, *The Authority of the Bible and the Rise of the Modern World* (London: SCM, 1984), 355–6.

[57] Stukeley to Wake, 3 June 1729, in Stukeley, *The Commentarys*, 141–2.

embraced classical authors as well as works by historians, theologians, natural philosophers, and travel writers of the seventeenth and early eighteenth centuries. These included such controversialists as the deist Edward Herbert and the pantheist John Toland, whose *Critical History of the Celtic Religion and Learning* was published posthumously in 1726, as well as the antitrinitarians Clarke and Whiston. He made an early attempt at incorporating the Trinity into his Avebury notes in an unpublished essay written at Stamford in 1732–4, titled 'Disquisitio de Deo. Or an Enquiry into the Nature of the DEITY.'[58] There he observed that 'All nations had a notion, no doubt, deriv'd from the Patriarchs, that the nature of the deity subsisted in a plurality of persons,' and proposed to show that 'The knowledg of the divine Trinity is not contrary to, nor above human reason: but discoverable from it & agreable to it.'[59] However, his defence of the reasonableness of the Trinity went only so far. Though he wrote: 'I believe it is possible for the human mind, of its own strength, to reach the knowledge of this great truth,' he hesitated, and added the codicil that it was only the discerning, gifted individual for whom the Trinity was discernible by reason. For the mass of mankind, trinitarian knowledge depended upon direct revelation. Only 'studious, reasoning, philosophical men, such as Pythagoras, Socrates, Zoroaster, Plato & the like' had had the strength of mind to reach the trinitarian truth, which had at first been imparted 'by direct revelation: & was at first spred over the whole globe with mankind itself'. It was a mistake of 'the learned, to say they had it from the jews. it was of much earlier date ... the heathen were acquainted with this plurality of persons in the deity either from the patriarchs of Abrahams family or earlier [from Noah]'. Thus this 'knowledg of the Trinity, I look upon to be of a mixt nature, partly from reason, partly from revelation'.[60] That the ancients had a notion of the Messiah was clear from their writings, particularly those of Plato, and for proof of this, 'we need goe no further than our own island' and the Druids' temple at Avebury, 'which fully shows ... that the Druids worshipt the true God, & that their idea's of religion were truly grand, sublime,

---

[58] Bodleian Library, MS Eng. misc. e. 650.
[59] Ibid. fo. iv, v.   [60] Ibid. fos. 6–8.

magnificent'.[61] This patriarchal notion being 'abusd brought up idolatry. to cure which the Mosaic System was introducd, both to be done away with by the light of truth in Christianity'.[62]

Like many of Stukeley's unpublished essays, the arguments in 'Disquisitio de Deo' are not always clear-cut, and are often circular and repetitive. But the manuscript illustrates the way in which he attempted to incorporate all his learning and knowledge into his written work, and the extent to which Avebury was an integral part of this argument. References and allusions were made to the works of Plato, Strabo, the Bible, and Stillingfleet, and refutations made of Clarke on the Trinity. Indeed, whilst Clarke is mentioned, Toland is not referred to, suggesting that Stukeley was aligning himself against the Arian Newtonians, and not 'priestcraft'. A note on the final page of the essay lists Stukeley's own trinity of influences: Cudworth, Kircher, and Andrew Ramsay. The last was a Scotsman who converted to Catholicism and spent most of his life in France, and studied mathematics under Newton's friend Fatio de Duillier in 1708. On a visit to England in 1729 he was made a fellow of the Royal Society, bringing with him his novel, *The Travels of Cyrus* (1729), a popular work influenced by Cudworth's *True Intellectual System*. In Ramsay's book the traveller Cyrus meets various ancient pagan philosophers whom, he discovers, all teach the same esoteric religious truths, including that of the Trinity, which they expressed symbolically in their religious rites.[63] In *Abury* Stukeley described Ramsay as one who had 'very laudably pursued the same track' in proposing that 'the ancients knew somewhat of the mysterious nature of the deity, subsisting in distinct personalities, which is more fully revealed to us in the christian dispensation'.[64] Yet Ramsay subsequently appeared in John Leland's *A View of the Principal Deistical Writers* (1754–56), which described him as a 'late ingenious author' who had 'endeavoured at large to show that some vestiges of the doctrines of the Trinity are to be found among the sages of all

[61] Bodleian Library, MS Eng. misc. e. 650, fo. iii. Bodleian Library MS Eng. misc. e. 554 also contains drafts of a number of sermons by Stukeley also on the subject of the Trinity and its antiquity. fos. 25–6. [62] Ibid. fo. 3v.

[63] See D. P. Walker, *The Ancient Theology: Studies in Christian Platonism from the Fifteenth to the Eighteenth Centuries* (London: Duckworth, 1972), 231–49.

[64] Stukeley, *Abury*, 6.

nations, times and religions'.[65] As the case of Ramsey—and as we saw earlier, Whiston—clearly shows, the relationship between the deist author and the 'orthodox' Christian was both paradoxical and potentially suspect.

In essence, Stukeley's argument at Avebury was that the stone circles and avenues had, when originally built by the Celtic Druids, represented a hieroglyph of a winged serpent passing through a circle. As Stukeley explained it, the snake was a representation of the Messiah, as 'All writers *jewish* and *christian* with one mouth assert'. The snake's practice of shedding its skin 'and returning to youth again' made it 'A fit emblem of [Christ's] resurrection from the dead, and of returning to an immortal life.'[66] The circle 'in hieroglyphs means, divine',[67] and was a clear symbol for God who, as described in the supposedly ancient texts of Hermes Trismegistus, was 'without beginning & ending whose center is every where & circumference no where'.[68] The 'wings'—the final part of the trinity which, Stukeley explained, were not actually physically portrayed at Avebury because of the difficulty of illustrating them in stones—represented the Holy Spirit, 'the moving & penetrative person of power of the deity'.[69] He claimed that although knowledge of hieroglyphs 'depends much on a knowledg of the Egyptian Philosophy and Theology' this was not a problem, 'because tis not materially different from what we have at this day. as nature is the same[,] true philosophy must beso [*sic*] too thro' all ages'. As he interpreted it,

the ancients, probably even from Adam's time, express'd in writing, the great idea of the deity ... [by] a circle with wings, and a snake proceeding from it. A figure excellently well design'd to picture out the intelligence they had, no doubt, by divine communication, of the mysterious nature of the deity ... By this means they produc'd a most effective prophylact ... which could not fail of drawing down the blessings of divine providence upon that place and country ...[70]

---

[65] See Alexander Ramsay, *The Philosophical Principles of Natural and Revealed Religion: Unfolded in a Geometrical Order* (2 vols.; Glasgow: printed and sold by Robert Foulis, 1748–9); John Leland, *A View of the Principal Deistical Writers that have Appeared in England in the Last and Present Century; With Observations upon them*, 2nd edn. (2 vols.; London: printed for B. Dod, 1755), ii. 600–1.

[66] Stukeley, *Abury*, 59–61.   [67] Ibid. 62.

[68] Stukeley, Bodleian Library, MS Eng. misc. c. 323, fo. 132.

[69] Ibid. fo. 230.   [70] Stukeley, *Abury*, 9.

Stukeley saw a precedence for such a symbolic structure: as Christian churches and cathedrals had been designed upon the shape of 'our saviour's body extended on the cross', so in ancient times 'they form'd them upon the geometrical figures or pictures, or manner of writing, by which they express'd the deity, and the mystical nature thereof.'[71] The 'symbol of the snake and circle' was 'the picture of the temple of *Abury*'.[72] It had been taken by the Egyptians together with 'hieroglyphic writing in general, from the common ancestors of mankind. This is sufficiently prov'd from the universality of the thing, reaching from *China* in the east, to *Britain* in the west, nay, and into *America* too.'[73]

Stukeley's belief that his Baconian-based antiquarians studies could, ultimately, transcend the corruption of texts was, of course, clearly flawed. There is much invention and hypothesis in his argument for the 'serpent-temple' at Avebury. But his interpretation, based as it was on extensive fieldwork at a time when many of the stones were being steadily destroyed for building materials, was to prove highly influential through the later eighteenth and nineteenth centuries, and it was taken by some of his readers as a defence of the antiquity of the doctrine of the Trinity. In the summer following the publication of *Abury* the Quaker physician John Fothergill visited Bath. As he told a friend, along the way 'I just took a transient view of the remains of the celebrated ancient temple at Avebury on Marlborough Downs, which, if it was what Dr Stukeley says it was, has been a most astonishing performance, and by what appears it seems not unlikely.'[74] The most interesting response, however, came from Roger Gale. He told Stukeley:

I have read over your Abury very carefully, & with great pleasure, having mett with the greatest satisfaction, I may allmost say demonstration, in it, that a subject of that nature is capable of receiving, either as to the architectonical or theological part. I little thought Dr. Tindal would have such a second to prove Christianity as old as the creation, though upon a different bottome and principles ...[75]

---

[71] Stukeley, *Abury*, 8.   [72] Ibid. 56.   [73] Ibid.

[74] Fothergill to Robert Key, London, 6 August 1744, in Christopher C. Booth and Betsy C. Corner (eds.), *Chain of Friendship: Selected Letters of Dr John Fothergill of London, 1735–1780* (London: Oxford University Press, 1971), 94–5.

[75] Gale to Stukeley, 20 May 1743, in Lukis, *Family Memoirs*, i. 359.

Stukeley's response to this statement is unknown, but he might have been surprised by the direct comparison with Matthew Tindal.[76] Tindal was a doctor in law and Fellow of All Souls' College, Oxford, and for a time he was one of the most notorious deists in England. The cause of his repute was the publication in 1730 of *Christianity as Old as the Creation: Or, The Gospel a Republication of the Religion of Nature.* Calling himself a 'Christian deist', Tindal aimed to show that natural religion 'differs not from Reveal'd, but in the Manner of its being communicated: The One being the Internal, as the Other the External Revelation of the same Unchangeable Will of a Being, who is alike at all Times infinitely Wise and Good'.[77] In the first pages of his book Tindal expressed the view that had been expressed over a hundred years earlier by Herbert of Cherbury—and it *is* essentially the same as Stukeley's thesis—that if Christianity was the 'Only True, and Absolutely Perfect Religion' (and what good Christian could disagree with that?) then

it follows, That the *Christian* Religion has existed from the Beginning; and that God, both *Then*, and *Ever Since*, has continu'd to give all Mankind sufficient Means to know It; and that 'tis their Duty to know, believe, profess and practice It; so that Christianity, tho' the Name is of a later Date, must be as old, and as extensive, as humane Nature; and as the Law of our Creation, must have been Then implanted in us by God himself.[78]

Tindal had carried the arguments of such pious and orthodox seventeenth-century scholars as Grotius and Stillingfleet to their natural conclusion. If God was good (a *sine qua non* of orthodox belief) then how could he have committed the thousands of souls born before Christ to eternal damnation? The answer would appear to be that a knowledge of Christ and Christianity had been an original part of human knowledge.

---

[76] One of the only times Stukeley mentions contemporary deists by name in his surviving correspondence is his advice in a letter of 1734 to an old school friend, the Revd Ambrose Pimlow, not to add his name 'to the number of those clergymen whose ingratitude to their patrons has done infinitely more mischief to religion than Tind[all] or [Anthony] Coll[ins].' Lukis, *Family Memoirs*, i. 274.

[77] Matthew Tindal, *Christianity as Old as the Creation: Or, The Gospel a Republication of the Religion of Nature* (London, 1730), 3.

[78] Ibid. 4.

Though there were numerous published refutations of Tindal's claim, if one followed the argument traced by Newton, Stukeley, and other contemporary writers that there had once been a worldwide *über*-religion, then one was drawn inevitably to the question of what role revelation had ever played. Even Stukeley came to the conclusion that certain 'studious, reasoning, philosophical men' had reached a knowledge of the Trinity without revelation. And the price of Stukeley's defence of the Trinity was a tacit 'accusation'—by a friend no less—of deism. It seems a harsh return for so many years of research aimed at exactly the opposite. Yet it is clear that in his attempts to defend both revealed religion and Newtonian natural philosophy, Stukeley sailed close to the ever-cloudier waters of eighteenth-century heterodoxy. He may have 'proved' the Trinity on archaeological grounds, he may even have 'claimed' Newton for the Church of England, but that Church which he conceived of was so broad that there must have been few believers it could ever have excluded. (And whatever the nature of his heterodoxy, Newton *was* a believer.) As such, Stukeley was an early example of the failure of the theologians to meet the challenges thrown up by advances in science. Yet in so doing—and at the same time—he did much to help found a new science, archaeology.

12

Joining Natural Philosophy to Christianity: The Case of Joseph Priestley

John Brooke

In his memoirs Joseph Priestley recalled that, from an early age, he had been 'much distressed' that he 'could not feel a proper repentance for the sin of Adam; taking it for granted that, without *this*, it could not be forgiven me'.[1] His deviation from orthodoxy was to extend in many directions during his life, but he was never to forget his mortification at being denied communion in the congregation he had always attended. The elders of the Independent Chapel at Heckmondwike in the West Riding of Yorkshire 'refused me, because, when they interrogated me on the subject of the *sin of Adam*, I appeared not to be quite orthodox'.[2] He could not think that the entire human race was liable to the wrath of God and the eternal pains of hell on account of that sin only.

Heterodoxy was a word that Priestley owned. At the Dissenting Academy in Daventry where he studied from 1752 to 1755, the style of theological disputation reflected the educational principles of Isaac Watts and Philip Doddridge. Both sides of a theological argument were represented in debate: Dr Ashworth, Priestley recalled, had taken the orthodox side of every question and Mr Clark, the sub-tutor, 'that of heresy, though always with the greatest modesty'.[3] Having been exposed to the pride of those who were sure that they, at least, were among the elect, Priestley was to be peculiarly susceptible

---

[1] Joseph Priestley, *Memoirs of Dr. Joseph Priestley* (London: Allenson, 1904), 7.
[2] Ibid.   [3] Ibid. 11.

to a modest heretic. He tells us that he 'saw reason to embrace what is generally called the heterodox side of almost every question'.[4]

Priestley will be best known to many as the discoverer of oxygen, even though his view of the gas was very different from that of Lavoisier who gave it its name. Priestley called it 'dephlogisticated air' because he believed its ability to support combustion derived from its propensity to absorb the phlogiston emitted from metals when they burned. Lavoisier's name for the gas reflected his belief that it was an acid producer—an essential component of all acids. Though neither theory survived, Lavoisier's name of oxygen endured. Not that Priestley himself has been forgotten. In the celebrations of 2004, marking the bicentenary of his death, his commitment to the utility of the sciences could not possibly be overlooked. He makes an irresistible test case for exploring the relations between science and religious heterodoxy. Connections have often been made in the literature, a recent commentator observing that, for Priestley, 'social progress is in part modelled on scientific progress' and both scientific knowledge and social improvement flourish best where there is free exchange of ideas.[5] The greatest barrier to social progress was state-imposed uniformity, whether the uniformity was religious, intellectual, or economic.

But there was more to it than that because, in Priestley's enthusiastic vision, scientific progress was not merely a model but a vehicle for social and religious reform. In a well-known passage he predicted 'this rapid progress of knowledge ... will, I doubt not, be the means under God of extirpating all error and prejudice, and of putting an end to all undue and usurped authority in the business of religion as well as of science'.[6] The reformation he sought included the abolition of Test and Corporation Acts under which dissenters were disadvantaged. He himself was never short of grievances: having to pay tithes to a church he had rejected was one. But he never admitted to being a

---

[4] Cited by Robert E. Schofield, *The Enlightenment of Joseph Priestley: A Study of his Life and Work from 1733 to 1773* (University Park: Pennsylvania State University Press, 1997), 51.

[5] Alan Tapper, 'Priestley on Politics, Progress and Moral Theology', in Knud Haakonssen (ed.), *Enlightenment and Religion: Rational Dissent in Eighteenth-Century Britain* (Cambridge: Cambridge University Press, 1996), 272–86, at 275.

[6] Cited by John G. McEvoy and J. E. McGuire, 'God and Nature: Priestley's Way of Rational Dissent', *Historical Studies in the Physical Sciences*, 6 (1975), 325–404, at 380.

political agitator. As he prepared to leave England for America, he was still avowing 'I never preached a political sermon in my life, unless such as, I believe, all Dissenters usually preach on the fifth of November, in favour of civil and religious liberty, may be said to be political.'[7] Priestley's reformation required a reformation of the mind. This could only be achieved through the ministry of the written word. His favourite parable was the parable of the sower, and he probably sowed more words than any other reformer of the eighteenth century. In his word-spinning, reference to the sciences played a strategic role: 'In nature we see no bounds to our inquiries. One discovery always gives hints of many more, and brings us into a wider field of speculation. Now why should this not be, in some measure, the case with respect to knowledge of a moral and religious kind?'[8] Believing that 'learned Unitarians increase, while learned Trinitarians decrease', he saw a direct parallel with the spread of Newton's science towards universal acceptance.[9]

For a historian of chemistry with interests in the relations between 'science' and 'religion' Priestley is alluring. When I first began to study him some twenty years ago he provoked the longest sentence of my writing career. I reproduce it here because it still explains why many find him so fascinating:

What is one to make of a man who proclaimed himself a Christian and denied the divinity of Christ; an apologist who considered this the best of all possible worlds and yet one which could be improved; a theist who denied that God could act directly on the human mind and yet who insisted that his God was more in control of human affairs than the God of religious orthodoxy; a Scriptural exegete who accepted the reality of certain biblical miracles as part of an argument to show that miracles did not occur; a philosophical determinist who believed that a denial of the autonomy of the human will made human beings more, not less, responsible for their actions; an advocate of toleration for Roman Catholics, whilst denouncing Catholic religion as 'properly anti-Christian' and a 'system of abomination little

[7] Joseph Priestley, *The Present State of Europe Compared with Antient Prophecies: A Sermon Preached at the Gravel Pit Meeting in Hackney on 28 February 1894* (London, 1994), Preface, xi.

[8] Joseph Priestley, *The Importance and Extent of Free Inquiry in Matters of Religion* (London: J. Johnson, 1785), 7.

[9] Joseph Priestley, *Reflections on the Present State of Free Inquiry in this Country* (Birmingham: J. Johnson, 1785), 51–9.

better than heathenism'; a materialist who did not believe in matter, certainly not solid matter as usually understood; an empiricist who, having discovered oxygen, not only considered it a compound, but supplied Lavoisier with an important clue for establishing it as an element; and overriding all, a radical in politics and religion, and yet so conservative in his chemical theory that he was left picking nits in the new French system?[10]

A closer look at Priestley's *science* would reveal numerous facets, most reflecting the importance he attached to simple experiments and the scientific instruments that made them possible.[11] We see this in his manipulation and identification of distinct gaseous species; for example his production of oxygen by heating what Lavoisier would call the oxide of mercury. In his defence of phlogiston as a principle of metallicity and combustibility, Priestley appealed to the simple fact that hydrogen (supposedly rich in phlogiston) when passed over red lead gave rise to the metal. He experimented with several gases, including those we call sulphur dioxide, ammonia, nitrous oxide, and nitrogen dioxide. A Leeds brewery was his laboratory for early experiments with 'fixed air', our carbon dioxide.[12] His experiments promised utility with a commercial twist: he had hopes that oxygen might be sold as a fashionable luxury item, that water infused with 'fixed air' might become a saleable cure for scurvy.

A member of the Lunar Society of Birmingham, Priestley saw that chemical analysis could have commercial value. The analysis of clays would provide assistance for Josiah Wedgwood's pottery.[13] A science popularizer as well as practitioner, Priestley enjoyed success with his *History of Electricity* (1767), though rather less with a subsequent history of optics.[14] Priestley's science was communicated as a form of

---

[10] John H. Brooke, ' "A Sower went Forth": Joseph Priestley and the Ministry of Reform', in A. Truman Schwartz and John G. McEvoy (eds.), *Motion Toward Perfection: The Achievement of Joseph Priestley* (Boston: Skinner House, 1990), 21–56, esp. 23–4.

[11] John R. Christie, 'Joseph Priestley: Science, Religion and Politics in the Age of Revolution', in R. Porter (ed.), *Man Masters Nature* (London: BBC, 1987), 88–100, 92.

[12] Ibid. 94.

[13] Jan Golinski, *Science as Public Culture: Chemistry and Enlightenment in Britain, 1760–1820* (Cambridge: Cambridge University Press, 1992), 65–8.

[14] Joseph Priestley, *The History and Present State of Electricity, With Original Experiments* (London: J. Dodsley, 1767); and *The History and Present State of Discoveries Relating to Vision, Light and Colours* (2 vols.; London: J. Johnson, 1772).

science most could perform: no special genius was required.[15] As with his theology, it was egalitarian. He described and prescribed experiments that could be performed at home. Jan Golinksi has observed that Priestley's distaste for the chemical system of Lavoisier was associated with an aversion to imperious theorizing and to the expensive apparatus that the Frenchman had at his disposal.[16] Such privilege took science out of the public domain.

To stress Priestley's empiricism is not to say that he had no developed theory of matter. He eventually favoured a model in which the properties of matter all stemmed from the interplay of attractive and repulsive forces. The solidity of an atom could not be a primary quality because there would always be the ulterior question: why did its parts cohere? Priestley's ontology of forces resembled that of the Jesuit natural philosopher Roger Boscovich, who was duly outraged when Priestley used it to eradicate the category of spirit from the world.[17]

A closer look at Priestley's *theology* would reveal that this, not science, was his primary interest, both chronologically and in terms of his identity as a dissenting minister. His private correspondence discloses a higher value placed on the identity and purification of Christianity than on the identity and purification of gases.[18] During his career Priestley was minister to five dissenting congregations, including one of the most opulent in England—Birmingham's 'New Meeting'.[19] What did he preach? Two principles above all. One was the liberty of religious expression, hence his involvement in setting up the first avowedly Unitarian Chapel under the charge of Theophilus Lindsey. The other was a doctrine of the free mercy of God to all who were penitent. Just that. There were no complications stemming from the supposed wrath of God or from a theology of atonement. Priestley happily proclaimed the message that God's intention was that all should be happy.

---

[15] John G. McEvoy, 'Electricity, Knowledge and the Nature of Progress in Priestley's Thought', *British Journal for the History of Science*, 12 (1979), 1–30.

[16] Golinski, *Science as Public Culture*, 83–7.

[17] A. Truman Schwartz, 'Priestley's Materialism: The Consistent Connection', in Schwartz and McEvoy, *Motion Toward Perfection*, 109–27, 120.

[18] See e.g. his letters to M. Van Marum in Robert E. Schofield, *A Scientific Autobiography of Joseph Priestley (1733–1804); Selected Scientific Correspondence Edited with Commentary* (Cambridge Mass.: MIT, 1966), 246 and 251.

[19] Schofield, *Enlightenment of Joseph Priestley*, 274.

A closer look at the connections *between* his scientific and religious ideas leads us straight into the questions that have provided the rationale for this book. Might heterodoxy in religion predispose one towards an interest in the sciences, perhaps even to heterodoxy as a scientific thinker? Conversely, might a commitment to the sciences lead to, or at least correlate with, heterodoxy in religion?

Rich and illuminating answers have been given in preceding chapters. We should, however, note the difficulty that can arise in deciding whether a piece of scientific work should be described as heterodox. Examples of deviation from established paradigms should not be difficult to chart; but, accepting for the moment Thomas Kuhn's term, there is an immediate problem at times of paradigm change. Interestingly, Priestley was used by Kuhn to support his thesis of incommensurability between competing paradigms and the complementary thesis that observations are theory-laden.[20] Both Priestley and Lavoisier looked at the same gas, but what they saw was different. Where Priestley saw dephlogisticated air, Lavoiser saw oxygen. But what is an 'orthodox' view if one is living through a chemical revolution and contributing to it, as Priestley did? With whom is the comparison to be drawn? To add to the difficulty, Priestley could be conservative, in that he defended phlogiston, and yet be radical in advancing a concept of matter that presaged the dynamical theories of Humphry Davy and Michael Faraday. Is it not then tempting to present Priestley as a spectacular counter-example to a supposed correlation between heterodoxies in science and religion: ultra-radical in religion, ultra-reactionary in chemistry? Tempting but not ultimately persuasive. As John McEvoy has insisted, it is incorrect to see him as a dogmatic champion of phlogiston. During the course of his controversy with Lavoisier, Priestley began to exploit the more subtle position that neither of the competing theories was ultimately demonstrable; both went beyond an empiricist analysis of material substances.[21] Moreover, as Simon Schaffer has indicated, there were

---

[20] Thomas S. Kuhn, *The Structure of Scientific Revolutions* (Chicago: University of Chicago Press, 1962).

[21] John G. McEvoy, 'Causes and Laws, Powers and Principles: The Metaphysical Foundations of Priestley's Concept of Phlogiston', in Robert Anderson and Christopher Lawrence (eds.), *Science, Medicine and Dissent: Joseph Priestley (1733–1804)* (London: Wellcome Trust/Science Museum, 1987), 55–71, 66.

at least two respects in which Priestley *was* radical in his scientific outlook.[22] He deviated from a tradition of popular lecturing in which the powers of nature, such as electricity, were routinely exhibited and manipulated as God's powers, but in displays that seemed to show the transfer of power from God to the experimental philosopher. By contrast, the duty of the lecturer or teacher, according to Priestley, was to display the rationality of God's creation. It was the interconnections and mutual adaptations of the powers of nature, not the powers themselves, which bore witness to the divine plan.

The second element of Priestley's radicalism, according to Schaffer, follows from this. His scientific outlook was one in which the natural world, embracing the human, was understood and celebrated as a *system*. Interpreting nature as an interlocking system conferred significance on scientific facts. As Priestley himself put it when discussing plant respiration, seemingly trivial observations could acquire 'the greatest dignity and importance; serving to explain some of the most striking phenomena in nature, respecting the general plan and constitution of the system, and the relation that one part of it bears to another'.[23] In this respect his theology was not an excrescence, for the system of nature had been devised as a self-replenishing system designed to sustain human life and to promote human happiness.

Although there may be problems in using the term heterodoxy in a scientific context, in Priestley's case they are not so pronounced on the religious front. His systematic rejection of Calvinism structured an emancipation that led to the very apotheosis of heterodoxy. Priestley himself repeatedly constructed an antithesis between what he called the 'orthodox system' and his 'rational system'. When he spoke of a 'dark hole' in the universe he was referring to the Calvinism with which he had grown up and struggled.[24] When he appealed to the 'serious and candid professors of Christianity' he identified five 'orthodox' doctrines that he believed were insupportable. These were that the unregenerate had no power to do God's will; that all humans were born into original sin through the sin of

[22] Simon Schaffer, 'Priestley and the Politics of Spirit', in Anderson and Lawrence, *Science Medicine and Dissent*, 39–53.

[23] F. W. Gibbs, *Joseph Priestley: Adventurer in Science and Champion of Truth* (London: Nelson, 1965), 123–4.

[24] Schofield, *Enlightenment of Joseph Priestley*, 14.

Adam; that only a predetermined elect would enjoy salvation; that Christ was fully divine; and that through his sacrificial death he had made atonement for human depravity.[25]

Priestley's 'rational' system could sound very rational. The forgiveness of a penitent brother, enjoined by Christ, would scarcely deserve the name of forgiveness if one insisted on any atonement. To expect a person to repent of the sin of Adam, or to feel anything like remorse for it, was blatantly unreasonable when, in Priestley's words 'he cannot but know that he never gave his consent to it'. High seriousness and an earnest morality underpinned Priestley's critique. Since the gospel was concerned with the reformation of character there was no room in his rational system for any doctrine that promised sudden acceptance with God. Deathbed conversions were simply not on. 'Some, indeed, are said to have been called at the *eleventh* hour', he noted, 'but none at the *twelfth*.'[26]

It is therefore an easy matter to delineate his heterodoxy with respect to Calvinism because he provided the necessary comparisons himself. And since many dissenters were themselves Calvinists, it was within his own circle that his heterodoxy was most harshly judged. Fiercely dissenting from orthodox dissent he attracted the question 'in the name of common sense, and rational religion what have the orthodox dissenters done to the Rev. Dr. Priestley, that he should set them forth in such a disagreeable point of view?'[27] Another measure of Priestley's heterodoxy was the scope he wished to give to religious toleration. His contention that even Roman Catholics should enjoy toleration worried fellow dissenters who feared that so accommodating a line would provoke reactions that could only jeopardize their own case for relief.[28]

Even when compared with other Unitarians, Priestley stands out as idiosyncratic. In his *Disquisitions Relating to Matter and Spirit* (1777), he rejected all conventional duality between body and soul,

---

[25] Joseph Priestley, *An Appeal to the Serious and Candid Professors of Christianity* (London: J. Johnson, 1772).

[26] Ibid. 5–11 and 18–21.

[27] John Macgowan, *Familiar Epistles to Rev. Dr. Priestley* (London: J. Johnson, 1771), 12.

[28] Martin Fitzpatrick, 'Joseph Priestley and the Cause of Universal Toleration', *The Price-Priestley Newsletter*, 1 (1977).

matter and spirit. He could do so because he invested matter with properties and propensities that had been ascribed to spirit. One consequence was a chemical account of the Resurrection: 'Death, with its concomitant putrefaction and dispersion of parts, is only a *decomposition*; whatever is decomposed, may be *recomposed* by the being who first composed it; and I doubt not but that, in the proper sense of the word, the same body that dies shall rise again.'[29] Such a view of the matter invited a predictable objection. Suppose some poor unfortunate were to drown in the Thames, to be eaten by eels, which in their turn were to grace a table:

> Poor Thomas in the Thames was drown'd
> And though long sought could not be found . . .
> At the last trumpet's solemn sound,
> How mangled will poor Tom be found![30]

Because Priestley's matter, constituted by attractive and repulsive forces, differed from conventional matter or spirit, he considered that it might as well be called spirit as matter. As I have indicated elsewhere, he would have agreed with the remark of a later materialist, John Tyndall, who, after rebuking the philosophers who had made it solid, impenetrable, and inert, complained that matter had been much maligned.[31] Priestley's contemporaries were for the most part mystified. A kindred spirit, Richard Price, repeatedly asked 'What is it that attracts and repels, and that is attracted and repelled?'[32] As for Priestley's account of the Resurrection, Price found it seriously wanting:

---

[29] Joseph Priestley, *Disquisitions Relating to Matter and Spirit* (London: J. Johnson, 1777); repr. edn. (New York: Arno Press, 1975), 161. The existence of chemical transformations in which substances could be recovered from the products into which they had been transformed had featured in earlier attempts to defend doctrines of resurrection: Fernando Vidal, 'Brains, Bodies, Selves and Science: Anthropologies of Identity and the Resurrection of the Body', *Critical Inquiry*, 28 (2002), 930–74, esp. 948 and 958.

[30] Alexander Bicknell, *The Putrid Soul. A Poetical Epistle to Joseph Priestley on his Disquisitions Relating to Matter and Spirit* (London: T. Bowen, 1780), 17–18.

[31] Brooke, ' "A Sower Went Forth" ', 40.

[32] Joseph Priestley, *A Free Discussion of the Doctrines of Materialism and Philosophical Necessity in a Correspondence between Dr. Price and Dr. Priestley* (London: J. Johnson and T. Cadell, 1778), 19.

It is ... implied, that the men who are to be raised from death, will be the same with the men who have existed in this world, only as a river is called the same, because the water, though different, has followed other water in the same channel... Did I believe this to be all the identity of man hereafter, I could not consider myself as having any concern in a future state.[33]

Heterodox by the standards of orthodox dissent and even among the Unitarians, Priestley was heterodox again in his attitude towards other religions. If Christianity were to be acceptable to a Muslim or a Jew, it had to be shorn of that which gave offence. Trinitarian doctrines could not pass that test, could not even be made intelligible to the common ploughman. The vision that sustained him was recorded in his *General History of the Christian Church*. Eventually every corruption of Christianity would be removed such that no impediments would remain to which any unbeliever, Jew or Muslim, could reasonably object. Rational Christianity would become the religion of the world. Not surprisingly he was dubbed 'half a Mahometan', though that and other abuse often missed the point. His hope was that, once the Trinitarian obstacle was removed, a rational dialogue between Christianity and Islam would ensue, establishing the one and destroying the other. Such was his confidence in human rationality that he thought less than a century might suffice.[34]

From this preliminary sketch we have caught a glimpse of a heterodox but passionate religious believer, and an experimental philosopher who made an indelible mark in both physical science and metaphysical reconstruction. Can we establish any connections between them? We must certainly be wary of strong claims to the effect that a dissenting education steered him inexorably towards the natural sciences. In his recent biography Robert Schofield observes that Priestley did not do any scientific work for ten years after leaving the Daventry Academy; and did not write as a philosopher of science for more than twenty. Priestley may even give the lie to that weaker correlation between science and religious dissent which suggests that dissenters moved into science by default as other doors were barred. He was, after all, employed at the Warrington Academy to teach

---

[33] Joseph Priestley, *A Free Discussion of the Doctrines of Materialism and Philosophical Necessity in a Correspondence between Dr. Price and Dr. Priestley* (London: J. Johnson and T. Cadell, 1778), 73.

[34] Priestley, *Reflections on Free Inquiry*, 48–9.

languages. If Priestley's induction into practical chemistry was through the lectures and demonstrations of Matthew Turner, who lectured at Warrington between 1763 and 1765, then there is even a certain irony because Turner was apparently notable as an atheist. As for other origins of Priestley's utilitarian interest in science, it has been suggested that it was through salt that he came to Bacon. While at Nantwich he took an interest in the local manufacture of Cheshire salt and, according to one biographer, probably came across William Brownrigg's *The Art of Making Common Salt* (1748).[35] This was a book with a Baconian preface, extolling a knowledge of the mechanic arts for the relief of man's estate. When Priestley looked forward to a social millennium he suggested it would be brought about by the commercial spirit *aided* by Christianity and true philosophy. But that was rather different from having the scientific or the commercial spirit derive from his religion.[36] This is not to deny that, during his early years at the Warrington Academy, there were opportunities for Priestley to develop his latent interest in the teaching of natural philosophy. Some of his friendships, as with John Seddon, were strengthened by a mutual interest in the sciences. He even gave some twenty lectures on anatomy.[37] But, as Schofield notes, if there was a shift in his interests during the early 1760s, it was more in the direction of history than experimental science.[38] It has even been proposed by Maurice Crosland that Priestley found solace in science as a refuge from religious polemics.[39] This may, however, be a precarious argument, since Priestley appears to have relished every opportunity for theological combat. In the 1780s he wrote that 'on no former occasion have I declined, but on the contrary I have rather courted, and provoked opposition, because I am sensible it is the only method of discovering truth.'[40]

[35] F. W. Gibbs, *Joseph Priestley* (London: Nelson, 1965), 13.

[36] On this and other historiographical complications concerning attempts to correlate scientific activity with religious dissent, see John H. Brooke, 'Joseph Priestley (1733–1804) and William Whewell (1794–1866): Apologists and Historians of Science', in Anderson and Lawrence, *Science, Medicine and Dissent*, 11–27; and 'Science and Dissent: Some Historiographical Issues', in Paul Wood (ed.), *Science and Dissent in England, 1688–1945* (Aldershot: Ashgate, 2004), 19–37.

[37] Schofield, *The Enlightenment of Joseph Priestley*, 137.   [38] Ibid. 138.

[39] Maurice Crosland, 'Priestley Memorial Lecture: A Practical Perspective on Joseph Priestley as a Pneumatic Chemist', *British Journal for the History of Science*, 16 (1983), 223–38, esp. 227–30.

[40] Cited by Gibbs, *Joseph Priestley*, 174.

These considerations suggest we have to be cautious about the kinds of claim we might want to make for connections between Priestley's 'science' and 'religion'. These very words might betray anachronism when torn from their contexts. Nevertheless, in the remainder of this chapter I want to suggest that, with due caution, two kinds of interpenetration can be discerned. In the first category are examples where one might plausibly argue that Priestley's religious commitment was relevant to his science or his science relevant to his religion. These are examples where it is possible to say in which direction the arrow of influence might fly. In the second category the connections are mediated by Priestley's philosophy and metaphysics and consequently a more holistic picture is required.

How might Priestley's religious belief be relevant to his science? It is not unduly contentious to observe that religious convictions might predispose a thinker towards one theory or one kind of theory rather than another.[41] This selective role has been common in the history of science and it shows up in Priestley's response to a theory of his contemporary, Erasmus Darwin. Darwin was speculating about spontaneous generation and versifying on the evolutionary transformation of living things. Priestley's theism, for all that it was radical, was not radical enough to accommodate Darwin's hypotheses. For Priestley the gap between organic and organized matter was so great that to postulate a transition was to affirm an effect without a cause. Advocates of spontaneous generation were hell-bent on denying miracles but were in effect proposing one. Priestley accused Darwin of exploiting an exploded doctrine.[42] Behind the accusation, as with his reaction to Hume's scepticism, was Priestley's conviction that all the beautifully adapted animals and plants in the world required an intelligent cause for their explanation.

In Priestley's natural theology we can see other elements that predisposed him towards some forms of scientific argument rather than others. Three examples stand out, though it would surely be possible to find others. A belief in nature as a designed system

---

[41] For a fuller discussion of salient examples, see John H. Brooke, *Science and Religion: Some Historical Perspectives* (Cambridge: Cambridge University Press, 1991).

[42] Harold. J. Abrahams, 'Priestley Answers the Proponents of Abiogenesis', *Ambix*, 12 (1964), 59.

appears to have led him to speculate about mechanisms for restoration, especially, as I noted earlier, for the replenishment of air fouled by breathing. His eventual conclusion was that vegetation was the key. It would be too much to claim that he understood the principles of photosynthesis; but his experimental work was regulated by what he presented as a systematic and sustained enquiry. In August 1771 he announced to Theophilus Lindsey that 'I have discovered what I have long been in quest of, *viz*, that process in nature by which air, rendered noxious by breathing, is restored to its former salubrious condition.'[43] When Sir John Pringle presented him with the Royal Society's Copley medal, he congratulated Priestley for discoveries which showed that 'no vegetable grows in vain'.[44] In the vitiation and restoration of air Priestley himself found a scientific parable of the transformation of evil into good.

A second example of Priestley's natural theology finding expression in his science concerns the economy of nature. If we ask why he found the phlogiston theory attractive it was surely in part because of its economy: the metals had properties in common because they shared the same ingredient, phlogiston. The quest for such unity and economy was to pervade much of nineteenth-century chemistry, with hydrogen a recurring candidate for the ultimate unit of matter.[45] Lavoisier's system may have prevailed over Priestley's but it must not be overlooked that, by making the metals elemental, Lavoisier could not explain why they displayed common properties.

My third example is simply that of a presupposition that came to the surface when Priestley contemplated the properties of his dephlogisticated air, our oxygen. It transpired that a mouse could survive in the new gas more than twice as long as in ordinary air. At first, Priestley found it very difficult to accept that there could be an air that supported respiration and combustion better than ordinary air. The presupposition, common in natural theology, that the natural must be the best, had made it difficult to accept that there might be something better. The shaping of science by religious preconceptions can sometimes be almost too subtle to notice. It can be found again in

[43] Schofield, *A Scientific Autobiography*, 133.
[44] Cited by Gibbs, *Joseph Priestley: Adventurer*, 81.
[45] David Knight, *The Transcendental Part of Chemistry* (Folkestone: Dawson, 1978).

Priestley's tendency to overestimate the restorative effects of shaking noxious airs with water, believing that such experiments mirrored a beneficent natural interaction between the atmosphere and the sea.[46]

What of the effects of science on his religious outlook? At the most obvious level it could help to eliminate superstition. Priestley saw no clash between science and religion when both were properly understood. That has been a common enough apologetic formula, but Priestley wished to say more—that science and religion were fighting on the same side against popular superstition. A telling example would be Priestley's assault on the doctrine that the human mind can be directly influenced by divine initiative.[47] Priestley had no time for this; and his conception of how the mind worked, taken largely from David Hartley, fortified him in that resolve. There were no gaps or spirits through which a spirit being might gain access. The causal nexus of nature, of which humans are part, was inviolable.

Through his science, Priestley could also stock up on metaphors that would enrich his rhetoric. Chemistry in particular provided explosions that erupted in his prose. Thus passive obedience to political authority he dismissed as an 'exploded doctrine'. In his verbal battles with the religious establishment he made good use of gunpowder in predicting the fall of the English hierarchy and the blasting of Anglican privilege.[48]

In these examples we can see a certain directness of relevance in the mutual bearings of Priestley's scientific and religious language. But there is a second category in which the mediation is more pronounced and a holistic analysis becomes the more appropriate. Perhaps it could be expressed like this—that the metaphysics to which Priestley was drawn in his maturity was congenial to both his scientific and religious convictions. Two aspects of his metaphysics are particularly revealing in this respect: his determinism and his monism.

Priestley preferred to speak of the doctrine of philosophical necessity rather than determinism, but its meaning was clear. Effects were

[46] John G. McEvoy, 'Joseph Priestley, "Aerial Philosopher": Metaphysics and Methodology in Priestley's Chemical Thought, 1772–1781', Part 1, *Ambix*, 25 (1978), 1–55; Part 2, ibid. 93–111; Part 3, ibid. 153–75; Part 4, ibid. 26 (1979), 16–38. Part 2, 100–1.

[47] Joseph Priestley, *The Doctrine of Divine Influence on the Human Mind Considered in a Sermon* (Bath: R. Cruttwell, 1779).

[48] Priestley, *Reflections on Free Inquiry*, 40–1. See also Joseph Priestley, *Letters to the Rev. Edward Burn of St. Mary's Chapel, Birmingham* (London: J. Johnson, 1790), p. ix.

physically bound to their causes by the very necessity that David Hume had denied. It was a doctrine consonant with a recurrent motif in Priestley's writing: an aversion to the arbitrary, where by 'arbitrary' he meant flowing from unjustified dictat. When disparaging Calvin's doctrine of predestination he would protest against the 'arbitrary decree'.[49] Following the revolution of 1789 he would refer to the 'late arbitrary government of France'.[50] It is not implausible to suggest that his presuppositions about the natural world were structured by the same deletion of the arbitrary. For if nature could be manipulated by a Sovereign will, what guarantee could there be of its uniformity? Surely the very possibility of a rational science of nature required a non-intervening rather than a manipulative deity? Priestley's conviction that miracles did not belong 'in this age of the world' was certainly of a piece with his scientific determinism.[51] The miracles that had authenticated Christ's ministry had simply rendered more miracles unnecessary. Scientific discoveries helped to disclose the interconnecting threads that were woven into the fabric of nature. There was necessity in the connections. Indeed, the existence of determinate relations between cause and effect was especially congenial for Priestley's account of human discipline and responsibility. In his own words: 'One principal reason why I reject the doctrine of philosophical liberty, is that exactly in the degree in which we suppose the mind not to be determined by motives, in that very degree do rewards and punishments lose their effect, and a man ceases to be a proper subject of moral discipline.'[52]

Priestley elaborated his views in *The Doctrine of Philosophical Necessity*—an appendix to his *Disquisitions on Matter and Spirit* (1777). His conviction was that

motives influence us in some definite and invariable manner: so that every volition or choice, is constantly regulated and determined by what precedes it. And this constant determination of the mind, according to the motives presented to it, is all that I mean by its necessary determination. This being admitted to be the fact, there will be a necessary connexion between all things past, present and to come, in the way of proper cause and effect, as

---

[49] Priestley, *An Appeal*, 10–11.
[50] Priestley, *Letters to the Rev. Edward Burn*, p. ix.
[51] Priestley, *The Doctrine of Divine Influence*, 9.
[52] Priestley, *A Free Discussion*, p. xxi.

much in the intellectual, as in the natural world; so that ... according to the established laws of nature, no event could have been otherwise than it has been, is, or is to be, and therefore all things past, present and to come, are precisely what the Author of nature really intended them to be, and has made provision for.[53]

In such passages we see the connections in Priestley's mind between his theology, and his understanding of causality and of the analogy between the workings of nature and those of the human mind. His was a metaphysics that even had pastoral pay-off because 'without this persuasion concerning the uniformity of the laws of nature respecting our minds ... minister and people will both be subject to great occasional despondency'.[54] We can begin to understand why the parable of the sower meant so much to him. It underlined the point that whether the seed germinated or not depended inexorably on the ground on which it fell. Accordingly, 'all the benefit we are authorised to expect from the gospel arises from the natural effect that the great truths and motives of it are calculated to produce upon the mind'.[55] In the last analysis the doctrine of philosophical necessity eventually bound together Priestley's understanding of nature and history. The whole of nature and the whole of history could be subsumed under divine decree. In this respect Priestley re-established the union of God's purpose in ordaining nature and the regularity of nature itself—a union broken by earlier attempts to separate general and special providence. All was ultimately ascribed to God; general and special providence were integrated without any violation of the natural order. Not surprisingly, Priestley would stress the unity of nature, prophesying that one great comprehensive law might one day be found to govern both the material and intellectual worlds. Even the corruption of Christianity fulfilled a divine purpose in making possible just that repurification to which he himself was so dedicated.[56]

In Priestley's monism there was a second metaphysical position that was congenial to both his scientific and religious commitments. It underpinned his assault on the world of spirits, his vehement defence of the doctrine of resurrection, and his exclusion of

---

[53] Joseph Priestley, *The Doctrine of Philosophical Necessity Illustrated.* Appendix to *Disquisitions Relating to Matter and Spirit* (London: J. Johnson, 1777), 7–8.
[54] Priestley, *The Doctrine of Divine Influence*, 8.   [55] Ibid. 1–2.
[56] Brooke, ' "A Sower Went Forth" ', 37–8.

immediate divine influence on the human mind. For his critique of a mind/matter dualism Priestley was able to adduce philosophical, religious, and scientific arguments. Philosophical in that if matter and spirit were such distinctive things as they were commonly made out to be, it was inconceivable how they could interact at all. Religious, because if the soul were immaterial and the body material, there was the insufferable difficulty whether the two came together at conception, birth, or whenever. And scientific in that chemistry had something to say about spirits. As in Priestley's work on gases, a vocabulary of 'airs' displaced a vocabulary of 'spirits', so the latter could by analogy be expunged from theology.[57]

For Priestley, monism and mortalism went hand in hand, serving to highlight the doctrine of bodily resurrection. At death there was no automatic survival of a separable immortal soul; but, by the grace of God, one had the promise of resurrection in God's own time. Priestley insisted that a unitary view of the human self was the biblical view and it helped him turn the tables on those who accused him of surrendering revelation to reason. Fernando Vidal has shown that during the seventeenth and eighteenth centuries there had been a shift away from the traditional view that the resurrected body had to be constituted by the same material components as its earthly predecessor. Robert Boyle, for example, had argued that since no one particular portion of matter determines personal identity, the sameness of the terrestrial and resurrected individual was not to be judged by material criteria.[58] With his holistic understanding of the human person, Priestley may have felt more constrained to believe that it would be the same body that would eventually be reconstituted after death. Either way, Priestley was adamant that the one essential article of Christianity *is* the doctrine of resurrection. Without it and without the prospect of rewards and punishment there could be no social control and no ultimate rationale for the reformation of character.[59] Such reformation would pave the way for the final perfecting of humanity in the afterlife, when even the wicked might yet prove capable of improvement.

---

[57] Ibid. 41.   [58] Vidal, 'Brain, Bodies, Selves, and Science', 955.

[59] Joseph Priestley, *Considerations on Differences of Opinion among Christians* (London: J. Johnson, 1769), 15.

It would be easy to give an account of Priestley in which his secularization of Christianity was a gradual but remorseless stripping away of doctrinal accretion until virtually nothing remained. But what Priestley did believe he believed with fervour and we can certainly misunderstand his heterodoxy if we are tempted to see in it any kind of religious indifference. Christianity had to be purged of its Platonist elements, but the residue could be proclaimed with real conviction, even to the French *philosophes* who Priestley believed had rejected a caricature of the faith and mistakenly thrown away the baby with the bathwater. His encounters with the French provide a concluding, irresistible anecdote: 'When I was dining at ... Turgot's table, M. de Chatellux ... in answer to an inquiry said the two gentlemen opposite me were the Bishop of Aix and the Archbishop of Toulouse, "But", said he, "they are no more believers than you or I". I assured him I was a believer; but he would not believe me.'[60]

Connections between science and secularization are a good deal more slippery than is often supposed. There is a real sense in which Priestley shows them to be so. Certainly in the practical details of a scientific experiment one might have to look very hard to discern any religious investment. Moreover, the separation of science from religious interests and control has been a favourite refrain in literature on secularization. But, as Amos Funkenstein observed, there can be other forms of secularization resulting from the fusion, not the separation, of scientific and religious concerns.[61] In his heterodoxies, Priestley arguably conforms as much to the latter model as the former. Certainly he thought so himself. In a letter from America of 3 April 1800, he declared that one of his primary objects had been to join (natural) philosophy to Christianity, from which it had been 'too much separated'.[62]

---

[60] Cited by A. D. Orange, 'Oxygen and One God: Joseph Priestley in 1774', *History Today*, 24 (1974), 773.

[61] Amos Funkenstein, *Theology and the Scientific Imagination from the Middle Ages to the Seventeenth Century* (Princeton: Princeton University Press, 1986).

[62] Priestley to B. Lynde Oliver, 3 April 1800, in Schofield, *A Scientific Autobiography*, 302.

Index